Stith Thompson's works concerning the folktale

*European Tales among the North American Indians*, 1919
*The Types of the Folktale* (with Antti Aarne) 1928,
    revised edition, 1961
*Tales of the North American Indians*, 1929
*Motif-Index of Folk-Literature*. 6 vols. 1932–36,
    new edition, 1955–58
*The Folktale*, 1946
*Oral Tales of India* (with Jonas Balys), 1958
*Types of Indic Folktales* (with W. E. Roberts), 1960

One Hundred Favorite Folktales

# One Hundred Favorite Folktales

*chosen by* Stith Thompson

*drawings by Franz Altschuler*

Indiana University Press
*Bloomington*

To my daughters

Dorothy Letsinger

Marguerite Hays

# Contents

# Foreword

Skilled story-tellers and eager listeners for many thousands of years in the Old World have developed a notable body of traditional narrative. From Ireland to India much of this is a common possession and many of the tales have been carried by emigrants to remote parts of the world. In the course of time some hundreds of stories have emerged and become a part of the repertory of many tellers of tales. Once all tales were told and listened to by the unlettered, but beginning some five or six thousand years ago the scribe and his writing began to influence the tradition.

Nevertheless, even today, for that group of full-length folktales which form this anthology, the oral teller and his audience are of primary importance. It is through them that these hundred stories have spread so widely over thousands of miles and have become favorites not only of unlettered adults but of the more sophisticated world both of children and of those who never grow old.

A body of narrative tradition is a gradual growth coming from many sources and taking many forms. The present selection has not concerned itself with local or historical traditions, nor with anecdotes or simple animal tales (whether of literary or oral origin), but only with favorite folktales of enough length to develop a recognizable plot. Of these there exist, of course, more than the hundred given here, but these at least have been recorded in scores of places and often hundreds of times.

The selection of the particular telling to use has come as the result of more than a half century of almost daily familiarity with these tales. The goal has been to find a version (1) that is representative of the well-recognized form of the tale-type, (2) that belongs in the geographical area where the tale is best known, and above all, (3) that is well told.

This anthology is in no sense a treatise on the folktale but is merely designed to furnish an adequate illustration of each tale chosen. It is recognized that many tales have been treated by writers as well as by story-tellers, and indeed for ancient times the only versions we have are from literature. Hence the appearance of a tale from ancient Egyptian papyri, one from Homer, and one from Herodotus. We shall never know just how the ancient story-tellers told them. And even in modern times certain authors have retold these popular tales in their own literary idiom and sometimes have almost driven out the original stories. For that reason one tale has been included from Basile in his highly artificial Neapolitan style (1634–36), and from the popular Charles Perrault (1697) and from Hans Christian Andersen. Aside from these six tales all were reported as heard from story-tellers.

The choice of these specimens has not been easy. Although the editor has twice revised and expanded the international list of folktales, he often found that out of hundreds of versions available few could serve his purposes. Sometimes language had kept versions from becoming "favorites." Such for example was often true of Irish or Finnish. And sometimes there was the obvious inadequacy of collections.

For help in the preparation of this anthology I owe thanks to the translators, Mrs. Barbro Sklute (Swedish), Mrs. Kirsten Streib (Danish), and my wife (some of the French). Mrs. Carol Madden, my occasional secretary, has been helpful at all stages of the work. Finally, I am grateful to the following publishers for permission to use coyright material: Southern Illinois University Press, Random House, University of Chicago Press, Oxford University Press, Dr. Waldemar Liungman, John Lane (the Bodley Head), and Oliver and Boyd, Ltd., Edinburgh. Specific acknowledgment will be made at appropriate places.

S.T.

One Hundred Favorite Folktales

*One*

# The Three Billy-Goats Gruff

*Norwegian*

Once on a time there were three billy-goats who were to go up to the hillside to make themselves fat, and the name of all three was "Gruff."

On the way up was a bridge over a burn they had to cross; and under the bridge lived a great ugly Troll, with eyes as big as saucers and a nose as long as a poker.

So first of all came the youngest billy-goat Gruff to cross the bridge.

"Trip, trap; trip, trap!" went the bridge.

"WHO'S THAT tripping over my bridge?" roared the Troll.

"Oh, it is only I, the tiniest billy-goat Gruff; and I'm going up to the hillside to make myself fat," said the billy-goat, with such a small voice.

"Now, I'm coming to gobble you up," said the Troll.

"Oh no, pray don't take me. I'm too little, that I am," said the billy-goat; "wait a bit till the second billy-goat Gruff comes, he's much bigger."

"Well, be off with you," said the Troll.

A little while after came the second billy-goat Gruff to cross the bridge.

"TRIP, TRAP! TRIP, TRAP! TRIP, TRAP!" went the bridge.

"WHO'S THAT tripping over my bridge?" roared the Troll.

"Oh, it's the second billy-goat Gruff, and I'm going up to the hillside to make myself fat," said the billy-goat, who hadn't such a small voice.

"Now, I'm coming to gobble you up," said the Troll.

"Oh no, don't take me; wait a little till the big billy-goat Gruff comes, he's much bigger."

"Very well, be off with you," said the Troll.

But just then up came the big billy-goat Gruff.

"TRIP, TRAP! TRIP, TRAP! TRIP, TRAP!" went the bridge, for the billy-goat was so heavy that the bridge creaked and groaned under him.

"WHO'S THAT tramping over my bridge?" roared the Troll.

"IT'S I! THE BIG BILLY-GOAT GRUFF," said the billy-goat, who had an ugly hoarse voice of his own.

"Now, I'm coming to gobble you up," roared the Troll.

> "Well, come along! I've got two spears,
> And I'll poke your eyeballs out at yours ears;
> I've got besides two curling-stones,
> And I'll crush you to bits, body and bones."

That was what the big billy-goat said; and so he flew at the Troll and poked his eyes out with his horns, and crushed him to bits, body and bones, and tossed him out into the burn, and after that he went up to the hillside. There the billy-goats got so fat they were scarce able to walk home again; and if the fat hasn't fallen off them, why, they're still fat; and so—

> Snip, snap, snout,
> This tale's told out.

*Two*

# The Ingrates

*Italian*

There was once a man who went into the forest to gather wood, and saw a snake crushed under a large stone. He raised the stone a little with the handle of his axe and the snake crawled out. When it was at liberty it said to the man: "I am going to eat you." The man answered: "Softly; first let us hear the judgment of some one, and if I am condemned, then you shall eat me."

The first one they met was a horse as thin as a stick, tied to an oak tree. He had eaten the leaves as far as he could reach, for he was famished. The snake said to him: "Is it right for me to eat this man who has saved my life?" The nag answered: "More than right. Just look at me! I was one of the finest horses. I have carried my master so many years, and what have I gained? Now that I am so badly off that I can no longer work they have tied me to this oak, and after I have eaten these few leaves I shall die of hunger. Eat the man, then; for he who does good is ill rewarded, and he who does evil must be well rewarded. Eat him, for you will be doing a good day's work."

They afterwards happened to find a mulberry tree, all holes, for it was eaten by old age; and the snake asked it if it was right to eat the man who had saved its life. "Yes," the tree answered at once, "for I have given my master so many leaves that he has raised from them the finest silkworms in the world; now that I can no longer stand upright, he has said that he is going to throw me into the fire. Eat him, then, for you will do well."

Afterwards they met the fox. The man took her aside and begged her to pronounce in his favor. The fox said: "The better to render judgment I must see just how the matter has happened." They all returned to the spot and arranged matters as they were at first; but as soon as the man saw the snake under the stone he cried out: "Where you are, there I will leave you." And there the snake remained.

The fox wished in payment a bag of hens, and the man promised them to her for the next morning. The fox went there in the morning, and when the man saw her he put some dogs in the bag, and told the fox not to eat the hens close by, for fear the mistress of the house would hear it. So the fox did not open the bag until she had reached a distant valley; then the dogs came out and ate her. And so it is in the world; for who does good is ill rewarded and who does evil is well rewarded.

*Three*

# John The Bear

*French*

Once upon a time there was a woodcutter and his wife. One day when she was taking soup to her husband she found herself caught by a branch in the midst of the woods. While she tried to get loose a bear rushed upon her and carried her into his den. Some time afterward the woman, who was pregnant, gave birth to a son who was half bear and half human. He was called John the Bear.

The bear took care of the mother and child. Each day he brought them food; he brought them apples and other wild fruits and everything suitable he could find.

When the child was four years old his mother told him to try to lift the stone before the entrance to the cave where the bear kept them, but the child was not yet strong enough. When he was seven, his mother said to him: "The bear is not your father. Try to lift the stone so that we can escape." "I will lift it," answered the child. The next morning, after the bear had left, he did lift the stone and escaped with his mother. At midnight they arrived at the woodcutter's house; the mother knocked on the door. "Open," she cried, "it is I, your wife." The husband got up and opened the door; he was astonished to see the wife he had thought dead. She said to him: "I had a frightful adventure; I was carried off by a bear. Here is the child which I carried then."

They sent the little boy to school. He was very naughty and had extraordinary strength. One day he gave one of his comrades such a blow with his fist that all the pupils were thrown to the other end of the bench. Then John the Bear threw the master, who had scolded him, through the window. After this feat he was expelled from school and his father said to him: "It is time for you to serve your apprenticeship." John, then fifteen, entered the service of a blacksmith, but his work was bad. At the end of three days he asked for his pay and then went to another blacksmith. He remained three weeks and had begun to learn the trade when the idea of leaving came to him. He left and entered the shop of a third blacksmith; there he became very skillful, and his master valued him highly.

One day John the Bear asked the blacksmith for iron to forge a cane. "Take what you need," his master said to him. John took all the iron he found in the shop and made himself a cane which weighed five hundred pounds. "I need still more iron," he said, "to make a ring for my cane." "Take all that you can find in the house," said the master; but there wasn't any more.

John the Bear then told the blacksmith goodbye and left with his cane. On his journey he met John of the Mill, who was playing quoits with a millstone. "Oh, oh," said John the Bear, "you are stronger than I. Will you come with me?" "Willingly," answered John of the Mill. A little farther they saw another young man who was holding up a mountain; he was named Hold-up-Mountain. "What are you doing there?" John the Bear asked him. "I am holding up this mountain; without me it would crumble." "Let us see," said John the Bear. The other had no sooner drawn back than the mountain fell down. "You are stronger than I," said John the Bear. "Will you come with me?" "I will indeed." When they arrived in a wood, they met another young man who was twisting an oak to tie his bundle of wood: he was called Oak-Twister. "Comrade," said John the Bear, "will you come with me?" "Gladly," answered Oak-Twister.

After walking two days and two nights through the woods, the four companions saw a beautiful castle. They entered it, and when they found in one of the rooms a table laden with fine food, they seated themselves and ate with good appetites. They drew lots as to who should remain in the castle while the others went hunting; he was to sound a bell to give his companions the signal for dinner.

John of the Mill was the first to guard the lodging. He was about to pour the soup on the bread when suddenly he saw a giant enter. "What are you doing here, boy?" the giant said to him. Then he knocked down John of the Mill and left. John of the Mill was covered with bruises and did not have the strength to ring the bell.

As his companions found the time long, they returned to the castle. "What has happened?" they asked John of the Mill. "I haven't been well; I believe that it is the smoke from the kitchen which has disagreed with me." "Is it only that?" said John the Bear; "that wouldn't make you very sick."

The following day Oak-Twister remained at the castle. As he was pouring the soup on the bread the giant arrived. "What are you doing here, boy?" he said to Oak-Twister, and after striking him down, he went away. John the Bear, having returned with his companions, said to Oak-Twister: "Why didn't you ring the bell?" "It's because," answered the other, "the smoke had made me ill." "Is that all?" said John the Bear. "Tomorrow it will be my turn."

The following day, just as John the Bear was about to ring the bell, the giant arrived. "What are you doing, boy?" he said to the young man and was about to throw himself upon him, but John the Bear did not give him time; he grasped his cane and split the giant in two. When his comrades returned to the castle, he scolded them for hiding their adventure. "I might have been killed," he said, "but I pardon you."

John the Bear then started to look about the castle. When he rapped with his cane upon the floor, it sounded hollow; he wanted to know why and discovered a great hole. His companions rushed forward. With the help of a rope they let down John of the Mill; he held in his hand a small bell. "When I ring it," he said, "pull me up." While he was going down he heard below him frightful howling; halfway down, he cried out that if he were not pulled up he would die. Then Hold-up-Mountain was lowered; also frightened at the shrieks which he heard, he soon rang the bell to be pulled back. Oak-Twister did the same.

John the Bear then descended with his cane. He reached the bottom without hearing anything and saw before him a fairy. "Have you no fear of the giant?" she asked him. "I have killed him," answered John the Bear. "You have done well," said the fairy. "Now you see this castle: there are devils in two rooms, eleven in the first and a dozen in the second; in another room you will find three beautiful princesses who are sisters." John the Bear entered the castle, which was even more beautiful than the other: there were magnificent gardens, trees loaded with golden fruit, meadows sprinkled with a thousand bright flowers.

When he reached one of the rooms, John the Bear knocked two or three times with his cane upon the gate which closed it, and made it fly into a thousand pieces; then he struck each of the little devils with his cane and killed them all. The gate to the other room was stronger; but John managed to break it and kill eleven devils. The twelfth asked mercy and begged to be allowed to live. "You will die like the others," said John the Bear, and he killed him.

Then he entered the room of the princesses. The youngest, who was also the most beautiful, gave him a little ball ornamented with pearls, diamonds, and emeralds. John the Bear went with her to the place where he had descended. He gave the signal and had them draw up the princess, whom John of the Mill quickly took away. John the Bear went to look for the second princess, who also gave him a little ball ornamented with pearls, emeralds, and diamonds. He had her drawn up like the first, and Hold-up-Mountain took her for himself. John the Bear returned to the third princess; he received from her the same gift, and had her pulled up like her sisters; Oak-Twister took her for himself. John the Bear then wished to return to the top himself; but his companions cut the rope. He fell to the bottom and broke his leg. Fortunately, he had a pot of ointment which the fairy had given him.

With it he rubbed his knee, and there were no longer signs of the wound.

He was wondering what to do, when the fairy again appeared to him and said: "If you wish to leave here, take this path which leads to the castle above; but do not look at the little light which will be behind you; otherwise the light will go out and you will no longer see your way."

John the Bear followed the advice of the fairy. Arriving at the top, he saw his comrades making up their bundles in order to depart with the princesses. "Away from here, rascals!" he cried, "or I will kill you! It was I who overcame the giant, I am master here." And he chased them away.

The princesses wished to take him to the king, their father, but he refused. "Perhaps some day," he said to them, "I shall enter into your country; then I shall come to see you." He put the three balls into his pocket and let the princesses leave. Once they had returned to the home of their father they no longer thought of him.

John the Bear began his travels again and came into the country of the king, father of the three princesses. He became a workman in the shop of a blacksmith; as he was very skillful, the shop soon became well known.

One day the king had the blacksmith brought to him and he said: "You must make me three small balls, for which this is the model. I will furnish everything and I will give you one million francs for your trouble; but if in the time allowed the balls are not ready, you shall die." The blacksmith told this to John the Bear, who answered that he would make it his business.

But as the time drew near, John the Bear had not worked any. He was at the table with his master. "The balls will not be ready," said the blacksmith. "Master, go now and bring out a jug." While he was in the cellar, John the Bear knocked on the anvil, then drew from his pocket the balls the princesses had given him. The job was done.

The blacksmith hastened to take the balls to the king. "Are they as you wished?" he said. "They are even more beautiful," answered the king. He counted out to the blacksmith the million promised, and went to show the balls to his daughters. They said to each other: "They are the balls which we gave to the young man who freed us." They told their father about this. He soon sent guards to find John the Bear; but John did not want to be bothered. The king sent other guards to tell him that if he did not come, he would die. Then John the Bear made his decision.

The king saluted him, and after many compliments and many thanks, he told him to choose as a wife the one of his three daughters who pleased him the most. John the Bear took the youngest, who was also the most beautiful. The marriage was celebrated three months later. As to the companions of John the Bear, they were burned in a great fire.

*Four*

# The Giant Who Had No Heart In His Body

*Norwegian*

Once on a time there was a king who had seven sons, and he loved them so much that he could never bear to be parted from them all; at least one must always be with him. Now, when they were grown up, six were to set off to woo, but as for the youngest, his father kept him at home, and the others were to bring back a princess for him to the palace. So the king gave the six the finest clothes you ever set eyes on, so fine that the light gleamed from them a long way off, and each had his horse, which cost many, many hundred dollars, and so they set off. Now, when they had been to many palaces, and seen many princesses, at last they came to a king who had six daughters; such lovely king's daughters they had never seen, and so they fell to wooing them, each one, and when they had got them for sweethearts, they set off home again, but they quite forgot that they were to bring back with them a sweetheart for Boots, their brother, who had stayed at home, for they were over head and ears in love with their own sweethearts.

But when they had gone a good bit on their way, they passed close by a steep hillside, like a wall, where the giant's house was, and there the giant came out, and set his eyes upon them, and turned them all into stone, princes and princesses and all. Now the king waited and waited for his six sons, but the more he waited the longer they stayed away; so he fell into great trouble, and said he should never know what it was to be glad again.

"And if I had not you left," he said to Boots, "I would live no longer, so full of sorrow am I for the loss of your brothers."

"Well, but now I've been thinking to ask your leave to set out and find them again; that's what I'm thinking of," said Boots.

"Nay, nay!" said his father; "that leave you shall never get, for then you would stay away too."

But Boots had set his heart upon it; go he would; and he begged and prayed so long that the king was forced to let him go. Now, you must know the king had no other horse to give Boots but an old broken-down jade, for his six other sons and their train had carried off all his horses; but Boots did not care a pin for that, he sprang up on his sorry old steed.

"Farewell, father," said he; "I'll come back, never fear, and like enough I shall bring my six brothers back with me"; and with that he rode off.

So, when he had ridden a while, he came to a raven, which lay in the road and flapped its wings, and was not able to get out of the way, it was so starved.

"Oh, dear friend," said the raven, "give me a little food, and I'll help you again at your utmost need."

"I haven't much food," said the prince, "and I don't see how you'll ever be able to help me much; but still I can spare you a little. I see you want it."

So he gave the raven some of the food he had brought with him.

Now, when he had gone a bit further, he came to a brook, and in the brook lay a great salmon, which had got upon a dry place, and dashed itself about, and could not get into the water again.

"Oh, dear friend," said the salmon to the prince; "shove me out into the water again, and I'll help you again at your utmost need."

"Well!" said the prince, "the help you'll give me will not be great, I daresay, but it's a pity you should lie there and choke"; and with that he shot the fish out into the stream again.

After that he went a long, long way, and met a wolf, which was so famished that it lay and crawled along the road on its belly.

"Dear friend, do let me have your horse," said the wolf; "I'm so hungry the wind whistles through my ribs; I've had nothing to eat these two years."

"No," said Boots, "this will never do; first I came to a raven, and I was forced to give him my food; next I came to a salmon, and him I had to help into the water again; and now you will have my horse. It can't be done, that it can't, for then I should have nothing to ride on."

"Nay, dear friend, but you can help me," said Graylegs the wolf; "you can ride upon my back, and I'll help you again in your utmost need."

"Well! the help I shall get from you will not be great, I'll be bound," said the prince; "but you may take my horse, since you are in such need."

So when the wolf had eaten the horse, Boots took the bit and put it into the wolf's jaw, and laid the saddle on his back; and now the wolf was so strong, after what he had got inside, that he set off with the prince like nothing. So fast he had never ridden before.

"When we have gone a bit farther," said Graylegs, "I'll show you the giant's house."

So after a while they came to it.

"See, here is the giant's house," said the wolf; "and see, here are your six brothers, whom the giant has turned into stone; and see here are their six brides, and away yonder is the door, and in at that door you must go."

"Nay, but I daren't go in," said the prince; "he'll take my life."

"No! no!" said the Wolf; "when you get in you'll find a princess, and she'll tell you what to do to make an end of the giant. Only mind and do as she bids you."

Well! Boots went in, but, truth to say, he was very much afraid. When he came in the giant was away, but in one of the rooms sat the princess, just as the wolf had said, and so lovely a princess Boots had never yet set eyes on.

"Oh! heaven help you! whence have you come?" said the princess, as she saw him; "it will surely be your death. No one can make an end of the giant who lives here, for he has no heart in his body.

"Well! well!" said Boots; "but now that I am here, I may as well try what I can do with him; and I will see if I can't free my brothers, who are standing turned to stone out of doors; and you, too, I will try to save, that I will."

"Well, if you must, you must," said the princess; "and so let us see if we can't hit on a plan. Just creep under the bed yonder, and mind and listen to what he and I talk about. But, pray, do lie as still as a mouse."

So he crept under the bed, and he had scarce got well underneath it, before the giant came.

"Ha!" roared the giant, "what a smell of Christian blood there is in the house!"

"Yes, I know there is," said the princess, "for there came a magpie flying with a man's bone, and let it fall down the chimney. I made all the haste I could to get it out, but all one can do, the smell doesn't go off so soon."

So the giant said no more about it, and when night came, they went to bed. After they had lain a while, the princess said—

"There is one thing I'd be so glad to ask you about, if I only dared."

"What thing is that?" asked the giant.

"Only where it is you keep your heart, since you don't carry it about you," said the princess.

"Ah! that's a thing you've no business to ask about; but, if you must know, it lies under the door-sill," said the giant.

"Ho! ho!" said Boots to himself under the bed, "then we'll soon see if we can't find it."

Next morning the giant got up cruelly early, and strode off to the wood; but he was hardly out of the house before Boots and the princess set to work to look under the door-sill for his heart; but the more they dug, and the more they hunted, the more they couldn't find it.

"He has balked us this time," said the princess, "but we'll try him once more."

So she picked all the prettiest flowers she could find, and strewed them over the door-sill, which they had laid in its right place again; and when the time came for the giant to come home again, Boots crept under the bed. Just as he was well under, back came the giant.

Snuff—snuff, went the giant's nose. "My eyes and limbs, what a smell of Christian blood there is in here," said he.

"I know there is," said the princess, "for there came a magpie flying with a man's bone in his bill, and let it fall down the chimney. I made as much haste as I could to get it out, but I daresay it's that you smell."

So the giant held his peace, and said no more about it. A little while after, he asked who it was that had strewed flowers about the door-sill.

"Oh, I, of course," said the princess.

"And, pray, what's the meaning of all this?" said the giant.

"Ah!" said the princess, "I'm so fond of you that I couldn't help strewing them, when I knew that your heart lay under there."

"You don't say so," said the giant; "but after all it doesn't lie there at all."

So when they went to bed again in the evening, the princess asked the giant again where his heart was, for she said she would so like to know.

"Well," said the giant, "if you must know, it lies away yonder in the cupboard against the wall."

"So, so!" thought Boots and the princess; "then we'll soon try to find it."

Next morning the giant was away early, and strode off to the wood, and so soon as he was gone Boots and the princess were in the cupboard hunting for his heart, but the more they sought for it, the less they found it.

"Well," said the princess, "we'll just try him once more."

So she decked out the cupboard with flowers and garlands, and when the time came for the giant to come home, Boots crept under the bed again.

Then back came the giant.

Snuff—snuff! "My eyes and limbs, what a smell of Christian blood there is in here!"

"I know there is," said the princess; "for a little while since there came a magpie flying with a man's bone in his bill, and let it fall down the chimney. I made all the haste I could to get it out of the house again; but after all my pains, I daresay it's that you smell."

When the giant heard that, he said no more about it; but a little while after, he saw how the cupboard was all decked about with flowers and garlands; so he asked who it was that had done that? Who could it be but the princess?

"And, pray, what's the meaning of all this tomfoolery?" asked the giant.

"Oh, I'm so fond of you, I couldn't help doing it when I knew that your heart lay there," said the princess.

"How can you be so silly as to believe any such thing?" said the giant.

"Oh yes; how can I help believing it, when you say it?" said the princess.

"You're a goose," said the giant; "where my heart is, you will never come."

"Well," said the princess; "but for all that, 'twould be such a pleasure to know where it really lies."

Then the poor giant could hold out no longer, but was forced to say—

"Far, far away in a lake lies an island; on that island stands a church; in that church is a well; in that well swims a duck; in that duck there is an egg, and in that egg there lies my heart—you darling!"

In the morning early, while it was still gray dawn, the giant strode off to the wood.

"Yes! now I must set off too," said Boots; "if I only knew how to find the way." He took a long, long farewell of the princess, and when he got out of the giant's door, there stood the wolf waiting for him. So Boots told him all that had happened inside the house, and said now he wished to ride to the well in the church, if he only knew the way. So the wolf bade him jump on his back, he'd soon find the way; and away they went, till the wind whistled after them, over hedge and field, over hill and dale. After they had traveled many, many days, they came at last to the lake. Then the prince did not know how to get over it, but the wolf bade him only not be afraid, but stick on, and so he jumped into the lake with the prince on his back, and swam over to the island. So they came to the church; but the church keys hung high, high up on the top of the tower, and at first the prince did not know how to get them down.

"You must call on the raven," said the wolf.

So the prince called on the raven, and in a trice the raven came, and flew up and fetched the keys, and so the prince got into the church. But when he came to the well, there lay the duck, and swam about backwards and forwards, just as the giant had said. So the prince stood and coaxed it and coaxed it, till it came to him, and he grasped it in his hand; but just as he lifted it up from the water the duck dropped the egg into the well, and then Boots was beside himself to know how to get it out again.

"Well, now you must call on the salmon, to be sure," said the wolf; and the king's son called on the salmon, and the salmon came and fetched up the egg from the bottom of the well.

Then the wolf told him to squeeze the egg, and as soon as ever he squeezed it the giant screamed out.

"Squeeze it again," said the wolf; and when the prince did so, the giant screamed still more piteously, and begged and prayed so prettily to be spared, saying he would do all that the prince wished if he would only not squeeze his heart in two.

"Tell him, if he will restore to life again your six brothers and their brides, whom he has turned to stone, you will spare his life," said the wolf. Yes, the giant was ready to do that, and he turned the six brothers into king's sons again, and their brides into king's daughters.

"Now, squeeze the egg in two," said the wolf. So Boots squeezed the egg to pieces, and the giant burst at once.

Now, when he had made an end of the giant, Boots rode back again on the wolf to the giant's house, and there stood all his six brothers alive and merry, with their brides. Then Boots went into the hillside after his bride, and so they all set off home again to their father's house. And you may fancy how glad the old king was when he saw all his seven sons come back, each with his bride. But the loveliest bride of all is the bride of Boots. "After all," said the king, "he shall sit uppermost at the table, with her by his side."

So he sent out, and called a great wedding-feast, and the mirth was both loud and long; and if they have not done feasting, why, they are still at it.

*Five*

# The Castle of No Return

*Spanish*

There was once a fisherman who went fishing every day. And one day he caught a fish and the fish said to him: "Listen, be sure not to take me now. Later I will be much better eating." So he threw the fish back into the water and left. Afterwards he caught another fish, who also said to him: "Don't take me now; later I will be much fatter." And the fisherman threw him back into the water and went on fishing. For a long time he did not catch anything, and he became somewhat annoyed and sorry about having thrown back the other fishes into the water. Then he cast his hook once more and caught a very large fish, who said to him: "I am going to be your good fortune. When you get home cut me up into pieces and give two of these pieces to your wife, two pieces to your female dog, two pieces to your mare, and two pieces you will bury in the yard."

The fisherman went very happily back home and when he arrived told his wife everything that had happened. He cut up the fish into eight parts and gave two pieces to his wife, two pieces to his female dog, two pieces to the mare, and buried two pieces in the yard, all according to what the fish had told him.

In the course of the year his wife gave birth to twins, the dog to two puppies, the mare to two colts, and in the yard there sprang forth two strong swords. When the twins grew up the elder of them said to his father: "Father, I know that we are poor people and I want to go out into the world and seek my fortune." And the younger one said: "But, see here, it is better that I should go since our parents are already old and they would miss you more." The father told them that they should draw lots to see who should leave. They did so, and it fell to the elder to leave home first. The elder took a bottle of water and said to his brother: "If the water stays clear that means that I am doing well, but if the water becomes troubled it means that things are going badly." Then he went and took one of the lances from the yard, saddled one of the colts, who were now horses, and set out into the world accompanied by one of his dogs.

In the course of his wanderings he came to a palace, where the neighbors told him: "Here in this palace there is an enchanted princess and they say that the king has said that whoever can disenchant her shall have her as wife." The youth said: "Then I am going to disenchant her." The neighbors told him not to enter into the enchanted palace since none who entered ever returned. But he paid no attention to them and went straight for the palace. When the doors were opened he came to where the princess was, and on seeing him she said: "Ah, why do you come here, unfortunate one?" The young man told her that he had come to disenchant her, and she said to him: "Now, listen; I am guarded by a serpent with seven heads who can see in all directions at once." As they were talking the serpent came out and she screamed: "Oh, leave here, or he will devour both of us." Then he set his dog on to the serpent and when the serpent was about to devour the dog he pulled out his sword and killed him forthwith. He seized and took out the seven tongues of the serpent and put them into a bag, and he said to the princess: "Now you are disenchanted. Go to the palace of the king your father, for I must travel about the world. But wait for me and I will return and marry you."

Around the village they said that the king's daughter had been disenchanted, and the serpent with seven heads who had kept her enchanted had been killed. A certain three went and found the dead serpent and cut off the heads and presented themselves in the king's palace, saying that they had killed the serpent. And the king said that the princess should marry one of them. But the princess said no, that this man was not the one who had disenchanted her and killed the serpent.

But the king said to his daughter that only the man who had killed the serpent could show the seven heads. And they made ready for her marriage with many celebrations and feasts.

On the first day of the feasts everybody came into the dining room and the princess was very sad because she did not see her lover. As they were seated at the table to eat, the false lover was about to take his first bite when the dog belonging to the young man came in and took the food from his hand. The princess, recognizing her lover's dog, arose and said: "Anyone who does not follow this dog cannot marry me." As they followed the dog, they noticed that she entered a house, and they went to the dog's master and told him that the king wanted to speak with him. The young man replied: "It is just as far from here to the king's palace as it is from the king's palace to my house." And they went and told this to the king. The king now came to the young man's house and asked him to be so good as to come out. The young man came out and the king invited him to eat with the others at the feast. The young man accepted and went to the palace to eat.

Now they were all seated around the table. The princess recognized her lover immediately but said nothing, and he likewise said nothing. Now the king said: "It is fallen to the fate of this man here to marry my daughter." And the young man said: "And what is the proof that he has killed the serpent?" The other man showed the seven heads of the serpent. And they all agreed that he was the one who should marry the princess, since among the three who had killed the serpent he was the one who had been chosen. Now the young man said to them: "Please examine the seven heads." They did so, and agreed that all the heads were all right. Then the young man opened the mouths and said to them: "Have you ever seen heads without tongues? Where are the tongues?" Now they all saw that the heads did not have tongues and that those who had cut off the heads of the serpent had not killed him. The young man then took out of his bag the seven tongues. They threw the other man out of the palace and the king said that the young man should immediately marry the princess. And they were married.

Sometime after they were married they were taking a walk and the young man observed a very beautiful palace which stood near to the king's. He said to his wife: "What palace is that?" And she answered: "The castle of no return." Then he said: "Well, I must see it." He told the princess that the next day he was going hunting with some friends, that he would stay all day and return in the evening. And the next morning he arose very early and went out on his horse with his lunch and his dog and his sword to seek for the castle of no return.

When he arrived at the palace and knocked on the door there came out to open the door an old witch. And the young man asked: "May I come in?" She answered: "Yes, please enter." As the young man came in he was put under an enchantment. His wife kept waiting and waiting but he did not return.

The brother who remained at home saw that the water in the bottle had become troubled and he said to his father: "The water is troubled. My brother is in difficulties and I must go to see if I can find him." And the father said: "Oh, my boy, don't go! You are the only son I have and if you leave what will happen to me?" And the younger son said: "Don't worry, father, that I will not return. I cannot remain at home when I know that my brother is in trouble and I can help him." And he took the other mare, the other sword, and the other dog and went off to hunt his brother.

After much traveling he reached the palace of the queen and when they saw him coming everybody believed that it was the princess' husband, and they went out to receive him very happily. He looked so much like his brother that the princess thought it was her husband, and she went out and said to him: "Hello! How did you find it in the castle of no return?" He said: "Well," but spoke little, and when the princess threw herself into his arms he did not embrace her. And she said: "Why is it that my husband does not want to embrace me?" When at night they went to bed, he put a sword between them, and she said to him: "Why do you

put that sword between us? You have never done that before."
And he told her that he had had to make a promise and until it
was carried out he could not sleep with her as usual.

The next day she said to him: "Would you not like to take a
walk?" He agreed and they went out for a walk in the palace
garden. Already he suspected that his brother was the husband of
this princess, and he saw the castle and asked: "See here, do you
know what castle that is?" And she answered: "It is the castle of
no return. Have you not just returned from there?" And then the
young man thought: "There certainly is my brother," but he did
not say anything to her. Then he said: "See here, I must go to
that castle." And she said to him: "Haven't you already been
there? Why do you want to go another time?" And he said to her:
"I have to go." And he immediately left for the castle.

He arrived just as his brother had and knocked at the door.
The old witch came out and bade him enter, and he said to her:
"If you don't give me my brother I will kill you with this sword."
And when the old woman also saw the dog which was with him
she said that she would obey, and she turned over to him his
brother alive. At the moment when he saw his brother he said:
"Listen, do you know what I have done? I have slept with your
wife." And the older brother without listening to any more words
took out his sword and stabbed him in the breast. And believing
that he had killed his brother he fled and left him there on the
ground.

When he arrived at the palace the princess, his wife, said to
him: "You got back early today in comparison to what you have
before. I am very happy." When they went to bed and he did not
put the sword between them, she said to him: "Have you carried
out the promise which you have made? The other time when you
came back from the castle you put the sword between us since you
had a promise to carry out and you kept away from me." And
then the young man said: "What a villain am I! I must go hunt
my brother." And immediately he left and found his brother, who
was screaming, but the old witch was helping him. He told the
old witch to cure him and she brought water in a bottle and did
cure him.

Then both of them left the castle and went to the palace. And
they looked alike and everything about them was alike—horses,
dogs, and swords. When they arrived the princess did not know
which was her husband, and when people asked her which was

her husband she could not say. Finally the older brother embraced her and said: "I am your husband." And he told her all about how he had gone to rescue his younger brother.

# The Danced-Out Shoes

*Russian*

There was once a widowed king who had twelve daughters, one more beautiful than the other. Every night these princesses went away, no one knew whither; and every night each of them wore out a new pair of shoes. The king could not get shoes for them fast enough and he wanted to know where they went every night and what they did there. So he prepared a feast, summoned kings and princes, noblemen, merchants, and simple people from all lands, and said: "Can anyone solve this riddle? He who solves it will receive his favorite princess in marriage and half the kingdom as a dowry." However, no one would undertake to find out where the princesses went at night, except one needy nobleman, who said: "Your Royal Majesty, I will find out." "Very well, find out."

Soon the needy nobleman began to doubt and thought to himself: "What have I done? I have undertaken to solve this riddle, yet I do not know how. If I fail now, the king will put me in prison." He went out of the palace and walked outside the town with a sad face. He met an old woman who asked him: "Why are you so sad, my good man?" He answered: "Grandmother, how can I help being sad? I have undertaken to find out for the king whither his daughters go every night." "Yes, that is a difficult task. But it can be accomplished. Here is an invisible cap; with its help you can find out many things. But mind you: when you go to bed, the princesses will give you a sleeping potion; however, turn your face to the wall, pour the drops into your bed, and do not drink them!" The nobleman thanked the old woman and returned to the palace.

From *Russian Fairy Tales*, edited and translated by Norbert Guterman. Copyright 1945 by Pantheon Books, Inc. Reprinted by permission of Pantheon Books, a Division of Random House, Inc.

At nightfall he was assigned a room next to the princesses' bedroom. He lay on his bed and made ready to watch. Then one of the princesses brought him sleeping drops in wine and asked him to drink to her health. He could not refuse, took the cup, turned to the wall, and poured it into his bed. On the stroke of midnight the princesses came to see whether he was asleep. The nobleman pretended to be sleeping so soundly that nothing could rouse him, but actually he was listening to every rustle. "Well, little sisters," said one of them, "our guard has fallen asleep; it is time for us to go to the ball." "It is time, high time!"

They dressed in their best garments; the oldest sister pushed her bed to one side and disclosed a passage to the underground kingdom, to the realm of the accursed king. They began to climb down a ladder. The nobleman quietly rose from his bed, donned his invisible cap, and followed them. Accidentally he stepped on the youngest princess' dress. She was frightened and said to her sisters: "Ah, little sisters, someone seems to have stepped on my dress; this is a bad omen." "Don't worry, nothing will happen to us." They went down the ladder and came to a grove where golden flowers grew. The nobleman picked one flower and broke off a twig, and the whole grove rumbled. "Ah, little sisters," said the youngest princess, "do you hear how the grove is rumbling? This bodes no good." "Fear not, it is the music in the accursed king's palace."

They came to the palace and were met by the king and his courtiers. The music began to play and they began to dance; they danced till their shoes were torn to shreds. The king ordered wine to be served to the guests. The nobleman took a goblet from the tray, drank the wine, and put the goblet in his pocket. At last the party was over; the princesses said farewell to their cavaliers, promised to come the next night, returned home, undressed, and went to sleep.

The next morning the king summoned the needy nobleman. "Well," he said, "have you discovered what my daughters do every night?" "I have." "Then where do they go?" "To the underground kingdom, to the accursed king, and there they dance all night." The king summoned his daughters and began to question them: "Where were you last night?" The princesses denied everything. "We did not go anywhere," they said. "Have you not been with the accursed king? This nobleman testifies against you and is ready to offer proof." "Father, he cannot offer proof, for he slept like the dead all night." The needy nobleman drew the golden flower and the goblet from his pocket. "Here," he said, "is the proof." The princesses had no choice but to confess everything to their father; he ordered the passage to the underground kingdom to be walled up, married the needy nobleman to his youngest daughter, and all of them lived happily ever afterward.

*Seven*

# The Maiden in the Tower

*French*

There was once a gentleman and his wife. They had been married a long time, but they had no children, though they wished for many, and they were much concerned because they did not have any. So they were advised to make a pilgrimage in order to have some. They therefore went on a pilgrimage to a place far from home. On the journey back the woman became pregnant. As they drove along one of the roads they noticed a beautiful garden. This garden was filled with magnificent fruit. The wife said to the husband:

"Oh, how I would like to eat some of that fruit and gather it myself."

The husband replied: "But if we should be seen!"

Then she said to him: "That would be too bad! Let me climb down and I will go and get some."

She went into the garden, ate some of the fruit, and then loaded some more into her carriage. While she was busy with loading the last of the fruit a pretty little woman appeared and asked her why she had just stolen her fruit. Then the wife explained her situation and why she had decided to steal it. Then the good woman said to her:

"As to the fact that you have stolen my fruit I shall say nothing to you; but I would like to be the godmother of your child. You are going to have a daughter."

She got back into the carriage and said to her husband:

"I promised that good woman that she might be godmother, but this will never be."

Finally the day came when she was due to have her child. She had a daughter, as the good woman had said she would. They baptised the child, but nobody invited the good woman.

The good woman went to see her sisters. She had two sisters who were fairies. She said to them:

"You know this woman who stole my fruit has had a child and did not make me godmother. She should be punished. The child must be stolen away."

She left with a big dog. When she arrived at the woman's door she rang, but no one was willing to open for her. Then she ordered her dog. He opened all the doors and went in to where the child was. She said to the dog:

"Carry off this child for me! And you, madame, the next time you will keep your promises; but you will never see your child again."

So she left with the baby and reached home. Immediately all the fairies of the country assembled and she was made godmother to the child, whom she named Parsilette. She gave her as a gift the power of singing so that she would be heard for seven leagues in all directions. The others gave her all sorts of gifts so that she would be beautiful and have many charms. Then they gave her a nurse and they had her reared so that she had everything of the best. When she grew up she was so beautiful that all of the gentlemen who passed stopped to look at her. She sang so well that everybody gathered to hear her. Then the good woman seeing this said to her sisters:

"It is absolutely necessary that we confine Parsilette in a tower, or someone will carry her off."

She put her in a tower three leagues from the house where she was. In that tower she had everything that could be useful and agreeable to her, even including a parrot who talked with her. Then the godmother said to her:

"Now when I come to bring anything to you I shall say: Parsilette, my dear, throw me your beautiful hair!"

This was to open the door; it was the password.

There was a prince in the neighborhood, seven leagues away. From where he was he heard her singing. He said:

"But who can it be that is singing so well as that? I must find out."

Then he learned about the direction from which the singing came and asked whose voice it was. He was told that it was a princess who was confined in a tower. He said: "I must see her and talk to her."

When he was walking around the tower he noticed the good woman who brought her food. He heard her say: "Parsilette, throw me your beautiful hair!"

He wrote this down so that he could remember the password and could use it himself. As soon as the good woman had left he said: "Parsilette, my dear, throw me your beautiful hair!" The young woman believed that it was her godmother who had forgotten something and let him in. When she saw the young man enter she wanted to escape, but she didn't know how. When he saw her he became so deeply in love with her that he would not leave, and he told her that if she would follow him he would make her a queen. She was tired of the tower and of always being alone with the parrot and was very willing. She promised that she would go along with him, and they were to leave the next day.

The good woman came again to bring the dinner. When Parsilette saw her godmother enter she hid the young man behind the curtain. But the parrot kept saying: "Godmother, lover hidden there." Then the godmother said to the girl: "What is it the parrot is saying to me?"

"Oh godmother, he only says what I teach him to say."

Since she suspected nothing the good woman left; and the other two also left. As she was leaving the good woman got to thinking about what the parrot had said to her, and she said to herself: "I believe the parrot has told me the truth and I must find out." She retraced her steps and when she came to the tower she called but no one answered. As she climbed to the top of the tower she saw Parsilette leaving on the arm of the young man.

She struck with her magic wand and the girl became as hideous as she had been beautiful, and all the gifts that had been given her disappeared. The young man did not know what to say when he saw her changed so much, and when she saw herself she said to him:

"I cannot go any further because I see my godmother in all of her anger. I must go back to her and beg her pardon."

Just as she said this the young man fell dead, and she went back to her godmother and begged pardon.

Then all her gifts returned to her and her godmother pardoned her. She remained with her godmother, but not in the tower. Later she married a rich prince, but she never did know her parents.

*Eight*

# How the Devil Married Three Sisters

*Italian*

Once upon a time the Devil was seized with a desire to marry. He therefore left Hell, took the form of a handsome young man, and built a fine large house. When it was completed and furnished in the most fashionable style, he introduced himself to a family where there were three pretty daughters, and paid his addresses to the eldest of them. The handsome man pleased the maiden, her parents were glad to see a daughter so well provided for, and it was not long before the wedding was celebrated.

When he had taken his bride home, he presented her with a very tastefully arranged bouquet, led her through all the rooms of the house, and finally to a closed door. "The whole house is at your disposal," said he, "only I must request one thing of you; that is, that you do not on any account open this door."

Of course the young wife promised faithfully; but equally, of course, she could scarcely wait for the moment to come when she might break her promise. When the Devil had left the house the next morning, under pretence of going hunting, she ran hastily to the forbidden door, opened it, and saw a terrible abyss full of fire that shot up towards her, and singed the flowers on her bosom. When her husband came home and asked her whether she had kept her promise, she unhesitatingly said "Yes"; but he saw by the flowers that she was telling a lie, and said: "Now I will not put your curiosity to the test any longer. Come with me. I will show you myself what is behind the door." Thereupon he led her to the door, opened it, gave her such a push that she fell down into Hell, and shut the door again.

A few months after, he wooed the next sister for his wife, and won her; but with her everything that had happened with the first wife was exactly repeated.

Finally he courted the third sister. She was a prudent maiden, and said to herself: "He has certainly murdered my two sisters;

but then it is a splendid match for me, so I will try and see whether I cannot be more fortunate than they." And accordingly she consented. After the wedding the bridegroom gave her a beautiful bouquet, but forbade her, also, to open the door which he pointed out.

Not a whit less curious than her sisters, she too opened the forbidden door when the Devil had gone hunting, but she had previously put her flowers in water. Then she saw behind the door the fatal abyss and her sisters therein. "Ah!" she exclaimed, "poor creature that I am; I thought I had married an ordinary man, and instead of that he is the Devil! How can I get away from him?" She carefully pulled her two sisters out of hell and hid them. When the Devil came home he immediately looked at the bouquet, which she again wore on her bosom, and when he found the flowers so fresh he asked no questions; but reassured as to his secret, he now, for the first time, really loved her.

After a few days she asked him if he would carry three chests for her to her parents' house, without putting them down or resting on the way. "But," she added, "you must keep your word, for I shall be watching you." The Devil promised to do exactly as she wished. So the next morning she put one of her sisters in a chest, and laid it on her husband's shoulders. The Devil, who is very strong, but also very lazy and unaccustomed to work, soon got tired of carrying the heavy chest, and wanted to rest before he was out of the street on which he lived; but his wife called out to him: "Don't put it down; I see you!" The Devil went reluctantly on with the chest until he had turned the corner, and then said to himself: "She cannot see me here; I will rest a little." But scarcely had he begun to put the chest down when the sister inside cried out: "Don't put it down; I see you still!" Cursing, he dragged the chest on into another street, and was going to lay it down on a doorstep, but he again heard the voice: "Don't lay it down, you rascal; I see you still!" "What kind of eyes must my wife have," he thought, "to see around corners as well as straight ahead, and through walls as if they were made of glass!" and thus thinking he arrived, all in a perspiration and quite tired out, at the house of his mother-in-law, to whom he hastily delivered the chest, and then hurried home to strengthen himself with a good breakfast.

The same thing was repeated the next day with the second chest. On the third day she herself was to be taken home in the chest. She therefore prepared a figure which she dressed in her own clothes, and placed on the balcony, under the pretext of being able to watch him better; slipped quickly into the chest, and had the maid put it on the Devil's back. "The deuce!" said he; "this chest is a great deal heavier than the others; and today, when she is sitting on the balcony, I shall have so much the less chance to rest." So by dint of the greatest exertions he carried it, without stopping, to his mother-in-law, and then hastened home to breakfast scolding, and with his back almost broken. But quite contrary to custom, his wife did not come out to meet him, and there was no breakfast ready. "Margerita, where are you?" he cried; but received no answer. As he was running through the corridors he at length looked out of a window, and saw the figure on the balcony. "Margerita, have you gone to sleep? Come down. I am as tired as a dog, and as hungry as a wolf." But there was no reply. "If you do not come down instantly I will go up and bring you down," he cried, angrily; but Margerita did not stir. Enraged, he hastened up to the balcony, and gave her such a box on the ear that her head flew off, and he saw that the head was nothing but a milliner's form, and the body a bundle of rags. Raging, he rushed down and rummaged through the whole house, but in vain; he found only his wife's empty jewel-box. "Ha!" he cried; "she has been stolen from me, and her jewels, too!" and he immediately ran to inform her parents of the misfortune. But when he came near the house, to his great surprise he saw on the balcony above the door all three sisters, his wives, who were looking down on him with scornful laughter.

Three wives at once terrified the Devil so much that he took his flight with all possible speed.

Since that time he has lost his taste for marrying.


*Nine*

# The White Cat

*French*

Once upon a time there was a young man named John; his parents were rich and did not need to work for a living. One day they gave him two thousand francs to go to a festival in a neighboring village; John lost them gambling. "If you wish," a comrade said to him, "I will lend you money." He lent him six thousand francs, and John lost them also; he was indeed disconsolate.

On his way back to his parents' home, he met a fine-looking man; it was the Devil. "What's the matter with you, my friend?" the Devil said to him; "you seem very unhappy." "I have just lost eight thousand francs." The Devil replied, "Wait, here are twenty thousand; but within a year and a day you must come to find me in the Black Forest."

Returning to his parents' home, John said to them: "I have lost a great deal of money gambling, but then I met a fine-looking man who gave me twenty thousand francs and told me to find him at the end of a year and a day in the Black Forest. "It is the Devil!" cried his parents, "you must run after him in order to return the money."

The young man mounted his horse and left immediately. When he had gone six hundred leagues, he asked some people whom he met: "Is it very far from here to the Black Forest?" "It is still six thousand leagues." "I am not nearly there," said John. Finally, just at the end of a year and a day, he arrived at the Black Forest, and near the Devil's house met a fairy who said to him: "There is a fountain in which three feathers are bathing: the Green Feather, the Yellow Feather, and the Black Feather; you will try to catch the Green Feather, take off her dress, and give her a kiss."

John went near the fountain, caught the Green Feather, and kissed her, in spite of her resistance. "The Devil is my father," she said to him then. "When you are in his house, if he offers you a chair, take another; if he says to you: 'Be seated at this table,' sit at another; if he says to you: 'Here is a plate,' do not take it; if he hands you a glass, refuse it; if he tells you to go to the room above, count the steps of the stairway up to the eighteenth; if he shows you a bed, sleep in the one beside it. And if he asks you why you have done all this, answer that it is the custom of your country."

The young man entered the Devil's house. "Good day, sir." "Good day," replied the Devil. "Here is a glass." "I will take that one." "Here is a plate." "I do not want anything." "You are indeed difficult." "People are like that in my country," the young man replied. "Come on, then, let me take you to the place where you will sleep."

While climbing the stairs, John counted the steps, one, two, three, up to eighteen. "Why are you counting thus?" "It is the custom of my country." They entered a room with two beds. "Sleep in this bed," said the Devil. "Good," said John, "I shall sleep there."

The Devil left, and John slept in the other bed. During all the night the Devil did not stop shaking and disturbing the bed in which he thought the young man had lain down. The next morning he entered the room. "Are you there?" he said to John; "you are not dead?" "No," said John. "Now," continued the Devil, "you are going to cut down my forest. Here is a pasteboard axe, a wooden saw, and a rubber bill hook. By this evening the wood must be cut, stacked in cords, and delivered to the king's courtyard."

The young man went sadly into the forest. Toward the middle of the day the Green Feather came bringing him food. "What's wrong with you, my friend?" she said to him. "Your father has commanded me to cut all his wood, to put it into cords, and to bring it this evening into the king's courtyard." The Green Feather gave a stroke of her wand; the wood was cut, placed in cords, and carried into the courtyard of the king.

When the Devil returned, he was indeed astonished. "You have done what I commanded you?" "Yes." "Oh! oh! you are stronger than I! Well, now you are going to build me a beautiful castle, well-carved, opposite my house, with a beautiful arrow in the middle."

The Green Feather came again to bring food to the young man and found him lying on the ground. "What's the matter with you?" she said to him; "what has my father commanded you to do?" "He has commanded me to build opposite his house a beautiful castle, well-carved, with a beautiful arrow in the middle." "Indeed!" said she, "I am going to change myself into a white cat. You will kill me; you will boil my skin in water; you will detach my bones, noticing well how they are placed because you must reassemble them later; you will find in my body a beautiful arrow, which you will put at the top of the castle."

The young man did all that she had told him to do; only, when he readjusted the bones, there was one little finger which was not well placed. With a stroke of the wand, the castle was built.

"You have done what I commanded you?" said the Devil. "Yes," said John. "Oh! oh! you are stronger than I!" Then he blindfolded John and said to him: "There are the Green Feather, the Yellow Feather, and the Black Feather. If you put your hand upon the one who has been changed into a white cat, you may have her in marriage." The young man put his hand upon the one in the middle; it was indeed the Green Feather.

The following evening, the Devil said to John: "You are going to sleep in this bed." John slept in the other. During the night, there arose a great wind; the Green Feather said to the young man: "Do you wish to flee with me?" "Yes, indeed I do," said John. So they flew away in the wind.

When they were near John's home, the Green Feather embraced the young man, and from being ugly he became handsome. "If your parents want to embrace you," she said to him, "do not let them, for your beauty will go away." When John entered the house, they wanted to embrace him, but he forbade it; but his old grandmother insisted upon it and soon he became ugly, as before. The Green Feather said to him: "I am going to embrace you again." She embraced him and he became handsome.

In the morning, the Devil, having climbed up to the room, found no one; he set out in pursuit of the two young people. On his way, he saw a breaker of stones. He said to him: "Have you seen a boy and a girl who flew with the wind?" "Ah! the stones are hard," the breaker of stones replied. "That is not what I asked you. Have you seen a boy and a girl who flew with the wind?" "They are certainly difficult to break," said the breaker of stones. "That is not what I am talking about."

The Devil continued on his way and met a plowman. "Have you seen a boy and a girl who flew with the wind?" "Oh! the ground is hard to break," said the plowman. "Have you seen a boy and a girl who flew with the wind?" asked the Devil again. "The work does not go well today." "I am not talking about that." The Devil, impatient, turned around.

However, a great many fine gentlemen, who did not know that White Cat was the wife of John, sought her in marriage. One came who gave her a hundred thousand francs. "Wait," she said to him, "I must leave; I have forgotten to close the door of the sideboard." When she went out, her husband, who had heard all, fell upon the suitor and beat him with his stick. Another came who gave twenty-four thousand francs to the White Cat. "Excuse me," she said to him, "I have forgotten to cover my fire." She left, and John came with a whip and whipped the good man unmercifully. A third came, who gave sixty thousand francs. "I must leave," the White Cat said to him; "I have left the door to my room open." John chased the wooer to the door with strokes of a bludgeon. They found themselves then quite rich, and they had a fine wedding feast.

*Ten*

# The Little Gardener with Golden Hair

*French*

A man and a woman who had just had a child duly found a godmother, but not a godfather. The man set out to seek one and met a fine gentleman, who was persuaded to be the godfather. He defrayed the expenses of the baptism, promised to send the child to school as soon as he could walk alone—that is to say, within a month—and he left money for the care of his godson, for whom he would return within a year and a day. The child developed very fast and went to school at the end of a month. He had nothing more to learn from his master after two months of classes and so he passed into two other schools, where he came to know more than his teachers knew.

The godfather returned at the appointed time, took John, his godson, and left money for his parents. A mare appeared on the road to lead them, and when they arrived at the castle, she jumped over the closed gate. The godfather showed John his stable where there was another horse and a mule; he was to be in charge of the castle during his godfather's absences, take excellent care of the two horses, and each day beat the mule with a big stick.

John received a little ring with which he had only to rap three times upon the table and it would be spread with whatever food he wanted. The boy immediately tried out the ring and sat down at the table with his godfather. During the meal the latter received a message that he must leave for two days. He repeated the orders to his godson and gave him the hundred keys to the hundred rooms of the castle. All these he could visit, with the exception of the hundredth. John began to visit the rooms, the first full of gold, the second full of silver, and the third full of jewels, and also to care for the horses and to beat the mule. The godfather returned and heard the boy's report, but during the meal received another message which compelled him to leave for eight days. John continued to visit the rooms, but this time he entered the hundredth. There he saw bloody corpses hanging from the ceiling and lying on the floor. His key fell into the blood and he tried his best to clean it; the more he rubbed it the larger the spot became. Later he thought of the books which he had seen in the room of corpses, and went to look at them. There he learned how to change himself into a beast, an ant, a butterfly, or a bird. In order to test his knowledge, he changed himself into an ant, and thought that in this form he could perhaps escape from his master. Returning into his human form, he cared for the horses and beat the mule; but the latter said to him:

"You would do better to give me something to drink and to eat. You have been into the hundredth room. . . . If you do not do what I am going to tell you, you will join the servants who went before you and did as you have done."

John agreed to follow the mule's advice. He gave the mule a large meal, brushed the horses with might and main, and then went into the garden taking sheets to muffle the bell, which would strike when something unusual occurred at the castle, and would thus warn the godfather even though he were a thousand leagues away. He then jumped into a fountain and came out with golden hair. Then, still following the advice of the mule, he left behind the gold, the silver, and the ring, and put upon the animal an old saddle and bridle, not the new ones which he would have preferred. Then he took his curry-comb, his brush, and his cork, jumped upon the mule, and they leaped over the gate.

Soon the mule warned John that the godfather had been told of their departure by the bell, which had struck hard and had torn the sheets. He had started in pursuit upon a horse much faster than the mule and John was to look back to let the mule know when he came near.

John at first saw nothing, then some smoke appeared. At the moment when this smoke was about to reach them, he obeyed the mule and threw the cork before them. It immediately formed a pond which was very narrow, but a hundred leagues around. The mule quickly crossed it, but the godfather had to go around.

Again John looked back but saw nothing. Then there was both fire and smoke, "which shows," said the mule, "that the godfather is to be feared more than the first time." When the fugitives were just about to be snatched, the mule told John to throw the brush. It formed a forest thirty leagues around but the width of only one league, and as thick as the bristles of the brush. The mule crossed at the center, while the godfather had to go around it.

A third time, the godfather, more terrible still, appeared as flashes of lightning and was about to catch up with John and the mule. This time John threw the curry-comb and there arose a mountain a kilometer high and ten leagues around. The mule climbed it easily, but the horse could not.

The mule walked a long time and became tired out. Again the godfather was just about to catch her when she reached a stream that marks the border of the land of mortals. With a leap she crossed it and the Devil, on the other side, could only snatch the half of her tail which was still within his reach.

Now that they were safe, the mule advised John to cover his hair with a cap as if he had scalded-head and to go see if the king needed a gardener. She also gave him a ring with which he had only to strike the ground and say, "On the strength of my little ring, come to me, my mule," and the animal would come immediately.

John went to the king's castle, and was made assistant gardener. He appeared before the main gardener, who was severe and jealous, and who told John to trim a vine, but gave him as his only tool an old wooden knife. John tried, but in vain; then out of anger he pulled up the vine and went to the gardener, and told him that it was trimmed. The gardener went to the king to complain, but meantime John had called the mule with his ring and told her what he had done. The mule, with the help of the ring, managed that the vine should be trimmed as if the best gardener had put his hand to it and that it be covered with the most beautiful grapes that had ever been seen. The king arrived with the gardener, who was stupefied and apologized for making a false report on a boy who deserved praise.

The main gardener then asked John to weed some carrots, but John pulled up the carrots and left the weeds. His master went again to complain to the king, but during the interval the mule had been called and wished with the ring that the place be decorated with carrots as large as an arm. The king was so discontented with the false reports of the master gardener that he dismissed him and gave the place to John. He offered him a staff as aid, but John refused and asked only that a small house be built for him near the gate.

John had three suits of clothes which the mule had given him. One was the color of the moon, one the color of the stars, and the third was the color of the sun. One night of the full moon, as he rode in the garden on his mule, wearing his suit the color of the sun, the youngest of the king's three daughters noticed him. She believed she recognized him and descended quickly to make sure, but John, with his ring, quickly made his suit and the mule disappear, shut himself in his house, and refused to open to the princess when she came knocking at the door. The next day as he rode again wearing his suit the color of the moon, the same thing happened, and the following day it happened again when he rode dressed in his suit the color of stars. In spite of his haste, the princess was now sure that she recognized him.

Since the eldest of the princesses wished to be married, the king decided to marry off his three daughters the same day. He gathered together the lords, the princes, the generals, and the admirals in the courtyard of the castle and gave to each of his daughters a golden ball which she was to throw at the feet of the chosen suitor. After the elder two had each chosen a prince, the third called out that not everybody was present; after the officers were brought in, she said the same; with the merchants and the workers, the same. Absent only was John the Scaldhead. The king sent for him and he came in heavy shoes and torn clothing. At his feet the third princess threw the golden ball. The king was unhappy, but he had given his word and he consented to their marriage. But he sent the couple to live in a distant house, although the two elder daughters and their husbands remained in the castle.

When he learned that his father-in-law had declared war, John the Scaldhead offered him his services, but the king gave him only a horse which walked on three legs and a rusty sword. John departed before the others, but his horse fell into a quagmire and he could not free it; his brothers-in-law, who came by on magnificent horses, followed by their armies, made fun of him in passing; but as soon as the army had passed, John called his mule, who had him put on his suit the color of the sun, and both left in grand style, passing the two brothers-in-law. They took John for a prince and wished to detain him. But John arrived alone before the enemy and strove so hard with his mule that the enemy king had to ask for a truce until the next day and gave John a paper on which he admitted having been beaten. John informed his brothers-in-law of his victory; they had turned around and found themselves in the quagmire where he had left his horse with three legs and his appearance as a scaldhead gardener.

The next day the same events occurred; John fought in his suit the color of the moon. And the following day he fought wearing his suit the color of stars. This time, John the Scaldhead destroyed almost all the enemy army, and demanded three million gold pieces, the flags, and the signing of peace.

On the return he stopped his brothers-in-law and showed them the signed treaty and the flags. These he agreed to yield to them, but beforehand he took a piece out of the middle of each flag, asked the two princes for their wedding rings, upon which their names were engraved, and finally, insisted that the mule's foot be imprinted upon each of their legs. Then he left, after accepting their invitation to come to see them, and rejoined his mired horse. His brothers-in-law made fun of John the Scaldhead in passing, spat upon him, and one of them hit him with his sword, the end of which broke and remained in the wound.

When he returned home, John was bedridden and was cared for by the king's doctor, who took out from the wound the piece of iron, and John put it carefully aside.

Several days later John had his wife invite the king to dinner, with her mother, her sisters and brothers-in-law, and the doctor. They were served a frugal menu—boiled potatoes, dark wheat cakes, and the like. At the end of a meal it was customary for each to tell a story. The king told of the marriage of his daughters, and the elder of the princes told of the victory which he and his brother had won, helped by an unknown prince.

"Would you recognize him?" asked John the Scaldhead.

"Yes, certainly, and we will see him again, as he has promised to come to see us."

John went out and called his mule and, when he had put on his suit the color of the sun, passed in front of the house. The princes and the king had him enter but did not recognize John the Scaldhead. The fine horseman bore witness to the victory of the princes, asked to see the flags, and stated that for each there was lacking a piece in the middle; he brought out the missing pieces

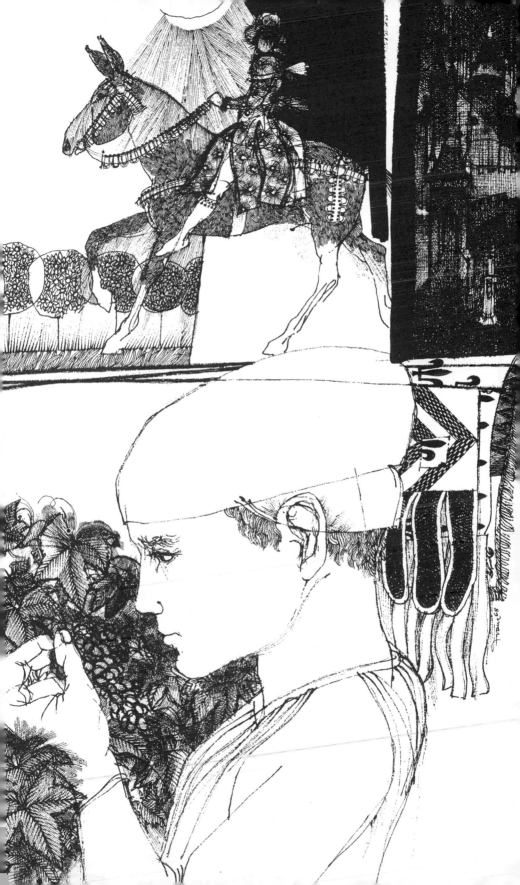

from a little box, offered the two rings of the sisters-in-law, and finally showed on the skin of the two princes the imprint of the mule's foot. Then he revealed his identity, told how one of his brothers-in-law had hit him with his sword, and took as witness the doctor who had pulled out the piece of the weapon, and they saw that the piece fitted one of the two swords. Then the king angrily sent away the two princes and condemned them to exile and decided that John the Scaldhead should remain near him and would have his crown.

*Eleven*

# Anpu and Bata

*Literary* (*Ancient Egyptian*)

Now there were once, they say, two brothers, of the same father and mother; Anpu was the name of the elder, and Bata the name of the younger. Now Anpu had a house and a wife, and his younger brother lived with him like a son. It was he who made clothes for him, and drove his cattle to the fields. And it was he who did the plowing and harvested for him, and he who did all the work that there is in fields. Now the younger brother was a comely lad; there was not his like in all the land; and the might of a god was in him.

And Anpu's younger brother tended his cattle according to his daily wont, and went home to his house each evening laden with all manner of herbs of the field, and with milk and wood, and all good things of the field, and set them down before his elder brother, who was sitting with his wife, and drank and ate, and went out to sleep in his cow-house among his cattle, alone.

Now when it had dawned and another day was come, the younger brother brought food which had been cooked and set it down before his elder brother, who gave him provisions for the fields; and he collected his cattle to pasture them in the fields, and he drove them out, and they said to him, "The grass of such-and-such a place is good," and he understood all that they said and

From *Land of Enchanters*, translated by Battiscombe Gunn. Used by permission of Harvill Press.

took them off to the good place with the grass that they desired. And the cattle that he tended became very fine, and they increased their calving very much.

Now at the time of plowing his elder brother said to him, "Make ready for us a good span of oxen for plowing, for the land has come forth and it is good for plowing. Also come to the field with seed-corn, for we shall be busy plowing tomorrow" —so he said to him. And his younger brother did just as his elder brother had told him to do.

Now when it had dawned and another day was come, they went to the field with their seed-corn, and busied themselves with plowing, and they were very happy in their work at the beginning of their labors.

Now some time after this they were in the field, and they were held up for seed-corn, and Anpu sent his younger brother, saying, "Go and fetch us seed-corn from the village." And Bata found his elder brother's wife sitting doing her hair; and he said to her, "Get up and give me some seed-corn, that I may go back to the field, because my elder brother will be waiting for me; don't make me wait." And she said to him, "Go and open the granary and bring away what you want; don't make me interrupt my hairdressing."

And the lad went into his cow-house, and brought a large vessel, wishing to take away much seed-corn; and he loaded himself up with barley and spelt and came out with them.

And she said to him, "What is the amount that's on your shoulder?" And he told her, "It's three bushels of spelt and two bushels of barley, five bushels in all, that are on my shoulder"— so he told her. And she talked with him, saying, "There is great strength in you; for I see your feats daily." And she desired to know him as a male is known, and she stood up and took hold of him, and said to him, "Come, let us spend an hour lying down. It will be well for you—then I will make you fine clothes."

And the lad became like a panther of southern Egypt for great anger at the evil speech that she had uttered to him. And she was very much afraid. And he talked with her, saying, "But see, you are like a mother to me, and your husband is like a father to me, and he, who is older than I, it is he who has brought me up. What is this great crime that you have mentioned to me? Do not say it to me again, and I will tell it to no one. I will not let it come out of my mouth to anyone." And he lifted up his burden and went off to the field. And he reached his elder brother, and they busied themselves in their labors.

Now afterwards, at evening-time, his elder brother went home to his house, while Bata tended his cattle and loaded himself with all manner of things of the field, and brought his cattle back before him to put them into their cow-house in the village for the night.

Now his elder brother's wife was afraid because of the speech that she had uttered; and she brought fat and grease, and feigned to have been beaten, with the intent to say to her husband, "It is your younger brother who has beaten me."

And her husband came back in the evening, according to his daily wont, and he reached his house, and found his wife lying down pretending to be in pain; she did not pour water over his hands according to his wont, nor had she lighted the lamp before he came in, and his house was in darkness, and she was lying vomiting. And her husband said to her, "Who has been speaking with you?" Then she said to him, "No one has been speaking with me except your younger brother. When he came to fetch away seed-corn for you and found me sitting alone he said to me, 'Come, let us spend an hour lying down. Put on your wig,' he said to me, and I did not listen to him. 'Am I not your mother, and is not your brother like a father to you?' I said to him. And he was afraid, and he beat me to prevent me from reporting it to you. Now if you let him live I will kill myself. See, when he comes back, do not speak to him, because if I were to make this ugly accusation (before him) he would turn it into an injury."

And his elder brother became like a panther of southern Egypt for anger, and he sharpened his spear, and took it in his hand, and he stood behind the door of his cow-house to kill his younger brother when he should return in the evening to drive his cattle into the cow-house.

Now when the sun set Bata loaded himself with all manner of herbs of the field, according to his daily wont, and came back; and the foremost cow entered the cow-house, and said to her herds-man, "See, your elder brother is standing in front of you with his spear to kill you. Flee before him." And he understood what his foremost cow had said; and the next one went in and said the same thing. And he looked under the door of his cow-house, and saw the feet of his elder brother as he stood behind the door with his spear in his hand. And he set his burden down on the ground and betook himself to speedy flight. And his elder brother went after him with his spear.

And his younger brother prayed to Rē-Harákhte, saying, "My good Lord, thou art he who judges between the evil-doer and the just man." Then Rē heard all his appeal, and created a great water between him and his elder brother, full of crocodiles, and one of them found himself on one side, the other on the other. And the elder brother struck twice on his hands because of not having killed him. And the younger brother called to him from the other side, saying, "Stay here until dawn, and when the sun rises you and I will be judged before him, and he will deliver the evil-doer to the righteous; for I will never live with you again, nor be in any place where you are. I will go to the Valley of the Cedar."

Now when it had dawned and another day was come, Rē-Harákhte arose, and they saw one another. And the lad spoke with his elder brother, saying, "Why did you pursue me to kill me wrongfully, before you had heard what I had to say? For I am indeed your younger brother, and you are like a father to m ., and your wife is like a mother to me; is it not so? Now when you sent me to fetch seed-corn for us, your wife said to me, 'Come, let us spend an hour lying down'; but see, to you she has turned it into the opposite."

And he informed him of everything that had happened between him and his wife; and he swore by Rē-Harákhte, saying, "Your coming with your spear to kill me wrongfully was at the bidding of a whore." And he took a reed-knife, and cut off his privy member, and threw it into the water, and a shad-fish swallowed it. And he grew faint and became weak. And his elder brother was very sorry for him, and stood weeping aloud for him; he was not able to cross the water to where his younger brother was, because of the crocodiles.

And his younger brother called to him, saying, "Though you remember one bad matter, do you not remember one good one, or one thing that I have done for you? Go home, and collect your cattle, for I will not stay in any place where you are. I will go to the Valley of the Cedar. Now what you shall do for me is to come to help me, if you know that anything is wrong with me, for I shall take out my heart, and place it on the top of the flower of the cedar. And if the cedar is cut down, and my heart falls to the ground and you come to seek it, even if you spend seven years in seeking it do not be discouraged. And if you find it, and put it into a jar of cold water, then I shall come to life, and will take vengeance for being sinned against. And you will know if anything is wrong with me, when a mug of beer is given into your hand and it foams up. Then do not delay. Certainly it will happen to you."

And he went off to the Valley of the Cedar; and his elder brother went off to his house with his hand laid on his head, which was smeared with dust. Then he arrived at his house, and he killed his wife, and threw her to the dogs. And he dwelt in mourning for his younger brother.

Now some time after this Bata was in the Valley of the Cedar, no one being with him; and he spent his days hunting the beasts of the desert, and in the evening he came back to lie down under the cedar, on the top of whose flower his heart was.

Now some time after this he built himself a castle with his own hands in the Valley of the Cedar, full of all good things, in order to set up a home for himself. Then he came out of his castle, and he encountered the Nine Gods, walking and ordering the affairs of the whole world. And the Nine told one of themselves to say to him, "Hail Bata, Bull of the Nine, are you here alone, having left your town, fleeing from the wife of Anpu, your elder brother? See, he has killed his wife, and you are avenged on him for all the injuries done you." And they were very sorry for him. And Rē-Harákhte said to Khnūm, "Do you fashion a spouse for Bata, that he may not dwell alone."

And Khnūm made him a spouse, who was more beautiful in body than any woman in all the world; the essence of every god was in her. And the Seven Hathors came to see her; and they said with one voice, "She will have a sharp death."

And he loved her very much; and she dwelt in his house, and he spent his days hunting the beasts of the desert, bringing them and laying them before her. And he said to her, "Do not go outside lest the sea carry you off; for I shall not be able to save you from it, because I am a woman like you. Now my heart lies on the top of the flower of the cedar, and if anyone else finds it I shall fight with him." And he described his heart to her in all its detail.

Now some time after this Bata went to hunt, after his daily wont. Then the girl went out to walk about under the cedar, which was beside her house. Then the sea saw her, its waves beating after her, and she betook herself to flight before it and went into her house. And the sea called to the cedar, saying,

"Seize her for me." And the cedar brought a lock of her hair. And the sea brought it to Egypt, and laid it at the place of the launderers of Pharaoh. And the smell of the lock of hair got into Pharaoh's clothes; and Pharaoh's servants quarrelled with Pharaoh's launderers, saying, "Pharaoh's clothes smell of unguent." And they fell to quarrelling with them every day, and they did not know what to do.

And Pharaoh's head launderer walked to the river-bank, and he was very wretched owing to the contention with him every day. And he stopped still and stood on the desert opposite the lock of hair, which was in the water; and he made a man go down, and he brought it to him. And he found its odour very sweet, and he took it to Pharaoh. And they fetched the scribes and learned men of Pharaoh; and they said to Pharaoh, "This lock of hair belongs to a daughter of Rē-Harákhte in whom is the essence of every god. Now it is a present to you from another country. Send messengers to every foreign land to seek her; but the messenger who goes to the Valley of the Cedar, send many people with him to bring her back." Then His Majesty said, "What you have said is very good"; and people were sent forth.

Now some time after this the people who had gone abroad came back to make report to His Majesty; but those who had gone to the Valley of the Cedar did not return, for Bata had killed them—but he spared one of them to make report to His Majesty. And His Majesty sent many foot-soldiers, and also chariotry, to fetch her back. And there was a woman among them into whose hand had been given all beautiful adornments of women. And the woman came back to Egypt with her, and there was rejoicing over her in all the land. And His Majesty loved her very much, and he gave her the rank of Great Favorite.

And he spoke with her to get her to describe her husband; and she said to His Majesty, "Have the cedar cut down and broken up." And he sent foot-soldiers with their weapons to cut down the cedar, and they reached the cedar and cut down the flower on which was Bata's heart, and he fell down dead at that very moment.

Now when it had dawned and another day was come, the cedar having been cut down, Anpu, the elder brother of Bata, went into his house and sat down to wash his hands. And a mug of beer was given to him, and it foamed up; and another, of wine, was given to him, and it turned sour. And he took up his staff and his sandals, also his clothes and his weapons, and set forth to journey to the Valley of the Cedar.

And he entered the castle of his younger brother, and found him lying on his couch, dead. And he wept when he saw his younger brother lying in death, and went to search for his heart under the cedar under which his younger brother went to sleep in the evening. And he spent three years in seeking it, without finding it. And when he had entered upon the fourth year, he longed to return to Egypt, and said, "I will go away tomorrow" —so he said in his heart.

Now when it had dawned and another day was come, he fell to walking under the cedar, and spent the day seeking the heart. And he went back in the evening, and spent a short time in seeking it again. And he found a berry, and went back with it. Now it was his younger brother's heart. And he fetched a jar of cold water and threw it into it, and he sat down according to his daily wont.

Now when night had come Bata's heart absorbed the water, and Bata quivered all over, and suddenly looked at his elder brother, while his heart was in the jar. And Anpu, his elder brother, took up the jar of cold water in which was his younger brother's heart, and the heart had drunk it, and his heart stood in its place, and he became as he had been. And they embraced one another, and each of them spoke with his fellow. And Bata said to his elder brother, "See, I will become a great bull, with all beautiful markings, one the nature of which will not be known; and you shall sit on my back until the sun rises, and we are in the place where my wife is, that I may take vengeance. And you shall take me to the place where the King is, for all good things will be done for you, and you will be rewarded with silver and gold for having taken me to Pharaoh, for I shall become a great wonder, and they will rejoice over me in all the land, and you will go away to your village."

Now when it had dawned and another day was come, then Bata took on the form which he had told his brother about, and Anpu, his elder brother, sat on his back until dawn, and he reached the place where the King was. And His Majesty was informed about him, and he saw him, and he was very glad about him. And he made a great feast because of him, saying, "This is a great marvel that has happened"; and they rejoiced over him in all the land. And the King loaded him with silver and gold for his elder brother, who dwelt in his village and the King gave him many people and much property, and Pharaoh loved him very much, more than anybody else in all the land.

Now some time after this the bull went into the dining-room, and stood where the Favorite was and he fell to talking with her, saying, "See, I am still alive." And she said to him, "Who, pray, are you?" And he said to her, "I am Bata. I know that when you had the cedar broken up for Pharaoh it was on my account, so that I should not live; but see, I am still alive, being a bull." And the Favorite was very frightened at the announcement that her husband had made to her. And he went out of the dining-room.

And His Majesty sat making holiday with her, and she poured out wine for His Majesty; and the King was very happy with her. And she said to His Majesty, "Swear to me by God, saying, 'What the Favorite may say I will obey for her sake'"; and he hearkened to all that she said. "Let me be allowed to eat some of the liver of this bull, for he will be of no use," she said to him. And the King was very much vexed at what she had said, and Pharaoh was very sorry for him.

Now when it had dawned and another day was come, the King announced a great feast with sacrifice of the bull, and the King sent one of his chief butchers to have the bull dispatched. And afterwards he was dispatched and while he was borne on the men's shoulders he shook his neck, and cast two drops of blood beside the two door-jambs of His Majesty—one of them fell on one side of the Great Portal of Pharaoh, and the other on the other side—and they grew into two large persea trees, and each of them was very fine. And they went to tell His Majesty, "Two large persea trees have grown up, a great marvel for His Majesty, in the night, beside His Majesty's Great Portal." And they rejoiced over them in all the land, and the King made offering to them.

Now some time after this His Majesty appeared at the Lapis-lazuli Window, with a garland of all manner of flowers at his neck; and he was in a gilded chariot, and he came out of the palace to see the persea trees. And the Favorite came out with horses, following Pharaoh. And His Majesty sat down under one of the persea trees, and the Favorite under the other. And Bata spoke with his wife, saying, "O you traitress, I am Bata, and I am alive in spite of you! I know of your having caused the cedar to be cut down for Pharaoh on my account, and I became a bull and you had me killed."

Now some time after this the Favorite stood pouring out wine for His Majesty, and the King was happy with her. And she said to His Majesty, "Swear to me by God, saying, 'What the Favorite may tell me I will obey for her sake,' so you shall say." And he hearkened to all that she said. And she said, "Have these two persea trees cut down, and made into beautiful furniture." And the King obeyed all that she said, and after a short time His Majesty sent cunning carpenters, and Pharaoh's persea trees were cut down. And the King's wife, the Favorite, watched. And a splinter flew up and entered the Favorite's mouth, and she swallowed it, and she conceived and became pregnant in the space of a moment. And the King did everything that she fancied with the trees.

Now some time after this she gave birth to a man-child, and they went to tell His Majesty, "A man-child has been born to you"; and he was fetched, and a nurse and female attendants were given him, and people rejoiced over him in all the land. And the King sat making holiday, and the people were jubilant. And His Majesty loved him at once, very much, and appointed him Viceroy of Nubia.

Now some time after this His Majesty made him Crown Prince of the whole land. Now some time after this, when he had spent many years as Crown Prince of the whole land, His Majesty flew up to heaven. And the new King said, "Let my great royal officials be brought to me, that I may inform them of everything that has happened to me." And his wife was brought to him, and he and she were judged before them, and they agreed with him. And his elder brother was brought to him, and he made him Crown Prince of the whole land. And he spent thirty years as King of Egypt, and then passed away to Life. And his elder brother arose in his place on the day of "landing."

*Twelve*

# The Doctor and His Pupil

*French*

There was once a poor man who had a twelve-year-old son. He sent him to find work.

The boy departed wearing a jacket that was red in front and white behind. He passed in front of a castle; it was the residence of a doctor, who happened to be standing at the window. As he needed a servant, the master of the castle called the boy.

"What are you looking for in these parts?"

"Since I'd like to make a living, I'm looking for work."

"Do you know how to read?"

"Yes, for I've been to school for six months."

"Then you won't do."

The boy went away; but in a few days he came back with his jacket on backwards and passed once more in front of the castle. Again the master was at his window.

"What are you looking for in these parts?"

"I'd like to make a living; I'm looking for work."

"Do you know how to read?"

"No, for I've never been to school."

"Well, then, come in; I'll hire you. I'll give you one hundred francs a year and board."

The boy entered and his master gave him something to eat. Then he showed him his book of secrets and gave him a duster.

"You will dust my book carefully every day, and that's all you'll have to do."

Then the doctor left on a trip and was gone a whole year. The boy took advantage of this absence to read his master's book and get acquainted with the doctor's skills.

The physician returned. He was very happy with his servant and departed for another year. During this second absence, the boy learned half of the book by heart.

The doctor returned and was so happy with his servant that he

From *The Borzoi Book of French Folk Tales*, by Paul Delarue and translated by Austin Fife. © Copyright 1956 by Alfred A. Knopf, Inc. Reprinted by permission of Alfred A. Knopf, Inc.

doubled his wages and departed for another year. During this third absence the young man learned the remainder of the book by heart. When his master returned he left the doctor's employ to return to his parents, who were as poor as ever.

On the eve of the village fair the young man said to his father: "Tomorrow go into the stable; you will find a beautiful horse that you must take to the fair. Sell him, but above all be sure to keep the halter."

The next day the father entered the stable and found a magnificent horse. He took it to the fair and buyers hastened around to admire the handsome animal. The father sold it for a good price, but he kept the halter and put it in his pocket. Then he set out on the road to his village and shortly he heard footsteps behind him: it was his son, who, having transformed himself into a horse and then retransformed himself into his natural shape while the buyer of the horse was celebrating in the tavern, was hastening to catch up with his father. And both were delighted with the fine deal they had made.

After a time there was no more money left in the house.

"Don't worry about it," said the boy to his father. "I'll see that you get more. Go in the stable tomorrow; you will find a steer that you can take to the fair. But when you sell it be sure to keep the rope that you are leading it with."

All took place at the fair as before, and the boy caught up with his father, whose appetite had been whetted by this money which was so easily earned, and who now proposed to take his son again to the next fair in the form of a horse.

But the doctor, by consulting his book, had become aware of what his former servant was doing. He went to the fair, recognized the horse, and bought it. He took the father to the inn to conclude the bargain and made him drink a great deal so that he forgot to keep the halter.

The doctor took the horse quickly away to a blacksmith. "Give him a good shoeing," he advised.

The horse was tied to the door. The children came out of school and a group of them came to hang around the blacksmith shop. The horse extended its muzzle toward a child and whispered to him:

"Untie me!"

The child was afraid and withdrew a bit; but the horse repeated: "Child, untie me!"

The schoolboy approached and untied him. Immediately the horse transformed itself into a hare and ran away. The doctor saw it and turned six boys into hunting dogs. The hare came to the edge of a reservoir, jumped in, and turned into a carp. The doctor arrived, bought all the fish in the reservoir, and had it fished clean. He recognized the carp and was about to grab it when it turned into a lark. He turned into an eagle and pursued the lark, which flew over a castle and fell down the chimney, where it turned into a grain of wheat, which rolled under the table in the bedroom of the girl of the castle.

The day passed. In the evening when the girl had gone to bed, the young man said:

"Mademoiselle, if you wish—"

The girl, hearing his voice, cried out to her parents, who came at once.

"What's the matter?"

"There's someone talking in here!"

But the young man turned back into a grain of wheat and rolled under the table. The parents turned on the lights, looked everywhere, and, finding nothing, departed.

The young man took his own shape and made more advances. The girl cried and her parents returned.

"There's been more talking in the room."

"Have you gone mad?" said the father.

"Well! Go to bed here if you want to hear it."

The father stayed a moment, then went away. The young man reappeared and the girl ended by acceding to him.

"Nights I shall sleep with you and days you may wear me as an engagement ring on your finger."

But the doctor found out all that was going on by consulting his books. He caused the father to become ill and came as a doctor to cure him.

"Heal me and I will pay you well," said the father.

"All I want is the ring on your daughter's finger."

The father promised. But the young man was aware of what was going on.

"The doctor is going to ask you for your ring," he said to the girl. "Don't give it to him; let it fall on the floor."

When the father was cured he called his daughter and told her to give the ring to the doctor. She took it off and let it fall; the ring turned into grains of wheat, which scattered out on the floor. The doctor turned into a rooster to pick them up. The young man turned into a fox and ate the rooster.

*Thirteen*

# A Tale of a Boy Who Set Out to Learn Fear

*German*

A father had two sons: of these the elder was bright and clever and knew how to get along everywhere, but the younger was dull and couldn't understand or learn anything, and when people saw him, they'd say, "He'll be a burden to his father." Whenever something was to be done, it was always the elder who had to do it. Nevertheless, if his father bade him fetch something late in the evening or even at night and if the way led across a churchyard or some other creepy place, he'd reply, "Oh, no, father, I won't go there; it makes me shudder," for he was afraid. Or, if of an evening stories were told by the fireside that made one shudder, those listening would sometimes say, "Oh, it makes me shudder." The younger son used then to sit in a corner and hear this and couldn't understand what it meant. "They keep saying, 'It makes me shudder, it makes me shudder'; it doesn't make me shudder, there must be some trick I don't understand."

Now his father once happened to say to him, "Listen, you over there in the corner, you're getting big and strong; you've got to learn something to earn your living by. See how hard your brother works while you're just hopeless." "Why, father," he replied, "I very much want to learn something; indeed, if possible, I'd like to learn shuddering; that's something I don't know anything about yet." On hearing that, the elder brother laughed and thought to himself: "Dear God, what a fool my brother is! He'll never get anywhere that way. As the twig is bent, the tree's inclined." The father heaved a sigh and answered, "You'll learn

From *German Folk Tales*, collected and edited by Grimm Brothers. Translated by Francis P. Magoun, Jr. and Alexander H. Krappe. Copyright © 1960, by Southern Illinois University Press. Reprinted by permission of the Southern Illinois University Press.

shuddering all right, but you won't earn your living that way."

Soon after that the sexton came to call, and the father told him his tale of woe, how his younger son was so ignorant in everything that he knew nothing and learned nothing. "Just think, when I asked him how he was going to earn his living, he actually asked to learn shuddering." "If that's all," answered the sexton, "he can learn that from me; turn him over to me and I'll plane off the rough edges all right." The father agreed, for he thought, "The boy'll at least be trimmed up a little." So the sexton took him into his home, and he had to ring the church bell. After a few days the sexton roused him at midnight, bade him get up, climb the steeple, and ring the bell. "You'll certainly learn what shuddering is," he thought, and went out secretly. When the boy was up in the steeple and turned around and was about to take hold of the bell rope, he saw a white form standing on the stairs opposite the sound hole. "Who's there?" he cried. But the form made no reply and neither moved nor stirred. "Answer me!" cried the boy, "or else get out; you've no business here at night." But the sexton remained motionless, so that the boy might think it was a specter. The boy called out a second time, "What do you want here? If you're an honest fellow, speak, or I'll throw you down the stairs." The sexton thought, "His bark's probably worse than his bite," didn't utter a sound, and stood stock-still. Then the boy called to him a third time, and when that did no good, made a dash and pushed the specter down the stairs so that it fell ten steps and lay in a corner. Then he rang the bell, returned home, and without saying a word went to bed and fell asleep. The sexton's wife waited a long time for her husband, but he didn't come back. Finally she got frightened and woke the boy up and asked, "Do you know where my husband has got to? He climbed the steeple ahead of you." "No," answered the boy, "but somebody was standing there on the stairs opposite the sound hole, and because he didn't answer me and wouldn't go away, I took him for a rogue and pushed him downstairs. Just go there and you'll see whether it was he; I'd be sorry if it were." The woman ran off and found her husband lying in a corner; he was groaning and had broken a leg.

She carried him down and then, crying loudly, hurried to the boy's father. "Your boy," she shouted, "caused a serious accident; he threw my husband downstairs so that he broke a leg. Get the good-for-nothing out of our house." The father was frightened, came on the run, and scolded the boy: "What kind of mischief have you been up to? The Evil One must have put you up to it." "Father," he answered, "just listen! I'm quite innocent; he was standing there in the night like someone with evil intentions. I didn't know who it was. Three times I told him to speak up or else go away." "Dear me!" said his father, "you only bring me misfortune. Get out of my sight! I don't want to see you any more." "All right, father, I'll do so quite willingly, only wait till morning then I'll get out and learn shuddering. Then I'll know at least one craft that I can earn my living by." "Learn whatever you like," said the father; "it's all the same to me. Here's fifty dollars. Take them and go out in the world, and don't tell anyone where you're from or who your father is, for I'm ashamed of you." "Yes, father, as you wish—so long as you ask for nothing more. That much I can easily keep in mind."

When day broke, the boy put the fifty dollars in his pocket, went out on the highway, and kept saying to himself, "If only I could shudder; if only I could shudder." Then a man came along who heard what the boy was saying to himself, and when they had gone a little farther so that one could see the gallows, the man said to him: "You see, there's the tree where seven men were wedded to the ropemaker's daughter and now are learning to fly. Sit down underneath it and wait till night comes; then you'll surely learn shuddering." "If that's all," answered the boy, "it's easy. If I learn shuddering that quickly, you shall have my fifty dollars. Just come back here tomorrow morning." The boy then went to the gallows, sat down underneath, and waited till nightfall. Because he was cold, he made a fire, but about midnight the wind got so cold that even with the fire he couldn't keep warm, and when the wind knocked the bodies of the hanged men against one another and they swung to and fro, he thought, "I'm cold down here by the fire; how frightfully cold and shivering they must be up there!" And because he took pity on them, he set up the ladder, mounted it, untied one after the other, and took all seven down. Then he stirred the fire, blew it up, and placed them around it, that they might get warm. But they sat there and didn't move, and their clothes caught fire. Then he said, "Look out, or I'll hang you up again." But the dead didn't hear, remained silent, and let their poor rags burn away. Then he lost his temper and said, "If you won't look out, I can't help you; I don't want to burn up with you," and hung them up again one after the other. Then he sat down by his fire and fell asleep. The next morning the man came to him, wanted the fifty dollars, and said, "Do you now know what shuddering is?" "No," he replied, "how should I? Those men up there didn't open their mouths and were so stupid that they let the few old rags they had on burn up." Then the man saw that he wouldn't get the fifty dollars that day and went off, saying, "I've never run into anyone like that."

The boy continued on his way and again began saying to himself, "Oh, if only I could shudder! oh, if only I could shudder!" A carter who was walking behind him overheard this and asked, "Who are you?" "I don't know," answered the boy. The carter continued to question him: "Where are you from?" "I don't know." "Who's your father?" "I mustn't tell." "What are you mumbling about all the time?" "Why," replied the boy, "I'd like to shudder, but no one can teach me how." "Stop your silly talk," said the carter; "come along with me and I'll see if I can put you up." The boy went with the carter, and in the evening they reached an inn where they planned to spend the night. On entering the taproom he again said aloud, "If only I could shudder! if only I could shudder!" Hearing that, the innkeeper laughed and said, "If that's what you want, there's a fine chance right here." "Oh, do be still," said the innkeeper's wife. "Many a Paul Pry has already lost his life; it would be a crying shame if his fine eyes should never see the light of day again." But the boy said, "Even if it's as hard as that, I want to learn it; that's why I left home." He gave the innkeeper no peace till the latter told him that not far off was an enchanted castle where one could certainly learn what shuddering was if he'd just stand watch there for three nights. He said that the king had promised his daughter in marriage to anyone who'd venture it, and that she was the most beautiful girl the sun shone upon. Furthermore, there were in the castle huge treasures guarded by evil spirits; this would then become free and would be enough to make a poor man rich. Many had, to be sure, gone in, but as yet no one had ever come out again. The next morning the boy went into the king's presence and said, "If it's allowed, I should very much like to keep watch for three nights in the enchanted castle." The king looked at him, and because he took a fancy to him, said, "You may ask for three things, but they must be inanimate objects; you may take them with you into the castle." Then he answered, "In that case, I ask for a fire, a lathe, and a carpenter's bench and knife."

The king had all this taken into the castle by daylight. As night drew near, the boy went up, kindled a bright fire in one of the rooms, set the carpenter's bench and the knife beside it, and sat down at the lathe. "Oh, if only I could shudder!" he said, "but I shan't learn it here, either." Toward midnight he wanted to stir up the fire, and as he was blowing into it, there came a cry from a corner, "Miaow, miaow, we're so cold!" "You fools," he shouted, "what are you crying for? If you're cold, come here and sit down by the fire and warm yourselves." No sooner had he said that than two big black cats came with a jump, sat down beside him and looked at him quite fiercely with their glowing eyes. After a while when they'd got warm, they said, "Shall we play a round of cards, pal?" "Why not?" he answered. "But first let's see your paws." Then they stretched out their claws. "My!" he said, "what long nails you've got! Wait a minute! I must first clip them for you." Thereupon he seized them by their necks, lifted them up onto the workbench, and made their paws fast in a vice. "I've had a look at your fingers," he said, "and I've lost all desire for cards." Then he killed them and threw them out into the pond. After he'd quieted those two and was about to sit down again by the fire, black cats and black dogs on glowing chains came out of every nook and corner—more and more and more—until he didn't know where to take refuge. They yowled horribly, trampled his fire, pulled it apart, and were about to put it out. He watched them quietly for a while, but when it got too bad, he seized his knife and shouted, "Get out, you scum!" and cut loose at them. Some of them ran away, the others he killed and threw out into the pond. When he came back, he blew up his fire afresh from the coals and warmed himself. As he was sitting thus, he couldn't keep his eyes open any longer and was overcome with a desire to sleep. Just then he looked about him and saw a big bed in a corner. "That's just the thing," he said, and lay down in it. As he was about to shut his eyes, the bed began to move of itself and traveled all through the castle. "Right you are," he said, "only faster!" Then as if drawn by six horses the bed rolled on over thresholds and up and down stairs. All of a sudden, bump, bump, it tipped over and lay upside down on top of him like a mountain. But he flung the covers and pillows into the air and climbed out, saying, "Anyone who wants to may take a ride." He lay down by the fire and slept until daybreak. In the morning the king came and, seeing him lying on the floor thought that the specters had killed him and that he was dead. So he said, "It's too bad about the fine-looking chap." The boy heard him, got up, and said, "It's not that bad." The king was astonished but very happy and asked him how he'd fared. "Very well," he answered. "One night's over; the other two will pass, also." When he got to the innkeeper's, the latter looked surprised. "I didn't think," he said, "that I'd see you alive again. Now have you learned what shuddering is?" "No," he replied, "it's all no use. If only someone could tell me!"

The second night he again went up into the old castle, sat down by the fire, and again started his old refrain, "If only I could shudder!" As midnight drew near, there was a rumbling, tumbling noise, first soft, then louder and louder; then it grew quiet for a bit. At last half a man came down the chimney with a loud cry and dropped right in front of him. "Hello!" he shouted, "there's still another half; this isn't enough." Then the noise began again: there was a roaring and howling and then the other half dropped down. "Wait a minute," he said; "let me first blow up the fire a little." When he'd done so and was looking about, the two pieces had put themselves together and a horrible man was sitting in his seat. "That's not what we bargained for," said the boy; "it's my bench." The man was about to shove him off, but the boy didn't stand for that; he pushed him off violently and sat down again at his place. Then still more men came tumbling down one after the other. They fetched nine dead men's bones and two dead men's skulls, set them up, and played ninepins. The boy wanted to play, too, and asked, "Listen, may I play, too?" "Yes, if you have money." "Plenty," he answered, "but your bowls aren't quite round." Then he took the dead men's heads, put them in the lathe, and turned them till they were round. "Now they'll roll better," he said; "hurray, now there'll be some fun!" He joined the game and lost a little money, but when the clock struck twelve, everything disappeared before his eyes. He lay down and quietly went to sleep. Next morning the king came and wanted to hear the news. "How did you fare this time?" he asked. "I played ninepins," he answered, "and lost a few farthings." "Didn't you shudder?" "Good heavens, no," he said. "I had a fine time. If only I might know what shuddering is!"

The third night he sat down again on his workbench and quite out of sorts said, "If only I could shudder!" When it got late, six tall men came in carrying a coffin. Then he said, "Ha! ha! That's no doubt my cousin who died only a few days ago." He beckoned with his finger and called out, "Come here, cousin, come here!" They set the coffin on the floor, and he stepped up and opened the lid: there was a dead man inside. He felt the face, but it was as cold as ice. "Just a minute," he said, "I'll warm you up a bit," went to the fire, warmed his hand, and laid it on the face. The dead man, however, remained cold. Then he took him out of the coffin, laid him by the fire, and putting him on his lap, rubbed his arms to get his blood circulating again. When even that did no good, he remembered that "when two people lie together in one bed, they warm each other up," put him in his bed, covered him, and lay down beside him. After a while the dead man got warm and began to move. Then the boy said, "Look here, cousin, suppose I hadn't warmed you?" But the dead man began to shout, "Now I'm going to strangle you." "What!" he said. "Is that the thanks I get? You're going right back into your coffin," picked him up, threw him into the coffin, and closed the lid. Then the six men came and carried it off again. "I simply can't shudder," he said. "I shan't learn it here as long as I live."

Then in came a man who was taller than all the rest and horrible looking; he was old and had a long white beard. "O you scoundrel," he cried, "now you'll soon learn what shuddering is, for you're going to die." "Not so fast!" answered the boy. "If I'm going to die, I must at least be present." "I'll catch you all right," said the monster. "Easy, easy, don't talk so big; I'm as strong as you and, indeed, even stronger." "We'll see," said the old man. "If you're stronger than I, I'll let you go. Come on, let's try." He led him through dark passageways to a smithy fire, took an ax, and with one blow drove one anvil right into the ground. "I can do better than that," said the boy, and stepped up to the other anvil. The old man took up a position close by in order to watch, and his white beard was flowing down. Then the boy seized the ax, split the anvil with one blow, wedging in the old man's beard. "Now I've got you!" said the boy; "now it's your turn to die." Then he seized an iron bar and pitched into the old man until he whimpered and begged him to stop, promising to bestow great riches upon him. The boy pulled out the ax and let him go. The old man led him back into the castle and showed him three chests full of gold in a cellar. "Of this," he said, "one part belongs to the poor, the other to the king, and the third is yours." Thereupon it struck twelve and the specter vanished so that the boy was alone in the darkness. "I'll be able to get out of here just the same," he said, groped about, found the way to his room, and fell asleep by his fire. The next morning the king appeared and said, "Now you must have learned what shuddering is." "No," he answered. "What is it really? My dead cousin was there, and a bearded man came who showed me a lot of money downstairs, but no one told me what shuddering is." Then the king said, "You've disenchanted the castle and are to marry my daughter."

"That's all very fine," he replied, "but I still don't know what shuddering is."

The gold was brought upstairs and the wedding celebrated, but the young king, fond as he was of his wife and happy as he was, still kept saying, "If only I could shudder, if only I could shudder." Finally she got tired of it. Her chambermaid said, "I'll manage it so he'll learn what shuddering is." She went to the brook that flowed through the garden and got herself a whole pail of minnows. In the night, as the young king was asleep, his wife pulled off the covers and poured over him the pail of cold water with the minnows so that the little fish wriggled around all over him. Then he woke up and cried out, "Oh, how I'm shuddering, how I'm shuddering, my dear! Yes, now I know what shuddering is."

*Fourteen*

# Haensel and Gretel

*German*

Near a large forest lived a poor woodcutter with his wife and two children. The boy's name was Haensel and the girl's Gretel. The woodcutter had little to eat, and once when a great famine swept the country, he was no longer able to earn even their daily bread. One evening when he was lying in his bed and tossing about and worrying, he sighed and said to his wife, "What's to become of us? How can we feed our poor children when we've nothing left for ourselves?" "Do you know what, husband," answered the

From *German Folk Tales*, collected and edited by Grimm Brothers. Translated by Francis P. Magoun, Jr. and Alexander H. Krappe. Copyright © 1960, by Southern Illinois University Press. Reprinted by permission of the Southern Illinois University Press.

wife, "the first thing tomorrow morning we'll take the children out into the densest part of the forest. There we'll kindle them a fire and give each a little piece of bread; then we'll go about our work and leave them there alone; they won't find the way back home, and we'll be rid of them." "No, wife," said the man, "that I won't do. How could I have the heart to leave my children alone in the forest; the wild animals would soon come and tear them to pieces." "O you fool," she said, "then all four of us will starve to death; you might as well start planing the boards for our coffins," and gave him no peace until he agreed. "But all the same I'm sorry for the poor children," said the man.

The two children hadn't been able to get to sleep, either, because they were hungry and heard what their stepmother said to their father. Gretel wept bitter tears and said to Haensel, "Now it's all up with us." "Be quiet, Gretel," said Haensel, "Don't worry, I'll get us out of this, of course." And when the mother and father had fallen asleep, he got up, put on his jacket, opened the lower half of the door, and crept out of the house. The moon was shining bright, and the white pebbles which were in front of the house gleamed like so many new silver coins. Haensel stooped down and put as many of them as he could in his jacket pocket. Then he went back and said to Gretel, "Don't worry, sister dear, and just go to sleep; God won't forsake us." Then he went to bed again.

When day dawned, even before sunrise the mother came and woke the children up, saying, "Get up, you lazybones, we're going into the forest to fetch wood." Then she gave each a piece of bread, saying, "Here's something for your dinner, but don't eat it beforehand; you're not getting anything else." Gretel put the bread in her apron because Haensel had the stones in his pocket. Then they all set out together for the forest. When they'd been walking a little while, Haensel stopped and looked back toward the house and did so again and again. The father said, "Haensel, what are you looking at there, and why are you lagging behind? Watch out or you'll be forgetting your legs." "Oh Father," said Haensel, "I'm looking at my white kitten; it's sitting on top of the roof and wants to say good-bye to me." The woman said, "You fool, that's not your kitten; it's the morning sun shining on the chimney." But Haensel hadn't been looking at the cat but was ever tossing one of the white pebbles from his pocket onto the path.

When they reached the middle of the forest, the father said, "Now gather some wood, children! I'll make a fire for you so you won't get cold." Haensel and Gretel gathered brush, quite a pile of it. The brush was kindled, and when the fire was blazing, the wife said, "Now lie down by the fire, children, and take a rest. We're going into the forest to cut wood when we're finished, we'll come back and fetch you."

Haensel and Gretel sat by the fire and when it was noon ate their piece of bread. And because they heard the blows of the ax, they thought their father was near by. But it wasn't the ax it was a branch he'd tied to a dead tree, which the wind was banging back and forth. When they'd been sitting for a long time, their eyes closed from weariness, and they fell fast asleep. When they finally woke up, it was already pitch-dark. Gretel began to weep and said, "How shall we get out of the forest now?" But Haensel consoled her, saying, "Just wait a bit till the moon's up then we'll easily find our way." When the full moon had risen, Haensel took his sister by the hand and followed the pebbles, which glittered like new silver coins and showed them the way. They kept walking all night and at daybreak were back at their father's house. They knocked at the door, and when the wife opened it and saw Haensel and Gretel, she said, "You naughty children, why did you sleep so long in the forest? We thought you weren't coming back at all." But the father was glad, for he was sorry he'd left them alone in the forest.

Not long after that there was again a famine everywhere, and one night the children heard their mother say in bed to their father, "Everything's been eaten up again; we've only got half a loaf of bread left and then we'll be at the end of our rope. The children must be sent away. Let's take them deeper into the forest to make sure they won't find the way out again. There's no other salvation for us." With heavy heart the man thought, "It'd be better to share your last morsel with your children," but the woman would listen to nothing he said, scolded him, and reproached him. But one step leads to another, and since he'd given in the first time, he had to the second, also.

The children, however, were still awake and heard the conversation. When the mother and father were asleep, Haensel again got up and was going out to pick up pebbles as before, but the wife had locked the door, and Haensel couldn't get out. Nevertheless, he consoled his sister and said, "Don't weep, Gretel, and just go to sleep; the dear Lord will surely help us."

Early in the morning the wife came and got the children out of bed. They received their piece of bread, but it was even smaller than last time. On their way to the forest Haensel crumbled it up in his pocket and, stopping often, scattered the crumbs on the ground. "Haensel, why are you stopping and looking around?" said his father; "go ahead." "I'm looking at my pigeon; it's sitting on the roof and wants to say good-bye to me," answered Haensel. "You fool!" said the woman, "that's not your pigeon; it's the morning sun shining on the chimney." Nevertheless, Haensel gradually scattered all the bread crumbs along the path.

The woman led the children still deeper into the forest, where they'd never been in all their lives. Then a big fire was again made, and the mother said, "Just sit there, children, and if you feel tired, you can take a little nap. We're going into the forest to cut wood and this evening when we're finished, we'll come and fetch you." When it was noon, Gretel shared her bread with Haensel, who'd scattered his piece along the way. Then they fell asleep, and the evening passed and no one came to get the poor children. They didn't wake up till it was pitch-dark, and Haensel consoled his sister, saying, "Just wait, Gretel, till the moon's up; then we'll see the bread crumbs I scattered. They'll show us the way home." When the moon rose, they set out but didn't find any bread crumbs, for the thousands of birds that fly about in forest and field had pecked them all up. Haensel said to Gretel, "We'll surely find the way," but they didn't find it. They walked all night and still another day from morning till evening but didn't get out of the forest. And they were very hungry, for they had nothing but a few berries that were on the ground, and because they were so tired that their legs wouldn't carry them any farther, they lay down under a tree and fell asleep.

By now it was already the third morning since they'd left their father's house. They began walking again but kept getting deeper and deeper into the forest, and unless help came soon, they were doomed to die of exhaustion. When it was noon, they saw a pretty snow-white bird perched on a branch; it sang so beautifully that they stopped and listened to it. And when it had finished, it flapped its wings and flew ahead of them; they followed it until they came to a cottage. There it lighted on the roof, and when they got quite near, they saw that the cottage was made of bread with a cake roof and that the windows were of sugar candy.

"Let's make for it," said Haensel, "and have a fine meal. I'll eat a piece of the roof and, Gretel, you may eat some of the window; that's sweet." Haensel reached up and broke off a little piece of the roof for himself to see how it tasted, and Gretel took her place at the windowpanes and nibbled at them. Then a shrill voice called out from the living room,

> "Nibble, nibble, nibble!
> Who's nibbling at my cottage?"

The children answered,

> "The wind, the wind,
> The Heavenly Child,"

and went on eating without being put off. Haensel, who quite liked the taste of the roof, pulled down a large piece, while Gretel took out a whole round windowpane, sat down, and ate it with relish. Then suddenly the door opened, and a very old woman leaning on a crutch came slinking out. Haensel and Gretel were so frightened that they dropped what they had in their hands. But the woman shook her head and said, "Well, well, you dear children, who brought you here? Come right in and stay with me; no harm will befall you." She took them both by the hand and led them into her cottage. They were served a good meal with milk, pancakes and sugar, apples, and nuts. Then she made up two pretty beds with white sheets, and Haensel and Gretel lay down in them and thought they were in Heaven.

The old woman was, however, only pretending to be kind; as a matter of fact, she was a wicked witch who lay in wait for children and who'd built the cottage of bread just to lure them to her. Once she got a child in her power, she'd kill it, cook it, and eat it, and that would be a red-letter day for her. Witches have red eyes and can't see far, but they've a keen sense of smell, just like animals, and scent the approach of human beings. As Haensel and Gretel were getting near her, she laughed wickedly and mockingly said, "I've got them! they shan't get away from me again!" Early in the morning before the children were awake, she was already up and, seeing them both sleeping so sweetly with their full rosy cheeks, muttered to herself, "That'll be a fine snack." Then with her withered hand she seized Haensel and carried him to a little pen and shut him up behind a grilled door. No matter how hard he cried, it did him no good. Then she went to Gretel, shook her till she woke up, and said, "Get up, you lazybones, fetch some water and cook something good for your brother; he's outside in the pen and must be fattened up. Once he's fat, I'll eat him." Gretel began to weep bitterly, but it was no use: she had to do what the wicked witch ordered her.

Now the best food was cooked for poor Haensel, but Gretel got nothing but crab shells. Every morning the old woman would slink out to the pen and cry, "Haensel! stick out your fingers so I can feel whether you'll be fat soon." But Haensel stuck out a little bone, and the old woman, whose eyesight was poor, couldn't see it and thought it was one of Haensel's fingers and was surprised he didn't get fat. When four weeks had passed and Haensel still stayed thin, she got impatient and wouldn't wait any longer. "Come on, Gretel!" she called out to the girl, "hurry up! bring some water! whether Haensel's fat or lean, I'm going to kill him tomorrow and cook him." Oh, how the poor little sister cried out when she had to carry the water, and how the tears rolled down her cheeks! "Dear Lord, please help us," she cried; "if only the wild animals in the forest had devoured us, then we at least should have died together." "Just stop your whining," said the old woman; "it won't do you any good at all."

Early in the morning Gretel had to go out and hang up the kettle full of water and kindle the fire. "First let's do some baking," said the old woman, "I've already heated up the oven and kneaded the dough." She pushed poor Gretel out to the oven, from which big flames already were leaping. "Crawl in!" said the witch, "and see whether it's properly hot, so we can put the bread in." Once Gretel was in, she intended to shut the oven and roast Gretel in it and then she was going to eat her up, too. But Gretel saw what she was up to and said, "I don't know how to. How do I get in?" "Stupid goose," said the old woman, "the opening's big enough. Why, I could get in myself," waddled up and stuck her head in the oven. Then Gretel gave her a shove so that she slid way in, shut the iron door, and shot the bolt. My! then she began to howl—something horrible! But Gretel ran away, and the wicked witch burned to death miserably.

Then Gretel went straight to Haensel, opened his pen, and called, "Haensel, we're saved! The old witch is dead!" Then Haensel jumped out like a bird from its cage when the door's opened. How happy they were! They fell on each other's necks, skipped about, and kissed one another, and because they didn't need to be afraid any more, they went into the witch's house, where there were chests of pearls and jewels in every nook and corner. "These are even better than pebbles," said Haensel, filling his pockets as full as he could, while Gretel said, "I want to bring something home, too," and filled her apron. "Now let's be off," said Haensel, "and get out of this enchanted forest." But when they'd been walking for a couple of hours, they reached a big body of water. "We can't get across," said Haensel; "I don't see any plank or bridge." "And there isn't any boat here," answered Gretel, "but there's a white duck. If I ask it, it'll help us across." Then she called out,

> "Duck, duck!
> Here's Haensel and Gretel.
> There's no plank or bridge;
> Take us on your white back."

As a matter of fact, the duck did come up, and Haensel got on it and told his sister to sit down beside him. "No," answered Gretel, "it'll be too heavy for the duck; it had better carry us over one at a time." The good creature did so, and when both were safely across and had gone a short distance, the forest kept getting more and more familiar to them, and finally they spied their father's house from afar. Then they began to run and rushed into the living room and fell on their father's neck. The man hadn't had a single happy hour since he'd left his children alone in the forest. The wife, however, had died. Gretel shook out her apron, and the pearls and jewels bounced about in the room, and Haensel threw one handful after the other from his pocket. Then all their troubles were at an end, and they lived most happily together.

My tale's done. There runs a mouse; whoever catches it may make a great big cap out of its fur.

*Fifteen*

# Boots and the Troll

*Norwegian*

Once on a time there was a poor man who had three sons. When he died, the two elder set off into the world to try their luck, but the youngest they wouldn't have with them at any price.

"As for you," they said, "You're fit for nothing but to sit and poke about in the ashes."

So the two went off and got places at a palace—the one under the coachman, and the other under the gardener. But Boots, he set off too, and took with him a great kneading-trough, which was the only thing his parents left behind them, but which the other two would not bother themselves with. It was heavy to carry, but he did not like to leave it behind, and so, after he had trudged a bit, he too came to the palace, and asked for a place. So they told him they did not want him, but he begged so prettily that at last he got leave to be in the kitchen, and carry in wood and water for the kitchen maid. He was quick and ready, and in a little while every one liked him but the two others were dull, and so they got more kicks than half-pence, and grew quite envious of Boots, when they saw how much better he got on.

Just opposite the palace, across a lake, lived a troll, who had seven silver ducks which swam on the lake, so that they could be seen from the palace. These the king had often longed for; and so the two elder brothers told the coachman:

"If our brother only chose, he has said he could easily get the king those seven silver ducks."

You may fancy it wasn't long before the coachman told this to the king; and the king called Boots before him, and said:

"Your brothers say you can get me the silver ducks; so now go and fetch them."

"I'm sure I never thought or said anything of the kind," said the lad.

"You did say so, and you shall fetch them," said the king, who would hold his own.

"Well, well," said the lad; "needs must, I suppose; but give me a bushel of rye and a bushel of wheat, and I'll try what I can do."

So he got the rye and the wheat, and put them into the kneading-trough he had brought with him from home, got in, and rowed across the lake. When he reached the other side he began to walk along the shore, and to sprinkle and strew the grain, and at last he coaxed the ducks into his kneading-trough, and rowed back as fast as ever he could.

When he got half over, the troll came out of his house and set eyes on him.

"Hallo!" roared out the troll; "is it you that has gone off with my seven silver ducks?"

"Ay! ay!" said the lad.

"Shall you be back soon?" asked the troll.

"Very likely," said the lad.

So when he got back to the king, with the seven silver ducks, he was more liked than ever, and even the king was pleased to say, "Well done!" But at this his brothers grew more and more spiteful and envious; and so they went and told the coachman that their brother had said if he chose, he was man enough to get the king the troll's bed-quilt, which had a gold patch and a silver patch, and a silver patch and a gold patch; and this time, too, the coachman was not slow in telling all this to the king. So the king said to the lad, how his brothers had said he was good to steal the troll's bed-quilt, with gold and silver patches; so now he must go and do it, or lose his life.

Boots answered, he had never thought or said any such thing; but when he found there was no help for it, he begged for three days to think over the matter.

So when the three days were gone, he rowed over in his kneading-trough, and went spying about. At last, he saw those in the troll's cave come out and hang the quilt out to air, and as soon as ever they had gone back into the face of the rock, Boots pulled the quilt down, and rowed away with it as fast as he could.

And when he was half across, out came the troll and set eyes on him, and roared out,—

"Hallo! It is you who took my seven silver ducks?"

"Ay! ay!" said the lad.

"And now, have you taken my bed-quilt, with silver patches and gold patches, and gold patches and silver patches?"

"Ay! ay!" said the lad.

"Shall you come back again?"

"Very likely," said the lad.

But when he got back with the gold and silver patchwork quilt every one was fonder of him than ever, and he was made the king's body-servant.

At this the other two were still more vexed, and to be revenged, they went and told the coachman:

"Now, our brother has said he is man enough to get the king the gold harp which the troll has, and that harp is of such a kind that all who listen when it is played grow glad, however sad they may be."

Yes; the coachman went and told the king, and he said to the lad:

"If you have said this you shall do it. If you do it you shall have the princess and half the kingdom. If you don't, you shall lose your life."

"I'm sure I never thought or said anything of the kind," said the lad; "but if there's no help for it, I may as well try; but I must have six days to think about it."

Yes, he might have six days, but when they were over he must set out.

Then he took a tenpenny nail, a birch-pin, and a waxen taper-end in his pocket, and rowed across, and walked up and down before the troll's cave, looking stealthily about him. So when the troll came out he saw him at once.

"Ho, Ho!" roared the troll; "is it you who took my seven silver ducks?"

"Ay! ay!" said the lad.

"And it is you who took my bed-quilt, with the gold and silver patches?" asked the troll.

"Ay! ay!" said the lad.

So the troll caught hold of him at once, and took him off into the cave in the face of the rock.

"Now, daughter dear," said the troll, "I've caught the fellow who stole the silver ducks and my bed-quilt with gold and silver patches; put him into the fattening coop, and when he's fat we'll kill him, and make a feast for our friends."

She was willing enough, and put him at once into the fattening coop, and there he stayed eight days, fed on the best, both in meat and drink, and as much as he could cram. So, when the eight days were over, the troll said to his daughter to go down and cut him in his little finger, that they might see if he were fat. Down she came to the coop.

"Out with your little finger!" she said,

But Boots stuck out his tenpenny nail, and she cut at it.

"Nay, nay! he's as hard as iron still," said the troll's daughter, when she got back to her father; "we can't take him yet."

After another eight days the same thing happened, and this time Boots stuck out his birchen pin.

"Well, he's a little better," she said, when she got back to the troll; "but still he'll be as hard as wood to chew."

But when another eight days were gone, the troll told his daughter to go down and see if he wasn't fat now.

"Out with your little finger," said the troll's daughter, when she reached the coop, and this time Boots stuck out the taper end.

"Now he'll do nicely," she said.

"Will he?" said the troll. "When, then, I'll just set off and ask the guests; meantime you must kill him, and roast half and boil half."

So when the troll had been gone a little while, the daughter began to sharpen a great long knife.

"Is that what you're going to kill me with?" asked the lad.

"Yes, it is," said she.

"But it isn't sharp," said the lad. "Just let me sharpen it for you, and then you'll find it easier work to kill me."

So she let him have the knife, and he began to rub and sharpen it on the whetstone.

"Just let me try it on one of your hair plaits; I think it's about right now."

So he got leave to do that; but at the same time that he grasped the plait of hair he pulled back her head, and at one gash cut off the troll's daughter's head; and half of her he roasted and half of her he boiled, and served it all up.

After that he dressed himself in her clothes, and sat away in the corner.

So when the troll came home with his guests, he called out to his daughter—for he thought all the time it was his daughter—to come and take a snack.

"No, thank you," said the lad, "I don't care for food, I'm so sad and downcast."

"Oh!" said the troll, "if that's all, you know the cure; take the harp, and play a tune on it."

"Yes!" said the lad; "but where has it got to; I can't find it."

"Why, you know well enough," said the troll; "you used it last;

where should it be but over the door yonder?"

The lad did not wait to be told twice; he took down the harp, and went in and out playing tunes; but, all at once he shoved off the kneading-trough, jumped into it, and rowed off, so that the foam flew around the trough.

After a while the troll thought his daughter was a long while gone, and went out to see what ailed her; and then he saw the lad in the trough, far, far out on the lake.

"Hallo! Is it you," he roared, "that took my seven silver ducks?"

"Ay, ay!" said the lad.

"Is it you that took my bed-quilt, with the gold and silver patches?"

"Yes!" said the lad.

"And now you have taken off my gold harp?" screamed the troll.

"Yes!" said the lad; "I've got it, sure enough."

"And haven't I eaten you up after all, then?"

"No, no! 'twas your own daughter you ate," answered the lad.

But when the troll heard that, he was so sorry, he burst; and then Boots rowed back, and took a whole heap of gold and silver with him, as much as the trough could carry. And so, when he came to the palace with the gold harp he got the princess and half the kingdom, as the king had promised him; and, as for his brothers, he treated them well, for he thought they had only wished his good when they said what they had said.

*Sixteen*

# The Master-Smith

*Norwegian*

Once on a time, in the days when our Lord and St. Peter used to wander on earth, they came to a smith's house. He had made a bargain with the Devil that the fiend should have him after seven years, but during that time he was to be the master of all masters in his trade, and to this bargain both he and the Devil had signed their names. So he had stuck up in great letters over the door of his forge,—

*"Here dwells the Master over all Masters."*

Now when our Lord passed by and saw that, he went in.

"Who are you?" he said to the smith.

"Read what's written over the door," said the smith "but maybe you can't read writing. If so, you must wait till some one comes to help you."

Before our Lord had time to answer him, a man came with his horse, which he begged the smith to shoe.

"Might I have leave to shoe it?" asked our Lord.

"You may try, if you like," said the smith "you can't do it so badly that I shall not be able to make it right again."

So our Lord went out and took one leg off the horse, and laid it in the furnace, and made the shoe red-hot; after that he turned up the ends of the shoe, and filed down the heads of the nails, and clenched the points; and then he put back the leg safe and sound on the horse again. And when he was done with that leg, he took the other foreleg and did the same with it; and when he was done with that he took the hind-legs—first the off, and then the near leg, and laid them in the furnace, making the shoes red-hot, turning up the ends, filing the heads of the nails, and clenching the points; and after all was done, putting the legs on the horse again. All the while the Smith stood by and looked on.

"You're not so bad a smith after all," said he.

"Oh, you think so, do you?" said our Lord.

A little while after came the smith's mother to the forge, and called him to come home and eat his dinner; she was an old, old woman, with an ugly crook on her back, and wrinkles in her face, and it was as much as she could do to crawl along.

"Mark now what you see," said our Lord.

Then he took the woman and laid her in the furnace, and smithied a lovely young maiden out of her.

"Well," said the smith, "I say now, as I said before, you are not such a bad smith after all. There it stands over my door—*Here dwells the Master over all Masters;* but for all that, I say right out, one learns as long as one lives"; and with that he walked off to his house and ate his dinner.

So after dinner, just after he had got back to his forge, a man came riding up to have his horse shod.

"It shall be done in the twinkling of an eye," said the smith, "for I have just learnt a new way to shoe; and a very good way it is when the days are short."

So he began to cut and hack till he had got all the horse's legs off, for he said, I don't know why one should go pottering back-wards and forwards—first with one leg, and then with another.

Then he laid the legs in the furnace, just as he had seen our Lord lay them, and threw on a great heap of coal, and made his mates work the bellows bravely; but it went as one might suppose it would go. The legs were burnt to ashes, and the smith had to pay for the horse.

Well, he didn't care much about that, but just then an old beggar-woman came along the road, and he thought to himself, "Better luck next time"; so he took the old dame and laid her in the furnace, and though she begged and prayed hard for her life, it was no good.

"You're so old, you don't know what is good for you," said the smith; "now you shall be a lovely young maiden in half no time, and for all that, I'll not charge you a penny for the job."

But it went no better with the poor old woman than with the horse's legs.

"That was ill done, and I say it," said our Lord.

"Oh! for that matter," said the smith, "there's not many who'll ask after her, I'll be bound; but it's a shame of the Devil, if this is the way he holds to what is written up over the door."

"If you might have three wishes from me," said our Lord, "what would you wish for?"

"Only try me," said the smith, "and you'll soon know."

So our Lord gave him three wishes.

"Well," said the smith, "first and foremost, I wish that any one whom I ask to climb up into the pear-tree that stands outside by the wall of my forge, may stay sitting there till I ask him to come down again. The second wish I wish is, that any one whom I ask to sit down in my easy chair which stands inside the workshop yonder, may stay sitting there till I ask him to get up. Last of all, I wish that any one whom I ask to creep into the steel purse which I have in my pocket, may stay in it till I give him leave to creep out again."

"You have wished as a wicked man," said St. Peter; "first and foremost, you should have wished for God's grace and good will."

"I durstn't look so high as that," said the smith; and after that our Lord and St. Peter bade him "Good-bye," and went on their way.

Well, the years went on and on, and when the time was up, the

Devil came to fetch the smith, as it was written in their bargain.

"Are you ready?" he said, as he stuck his nose in at the door of the forge.

"Oh," said the smith, "I must just hammer the head of this tenpenny nail first; meantime you can just climb up into the pear-tree, and pluck yourself a pear to gnaw at; you must be both hungry and thirsty after your journey."

So the devil thanked him for his kind offer, and climbed up into the pear-tree.

"Very good," said the smith; "but now, on thinking the matter over, I find I shall never be able to have done hammering the head of this nail till four years are out at least, this iron is so plaguy hard; down you can't come in all that time, but may sit up there and rest your bones."

When the Devil heard this, he begged and prayed till his voice was as thin as a silver penny that he might have leave to come down; but there was no help for it. There he was, and there he must stay. At last he had to give his word of honor not to come again till the four years were out, which the smith had spoken of, and then the smith said, "Very well, now you may come down."

So when the time was up, the Devil came again to fetch the smith.

"You're ready now, of course," said he; "you've had time enough to hammer the head of that nail, I should think."

"Yes, the head is right enough now," said the smith; "but still you have come a little tiny bit too soon, for I haven't quite done sharpening the point; such plaguy hard iron I never hammered in all my born days. So while I work at the point, you may just as well sit down in my easy chair and rest yourself; I'll be bound you're weary after coming so far."

"Thank you kindly," said the Devil, and down he plumped into the easy chair; but just as he had made himself comfortable, the smith said, on second thoughts he found he couldn't get the point sharp till four years were out. First of all, the Devil begged so prettily to be let out of the chair, and afterwards, waxing wroth, he began to threaten and scold; but the smith kept on, all the while excusing himself, and saying it was all the iron's fault, it was so plaguy hard, and telling the Devil he was not so badly off to have to sit quietly in an easy-chair, and that he would let him out to the minute when the four years were over. Well, at last there was no help for it, and the Devil had to give his word of honor not to fetch the smith till the four years were out; and then the smith said:

"Well now, you may get up and be off about your business," and away went the Devil as fast as he could lay legs to the ground.

When the four years were over the Devil came again to fetch the smith, and he called out, as he stuck his nose in at the door of the forge:

"Now, I know you must be ready."

"Ready, ay, ready," answered the smith; "we can go now as soon as you please; but hark ye, there is one thing I have stood here and thought, and thought I would ask you to tell me. Is it true what people say, that the Devil can make himself as small as he pleases?"

"God knows, it is the very truth," said the Devil.

"Oh!" said the smith; "it *is* true, is it? then I wish you would just be so good as to creep into this steel purse of mine, and see whether it is sound at the bottom, for, to tell you the truth, I'm afraid my traveling money will drop out."

"With all my heart," said the Devil, who made himself small in a trice, and crept into the purse; but he was scarce in when the smith snapped to the clasp.

"Yes," called out the Devil inside the purse; "it's right and tight everywhere."

"Very good," said the smith; "I'm glad to hear you say so, but 'More haste the less speed,' says the old saw, and 'Forewarned is forearmed,' says another; so I'll just weld these links a little together, just for safety's sake"; and with that he laid the purse in the furnace, and made it red hot.

"Ow! Ow!" screamed the Devil, "are you mad? don't you know I'm inside the purse?"

"Yes, I do!" said the smith; "but I can't help you, for another old saw says, 'One must strike while the iron is hot' "; and as he said this, he took up his sledgehammer, laid the purse on the anvil, and let fly at it as hard as he could.

"Ow! Ow! Ow!" bellowed the Devil, inside the purse. "Dear friend, do let me out, and I'll never come near you again."

"Very well!" said the smith; "now, I think, the links are pretty well welded, and you may come out"; so he unclasped the purse, and away went the Devil in such a hurry that he didn't once look behind him.

Now, some time after, it came across the smith's mind that he had done a silly thing in making the Devil his enemy, for he said to himself:

"If, as is like enough, they won't have me in the kingdom of Heaven, I shall be in danger of being houseless, since I've fallen out with him who rules over Hell."

So he made up his mind it would be best to try to get either into Hell or Heaven, and to try at once, rather than to put it off any longer, so that he might know how things really stood. Then he threw his sledgehammer over his shoulder and set off; and when he had gone a good bit of the way, he came to a place where two roads met, and where the path to the kingdom of Heaven parts from the path that leads to Hell, and here overtook a tailor, who was pelting along with his flatiron in his hand.

"Good day," said the smith; "whither are you off to?"

"To the kingdom of Heaven," said the Tailor, "if I can only get into it; but whither are you going yourself?"

"Oh, our ways don't run together," said the smith; "for I have made up my mind to try first in Hell, as the Devil and I know something of one another from old times."

So they bade one another "Good-bye," and each went his way; but the smith was a stout strong man, and got over the ground far faster than the tailor, and so it wasn't long before he stood at the gates of Hell. Then he called the watch, and bade him go and tell the Devil there was some one outside who wished to speak a word with him.

"Go out," said the Devil to the watch, "and ask him who he is?" So that when the watch came and told him that, the smith answered:

"Go and greet the Devil in my name, and say it is the smith who owns the purse he wots of; and beg him prettily to let me in at once, for I worked at my forge till noon, and I have had a long walk since."

But when the Devil heard who it was he charged the watch to go back and lock up all the nine locks on the gates of Hell.

"And, besides," he said, "You may as well put on a padlock, for if he only once gets in, he'll turn Hell topsy-turvy!"

"Well!" said the smith to himself, when he saw them busy

bolting up the gates, "there's no lodging to be got here, that's plain; so I may as well try my luck in the kingdom of Heaven"; and with that he turned round and went back till he reached the cross-roads, and then he went along the path the tailor had taken. And now, as he was cross at having gone backwards and forwards so far for no good, he strode along with all his might, and reached the gate of Heaven just as St. Peter was opening it a very little, just enough to let the half-starved tailor slip in. The smith was still six or seven strides off the gate, so he thought to himself, "Now there's no time to be lost"; and grasping his sledgehammer, he hurled it into the opening of the door just as the tailor slunk in; and if the smith didn't get in then, when the door was ajar, why I don't know what has become of him.


*Seventeen*

# The Child Sold to the Devil

*French*

A man and his wife already had many children, and they were going to have another. In order to support him they promised him to the Devil. When the child was born the Devil came to see his father and mother and told them that they would never lack for money, but that he would take the child when he was seven years old.

When the mother was cutting bread for her children, she always wept when she came to the child who had been promised to the Devil. She now felt that she had committed a great sin, but it was too late. The boy kept noticing his mother's tears and one day he asked her the reason for her crying. For a long time she refused to explain, but at last she told him that he had been promised to the Devil and that he would be taken away when he was seven years old.

The boy said to his mother, "Give me a little bag and I will leave the country so that the Devil cannot find me. I will live as a beggar."

The mother gave her son a little bag, embraced him many times, and told him always to love God so that he would not be carried off by the Devil. The boy promised to obey her and left.

He lived as a beggar. After he had traveled a long way he met the Devil and they began to speak to each other.

"I understand," said the boy, "that you are able to make yourself little, as little as a mouse?"

"Very easily," said the Devil,

"Then turn yourself into a mouse."

The Devil turned himself into a mouse. The boy opened his bag in front of the Devil and he walked into it. And now the Devil was in the bag. The boy tied up the string to the bag and found two blacksmiths. He put the bag on the anvil and told the blacksmiths to strike down with their heavy hammers. The Devil begged pity, and finally the boy said to him:

"I will put you at liberty if you will promise me never to have any rights over me or mine to the seventh generation."

"I agree to all that, but let me out."

And the boy released the Devil.

*Eighteen*

# Godfather Death

*Swedish*

Once there was a poor man whose wife had a son. But since they had seven children already, they were not happy about the birth of the eighth. The man went out begging and collected some clothes and food for the christening, but nobody wanted to be godfather to the beggar's son. Nor did they want to give any christening gift. Weeping, the man went into a big forest; he felt very unhappy and abandoned. There he met a man who was fair and beautiful. His eyes were sparkling and blue as the spring sky, his hair was like gold, and his voice like sweet music when he asked:

"Why do you weep so bitterly?"

"Nobody wants to be godfather to my little son," said the man.

"I will be godfather," said the shining one.

"Who are you then?" asked the man.

"I am the good Lord," he answered, and the flowers gave out

Translated from *Sveriges Samtliga Folksagor* by Waldemar Liungman. Used by permission.

their scent and the birds sang sweeter still.

"No," said the beggar. "I don't want you as godfather if you are God, because you are not just. To some you give wealth and happiness, to others poverty and want." Weeping, he continued on his way.

Then he met a man whose eyes shone like balls of fire. The flowers wilted wherever he went and snakes coiled in the grass around him.

"Why do you weep?" he said and a foul stench of sulphur came from his mouth.

"Nobody wants to be godfather to my son," said the beggar.

"I will be godfather," said the gloomy man he was talking to.

"Who are you?" asked the beggar.

"I am the Devil," said the man and smiled wickedly.

"Then I don't want you as my son's godfather, because at the end you reward badly those who serve you by tormenting them eternally."

The beggar then met a tall, thin man with a scythe on his shoulder. A chilly fog seemed to escape from his mouth and flowers and grass seemed to stiffen wherever he went.

"Why do you weep so bitterly?" he said with a hollow voice.

"I have a son to be christened, but nobody wants to be godfather," said the beggar.

"I will be godfather to your son," said the sinister man.

"Who are you?" asked the beggar.

"I am Death," said the man, and a cold breath came out of his mouth. Then the beggar was happy and said:

"Yes, gladly would I have you as godfather, because you give the same to all and make no distinction between high and low."

So Death carried the beggar's son to the christening and said afterwards:

"Take my godson with you on the day he is eighteen years old and meet me at the place where we first saw each other and I shall give him a christening gift."

The boy grew up and when he was eighteen years old his father brought him to the place where he had met his godfather. He was there to meet them and said:

"My godson shall become a doctor and as a christening gift I am giving him the ability to see if a sick man will die or regain health. If my godson sees me standing at the head of the bed the sick man will die, but if I stand at his feet he will live."

The boy became famous as a doctor, since he could tell immediately upon seeing a sick man whether he would get well or die, and it never happened that he made a mistake. But once the king's chief councilor got sick. The king was beside himself, because he could not rule his kingdom without him. He offered to give two barrels of gold to the man who cured him. When the doctor came near the sick man, his godfather was standing at the head of the bed. The doctor begged and beseeched him to be reasonable and move to the foot of the bed, but he couldn't be persuaded. Therefore the godson decided to try to cheat Death and turned the bed so that Death came to stand at the foot instead, and immediately the sick man came to life. He recovered and the doctor received the promised reward.

But Death was very angry because his godson had cheated him out of his victim.

"If you try this trick again, you shall die yourself," he said.

After some time the king's only daughter got sick. Now the king was in despair and said that he couldn't live without his daughter. He promised half the kingdom and the hand of the princess to the man who could cure her. When Death's godson entered the princess' room, he saw his godfather standing at the head of her bed. He fell down on his knees before Death and ardently beseeched him to place himself at the princess' feet, but he remained firm. Then the doctor decided to use his cunning once more and again he turned the bed so that Death stood at her feet. The princess recovered and, according to the king's promise, a wedding was prepared for her and the doctor who had cured her.

On the wedding night, when the doctor was sleeping with his beautiful bride, there was a knock at the door and his godfather entered and beckoned to his godson. He stood up and followed his godfather and was brought to a cave deep down in the earth. A countless number of candles were burning there, some newly lit, others almost burned out in their holders.

"What does this mean?" asked Death's godson.

"Those are life-lights of men," said the godfather.

"Whose is that?" asked the godson and pointed to a light which had almost burned out and merely flickered in its holder.

"Your own," said Death and pointed to a larger candle which had been lit so recently that the flame still had not seized hold firmly.

"This newly kindled light is your son's."

The godson then fell down before his godfather and, filled with anguish, he pleaded with him to put a new candle on his own holder quickly, but Death did not answer. And now the light flickered for the last time and went out, and at that moment the godson fell down dead before his godfather's feet.

We find from this that you can neither persuade nor cheat Death.

*Nineteen*

# Little Red Riding-Hood

*French (literary)*

Once upon a time there was a little country girl, the prettiest ever seen; her mother was excessively fond of her, and the grandmother still more fond. This good woman had made for her granddaughter a little red cap, which suited her so well that everywhere she was called little Red Riding-Hood.

One day her mother made some cakes and said to her:

"Go see how your grandmother is, for I have heard that she is sick. Take her a cake and this little pot of butter."

Little Red Riding-Hood soon left to see her grandmother, who lived in another village. As she passed through a wood, she met Mr. Wolf, who wanted to eat her but did not dare because of some woodcutters who were in the forest. He asked her where she was going. The poor child, who did not know that it was dangerous to stop to talk to a wolf, said to him:

"I am going to my grandmother, and I am carrying her a cake with a little pot of butter, which my mother is sending her."

"Does she live far from here?" the wolf asked her.

"Oh yes," said little Red Riding-Hood; "it is beyond the mill which you see over there, in the first house of the village."

"Indeed!" said the wolf, "I also wish to go see her. I will go there by this path, and you take that path and we will see who gets there first."

The wolf began to run as fast as possible along the path which was the shortest, and the little girl went on the longer path, gathering nuts, running after butterflies, and making bouquets of little flowers which she had picked.

The wolf soon arrived at the house of the grandmother. He rapped on the door: knock, knock.

"Who is there?"

"It is your little girl, Little Red Riding-Hood," said the wolf, disguising his voice, "who is bringing you a cake and a little pot of butter, which my mother sends you."

The good grandmother, who was in bed because she did not feel well, called to him:

"Pull the pin, the latch will open."

The wolf pulled the pin and the door opened. He pounced upon the good woman, and devoured her in no time at all because it was three days since he had eaten. Then he closed the door, lay down in the grandmother's bed and waited for Little Red Riding-Hood. Some time later she came rapping at the door: knock, knock.

"Who is there?"

Little Red Riding-Hood, who heard the deep voice of the wolf, was at first afraid, then believing that her grandmother had a cold, she answered:

"It is your little girl, Little Red Riding-Hood, who is bringing you a cake and a little pot of butter, which my mother sends you."

The wolf called to her, softening a little his voice:

"Pull the pin, the latch will open."

Little Red Riding-Hood pulled the pin and the door opened.

The wolf, seeing her enter, hiding down in the bed under the covers, said to her:

"Put the cake and the little pot of butter on the bread-bin, and come lie down with me."

Little Red Riding-Hood undressed and started to get into the bed, when she was astonished to see how her grandmother appeared undressed. She said to her:

"Grandmother, what big arms you have!"

"The better to embrace you, my child!"

"Grandmother, what big legs you have!"

"The better to run, my child!"

"Grandmother, what big ears you have!"

"The better to hear you, my child!"

"Grandmother, what big eyes you have!"

"The better to see you, my child!"

"Grandmother, what big teeth you have!"

"The better to eat you!"

And, saying these words, the bad wolf pounced upon Little Red Riding-Hood, and ate her.


*Twenty*

# Maid Lena

*Danish*

Once upon a time there was a farmer who had three sons. The eldest was called Peter, the second Paul, and the third Esben. Now Peter and Paul were a couple of strong, wide-awake lads; they could hear, and see, and laugh, and play, and sow, and reap, so they were very useful to their father. But the youngest was a poor sort of do-nothing fellow, who never had a word to say, but went mooning about like one in a dream, or sat over the fire and raked up the ashes; so they called him Esben-Ash-rake.

The farm stood amid fertile fields and fair green meadows; but in their midst lay a tract of barren, worthless moorland, strewn over with stones and overgrown with heather. Here Esben loved to lie asleep and dreaming, or staring up at the sky.

Peter and Paul, however, could not bear to see that bit of waste land, so their father gave them leave to see what they could do with it. True, there was an old story about the land belonging to the fairies, but, of course, that was all nonsense. So Peter and Paul set to work with a will; they dug up all the stones, and put them in a heap on one side; and they plowed and sowed their new field. They sowed it with wheat, and it did well all through the winter, and in the spring gave promise of a splendid crop.

Not one of their other fields looked half so well, until Midsummer Eve, when there came a sudden end to all their satisfaction —for on Midsummer Eve the whole crop was utterly destroyed. The entire field looked as if it had been trodden under foot; every blade of wheat was so crushed and beaten down that it could never recover or lift itself up again.

No one could understand how such a thing had happened. So there remained nothing to do but plow the field afresh, and let the grass grow.

Next spring there was finer and better grass there than in any of their meadows, but just the same thing happened again. On Midsummer Eve all the grass was trodden down and beaten out as if with a flail, so they got no profit out of the field that year. Then they plowed it once more, let it lie fallow through the winter, and in the spring sowed their field with flax. It came up beautifully, and before Midsummer Eve was in full flower. It was a pretty sight, and Peter and Paul surveyed it with pride and joy; but, remembering what had taken place the two former years, they agreed that one of them should keep watch there on Midsummer Eve. Peter, as the eldest, wished to undertake this duty; so, arming himself with a stout cudgel, he sat down on the great bank of stones he had helped to pile up when they cleared the land.

It was a beautifully mild evening, clear and still. Peter quite meant to keep wide awake. For all that, however, he fell asleep, and never woke till midnight, when there came a fearful rushing and roaring overhead, that made the ground beneath him shake and tremble; and when he tried to look about him the whole sky was pitchy black. But in the midst of it all, there shone something red that looked like a fiery dragon, and the whole field seemed to roll from side to side, till he began to feel as if he were being tossed in a blanket; and there was such a roaring and buzzing in his ears that at last he became completely dazed. He could not bear it any longer, but was glad enough to escape with a whole skin, and get safely home.

Next day the flax lay there, trodden down and beaten out, till the whole field looked as smooth and bare as a deal board. So after that neither Peter nor Paul cared to bestow any more labor upon the land, and the next spring the whole place was overgrown with grass and wild-flowers. There were white ladysmocks, blue corn-flowers, and scarlet poppies; the heather, too, came creeping and peeping up everywhere amongst the stones and flowers. For while the brothers were working away so hard with plow and harrow, the heather had lain snugly hidden in little nooks and crannies.

And now nobody troubled himself any further about the field except Esben, who liked it far better this year than he had done the three previous summers, and he used to go there oftener than ever and lie staring up at the blue sky.

Late on Midsummer Eve he slipped out of the house (after having slept most of the day), for he meant to keep watch all that night. He wanted to know what it was that went on there every Midsummer Eve, and whether it was the work of fairy-folk or other folk.

Close to the heap of stones there stood a tall tree, an old ash that had stood there many hundred years. Esben climbed up into this tree, sat very still, and kept wide awake till midnight. Then he, too, heard a roaring and a rushing that seemed to fill the air, and he, too, saw the sky grow as dark as if a carpet were spread out over it; and out of the black sky he saw a red gleam come. It came nearer and nearer till it took the form of a fiery dragon, with three heads and three long necks. As the dragon drew nearer, the storm increased, and a whirlwind rushed round and round the field, until each single blade and stalk lay there crushed and ground down, as if it had been trampled underfoot. The old ash-tree lashed about him with its branches, while its aged trunk swayed to and fro so violently that Esben had to hold on tight, lest the whirlwind should blow him away.

Then all at once it grew quite still and quiet the sky was clear again, and instead of a dragon with three heads, Esben now saw what looked like three large swans. But as they came nearer he saw they were three young girls, partly disguised in the form and plumage of swans, with great white wings and long, flowing veils; and they sank slowly down through the air to the foot of the old ash where Esben was. Then they cast aside their feathery disguise; the wings folded themselves together, and there, at the foot of the tree, lay three white veils as fine as cobwebs. They themselves, however, rose and danced, hand in hand, round and round the field, singing all the while.

Never had Esben heard anything so enchanting, never had he seen anything so beautiful, as these young girls in their white robes and with golden crowns upon their heads. For a long time he was afraid to move, lest he should frighten them away; but at length he slipped softly down, picked up the three white veils, and climbed as noiselessly up again.

The three swan-princesses had not noticed anything, but went on dancing round and round the meadow until three hours after midnight. Then they came back to the tree, and wanted to put on their veils again. But there were no veils to be found. They ran about, looking and looking, till at last they saw Esben up in the tree. They spoke to him, and said they were sure he had taken their veils.

"Yes," Esben told them, he had them.

Then they entreated him to let them have them again, or they should be utterly ruined, they said. And they wept and implored, and promised to give him so much money for the veils that he would be richer than any king in the land.

Esben sat and gazed at them. How beautiful they were! So he told them they should not have their veils unless one of them would consent to be his wife.

"Ah, no," said one.

"Certainly not!" cried the second.

But the third and youngest Princess said:

"Yes, only bring us our veils."

Esben gave the other two their veils, but refused to let the third have hers until she gave him her hand and a kiss, and put a ring on his finger, and promised to come and be married to him next Midsummer Eve.

"We are three sisters," answered the Princess, "and were brought up in a castle that used to stand on this very spot. But a long, long time ago we were carried off by a wicked fairy, who keeps us imprisoned ten thousand miles from here, and only on Midsummer Eve are we allowed to revisit our old home. Now you must build a castle on this very spot, where our marriage also can take place, and everything must be arranged on a princely scale. You may invite as many guests as you please, only not the King of the land. You shall not lack money. Break off a twig from the ash-tree you climbed, strike the largest of the stones lying at its root, and say, 'For Maid Lena!' The stone will roll back, and under it you will find all you may require. You can open and shut your treasure-house, as often as you like to repeat these words, with a stroke of the ash-twig. And so farewell till then," she said; and she wound her veil about her head, as her sisters had already done; then it spread out like two white wings, and all three princesses flew away.

At first they looked like three white swans; but they rose higher and higher till they were nothing but little white specks, and then they were lost to sight, and at the same moment the first ray of sunlight fell across the field.

For a long time Esben stood gazing after them, quite stunned with all he had seen and heard. At last he roused himself, tore a twig from the ash-tree and struck the stone, with the words, "For Maid Lena!"

Immediately the stone rolled back, and beneath it was the entrance to a royal treasure-house, full of silver and gold, and precious stones and costly jewels, and goblets and dishes, and candelabra, all of the most artistic form and design—in short, everything was there that could adorn a king's table.

Esben took as many gold and silver coins as he could carry, struck the stone again, repeating the same words, and then went back to the farm. His father and brothers hardly knew him again, he wasn't like the same man. He walked with head erect, his hair was thrown back from his forehead, his eyes were shining, and he looked full of life and energy.

Then he told them he knew now who it was that had destroyed their harvest the three previous summers. That piece of land was not to be cultivated; but he intended building a castle there, and there his wedding was to take place next Midsummer Eve.

At first they thought he had lost his wits; but when they saw all the silver and gold he had brought with him, they changed their opinions, and let him give what orders he pleased.

And now began a busy time, the like of which was never seen, with axe and saw, and hammer and plane, and line and trowel, so that on Midsummer Eve the castle stood complete, with tower and turret, and roof and pinnacle all glittering with gold.

Now it so happened that just before Midsummer Eve, after all the invitations were out, Esben's father and mother met the King, who had arranged a little trip into the country, and had contrived that his route should take him past the castle of which he had heard so much. Of course the farmer took off his hat to the King, who lifted his in return, and said he had heard of the grand wedding that was being prepared for his youngest son, and added:

"I should like to see him and his young bride."

Well, the farmer did not see that he could do otherwise than say that they would feel it a very great honor if the King would come to the wedding.

So then the King thanked him, and said that it would give him great pleasure, and then he rode on.

The wedding-day came, and the guests came, and the King came too.

Esben was there, but as yet no bride had appeared. People began to whisper that things were not quite right, that Esben's bride had come to him in a dream, and vanished with the dream.

About sunset Esben went and stood in front of the castle, and gazed up into the air.

"Oho!" said the folks, "she is to come that road, is she? Then she is neither more nor less than one of the crazy fancies Esben's head is always full of."

But Esben remained quite undisturbed; he had seen the swans coming flying through the air, and now he knew that she was near at hand.

Directly afterwards there came rolling up to the castle gates a magnificent golden chariot, drawn by six white horses.

Esben sprang to the carriage door, and there sat the bride, radiantly beautiful. But the first thing she said was:

"Is the King come?" and Esben was obliged to say, "Yes; but he invited himself, we did not ask him."

"That makes no difference," she said. "If I were to become a bride here to-day, the King would have to be the bridegroom, and it would cost you your life, which would make me most unhappy, for I wish to marry you, and no one else. And now you will have to come to me, if you can, and that before the year is out, or it will be too late. I live ten thousand miles from here, in a castle south of the sun, west of the moon, and in the center of the earth."

When she had thus spoken, she drove off at a tremendous pace, and directly afterwards Esben saw a flock of swans rise up in the air and disappear among the clouds.

So he took his staff in his hand, left everything, and set off on his wanderings through the wide, wide world to seek and find his bride. He made straight for the south, and he wandered for days and for weeks, and wherever he came he asked people if they knew the castle, but there was no one who had ever even heard the name.

So at last, one day, out in a wood, he came upon two terribly grim-looking fellows fighting. Esben stopped and asked them what they were fighting about. They told him they were fighting for an old hat that was lying close by; their father was dead, and now they wanted to divide their inheritance, but the hat they could not divide.

"The hat is not worth much," said Esben.

But the dwarfs said this hat was not like other hats, for it possessed this peculiarity: whoever put it on became invisible, and so they both wanted to have it.

And then they fell to again, and fought and struggled.

"Well, fight away till you are friends again," said Esben, as he snatched up the hat, put it on his head, and went his way.

When he had gone some little distance he came upon two other dwarfs, who were fighting savagely. They also wanted to divide their father's property, which consisted solely in a pair of boots, but whoever put them on went a hundred miles with each step, so they both wanted them.

Esben got into conversation with them, and when he had learned the state of affairs he advised them to run a race for the boots.

"Now, I will throw a stone," said he, "and you must run after it, and whoever gets there first shall have the boots."

This they agreed to, so Esben threw the stone, and they set off running.

Meanwhile Esben had put on the boots, and the first step carried him a hundred miles away.

Once again he came upon two dwarfs quarreling over their inheritance, which could not be divided, and which both wanted to have. This was a rusty old clasp-knife. But it possessed this virtue, they said: If you opened it, and just pointed at any one with it, they fell down dead and then if you shut it up again and touched them with it, they became alive again directly.

"Let me look at the knife," said Esben "I shall be able to advise you, for I have settled such quarrels before."

When he had got it, he wanted to prove it, so he opened it, and pointed it at the two dwarfs, who immediately fell down dead.

"That's right," said Esben; so he shut up the knife and touched them with it, and they jumped up again directly.

Esben put the knife in his pocket, said good-bye, put the hat on his head, and in another second was a hundred miles away.

He went on and on till evening, when he came to a little house that stood in the middle of a thick wood. A very old woman lived there; she was so old that she was all overgrown with moss.

Esben greeted her politely, and asked if she could tell him where the castle was that stood south of the sun, west of the moon, and in the center of the earth.

"No," she said; "she had never heard of such a castle. But she ruled over all the beasts of the field, and she could call them together, and ask if any one of them knew." So she blew her whistle, and wild beasts came gathering round them from all sides. They came running at full speed, all except the fox; he came sneaking behind in a very bad temper, for he was just going to catch a goose when he heard the whistle, and was obliged to come away and leave it. But neither the fox nor any one of the animals knew anything about the castle.

"Well, then, you must go to my sister," said the old woman; "she rules over all the birds of the air. If she cannot help you, no one can. She lives three hundred miles south of this, on the top of a high mountain. You cannot miss your way."

So Esben set off again, and soon came to the bird mountain.

The old woman who lived there had never heard of the castle south of the sun, west of the moon, and in the center of the earth; but she whistled with her pipe, and all the birds came flocking from all four corners of the earth. She asked them if they knew the castle, but there was not one of them who had ever been so far.

"Ah! but the old eagle is not here," she said, and whistled again.

At last the old eagle came sailing heavily along, his wings whirring and whizzing, and he alighted on the top of a tree.

"Where do you come from?" said the old woman. "You come too late; your life must pay the forfeit."

"I come from the castle south of the sun, west of the moon, and in the center of the earth," said the eagle. "I have a nest and young ones there, and I was obliged to see after them a little before I could leave them and fly so far away."

The old woman answered that his life should be spared if he would conduct Esben to the castle.

The eagle thought he could manage that, if he were allowed to stop and rest the night.

Next morning Esben got up on the eagle's back, and the eagle flew away with him—high, high up in the air, and far away over the stormy ocean.

When they had gone a long, long way, the eagle said:

"Do you see anything out yonder?"

"I see something like a high, black wall close upon us!"

"Ah! that is the earth; we have to go through that. Hold fast; for if you were to get killed, my life would have to pay the forfeit."

So they flew straight into the pitch-dark cave. Esben held fast, and almost directly afterwards he saw daylight again.

When they had gone a little farther, the eagle said again:

"Do you see anything out yonder?"

"I see something like a great glass mountain," said Esben.

"That is water," said the eagle; "we have to go through that. Hold fast; for if you were to get killed, my life would have to pay the forfeit."

So they plunged right into the water, and got safely through. Then they flew some distance through the air, and then the eagle said again:

"Do you see anything out yonder?"

"I only see flames of fire," said Esben.

"We have to go through that," said the eagle. "Creep well under my feathers, and hold fast; for if you should get killed, my life would have to pay the forfeit."

So they flew straight into the fire, but they got safely through. Then the eagle sank slowly down, and alighted on the land.

"Now," said he, "I must rest awhile; but we have five hundred miles farther to go."

"Ah! now I can carry you," said Esben; so he took the eagle on his back, and with five strides they were there.

"Now we have come too far," said the eagle. "Can you step ten miles backward?"

"No, I can't do that," said Esben.

"Then we must fly those ten miles," said the eagle.

So they arrived safe and sound at the castle south of the sun, west of the moon, and in the center of the earth. That *was* a castle, the like of which was not to be found in all the world. It shone from top to bottom like pure gold.

When Esben came to the castle gate, he sat down, and presently a serving-maid passed him on her way into the castle. He called to her:

"Greet Maid Lena, and beg her for a goblet of wine for a weary wayfarer."

The girl brought the message to the Princess, who ordered her own golden goblet to be filled with wine, and sent the girl out with it.

When Esben had drunk the wine, he threw his ring into the goblet—the ring she had given him the day they first met. The Princess recognized the ring directly, so she ran down and embraced Esben, and led him into the castle.

"Now I have got you, I must let you go again directly," she said; "and you must journey all the long way back in my swan-garb, for if the witch who has enchanted us should catch sight of

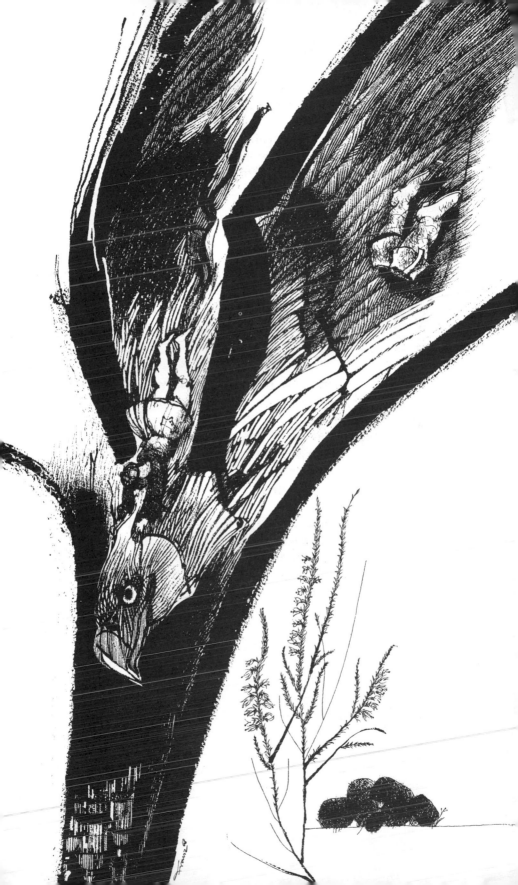

you, she would change you into stone with a single glance."

"There is a remedy for that," said Esben; "only take me to her."

So Esben put on his invisible hat, took his knife in his hand, went up to the old witch, and just pointed at her, and she fell down dead. So he had her buried forty fathoms underground, and then he married his Princess, and he is married to her still.

*Twenty-one*

# The Three Princesses of Whiteland

*Norwegian*

Once on a time there was a fisherman who lived close by a palace, and fished for the king's table. One day when he was out fishing he just caught nothing. Do what he would—however he tried with bait and angle—there was never a sprat on his hook. But when the day was far spent a head bobbed up out of the water, and said:

"If I may have what your wife bears under her girdle you shall catch fish enough."

So the man answered boldly, "Yes"; for he did not know that his wife was going to have a child. After that, as was like enough, he caught plenty of fish of all kinds. But when he got home at night and told his story, how he had got all that fish, his wife fell a-weeping and moaning, and was beside herself for the promise which her husband had made, for she said, "I bear a babe under my girdle."

Well, the story soon spread, and came up to the castle; and when the king heard the woman's grief and its cause, he sent down to say he would take care of the child, and see if he couldn't save it.

So the months went on and on, and when her time came the fisher's wife had a boy; so the king took it at once, and brought it up as his own son, until the lad grew up. Then he begged leave one day to go out fishing with his father; he had such a mind to go, he said. At first the king wouldn't hear of it, but at last the lad had his way, and went. So he and his father were out the whole day, and all went right and well till they landed at night. Then the lad remembered he had left his handkerchief, and went to look for it; but as soon as ever he got into the boat it began to move off with him at such speed that the water roared under the bow, and all the lad could do in rowing against it with the oars was no use; so he went and went the whole night, and at last he came to a white strand, far, far away.

There he went ashore, and when he had walked about a bit, an old, old man met him, with a long white beard.

"What's the name of this land?" asked the lad.

"Whiteland," said the man, who went on to ask the lad whence he came, and what he was going to do. So the lad told him all.

"Ay, ay!" said the man; "now when you have walked a little farther along the strand here, you'll come to three princesses, whom you will see standing in the earth up to their necks, with only their heads out. Then the first—she is the eldest—will call out and beg you so prettily to come and help her; and the second will do the same; to neither of these shall you go; make haste past them, as if you neither saw nor heard anything. But the third you shall go to, and do what she asks. If you do this you'll have good luck, that's all."

When the lad came to the first princess she called out to him and begged him so prettily to come to her, but he passed on as though he saw her not. In the same way he passed by the second; but to the third he went straight up.

"If you'll do what I bid you," she said, "you may have which of us you please."

"Yes"; he was willing enough; so she told him how three trolls had set them down in the earth there; but before they had lived in the castle up among the trees.

"Now," she said, "you must go into that castle, and let the trolls whip you each one night for each of us. If you can bear that you'll set us free."

Well, the lad said he was ready to try.

"When you go in," the princess went on to say, "you'll see two lions standing at the gate; but if you'll only go right in the middle between them they'll do you no harm. Then go straight on into a little dark room, and make your bed. Then the troll will come to whip you; but if you take the flask which hangs on the wall, and rub yourself with the ointment that's in it, wherever his lash falls you'll be as sound as ever. Then grasp the sword that hangs by the side of the flask and strike the troll dead."

Yes, he did as the princess told him; he passed in the midst between the lions, as if he hadn't seen them, and went straight into the little room, and there he lay down to sleep. The first night there came a troll with three heads and three rods, and whipped the lad soundly; but he stood it till the troll was done; then he took the flask and rubbed himself, and grasped the sword and slew the troll.

So, when he went out next morning, the princesses stood out of the earth up to their waists.

The next night 'twas the same story over again, only this time the troll had six heads and six rods, and he whipped him far worse than the first; but when he went out next morning the princesses stood out of the earth as far as the knee.

The third night there came a troll that had nine heads and nine rods, and he whipped and flogged the lad so long that he fainted away; then the troll took him up and dashed him against the wall; but the shock brought down the flask, which fell on the lad, burst and spilled the ointment all over him, and so he became as strong and sound as ever again. Then he wasn't slow; he grasped the sword and slew the troll; and next morning when he went out of the castle the princesses stood before him with all their bodies out of the earth. So he took the youngest for his queen, and lived well and happily with her for some time.

At last he began to long to go home for a little to see his parents. His queen did not like this; but at last his heart was so set on it, and he longed and longed so much, there was no holding him back, so she said:

"One thing you must promise me. This.—Only to do what your father begs you to do, and not what your mother wishes"; and that he promised.

Then she gave him a ring, which was of that kind that any one who wore it might wish two wishes. So he wished himself home, and when he got home his parents could not wonder enough what a grand man their son had become.

Now, when he had been at home some days, his mother wished him to go up to the palace and show the king what a fine fellow he had come to be. But his father said:

"No! don't let him do that; if he does, we shan't have any more joy of him this time."

But it was no good, the mother begged and prayed so long, that at last he went. So when he got up to the palace, he was far braver, both in clothes and array, than the other king, who didn't quite like this, and at last he said:

"All very fine; but here you can see my queen, what she is like, but I can't see yours, that I can't. Do you know I scarce think she's so good-looking as mine."

"Would to Heaven," said the young king, "she were standing here; then you'd see what she was like." And that instant there she stood before them.

But she was very woeful, and said to him:

"Why did you not mind what I told you; and why did you not listen to what your father said? Now, I must away home, and as for you, you have had both your wishes."

With that she knitted a ring among his hair with her name on it, and wished herself home, and was off.

Then the young king was cut to the heart, and went, day out day in, thinking and thinking how he should get back to his queen. "I'll just try," he thought, "if I can't learn where Whiteland lies"; and so he went out into the world to ask. So when he had gone a good way he came to a high hill, and there he met one who was lord over all the beasts of the wood, for they all came home to him when he blew his horn; so the king asked if he knew where Whiteland was.

"No, I don't," said he, "but I'll ask my beasts." Then he blew his horn and called them, and asked if any of them knew where Whiteland lay; but there was no beast that knew.

So the man gave him a pair of snow-shoes.

"When you get on these," he said, "you'll come to my brother, who lives hundreds of miles off; he is lord over all the birds of the air. Ask him. When you reach his house, just turn the shoes, so that the toes point this way, and they'll come home of themselves." So when the king reached the house he turned the shoes as the lord of the beasts had said, and away they went home of themselves.

So he asked again after Whiteland, and the man called all the birds with a blast of his horn, and asked if any of them knew where Whiteland lay; but none of the birds knew. Now, long, long after the rest of the birds, came an old eagle, which had been away ten round years, but he couldn't tell any more than the rest.

"Well! well!" said the man, "I'll lend you a pair of snow-shoes, and when you get them on they'll carry you to my brother, who lives hundreds of miles off; he's lord of all the fish in the sea; you'd better ask him. But don't forget to turn the toes of the shoes this way."

The king was full of thanks, got on the shoes, and when he came to the man who was lord over the fish of the sea, he turned the toes round, and so off they went home like the other pair. After that, he asked again after Whiteland.

So the man called the fish with a blast, but no fish could tell where it lay. At last came an old pike, which they had great work to call home, he was such a way off. So when they asked him he said:

"Know it! I should think I did. I've been cook there ten years, and tomorrow I'm going there again; for now, the queen of Whiteland, whose king is away, is going to wed another husband."

"Well!" said the man, "as this is so, I'll give you a bit of advice. Hereabouts, on a moor, stand three brothers, and here they have stood these hundred years, fighting about a hat, a cloak, and a pair of boots. If any one has these three things he can make himself invisible, and wish himself anywhere he pleases. You can tell them you wish to try the things, and after that you'll pass judgment between them, whose they shall be."

Yes, the king thanked the man, and went and did as he told him.

"What's all this?" he said to the brothers. "Why do you stand here fighting for ever and a day? Just let me try these things, and I'll give judgment whose they shall be."

They were very willing to do this; but as soon as he had got the hat, cloak, and boots, he said:

"When we meet next time I'll tell you my judgment," and with these words he wished himself away.

So as he went along, up in the air, he came up with the North Wind.

"Whither away?" roared the North Wind.

"To Whiteland," said the king; and then he told him all that had befallen him.

"Ah," said the North Wind, "you go faster than I—you do; for you can go straight, while I have to puff and blow round every turn and corner. But when you get there, just place yourself on the stairs by the side of the door, and then I'll come storming in, as though I were going to blow down the whole castle. And then when the prince, who is to have your queen, comes out to see what's the matter, just you take him by the collar and pitch him out of doors; then I'll look after him, and see if I can't carry him off."

Well—the king did as the North Wind said. He took his stand on the stairs, and when the North Wind came, storming and roaring, and took hold of the castle wall, so that it shook again, the prince came out to see what was the matter. But as soon as ever he came, the king caught him by the collar and pitched him out of doors, and then the North Wind caught him up and carried him off. So when there was an end of him, the king went into the castle, and at first his queen didn't know him, he was so wan and thin, through wandering so far and being so woeful; but when he showed her the ring, she was as glad as glad could be; and so the rightful wedding was held and the fame of it spread far and wide.

*Twenty-two*

# The Frog Princess

*Russian*

Long ago, in ancient times, there was a king who had three sons, all of them grown. The king said: "My children, let each of you make a bow for himself and shoot an arrow. She who brings back your arrow will be your bride; he whose arrow is not brought back will not marry." The eldest son shot his arrow, and a prince's daughter brought it back to him. The middle son shot his arrow, and a general's daughter brought it back to him. But little Prince Ivan's arrow was brought back from the marsh by a frog who held it between her teeth. His brothers were joyous and happy, but Prince Ivan became thoughtful and wept: "How will I live with a frog? After all, this is a life task, not like wading across a river or walking across a field!" He wept and wept, but there was no way out of it, so he took the frog to wife. All three sons and their brides were wed in accordance with the customs of

From *Russian Fairy Tales*, edited and translated by Norbert Guterman. Copyright 1945 by Pantheon Books, Inc. Reprinted by permission of Pantheon Books, a Division of Random House, Inc.

their country; the frog was held on a dish.

They began living together. One day the king asked that all three brides make him gifts, so that he could see which of them was the most skillful. Prince Ivan again became thoughtful and wept: "What can my frog make? Everyone will laugh at me!" The frog only hopped about on the floor and croaked. When Prince Ivan fell asleep, she went out into the street, cast off her skin, turned into a lovely maiden, and cried: "Nurses, nurses! Make something!" The nurses at once brought a finely woven shirt. She took it, folded it, placed it beside Prince Ivan, and again turned herself into a frog, as though she had never been anything else! Prince Ivan awoke, was overjoyed with the shirt, and brought it to the king. The king received it, examined it, and said: "Well, this is indeed a shirt to wear on holidays!" Then the second brother brought a shirt. The king said: "This one is good only to wear to the bath!" And of the shirt the eldest brother brought he said: "This one is fit to be worn only in a lowly peasant hut!" The king's sons left, and the two elder ones decided between themselves: "We were wrong to make fun of Prince Ivan's wife; she is not a frog, but a cunning witch!"

The king again issued a command to his daughters-in-law—this time that they should bake bread, and show it to him, so that he might see which of them baked best. Before the first contest, the brides of the two elder sons had made fun of the frog; but now they sent a chambermaid to spy on her and see how she would go about baking her loaf. The frog was aware of this, so she mixed her dough, rolled it, hollowed out the oven from above, and poured her dough right there. The chambermaid saw this and ran to tell her mistresses, who forthwith did the same. But the cunning frog had deceived them; the moment the chambermaid left, she dug the dough out of the oven, cleaned and plastered up everything as though nothing had happened, then went on the porch, got out of her frog's skin, and cried: "Nurses, nurses! Bake me such a loaf of bread as my dear father ate only on Sundays and holidays!" The nurses brought the bread at once. She took it, placed it beside the sleeping Prince Ivan, and turned into a frog again. Prince Ivan awoke, took the bread, and went with it to his father. Just then the king was examining the loaves of bread brought by his elder sons. Their wives had dropped the dough into the oven just as the frog had, and all they had pulled out was formless lumps. First the king took the eldest son's loaf, looked at it, and sent it back to the kitchen; then he took the second son's loaf and sent it back too. Then came Prince Ivan's turn: he presented his loaf. The father received it, examined it, and said: "Now this bread is good enough for a holiday! It is not slack-baked, like that of my elder daughters-in-law!"

After that the king decided to hold a ball in order to see which of his daughters-in-law danced best. All the guests and the daughters-in-law assembled, and also the sons, except Prince Ivan, who became thoughtful: how could he go to a ball with a frog? And our Prince Ivan began to sob. The frog said to him: "Weep not, Prince Ivan! Go to the ball. I will join you in an hour." Prince Ivan was somewhat heartened when he heard the frog's words; he left for the ball, and the frog cast off her skin, and dressed herself in marvelous raiment. She came to the ball; Prince Ivan was overjoyed, and all the guests clapped their hands when they beheld her; what a beauty! The guests began to eat and drink; the princess would pick a bone and put it in her sleeve; she would drink of a cup and pour the last drops into her other sleeve. The wives of the elder brothers saw what she did, and they too put the bones in their sleeves, and whenever they drank of a cup, poured the last drops into their other sleeves. The time came for dancing; the tsar called upon his elder daughters-in-law, but they deferred to the frog. She straightway took Prince Ivan's arm and came forward to dance. She danced and danced, and whirled and whirled, a marvel to behold! She waved her right hand, and lakes and woods appeared; she waved her left hand, and various birds began to fly about. Everyone was amazed. She finished dancing, and all that she had created vanished. Then the other daughters-in-law came forward to dance. They wanted to do as the frog had done: they waved their right hands, and the bones flew straight at the guests; and from their left sleeves water spattered, that too on the guests. The king was displeased by this and cried: "Enough, enough!" The daughters-in-law stopped dancing.

The ball was over. Prince Ivan went home first, found his wife's skin somewhere, took it and burned it. She arrived, looked for the skin, but it was gone, burned. She lay down to sleep with Prince Ivan, but before daybreak she said to him: "If you had waited a little, I would have been yours; now only God knows when we will be together again. Farewell! Seek me beyond the thrice ninth land, in the thrice tenth kingdom!" And the princess vanished.

A year went by, and Prince Ivan longed for his wife. In the second year, he made ready for his journey, obtained his father's and mother's blessing, and left. He walked a long time and suddenly he saw a little hut standing with its front to the woods and its back to him. He said: "Little hut, little hut, stand the old way, as thy mother stood thee, with thy back to the woods and thy front to me!" The hut turned around. He entered. An old woman was sitting there, who said: "Fie, fie! Of a Russian bone not a sound was heard, not a glimpse was seen, and now a Russian bone has come to my house of its own free will. Whither goest thou, Prince Ivan?" "First of all, old woman, give me to eat and to drink, then ask me questions." The old woman gave him to eat and to drink and put him to bed. Prince Ivan said to her: "Little grandmother, I have set out to find Elena the Fair." "Oh, my child, how long you have been away! At the beginning she often remembered thee, but now she no longer remembers thee, and has not come to see me for a long time. Go now to my middle sister, she knows more than I do."

In the morning Prince Ivan set out, came to a hut, and said: "Little hut, little hut, stand the old way, as thy mother stood thee, with thy back to the woods and thy front to me." The hut turned around. He entered, and saw an old woman sitting there, who said: "Fie, fie! Of a Russian bone not a sound was heard, not a glimpse was seen, and now a Russian bone has come to my house of its own free will. Whither goest thou, Prince Ivan?" "To get Elena the Fair, little grandmother." "Oh, Prince Ivan," said the old woman, "thou hast been long a-coming! She has begun to forget thee, she is marrying someone else; the wedding will take place soon! She is now living with my eldest sister. Go there, but be careful. When thou approachest their house, they will sense it; Elena will turn into a spindle, and her dress will turn into gold thread. My sister will wind the gold thread; when she has wound it around the spindle, and put it into a box and locked the box, thou must find the key, open the box, break the spindle, throw the top of it in back of thee, and the bottom of it in front of thee. Then she will appear before thee."

Prince Ivan went, came to the third old woman's house, and entered. The old woman was winding gold thread; she wound it around the spindle and put it in a box, locked the box, and put the key somewhere. He took the key, opened the box, took out the spindle, broke it just as he had been told, cast the top in back of him and the bottom in front of him. Suddenly Elena the Fair stood before him and greeted him: "Oh, you have been a long time coming, Prince Ivan! I almost married someone else." And she told him that the other bridegroom was expected soon. Elena the Fair took a magic carpet from the old woman, sat on it with Prince Ivan, and they took off and flew like birds. The other bridegroom suddenly arrived and learned that they had left. He too was cunning! He began to pursue them, and chased and chased them, and came within ten yards of overtaking them: but on their carpet they flew into Russia, and for some reason he could not get into Russia, so he turned back. The happy bride and groom came home; everyone rejoiced, and soon Ivan and Elena began to live and prosper, for the glory of all the people.

*Twenty-three*

# The White Bride and the Black Bride

*Swedish*

Once there was a king who had only one daughter. She was so beautiful and fair that she was loved by everyone who saw her. The king's spouse, the queen, also had one daughter. But she was so ugly and so wicked that nobody could speak well about her. The queen was most indignant about this and wished the king's daughter nothing good. Then, after the king had died, the queen became very cruel to her stepdaughter and gave her all sorts of lowly tasks. The poor girl never complained, but was always patient and obedient.

One day it so happened that the queen sent her stepdaughter up to the loft to keep watch over the grain. While she was sitting there watching, the little birds of the heavens came flying and chirping; they flew around the heap of grain as if they were asking to get some grains from it. The king's daughter felt sorry for the little creatures and she threw them grains from the bin. She said:

"My poor little birds! Are you so hungry? Here you have grains; pick nicely and eat yourselves full."

When the sparrows had eaten they flew away, sat down on the roof, and took counsel as to how they would reward the maiden for her good heart. Then one bird said:

"I shall grant her that wherever she puts her foot on the ground red roses shall grow." The other one said:

"I shall grant her that she shall be more and more beautiful each day that she lives."

"And I," added the third, "shall grant her that each time she smiles a ring of red gold shall come out of her mouth."

After they had spoken they flew away, but everything was fulfilled as they had said and from that day on the king's daughter was even fairer than before so that a lovelier woman was not to be found in seven kingdoms.

When the queen saw this she became even more jealous than before and considered how her daughter could become as beautiful as her stepsister. For that purpose she sent the princess as well to keep watch over the grain up in the loft. The girl went although she was greatly annoyed that anyone would give her such lowly tasks. Now as she was sitting there the birds of the heavens came flying and chirping; they flew around the heap of grain as if they were begging for some grains from it. Then the wicked maiden lost her temper. She grabbed the broom, chased away the little birds and said in anger:

"What do you want here, you nasty birds! You don't imagine that a noble maiden like me would soil my hands feeding you, do you?" The sparrows flew away, sat down on the roof and took counsel how they would punish the wicked princess for her harsh words. Then one of them said:

"I shall grant her that each time she puts her foot on the ground thistle and thorn shall grow there." Another one said:

"I shall grant her that she shall become uglier and uglier each day that she lives."

"And I," added the third, "shall grant her that each time she laughs toads and frogs shall jump out of her mouth." After they had said this they flew away, but everything was fulfilled as the sparrows had said and from that day on the queen's daughter was uglier still to look at and still more wicked than she had been before.

The stepmother and her wicked daughter now could not stand seeing the king's lovely daughter in front of their eyes, so they sent her to tend the cattle in the forest. So the poor maiden had to

another task

wander there back and forth like other farm-maids and often it seemed to her that she suffered from great want and injustice. But the wicked princess stayed with her mother at the royal castle and rejoiced in her false heart that nobody could see the king's fair daughter or hear about her beauty.

One day it so happened that the beautiful farm-maid was sitting in the forest knitting a mitten while her cattle were grazing. Then some young squires came passing by. When they saw the lovely lass sitting there working so diligently they were struck by her beauty, walked up to her, greeted her courteously and said:

"Why do you sit here, fair maiden, knitting so diligently?" The king's daughter answered:

> Bite, bite in the glove
> The prince of Denmark I shall have.

The squires were very puzzled at this reply and asked the damsel to come along to the royal castle. But the maiden would not listen to their speech. She only gave them rings of red gold so that they would leave her alone. So the squires went their way and reached home. But they never tired of telling about the beautiful farm-maid whom they had met in the forest; as a consequence, her beauty and wealth were spoken about a great deal all around the royal castle.

When this talk reached the ears of the king's young son he had an ardent desire to see the beautiful maiden and to know if all that the squires had told was true. Therefore he set out hunting with his falcons and dogs and went far out into the forest to that place where the king's daughter sat knitting on her mitten. The prince walked up to her, greeted her courteously, and said:

"Why do you sit here, fair maiden, knitting so diligently?" The maiden answered:

> Bite, bite in the glove
> The prince of Denmark I shall have.

When the king's son heard this he felt strange and asked if the farm-maid would not want to go home with him. Then the princess smiled. At that moment a ring of red gold fell out of her mouth and when she got up to leave red roses sprang up in her footsteps. Now the king's son's desire turned so much toward her that he confessed who he was and asked if the young maiden would not want to be his queen. The princess answered yes to this, and let him also understand that she was not inferior to him in family and origin. After that they left together for the king's castle and the king's daughter became the prince's spouse. Everybody wished her well and the king's son held her dearer than anything else in the world.

Because of all this the wicked stepmother became even more jealous in her heart and thought of nothing so much as how she would be able to cause her stepdaughter's misfortune and make her own daughter queen in her place. Then it so happened that there was a great war, so the king's son had to leave. But the queen was pregnant and about to give birth. The stepmother took this opportunity, left for the castle, and showed herself very friendly toward everybody. But when the young queen got sick and nobody was with her the stepmother used trickery, put her own daughter in her stepdaughter's place, and transformed the real queen into a little duck swimming in the river outside the royal castle.

Some time afterwards the war had come to an end and the young king went home full of longing to see his beautiful bride again. But when he entered the bedchamber and found the wicked stepsister in the bed he became very sad and asked how his wife's appearance could have changed so much. The treacherous stepmother was immediately prepared and answered:

"That is because of her sickness and will probably disappear." The king asked further:

"Formerly rings of gold flowed out every time my queen smiled, now toads and frogs jump out; formerly red roses grew up in her footsteps, now thistle and thorn grow. What could be the reason for all this?" But the wicked queen chose her words well and answered:

"The way she is she will remain and not otherwise until the king can take blood from a little duck which is swimming around in the river." The king said:

"How can I get blood from that duck?" The stepmother answered:

"Well, it must be taken between a waning and a waxing moon." The king now gave orders that the little duck be caught. But the bird escaped all traps, however they were laid.

The following Thursday night while everybody was asleep the watchmen noticed that a white phantom which in every way resembled the queen arose from the river and went into the kitchen wing. The princess had owned a little dog which she loved very much. He was called Nappe. When the phantom entered the kitchen, she said:

"Little Nappe my dog, do you have any food to give to me tonight?"

"Oh no, that I have not, my mistress!" answered the dog. The king's daughter said:

"I suppose that the witch is sleeping with my young little prince in the high loft?"

"Oh yes, so she does, my mistress," said the dog. The king's daughter spoke again:

"Now I shall come here two more Thursday nights and then never again." After that she sighed heavily, walked down to the river, and was transformed into a little duck as before.

The next Thursday night everything passed in the same way. After everyone had gone to rest, the watchmen noticed a white phantom which came up from the river and walked into the kitchen wing. Now, since everybody held the young queen dear they wondered very much over this and went secretly to listen to what she would say and do. And when the king's daughter had entered the kitchen she said:

"Little Nappe my dog, do you have any food to give to me tonight?"

"Oh no, that I have not, my mistress!" answered the dog. The king's daughter spoke again:

"I suppose that the witch is sleeping with my young little prince in the high loft?"

"Oh yes, so she does, my mistress!" answered the dog. The queen continued:

"Now I shall come here one more Thursday evening and never again after that." Then she began to weep bitterly and returned to the river where she was transformed into a little duck playing in the water. But when the men learned all this it seemed so strange to them that they went to their master in secrecy and told him what they had heard and seen. Then the king fell into deep thought and ordered the watchmen to send for him when the phantom appeared for the third time.

On the third Thursday night after everybody had gone to rest, the king's daughter again arose from the water and walked up to the royal castle. When she had entered the kitchen wing as her custom was, she spoke to her dog and said:

"Little Nappe my dog, do you have any food to give to me tonight?"

"Oh no, that I have not, my mistress," answered the dog. The king's daughter spoke again:

"I suppose that the witch is sleeping with my young little prince in the high loft?"

"Oh yes, so she does, my mistress!" answered the dog.

Then the queen sighed heavily and said:

"Now I shall come here no more."

Then she began to weep bitterly and walked out to return down to the river. But the king had been standing behind the door listening to their conversation. Now that the phantom was about to depart he took his knife inlaid with silver and wounded her left little finger so that three drops of blood seeped out there. Then the spell was broken and the queen woke up as from a bad dream and said:

"Oh, oh, do *you* stand here?" Then she happily threw her arms around her husband's neck and he carried her up to her bedchamber in the high loft.

The king's young daughter now told her spouse everything that had befallen her and their hearts rejoiced that they could have each other again. The king then walked to the stepmother as she was sitting at her daughter's bedside, but the false queen had the child in her arms and pretended to be very weak after her confinement. Now that the king entered he greeted the old witch and said:

"If someone wanted to destroy my sick queen and throw her into the river, tell me, what would he deserve in return?"

The wicked stepmother did not think that her deceit had been revealed and answered immediately:

"That one would deserve to be put into a spiked barrel and be rolled down the mountain."

Then the king got angry, stood up, and said:

"Thus you have now proclaimed your own sentence and it shall happen to you as you have said yourself."

The witch was then put into a spiked barrel and was rolled down the mountain and her daughter, the false queen, had to take the same trip. But the king took his true queen and lived with her in peace and happiness. But after this I was not around any more.

*Twenty-four*

# The Three Citrons

*Italian (literary)*

The king of Torrelunga had a son who was his right eye and on whom he had built all his hopes. He longed for the time when he should find a good match for him and hear himself called grandfather. But such ideas were so alien to the prince's mind that if anyone spoke of a wife for him he would shake his head, and one would feel that his thoughts were a hundred miles away. The father, seeing his son so wayward and obstinate, felt his posterity was endangered, and was more vexed and bitter than a courtesan who has lost her client, or a merchant whose correspondent has failed him, or a peasant whose ass has died. The tears of the father did not move the prince, he was insensible to the prayers of his subjects, nor could the counsels of the wise men of the kingdom induce him to yield. In vain they urged the wishes of his father, and pointed out the needs of his subjects and his own interest, since he would be the last of the royal line. With determined obstinacy, like an old she-mule with a skin three inches thick over every sensitive part, he put his feet down resolutely, closing his heart and stopping up his ears. It would have been useless to call: "To your arms!" even; he would not have answered.

But frequently more will happen in a single hour than in a hundred years, and one can never say: "I shall not travel along that road." And so it happened that one day, when all were seated at table, the prince was about to cut a cream cheese in half, but, being distracted watching some jackdaws flying about, he unfortunately cut his finger, and two drops of blood fell on the cheese. This produced such a beautiful combination of colors that the prince was seized with the desire to have a wife as white and red as the cheese dyed with his blood. This was perhaps the punishment of Love, watching to catch him; or else the will of Heaven to comfort the good man, his father, who had never suffered such

From *The Pentamerone of Basile*, edited by N. M. Penzer. Reprinted by permission of The Bodley Head.

domestic worry as he had from this obstinate colt of his. The prince turned to his father and said: "Sire, if I cannot find a wife with coloring like this, I am lost. Never before have I desired women, but now I long for one the color of my own blood. Therefore, if you wish to see me alive and well, give me the means to travel through the world in search of beauty and color which can be compared exactly with this cream cheese. If not, my race is run, and I shall pass over to the land of shades." When the king heard this mad resolve, he thought the house was tumbling about his ears, and stood dismayed, changing color from red to white and from white to red. "My son," he said at last, "entrails of my soul, core of my heart, prop of my old age, what has turned your head? Have you gone out of your mind? Have you lost your senses? You want all or nothing; first you would not have a wife, and would deprive me of an heir, and now you are seized with a whim which will be the death of me. Where do you want to wander off to, without any help, wasting your life? How can you wish to leave your hearth and home? You do not know to what dangers and hardships travellers are exposed! Let this madness pass, my son; be sensible. You cannot wish to see my life destroyed and this house and the kingdom brought to ruin!"

These words and others to the same effect went in at one ear and out at the other; they were all thrown into the sea. The unhappy king, seeing his son was like a rook on a belfry-tower, gave him a heap of crown pieces and two or three servants and granted him permission to go. But he felt as if his heart was being torn from his body, and, weeping bitterly, watched his son from a balcony till he lost sight of him.

The prince rode through woods and fields, mountains and valleys, plains and hills, seeing many countries, meeting many people, and always keeping his eyes open in case he should find the object of his desire. At the end of four months he came to the sea-coast of France, and, leaving his servants in a hospital because they were suffering from sore feet, he embarked alone in a Genoese coasting-vessel, and sailed to the Straits of Gibraltar, where he took a larger ship and sailed on to the Indies. In every kingdom, in every province, in every countryside, in every street, in every house, and in every cottage he sought the original of the beautiful image engraven on his heart.

After much voyaging, the ship came to the island of the ogresses, where they cast anchor and the prince landed. Here he found an old, old woman, all shriveled up, with a most hideous face, to whom he told the reason of his coming to that country. The old woman was amazed on hearing of the whim and the strange fancy of the prince, and of the risks and hardships he had suffered seeking to satisfy his desire, and said to him: "My son, away with you. For if my three sons, who are butchers of human flesh, catch sight of you, they will not value your life at more than a few pence; half alive and half cooked, your bier will be a frying-pan and a belly will be your grave. So fly like a hare, but you will not go far before you find fortune." On hearing this, the prince was overcome, aghast, dismayed and terrified. He took to his heels without even stopping to say "Good-bye," and ran on and on till he came into another country. Here he found another old woman uglier than the first, to whom he told his story from beginning to end, and she also said: "Be off from here as quick as you can if you do not wish to make a meal for my daughters, the ogresses. Run, night is upon you! Only a little further on you will find fortune awaiting you."

The prince again took to his heels as if he had a blistered tail, and went on and on till he found another old woman, who was sitting on a wheel with a basket on her arm full of cakes and sweets. With these she was feeding a number of asses, who began prancing about on the bank of a river and kicking some unfortunate swans. The prince politely saluted her a thousand times, and related the story of his pilgrimage, and the old woman comforted him with kindly words and gave him the sort of meal that makes one want to lick one's fingers. When they left the table she presented him with three citrons which seemed to have been just picked from the tree, and also a fine knife, and said: "You can return to Italy, for your spindle is full and you have found what you sought. Go, then, and when you have nearly reached your own country, stop beside the first fountain you come to and cut open one of these citrons. A beautiful fairy will step out and will say: 'Give me something to drink.' You must be quick with some water, or she will slip away like quicksilver. If you have not been quick enough with the first or the second fairy, keep your wits about you, and be careful with the third. Give her water to drink at once, so that she does not escape you, and you will have a wife after your own heart."

The prince was delighted, and kissed the old woman's hairy hand, which was like a porcupine's back, a hundred times. Then, taking his leave of her, he went back to the coast and sailed for the Pillars of Hercules and entered our waters. After a thousand storms and dangers he came to a port only a day's journey from his own kingdom. Here he landed and came to a beautiful little wood, where the shades made a place for the meadows to shelter them from the sun. He dismounted from his horse beside a fountain, which with crystal-tongued whisperings invited the passers-by to come and refresh their throats, and, seating himself on a Syrian carpet woven by the flowers and grasses, he took the knife out of its sheath and began to cut the first citron. Lo, and behold! there stepped out of it a beautiful maiden as fair as cream and as red as a strawberry, who said: "Give me something to drink." The Prince was so entranced that he could only gaze open-mouthed, and was not quick enough in getting the water; for she appeared and vanished again in the same moment.

That this was a stunning blow on the prince's head anyone will realize who, after greatly longing for something, loses it directly he gets it into his hands! But on cutting the second citron he received a second blow, for the same thing happened again, so that his eyes became two streams, and his tears fell, keeping pace with the fountain, head to head, face to face, tit for tat, drop for drop, while he lamented bitterly, saying: "Woe is me! Twice I have let her slip through my hands as if they were benumbed and paralysis were creeping over me! I sit like a stone when I should run like a greyhound. A fine mess I have made of it! Rouse yourself, wretched man! There is one more chance, and the third chance is the lucky one: either the knife will yield me the fairy or I shall yield to my fate." Then he cut the third citron, and out came a fairy, who said: "Give me something to drink," and the Prince, as quick as lightning, fetched her some water, and behold, there stood before him a beautiful young girl as fair as junket streaked with red, looking like an Abruzzi ham or a Nola sausage: such a sight as never before had been seen, beauty beyond all measure, fairer than the fairest, more gracious than the most gracious. Jupiter had rained down gold on that hair of which Cupid made his shafts to pierce all hearts; the god of Love had tinged that face so that some innocent soul should be hanged on the gallows of desire; the sun had lit two fires in those eyes which, by setting light to the powder casks in the breasts of all beholders, should bring forth in volleys squibs and crackers of sighs; Venus had tinted those lips—roses whose thorns would pierce a thou-

sand hearts; Juno had transfused her milk into those breasts that
they should nourish human desire—the maiden, in a word, was so
beautiful from head to foot that nothing more fascinating and
wonderful could possibly be seen.

The prince gazed in bewilderment at this fair offspring of a
citron, this lovely slice of femininity sprung into being from the
slice of a fruit, and said to himself: "Are you asleep or awake,
Cenzullo? Has your sight become bewitched or have your eyes
got topsy-turvy? What is this white creation that has come from a
yellow rind? What sweet pastry from the bitterness of a citron!
How fair a shoot from such a pip!" But at last, finding it was real
earnest and no dream, he embraced the fairy, giving her hundreds
of kisses and little pinches, and a thousand loving words passed
between them—words which were the *canto fermo* to a counter-
point of honeyed kisses. Then the prince said: "My soul, I will
not take you to my father's kingdom till you can be arrayed as
befits so beautiful a person, and can have, as is your due, an escort
worthy of a queen. Therefore climb into this oak-tree, where
Nature seems to have made on purpose for us a hollow like a little
room, and there await my return." Then he spat on the ground
and, promising that before it should dry he would come back to
take her with suitable apparel and with a fitting escort to his
kingdom, he took leave of her with due ceremony.

At the same time it happened that a black slave had been sent
by her mistress with a pitcher to fetch water from this fountain.
When the slave saw the reflection of the fairy in the water, she
thought it was her own and exclaimed in astonishment: "What
see poor Lucia, you so pretty and mistress send me water fetch!
Poor Lucia, me not stand it longer!" And with these words she
smashed the pitcher to pieces and went home.

When her mistress asked her why she had done such a mischie-
vous thing, she answered: "Me gone to fountain and pitcher
broke on stones." The mistress swallowed this stale cake of a
story and gave the slave a fine cask to go and fill with water. But
when she returned to the fountain and saw the beautiful reflection
in the water, again she heaved a great sigh and said: "Me no be
slave no longer! Me no be web-footed goose with waddling be
hind! Me all nice, yet must go carry cask to fountain!" and she
threw down the cask, and smashed it into a thousand pieces; and
when she got back to her mistress muttered angrily: "Donkey go
by, kick cask, cask fall and all break."

This time the mistress could no longer keep calm and, seizing a broom-handle, belabored the slave so that she felt it for many days; then, giving her a leather bottle, she said: "Now run, break your neck, you wretched slave, you grasshopper legs! Run, don't wait an instant or stop on the road, and none of your Lucia tricks! Bring this back full of water, or I will pound you to a jelly and give you such a thrashing that you'll have something to talk about! Run, fling up your heels to your shoulders!"

The slave, who had seen the lightning and now feared the thunder, ran off, but while she was filling the leather bottle she saw the beautiful image once more, and exclaimed: "Me burst than fetch water! Me find fortune and husband, me too fine to come bad end and serve bad mistress." Then, taking a large pin from her head, she pierced the bottle in many places, so that the water made a hundred little jets like a fountain in a garden square.

The sight of this made the fairy laugh aloud, and the slave, looking up, saw the hiding-place, and said to herself: "Ah, you be cause mistress beat me! But no you mind!" Then she said aloud to the fairy: "What do you up there, my pretty maid?" The fairy, who was the very mother of courtesy, told the whole of her story, leaving out nothing about her meeting with the prince, whom she was now expecting every hour, every moment, to come back with the apparel and the company to escort her to the kingdom of his father to celebrate their wedding.

The slave listened with malicious glee to this story, and felt sure she could secure the prize for herself with a turn of the hand, so she said to the fairy: "If husband waiting, me come up comb hair and make you fine." The fairy replied: "You are as welcome as the first of May," and to help the slave climb up she stretched out her white, white hand which looked like a crystal mirror in an ebony frame when it was grasped by the black paw. As soon as the slave got into the tree, pretending to dress the fairy's hair she dug a big pin into her head, and the fairy, when she felt her head being pierced, called out: "Dove, dove!" and changing into a dove, flew away.

The slave stripped herself of her rags and, making them into a bundle, threw them a mile away; then she settled down into the tree as naked as when she was born, a statue of jet in a house of emeralds.

Shortly afterwards the prince returned with a great cavalcade, and when he found a band of dark caviare where he had left a pan of white milk, he was for a time beside himself. At last he said: "Who has made this blot of ink on the fair white sheet on which I thought to write my happiest days? Who has draped with mourning the freshly white-washed house in which I hoped to find all my joy? Why do I find this black touchstone when I left a mine of silver that would make me rich and happy?"

The cunning slave, seeing the prince's bewilderment, said: "Do not wonder, my Prince, me is bewitched and turned into blackamoor—one year black and one year white." Since there was no help for it, the poor prince resigned himself, like the ox to his horns, and swallowed the pill. He bade the slave come down, and had her dressed from head to foot in new clothes and decked out with ornaments. Then, downcast, swelling with rage, and with a long face, he took his way back to his own country, and was received by the king and queen, who had come out six miles to meet them, with the same pleasure as the prisoner feels when he hears the sentence of death. Although they saw the clear proof of the folly of their son, who had sought the whole world for his white dove and had only brought back a black slave, they felt they could do no less than give up their crown to the bride and bridegroom, and placed the tripod of gold on the coal-black head.

Now while astonishing feasts and banquets were being prepared and the cooks were busy plucking geese, killing sucking-pigs, flaying goats, basting the joints, skimming the sauces in the pans, making forcemeat, stuffing fowls, and making a thousand dainty dishes, a beautiful dove came to the kitchen window and sang:

> Oh, cook, cook in the kitchen tell me, I pray,
> What the Prince and his Moor are doing today.

At first the cook paid no heed, but when the dove sang the verse a second and even a third time, he ran to tell the banqueters this strange thing. The princess, as soon as she heard the verse, gave orders that the dove should be caught and made into a hash. The cook, obedient to the commands of the spiteful vixen, succeeded in catching the bird, and when he had scalded it to get its feathers off, he threw the water and the feathers out from the balcony on to the ground.

Before three days had passed a fine citron-tree began to shoot up, and grew rapidly from day to day, and the king, standing one day at a window which looked out that way, happened to notice it. As he had never seen it there before, he called the cook and asked who had planted it. When Master Cook told him all that had happened, the king began to suspect some mystery, and commanded, under pain of death, that no one should touch the tree, and that it should be tended with every care.

In a few days' time beautiful citrons began to form on the tree, just like those the ogress had given the prince. As soon as they were ripe the prince had them gathered and, shutting himself into a room with a large glass of water, he prepared to cut them open with the old woman's knife, which he always carried at his side. Just as had happened before, the first and second fairies disappeared in a flash; but when he cut the third he gave the water to the maiden who stepped out of it, and there stood before him the same fairy he had left in the tree, who at once told him the story of the black slave's deceit.

Who could describe even a part of the joy felt by the king at this good fortune? Who could describe the exultant happiness, the gaiety and gladness, the laughter and the tears? He swam on a stream of bliss, he was beside himself with joy, and thrilled with an ecstasy of tenderness and love. He clasped the fairy in his arms; then, when he had had her suitably clothed and adorned, he led her by the hand into the middle of the hall where all the courtiers and nobles were assembled in honor of the wedding festival.

One by one the king asked the assembled company: "What penalty should a person deserve who would harm such a beautiful lady?" One answered, a collar of hemp; another, to be stoned; another, a sledgehammer blow on the stomach; another, a draught of scammony; another, a necklace of mill-stones; and one suggested one thing and one another.

At last the king called the unfortunate queen, and when he put the question to her she answered: "Deserve burning and ashes thrown down from the castle." Then the king said: "With your own pen you have written down your own fate; you have chopped your own foot; you have forged your own fetters, sharpened the knife, mixed the poison, for no one has done more evil than you, you black dog! Do you know that this is the beautiful maiden whose head you pierced with your big pin? Do you know that this is the rare dove who by your orders was killed and cooked in a stew? What do you answer to this? This is a foul deed that you have done, and he who does evil must expect evil in return—you shall reap as you have sown."

Then he ordered her to be carried off and placed alive on a huge pile of wood and burnt to ashes, and that the ashes should be scattered to the wind from the top of the castle. Thus was shown the truth of the saying that:

*He who sows thorns must not go barefoot.*

*Twenty-five*

# Sleeping Beauty
*Swedish*

Once upon a time there were a king and a queen who lived happily in their country. But they would have been even happier if they had had children. After a long time they finally had a little daughter. The king and queen were so overjoyed that they invited half the people in the kingdom to be godparents. Among them were twelve fairies but the thirteenth was not invited for there were only twelve gold plates to eat from. At any rate, when the princess had been christened the thirteenth fairy arrived and was much upset that she had not been invited. She then said that the princess would stick herself on a spindle when she was fifteen years of age and die.

The other fairies were very sorry but they could not change the prophecy. However they could arrange it so that she would sleep for a hundred years instead of dying, and if a prince should happen to arrive during that time it should be possible to awaken her. The twelve fairies in addition gave the princess each a gift: beauty, wisdom, wealth, kindness, and the like.

The king, who had heard the prophecy, sent word all over the country that all spindles should be burned. But on her fifteenth birthday the princess was walking through the castle and unknowingly entered the tower. There she found a door with a rusty key in the lock. She opened the door and stepped in. An old woman was sitting there spinning with a spindle.

Translated from *Sveriges Samtliga Folksagor* by Waldemar Liungman. Used by permission.

"What are you doing here, old woman?" asked the princess.

"I am spinning, as you can see."

"May I spin too?"

The princess was allowed to try, but she pricked herself and immediately fell asleep. The king and the queen went to sleep too, and the cook in the kitchen, who had just put his hands on the hair of the kitchen boy, preparing to strike him, fell asleep together with the boy. The maid who was plucking a black hen went to sleep too, and the fire in the hearth and the roast in the oven and the pigeons on the roof and the horse in the stable and the dogs in the courtyard, they all went to sleep.

A hedge of hawthorn now grew up around the castle. Many people came during the hundred years and tried to awaken the princess, but they could not get through the hedge. One hundred years later to the day a prince arrived and wanted to get in, but the people in the area warned him and told him how the people who had tried earlier had had accidents and had cut themselves. But when the prince came to the hedge he found no resistance. The hedge opened and he was let in together with his followers. He wandered through the castle, came up into the tower, and entered the room where the sleeping princess was.

He stood for a long while and looked at her and saw how beautiful she was. Then he bent down and gave her a kiss. She woke up, opened her eyes, and looked at him. He gave her another kiss and she got up. He took her arm and led her through the castle. Then both the king and the queen and all of the court people woke up. Presently they walked into the kitchen, where the cook woke up and started to strike the kitchen boy. The maid woke up also and started to pluck her black hen. The fire in the hearth began to burn and the roast in the oven started to sizzle. Later they walked into the courtyard. The dogs woke up and began to bark. The pigeons on the roof woke up and began to coo, the horses in the stable stamped and neighed. There was great happiness at the castle. Later a large wedding was arranged and the prince married the princess.

*Twenty-six*

# East o' the Sun and West o' the Moon

*Norwegian*

Once on a time there was a poor husbandman who had so many children that he hadn't much of either food or clothing to give them. Pretty children they all were, but the prettiest was the youngest daughter, who was so lovely there was no end to her loveliness.

So one day, 'twas on a Thursday evening late at the fall of the year, the weather was so wild and rough outside, and it was so cruelly dark, and rain fell and wind blew, till the walls of the cottage shook again. There they all sat round the fire busy with this thing and that. But just then, all at once something gave three taps on the window-pane. Then the father went out to see what was the matter; and, when he got out of doors, what should he see but a great big white bear.

"Good evening to you," said the white bear.

"The same to you," said the man.

"Will you give me your youngest daughter? If you will, I'll make you as rich as you are now poor," said the bear.

Well, the man would not be at all sorry to be so rich; but still he thought he must have a bit of a talk with his daughter first; so he went in and told them how there was a great white bear waiting outside, who had given his word to make them so rich if he could only have the youngest daughter.

The lassie said "No!" outright. Nothing could get her to say anything else; so the man went out and settled it with the white bear, that he should come again the next Thursday evening and get an answer. Meantime he talked his daughter over, and kept on telling her of all the riches they would get, and how well off she would be herself; and so at last she thought better of it, and washed and mended her rags, made herself as smart as she could, and was ready to start. I can't say her packing gave her much trouble.

Next Thursday evening came the white bear to fetch her, and she got upon his back with her bundle, and off they went. So, when they had gone a bit of the way, the white bear said:

"Are you afraid?"

No! she wasn't.

"Well! mind and hold tight by my shaggy coat, and then there's nothing to fear," said the bear.

So she rode a long, long way, till they came to a great steep hill. There, on the face of it, the white bear gave a knock, and a door opened, and they came into a castle, where there were many rooms all lit up; rooms gleaming with silver and gold; and there too was a table ready laid, and it was all as grand as grand could be. Then the white bear gave her a silver bell; and when she wanted anything, she was only to ring it, and she would get it at once.

Well, after she had eaten and drunk, and evening wore on, she got sleepy after her journey, and thought she would like to go to bed, so she rang the bell; and she had scarce taken hold of it before she came into a chamber, where there was a bed made, as fair and white as any one would wish to sleep in, with silken pillows and curtains, and gold fringe. All that was in the room was gold or silver; but when she had gone to bed, and put out the light, a man came and laid himself alongside her. That was the white bear, who threw off his beast shape at night; but she never saw him, for he always came after she had put out the light, and before the day dawned he was up and off again. So things went on happily for a while, but at last she began to get silent and sorrow-ful; for there she went about all day alone, and she longed to go home to see her father and mother, and brothers and sisters. So one day, when the white bear asked what it was that she lacked, she said it was so dull and lonely there, and how she longed to go home to see her father and mother, and brothers and sisters, and that was why she was so sad and sorrowful, because she couldn't get to them.

"Well, well!" said the bear, "perhaps there's a cure for all this; but you must promise me one thing, not to talk alone with your mother, but only when the rest are by to hear; for she'll take you by the hand and try to lead you into a room alone to talk; but you must mind and not do that, else you'll bring bad luck on both of us."

So one Sunday the white bear came and said now they could set off to see her father and mother. Well, off they started, she sitting on his back; and they went far and long. At last they came to a grand house, and there her brothers and sisters were running about out of doors at play, and everything was so pretty, 'twas a joy to see.

"This is where your father and mother live now," said the white bear; "but don't forget what I told you, else you'll make us both unlucky."

No! bless her, she'd not forget; and when she had reached the house, the white bear turned right about and left her.

Then when she went in to see her father and mother, there was such joy, there was no end to it. None of them thought they could thank her enough for all she had done for them. Now, they had everything they wished, as good as good could be, and they all wanted to know how she got on where she lived.

Well, she said, it was very good to live where she did; she had all she wished. What she said beside I don't know; but I don't think any of them had the right end of the stick, or that they got much out of her. But so in the afternoon, after they had done dinner, all happened as the white bear had said. Her mother wanted to talk with her alone in her bed-room; but she minded what the white bear had said, and wouldn't go up stairs.

"Oh, what we have to talk about will keep," she said, and put her mother off. But somehow or other, her mother got round her at last, and she had to tell her the whole story. So she said, how every night, when she had gone to bed, a man came and lay down beside her as soon as she had put out the light, and how she never saw him, because he was always up and away before the morning dawned; and how she went about woeful and sorrowing, for she thought she should so like to see him, and how all day long she walked about there alone, and how dull, and dreary, and lonesome it was.

"My!" said her mother; "it may well be a troll you slept with! But now I'll teach you a lesson how to set eyes on him. I'll give you a bit of candle, which you can carry home in your bosom; just light that while he is asleep, but take care not to drop the tallow on him."

Yes! she took the candle, and hid it in her bosom, and as night drew on, the white bear came and fetched her away.

But when they had gone a bit of the way, the white bear asked if all hadn't happened as he had said.

Well, she couldn't say it hadn't.

"Now, mind," said he, "if you have listened to your mother's advice, you have brought bad luck on us both, and then, all that has passed between us will be as nothing."

No, she said, she hadn't listened to her mother's advice.

So when she reached home, and had gone to bed, it was the old story over again. There came a man and lay down beside her; but at dead of night, when she heard he slept, she got up and struck a light, lit the candle, and let the light shine on him, and so she saw that he was the loveliest prince one ever set eyes on, and she fell so deep in love with him on the spot, that she thought she couldn't live if she didn't give him a kiss there and then. And so she did, but as she kissed him, she dropped three hot drops of tallow on his shirt, and he woke up.

"What have you done?" he cried; "now you have made us both unlucky, for had you held out only this one year, I had been freed. For I have a stepmother who has bewitched me, so that I am a white bear by day, and a man by night. But now all ties are snapt between us; now I must set off from you to her. She lives in a castle which stands East o' the Sun and West o' the Moon, and there, too, is a princess, with a nose three ells long, and she's the wife I must have now."

She wept and took it ill, but there was no help for it; go he must.

Then she asked if she mightn't go with him.

No, she mightn't.

"Tell me the way, then," she said, "and I'll search you out; *that* surely I may get leave to do."

Yes, she might do that, he said; but there was no way to that place. It lay East o' the Sun and West o' the Moon, and thither she'd never find her way.

So next morning, when she woke up, both prince and castle were gone, and then she lay on a little green patch, in the midst of the gloomy thick wood, and by her side lay the same bundle of rags she had brought with her from her old home.

So when she had rubbed the sleep out of her eyes, and wept till she was tired, she set out on her way, and walked many, many days, till she came to a lofty crag. Under it sat an old hag, and played with a gold apple which she tossed about. Her the lassie asked if she knew the way to the prince, who lived with his stepmother in the castle that lay East o' the Sun and West o' the

Moon, and who was to marry the princess with a nose three ells
long.

"How did you come to know about him?" asked the old hag;
"but maybe you are the lassie who ought to have had him?"

Yes, she was.

"So, so; it's you, is it?" said the old hag. "Well, all I know
about him is, that he lives in the castle that lies East o' the Sun
and West o' the Moon, and thither you'll come, late or never; but
still you may have the loan of my horse, and on him you can ride
to my next neighbor. Maybe she'll be able to tell you; and when
you get there, just give the horse a switch under the left ear, and
beg him to be off home; and, stay, this gold apple you may take
with you."

So she got upon the horse, and rode a long long time, till she
came to another crag, under which sat another old hag, with a
gold carding-comb. Her the lassie asked if she knew the way to
the castle that lay East o' the Sun and West o' the Moon, and she
answered, like the first old hag, that she knew nothing about it,
except it was east o' the sun and west o' the moon.

"And thither you'll come, late or never; but you shall have the
loan of my horse to my next neighbor; maybe she'll tell you all
about it; and when you get there, just switch the horse under the
left ear, and beg him to be off home."

And this old hag gave her the golden carding-comb; it might
be she'd find some use for it, she said. So the lassie got up on the
horse, and rode a far far way, and a weary time; and so at last she
came to another great crag, under which sat another old hag,
spinning with a golden spinning-wheel. Her, too, she asked if she
knew the way to the prince, and where the castle was that lay
East o' the Sun and West o' the Moon. So it was the same thing
over again.

"Maybe it's you who ought to have had the prince?" said the
old hag.

Yes, it was.

But she, too, didn't know the way a bit better than the other
two. "East o' the sun and west o' the moon it was," she knew—
that was all.

"And thither you'll come, late or never; but I'll lend you my
horse, and then I think you'd best ride to the East Wind and ask
him; maybe he knows those parts, and can blow you thither. But
when you get to him, you need only give the horse a switch under

the left ear, and he'll trot home of himself."

And so, too, she gave her the gold spinning-wheel. "Maybe you'll find a use for it," said the old hag.

Then on she rode many many days, a weary time, before she got to the East Wind's house, but at last she did reach it, and then she asked the East Wind if he could tell her the way to the prince who dwelt East o' the Sun and West o' the Moon. Yes, the East Wind had often heard tell of it, the prince and the castle, but he couldn't tell the way, for he had never blown so far.

"But, if you will, I'll go with you to my brother the West Wind, maybe he knows, for he's much stronger. So, if you will just get on my back, I'll carry you thither."

Yes, she got on his back, and I should just think they went briskly along.

So when they got there, they went into the West Wind's house, and the East Wind said the lassie he had brought was the one who ought to have had the prince who lived in the castle East o' the Sun and West o' the Moon; and so she had set out to seek him, and how he had come with her, and would be glad to know if the West Wind knew how to get to the castle.

"Nay," said the West Wind, "so far I've never blown; but if you will, I'll go with you to our brother the South Wind, for he's much stronger than either of us, and he has flapped his wings far and wide. Maybe he'll tell you. You can get on my back, and I'll carry you to him."

Yes! she got on his back, and so they traveled to the South Wind, and weren't so very long on the way, I should think.

When they got there, the West Wind asked him if he could tell her the way to the castle that lay East o' the Sun and West o' the Moon, for it was she who ought to have had the prince who lived there.

"You don't say so! That's she, is it?" said the South Wind.

"Well, I have blustered about in most places in my time, but so far have I never blown; but if you will, I'll take you to my brother the North Wind; he is the oldest and strongest of the whole lot of us, and if he doesn't know where it is, you'll never find any one in the world to tell you. You can get on my back, and I'll carry you thither."

Yes! she got on his back, and away he went from his house at a fine rate. And this time, too, she wasn't long on her way.

So when they got to the North Wind's house, he was so wild and cross, cold puffs came from him a long way off.

"Blast you both, what do you want?" he roared out to them ever so far off, so that it struck them with an icy shiver.

"Well," said the South Wind, "you needn't be so foul-mouthed, for here I am, your brother, the South Wind, and here is the lassie who ought to have had the prince who dwells in the castle that lies East o' the Sun and West o' the Moon, and now she wants to ask you if you ever were there, and can tell her the way, for she would be so glad to find him again."

"Yes, I know well enough where it is," said the North Wind; "once in my life I blew an aspen-leaf thither, but I was so tired I couldn't blow a puff for ever so many days after. But if you really wish to go thither, and aren't afraid to come along with me, I'll take you on my back and see if I can blow you thither."

Yes! with all her heart; she must and would get thither if it were possible in any way; and as for fear, however madly he went, she wouldn't be at all afraid.

"Very well, then," said the North Wind, "but you must sleep here tonight, for we must have the whole day before us, if we're to get thither at all."

Early next morning the North Wind woke her, and puffed himself up, and blew himself out, and made himself so stout and big, 'twas gruesome to look at him; and so off they went high up through the air, as if they would never stop till they got to the world's end.

Down here below there was such a storm; it threw down long tracts of wood and many houses, and when it swept over the great sea, ships foundered by hundreds.

So they tore on and on—no one can believe how far they went —and all the while they still went over the sea, and the North Wind got more and more weary, and so out of breath he could scarce bring out a puff, and his wings drooped and drooped, till at last he sunk so low that the crests of the waves dashed over his heels.

"Are you afraid?" said the North Wind.

No! she wasn't.

But they weren't very far from land; and the North Wind had still so much strength left in him that he managed to throw her up on the shore under the windows of the castle which lay East o' the

Sun and West o' the Moon; but then he was so weak and worn out, he had to stay there and rest many days before he could get home again.

Next morning the lassie sat down under the castle window, and began to play with the gold apple; and the first person she saw was the long-nose who was to have the prince.

"What do you want for your gold apple, you lassie?" said the long-nose, and threw up the window.

"It's not for sale, for gold or money," said the lassie.

"If it's not for sale for gold or money, what is it that you will sell it for? You may name your own price," said the princess.

"Well! if I may get to the prince, who lives here, and be with him tonight, you shall have it," said the lassie whom the North Wind had brought.

Yes! she might; that could be done. So the princess got the gold apple; but when the lassie came up to the prince's bed-room at night he was fast asleep; she called him and shook him, and between whiles she wept sore; but all she could do she couldn't wake him up. Next morning as soon as day broke, came the princess with the long nose, and drove her out again.

So in the day-time she sat down under the castle windows and began to card with her golden carding-comb, and the same thing happened. The princess asked what she wanted for it; and she said it wasn't for sale for gold or money, but if she might get leave to go up to the prince and be with him that night, the princess should have it. But when she went up she found him fast asleep again, and all she called, and all she shook, and wept, and prayed, she couldn't get life into him; and as soon as the first gray peep of day came, then came the princess with the long nose, and chased her out again.

So in the day-time the lassie sat down outside under the castle window, and began to spin with her golden spinning-wheel, and that, too, the princess with the long nose wanted to have. So she threw up the window and asked what she wanted for it. The lassie said, as she had said twice before, it wasn't for sale for gold or money; but if she might go up to the prince who was there, and be with him alone that night, she might have it.

Yes! she might do that and welcome. But now you must know there were come Christian folk who had been carried off thither, and as they sat in their room, which was next the prince, they had heard how a woman had been in there, and wept and prayed, and called to him two nights running, and they told that to the prince.

That evening, when the princess came with her sleepy drink, the prince made as if he drank, but threw it over his shoulder, for he could guess it was a sleepy drink. So, when the lassie came in, she found the prince wide awake; and then she told him the whole story how she had come thither.

"Ah," said the prince, "you've just come in the very nick of time, for tomorrow is to be our wedding-day; but now I won't have the long-nose, and you are the only woman in the world who can set me free. I'll say I want to see what my wife is fit for, and beg her to wash the shirt which has the three spots of tallow on it; she'll say yes, for she doesn't know 'tis you who put them there; but that's a work only for Christian folk, and not for such a pack of trolls, and so I'll say that I won't have any other for my bride than the woman who can wash them out, and ask you to do it."

So there was great joy and love between them all that night. But next day, when the wedding was to be, the prince said:

"First of all, I'd like to see what my bride is fit for."

"Yes!" said the stepmother, with all her heart.

"Well," said the prince, "I've got a fine shirt which I'd like for my wedding shirt, but some how or other it has got three spots of tallow on it, which I must have washed out; and I have sworn never to take any other bride than the woman who's able to do that. If she can't, she's not worth having."

Well, that was no great thing they said, so they agreed, and she with the long nose began to wash away as hard as she could, but the more she rubbed and scrubbed, the bigger the spots grew.

"Ah!" said the old hag, her mother, "you can't wash; let me try."

But she hadn't long taken the shirt in hand, before it got far worse than ever, and with all her rubbing, and wringing, and scrubbing, the spots grew bigger and blacker, and the darker and uglier was the shirt.

Then all the other trolls began to wash, but the longer it lasted, the blacker and uglier the shirt grew, till at last it was as black all over as if it had been up the chimney.

"Ah!" said the prince, "you're none of you worth a straw: you can't wash. Why there, outside, sits a beggar lassie, I'll be bound she knows how to wash better than the whole lot of you. Come in, lassie!" he shouted.

Well, in she came.

"Can you wash this shirt clean, lassie, you?" said he.

"I don't know," she said, "but I think I can."

And almost before she had taken it and dipped it in the water, it was as white as driven snow, and whiter still.

"Yes; you are the lassie for me," said the prince.

At that the old hag flew into such a rage, she burst on the spot, and the princess with the long nose after her, and the whole pack of trolls after her—at least I've never heard a word about them since.

As for the prince and princess, they set free all the poor Christian folk who had been carried off and shut up there; and they took with them all the silver and gold, and flitted away as far as they could from the castle that lay East o' the Sun and West o' the Moon.

*Twenty-seven*

# King Bean

*Italian*

There was once an old man who had three daughters. One day the youngest called her father into her room, and requested him to go to King Bean and ask him whether he wished her for his wife. The poor old man said: "You want me to go, but what shall I do; I have never been there?" "No matter," she answered; "I wish you to obey me and go." Then he started on his way, and asked (for he did not know) where the king lived, and they pointed out the palace to him. When he was in the king's presence he said: "Your Majesty's servant." The king replied: "What do you want of me, my good old man?" Then he told him that his daughter was in love with him, and wanted to marry him. The king answered: "How can she be in love with me when she has never seen or known me?" "She is killing herself with weeping, and cannot stand it much longer." The king replied: "Here is a white handkerchief; let her dry her tears with it."

The old man took back the handkerchief and the message to his daughter, who said: "Well, after three or four days you must go back again, and tell him that I will kill myself or hang myself if he will not marry me."

The old man went back, and said to the king: "Your Majesty, do me the favor to marry my daughter; if not, she will make a great spectacle of herself." The king replied: "Behold how many handsome portraits I have here, and how many beautiful young girls I have, and not one of them suits me." The old man said: "She told me also to say to you that if you did not marry her she would kill herself or hang herself." Then the king gave him a knife and a rope, and said: "Here is a knife if she wants to kill herself, and here is a rope if she wants to hang herself."

The old man bore this message back to his daughter, who told her father that he must go back to the king again, and not leave him until he obtained his consent. The old man returned once more, and, falling on his knees before the king, said: "Do me this great favor: take my daughter for your wife; do not say no, for the poor girl is beside herself." The king answered: "Rise, good old man, and I will consent, for I am sorry for your long journeys. But hear what your daughter must do first. She must prepare three vessels: one of milk and water, one of milk, and one of rose-water. And here is a bean; when she wants to speak with me, let her go out on the balcony and open the bean, and I will come."

The old man returned home this time more satisfied, and told his daughter what she must do. She prepared the three vessels as directed, and then opened the bean on the balcony, and saw at once something flying from a distance towards her. It flew into the room by the balcony, and entered the vessel of water and milk to bathe; then it hastened into the vessel of milk, and finally into that containing the rose-water. And then there came out the handsomest youth that was ever seen, and made love to the young girl. Afterward, when they were tired of their love-making, he bade her good-night, and flew away.

After a time, when her sisters saw that she was always shut up in her room, the oldest said: "Why does she shut herself up in her room all the time?" The other sister replied: "Because she has King Bean, who is making love to her." The oldest said: "Wait until she goes to church, and then we will see what there is in her room." One day the youngest locked her door, and went to church. Then the two sisters broke open the door, and saw the three vessels prepared, and said: "This is the vessel in which the king goes to bathe." The oldest said: "Let us go down into the store, and get some broken glass, and put a little in each of the three vessels; and when the king bathes in them, the glass will pierce him and cut all his body."

They did so, and then left the room looking as it did first. When the youngest sister returned, she went to her room, and wished to talk with her husband. She opened the balcony, and then she opened the bean, and saw at once her husband come flying from a distance, with his arms open to embrace her. He flew on to the balcony, and threw himself into the vessel of milk and water, and the pieces of glass pierced his body; then he entered the vessel of milk and that of rose-water, and his body was filled with the fragments of glass. When he came out of the rose-water, he flew away. Then his wife hastened out on the balcony, and saw a streak of blood wherever he had flown. Then she looked into the vessels, and saw all three full of blood, and cried: "I have been betrayed! I have been betrayed!"

She called her father, and told him that she had been betrayed by her sisters, and that she wished to go away and see whether she could cure her husband. She departed, and had not gone far when she found herself in a forest. There she saw a little house, with a little bit of a door, at which she knocked, and heard a voice saying, "Are you Christians?" She replied, "Yes." Then the door opened, and she saw a holy hermit, who said: "Blessed one, how did you get here? In a moment the witches will come who might bewitch you." She replied: "Father, I am seeking King Bean, who is ill." The hermit said: "I know nothing about him. Climb that tree; the witches will soon come, and you will learn something from them. If you want anything afterward, come to me, and I will give it to you."

When she was up the tree she heard a loud noise and the words, "Here we are! here we are!" and all the witches ran and seated themselves on the ground in the midst of the forest, and began to say: "The cripple is not here! Where has that cursed cripple gone?" Some one answered: "Here she is coming!" Another said: "You cursed cripple, where have you been?" The cripple answered: "Be still; I will tell you now. But wait a moment until I shake this tree to see whether there is any one in it." The poor girl held on firmly so as not to fall down. After she had shaken it this cripple said to her companions: "Do you want me to tell you something? King Bean has only two hours to live." Another witch said: "What is the matter with him?" The cripple answered: "He had a wife, and she put some broken glass in the three vessels, and he filled his body with it." Another witch asked: "Is there nothing that can cure him?" The cripple replied: "It is very difficult." Another said: "What would be necessary?" The cripple said: "Listen to what it needs. One of us must be killed, and her blood put in a kettle, and have added to it the blood of one of these doves flying about here. When this blood is well mixed, it must be heated, and with this blood the whole body of the king must be anointed. Another thing yet is necessary. Under the stone you see there is a flask of water. The stone must be removed, a bottle of the water must be poured over the king, and all the bits of glass will come out of him, and in five minutes he will be safe and sound."

Then the witches ate and drank until they were intoxicated and tired, and then threw themselves down on the ground to sleep. When the young girl saw that they were asleep, she descended quietly from the tree, knocked at the hermit's door, told him what the witches had said, and asked him for a kettle, knife, and bottle. He gave them to her, and caught a dove, which he killed and bled, and put the blood in a kettle.

The young girl did not know which one of the witches to kill, but finally she decided to kill the cripple who had spoken, and put her blood in the kettle. Afterward she lifted the stone, found the flask of water, and filled her bottle with it. She then returned to the hermit, and told him all she had done. He gave her a physician's dress, which she put on, and went to the palace of King Bean. There she asked the guards to let her pass, for she was going, she said, to see about curing the king. The guards refused at first, but, seeing her so confident, allowed her to enter. The king's mother went to her at once and said: "My good physician, if you can cure my son, you shall mount the throne, and I will give you my crown." "I have come in haste from a distance," said the physician, "and will cure him."

Then the physician went to the kitchen, put the kettle on the fire, and afterward entered the room of the king, who had but a few minutes to live, anointed his whole body with the blood, and then poured the bottle of water all over him. Then the glass came out of his body, and in five minutes he was safe and sound. The king said: "Here, physician, is my crown. I wish to put it on your head." The physician answered: "How did Your Majesty come to have this slight trouble?" The king said: "On account of my wife. I went to make love to her, and she prepared for me three vessels of water and milk, of milk, and of rose-water, and put broken glass in them, so that I had my body full of it." Said the physician: "See whether it was your wife who worked you this treason! Could it not have been some one else?" "That is impossible," said the king; "for no one entered her room." "And what would you do," said the physician, "if you had her now in your hands?" "I would kill her with a knife." "You are right," said the physician; "because, if it is true that she has acted thus, she deserves nothing but death."

Then the physician said he must depart; but the king's mother said: "No, no! It shall never be said that after saving my son's life you went away. Here you are, and here I wish you to stay; and, on account of the promise I made you, I wish my crown to come upon your head." "I want but one thing," said the physician. "Command, doctor; only say what you desire." "I wish the king to write on the palm of one of my hands my name and surname, and on the other his name and surname." The king did so, and the physician said: "Now I am going to make some visits, then I will return."

Instead of returning, the pretended physician went to her own home, and threw away the water and milk in the three vessels, and put in other pure water and milk and rose-water. Then she went out on the balcony, and opened the bean. The king, who felt his heart opened, seized his dagger, and hastened to his wife to kill her. When she saw the dagger, she raised her hands, and the king beheld his name and hers. Then he threw his dagger away, bathed in the three vessels, and then threw his arms about his wife's neck, and exclaimed: "If you are the one who did me so much harm, you are also the one who cured me." She answered: "It was not I. I was betrayed by my sisters." "If that is so," said he, "come at once to my parents' house, and we will be married there." When she arrived at the king's palace, she related everything to his parents, and showed them her hands with her name and surname. Then the king's parents embraced her, and gave her a wedding, and she and the king loved each other as long as they lived.

*Twenty-eight*

# King Lindorm

*Swedish*

Once upon a time there was a poor wood-cutter who had two daughters. Once when he was in the forest he forgot his coat, which he had left near a tree; and so he asked his oldest daughter to go out and get it for him. But she came back and told him that there was a white snake on the coat and she was afraid of picking it up. Now the youngest daughter had to go and get the coat, but the white snake was still there when she got there, and it said to her:

"Get up on my back and we will set out on a journey!"

She did as she was told. They soon came to a large lake. There he asked her if she could see any land on the other side, and she answered that she could see a large yellow farmhouse. He then said:

"We are going there tonight and when you enter you shall bring greetings from King Lindorm and say that he is traveling and on his way home. After that you will receive both food and lodging but you must not forget to drop some food for me. I will be under the table although no one will see me."

Everything went as the snake had said. They spent that night at the yellow house.

But the following morning they again came to a large lake. He asked:

"Do you see land?" She answered that she saw a large blue house.

"We are going there tonight," he said, "and you shall bring greetings from King Lindorm and say that he is traveling and on his way home. But do not forget to drop some food down for me."

And they spent that night at the blue house.

The next morning they again traveled for a long time across a large lake, and the snake asked:

"Do you see any land?" She answered that she saw a large white house. The snake said:

Translated from *Sveriges Samtliga Folksagor* by Waldemar Liungman. Used by permission.

"We are going there tonight. We are going to stay there for some days. But you shall bring greetings from King Lindorm and say that he is traveling and on his way home."

And in the evening when the girl was getting ready to lie down the snake said to her:

"Take the kitchen ax with you," and when she had gone to bed, he said:

"Chop off my head!" She answered:

"I cannot do that!" But he said:

"If you do not do it our journey will have been in vain!" Then she did it and the snake turned into a real prince and the girl became his bride.

Many years later they traveled to see her parents. They did not recognize her but lamented that their oldest daughter had died and that their youngest daughter had disappeared when she was fifteen years old.

"We do not know where she is," they said. But then she told them who she was and everything turned out well.


*Twenty-nine*

# The Frog King

*German*

In days of old when wishing still did some good, there lived a king whose daughters were all beautiful; but the youngest was so beautiful that the sun itself, which has, to be sure, seen so many things, was astonished every time it shone in her face. Near the royal manor was a big dark forest, and in that forest under an old linden was a well. Now whenever the day was quite hot, the king's daughter used to go out into the forest and sit down by the cool well. If time hung too heavy on her hands, she would take a golden ball, toss it up in the air, and catch it again; and this was her favorite pastime.

From *German Folk Tales*, collected and edited by Grimm Brothers. Translated by Francis P. Magoun, Jr. and Alexander H. Krappe. Copyright © 1960, by Southern Illinois University Press. Reprinted by permission of the Southern Illinois University Press.

Now it once happened that the golden ball of the king's daughter did not drop into the little hand which she held up but fell to the ground and rolled straight into the water. She followed it with her eyes; but the ball disappeared, and the well was deep, so deep that one couldn't see the bottom. Then she began to weep and wept louder and louder and was unconsolable. And as she was thus lamenting, someone called out to her: "What is the matter, king's daughter? You're crying hard enough to move a stone to pity." She looked about in the direction of the voice and then saw a frog sticking its big ugly head out of the water. "Oh, it's you, old water-splasher," she said. "I'm weeping over my golden ball which fell into the well." "Be quiet and don't weep," answered the frog. "I can certainly help you. But what will you give me if I fetch your plaything up again?" "Anything you wish, dear frog," she said, "my clothes, my pearls and jewels, and even the golden crown I'm wearing." The frog answered, "I don't want your clothes, your pearls and jewels, and your golden crown; but if you'll love me and let me be your companion and playmate, sit beside you at your table, eat from your golden plate, drink out of your cup, and sleep in your bed—if you'll promise me that, I'll go down and bring up your golden ball." "Oh, yes," she said, "I'll promise you everything you want, if you'll only bring back the golden ball." She thought to herself, however, "How foolishly the silly frog's talking; it sits in the water with its kind and croaks and can't be anybody's companion."

On receiving her promise the frog dived in headfirst and in a short time came paddling up again; it had the ball in its mouth and threw it on the grass. The king's daughter was very glad to see her pretty plaything again, picked it up, and ran off with it. "Wait, wait!" cried the frog, "take me with you; I can't run like you." But what good did it do to croak after her, no matter how loud! She didn't listen but hurried home and soon forgot the poor frog, who had to crawl down again into its well.

The next day when she sat down to dinner with the king and all his court and was eating from her golden plate, suddenly, plump, plump, something came crawling up the marble stairs, and when it reached the top, there was a knock at the door and a voice cried, "King's daughter, youngest daughter! Open the door for me." She ran to see who might be outside, and when she opened the door, there was the frog. Then she hurriedly shut the door, sat down again at the table, and was quite frightened. The king saw clearly that her heart was beating furiously and said, "My child, what are you frightened of? There isn't by chance a giant at the door who wants to take you away?" "Oh, no," she answered, "it isn't a giant; it's a nasty frog." "What does the frog want of you?" "Oh, father dear, yesterday as I was sitting in the forest near the well and was playing, my golden ball fell into the water, and because I wept so hard, the frog fetched it up again. And because it insisted, I promised that it should be my companion, though I never thought it could get out of the water. Now it's outside and wants to come in here to me." Meanwhile there was a second knock, and a voice cried:

> "King's daughter, youngest daughter,
> Let me in.
> Don't you know what yesterday
> You told me
> By the cool water of the well?
> King's daughter, youngest daughter,
> Let me in."

Then the king said: "You must keep your promise. Go now and let it in." She went and opened the door; then the frog hopped in right behind her to her chair. There he sat and cried, "Lift me up." She hesitated, till finally the king commanded her to do so. Once the frog was on the chair, it wanted to get onto the table, and when it was sitting there, it said: "Now push your golden plate nearer me so that we may eat together." She even did this, but it was clear she didn't like doing it. The frog enjoyed its meal, but nearly every morsel stuck in her throat. Finally it said, "Now I have eaten my fill and am tired, so carry me to your room and make ready your silken bed; then we'll lie down to sleep." The king's daughter began to weep and was afraid of the cold frog, which she didn't dare touch and which was now to sleep in her pretty, clean bed. But the king grew angry and said, "You mustn't despise anyone after he has helped you when you were in trouble." Then she took it between her two fingers, carried it up, and put it in a corner; but when she was in her bed, it crawled up and said, "I'm tired and want to sleep as well as you; pick me up or I'll tell your father." Then she got very angry, picked it up, and threw it with all her might against the wall: "Now you can take a rest, you nasty frog!"

But when it fell it wasn't a frog but a king's son, with handsome kindly eyes. Now, as her father wished, he became her dear companion and husband. Then he told her how a wicked witch had laid a spell upon him and how no one could have disenchanted him out of the well except herself, and the next day they'd go together to his kingdom. Then they fell asleep, and the following morning when the sun woke them up, a coach came with a team of eight white horses with white ostrich plumes on their heads and harnessed with golden chains, and behind stood the young king's servant. That was Faithful Henry. Faithful Henry had been so distressed when his lord was transformed into a frog that he'd had three iron bands put around his heart lest it should break from sorrow and sadness. The coach, on the other hand, was to take the young king to his kingdom. Faithful Henry helped them both into the coach, once again took up his place behind, and was very happy about the disenchantment. When they had gone some distance, the king's son heard a cracking noise behind him as if something had broken. He turned around and said:

> "Henry, the coach is breaking."
> "No, my lord, not the coach;
>   It's a band from my heart
>   Which suffered sorely
>   While you were sitting in the well,
>   While you were a frog."

Again and again on the way there was a cracking noise, and every time the king's son thought that the coach was breaking; but it was only the bands snapping from Faithful Henry's heart because his lord was now disenchanted and happy.

*Thirty*

# Sister Alionushka, Brother Ivanushka

*Russian*

Once there lived a king and a queen; they had a son and a daughter, called Ivanushka and Alionushka. When their parents died the children remained alone and went wandering in the wide world. They walked and walked and walked till they saw a pond, and near the pond a herd of cows was grazing. "I am thirsty," said Ivanushka. "I want to drink." "Do not drink, little brother, or you will become a calf," said Alionushka. The brother heeded her and they went on farther; they walked and walked and saw a river, and near it a drove of horses. "Ah, little sister," Ivanushka said, "if you only knew how thirsty I am!" "Do not drink, little brother, or you will become a colt." Ivanushka heeded her, and they went on farther; they walked and walked and saw a lake, and near it a flock of sheep. "Ah, little sister, I am terribly thirsty," Ivanushka said. "Do not drink, little brother, or you will become a sheep." Ivanushka heeded her and they went on farther; they walked and walked and saw a stream, and near it pigs were feeding. "Ah, little sister, I must drink," Ivanushka said. "I am frightfully thirsty." "Do not drink, little brother, or you will become a piglet." Ivanushka heeded her again and they went on farther; they walked and walked and saw a flock of goats grazing near a well. "Ah, little sister, now I must drink," Ivanushka said. "Do not drink, little brother, or you will become a kid." But he could not restrain himself and did not heed his sister; he drank from the well, and became a kid. He leaped before Alionushka and cried: "Maa-ka-ka! maa-ka-ka!"

Alionushka tied him with a silken belt and led him on, shedding tears, bitter tears. The kid ran and ran till he ran into the garden of a certain king. The servants saw him and at once reported to the king. "Your Majesty," they said, "in our garden there is a kid; a maiden is leading him on a belt, and she is a great beauty." The king ordered them to find out who she was. The servants asked her whence she came and of what parentage she was. "There were a king and a queen and they died," said Alionushka. "We children remained—I, the princess, and my little brother, the prince. He could not restrain himself, drank water from a well, and became a kid." The servants reported all this to the king. He called Alionushka before him and questioned her about everything; she pleased him and he wanted to marry her. Soon they celebrated their wedding and began to live together, and the kid lived with them; he walked in the garden and ate and drank with the king and queen.

One day the king went hunting. While he was away a sorceress came and cast a spell on the queen; Alionushka fell ill and became thin and pale. Everything became gloomy at the king's palace; the flowers in the garden began to fade, the trees to dry, and the grass to wither. The king returned and asked the queen: "Are you sick?" "Yes, I am sick," answered the queen. Next day the king again went hunting. Alionushka lay ill; the sorceress came to her and said: "Do you want me to heal you? Go to such and such a sea at twilight and drink water there." The queen heeded her and at twilight went to that sea. The sorceress was waiting for her, seized her, tied a stone around her neck, and cast her into the sea. Alionushka sank to the bottom; the kid ran to the shore and wept bitterly. But the sorceress turned herself into the likeness of the queen and went back to the palace.

The king came home and was overjoyed to find that the queen was well again. They set the table and began to dine. "But where is the kid?" asked the king. "We don't want him with us," said the sorceress. "I gave orders that he be shut out; he has a goatlike smell." Next day, as soon as the king went hunting, the sorceress beat and beat the kid and threatened: "When the king returns I will ask him to slaughter you." The king returned and the sorceress begged him over and over again to have the kid slaughtered. "I am annoyed with him, I am tired of him," she said. The king pitied the kid, but there was nothing to be done; the queen insisted and urged him so much that in the end he consented and gave leave to have the kid slaughtered. The kid saw that steel knives were being sharpened for him, and he wept. He ran to the king and implored him: "King, give me leave to go to the sea, to

drink water, to rinse my insides." The king let him go. The kid
ran to the sea, stood on the shore, and cried plaintively:

> "Alionushka, my little sister,
> Come up, come up to the shore.
> Hot fires are burning,
> Big kettles are boiling,
> Steel knives are being sharpened—
> They want to slaughter me!"

She answered him:

> "Ivanushka, my little brother,
> The heavy stone is pulling me down,
> The cruel serpent has sucked out my heart."

The kid wept and returned home. In the middle of the day he
again asked the king: "King, give me leave to go to the sea, to
drink water and rinse my insides." The king allowed him to go.
The kid ran to the sea and cried plaintively:

> "Alionushka, my little sister,
> Come up, come up to the shore.
> Hot fires are burning,
> Big kettles are boiling,
> Steel knives are being sharpened—
> They want to slaughter me!"

She answered him:

> "Ivanushka, my little brother,
> The heavy stone is pulling me down,
> The cruel serpent has sucked out my heart."

The kid wept and returned home. The king wondered why the
kid kept running to the sea. Now the kid asked him for the third
time: "King, give me leave to go to the sea, to drink water and
rinse my insides." The king let him go and followed him. When
he came to the sea he heard the kid calling to his sister:

> "Alionushka, my little sister,
> Come up, come up to the shore.
> Hot fires are burning,
> Big kettles are boiling,
> Steel knives are being sharpened—
> They want to slaughter me!"

She answered him:

> "Ivanushka, my little brother,
> The heavy stone is pulling me down,
> The cruel serpent has sucked out my heart."

The kid again called to his sister. Alionushka swam up and came to the surface. The king snatched her, tore the stone from her neck, pulled her ashore, and asked her how all this had happened. She told him everything. The king was overjoyed and so also was the kid; he capered, and everything in the garden grew green and blossomed again. The king ordered the sorceress to be put to death; a stake of wood was set up in the courtyard and she was burned. After that the king, the queen, and the kid began to live happily and to prosper and to eat and drink together as before.

*Thirty-one*

# The Six Swans

*Swedish*

Once there was a king who ruled over a great kingdom. He was happily married to his queen. They had seven children—six princes and one princess. But then his queen died and he was left alone with all his children. When a few years had passed he decided to get another mother for the children. The new queen was outwardly friendly enough toward the children, but inwardly she resented them. She also knew witchcraft and she certainly would have gotten rid of them if she could only have been sure that she wouldn't be discovered. Once it happend that the king went away on a trip and took the little princess along. When the king had gone, she took the princes up in the tower to show them something marvelous. And when they got there she opened a window and transformed them into birds and a moment later six most beautiful swans soared into the wide heavens. When the king came home there was great commotion in the castle. Nobody knew what had become of the princes. The king had his whole kingdom searched, but in vain.

Translated from *Sveriges Samtliga Folksagor* by Waldemar Liungman. Used by permission.

Some time later the princess was walking in the forest, lonely and sad. Then she met an old man who spoke to her and said that he knew what caused her sorrow and that he could teach her how she could deliver her brothers. He told her that they had been transformed into swans and that they had been at the castle several times. She would be able to speak to them and they would understand very well what she said although they couldn't answer. She was also told that it was the queen who had transformed them. If the princess wished to deliver them, she would have to make them each a shirt out of nettles with her bare hands and without needle and thread. But nobody must see it or know about it, for then it would be of no use. And the shirts had to be finished so that the princes could get them within seven years from the transformation, or else it would be too late. The princess was happy, but also worried, because a few years had already passed since the transformation. She thanked the old man, hurried home and sought out a cellar which was no longer used. Then she learned where she could find nettles and gathered them at night. After that she worked every night for a few hours. The queen often sneered at her rough, sore hands, but the princess avoided the wicked stepmother as much as she could. She slipped out into the forest whenever she saw the swans, and then she spoke to her brothers and comforted them in their grief and asked them to come behind the castle as often as they dared to.

Finally the last day had arrived and the princess had all the shirts ready except the one for the youngest brother. A sleeve was missing on that one because the princess had been watched lately. Now the swans came flying, and the princess ran to get the shirts and threw them over them, and right then the brothers regained human shape, but the youngest had to keep one wing because one sleeve was missing. When the princess and her brothers entered the castle and the queen saw them, she became so terrified that she was changed into a black raven. It flew out through the door and since then nobody has seen it. But the king's happiness was great and the princess was honored throughout the kingdom for her devoted work.

*Thirty-two*

# The Rich Man and His Son-in-Law

*Swedish*

Per the Rich Merchant had a daughter who promised to be both fair and beautiful, but there was no suitor around who could compare with him in wealth. When he traveled to the capital of the country to consult astrologers, they answered that his daughter was to get married to his miller's son. Per the Rich Merchant found this impossible and returned home enraged. However, he went down to the miller and his wife to buy their little son, but since the miller had no other child they were reluctant to let him go. Per the Rich Merchant then promised to give them the house and the land if he could have their son. The miller found this a good suggestion and let Per the Rich Merchant have him. But Per the Rich Merchant wanted the miller's son only so that he could get rid of him. He made a box and in it he placed the little boy, nailed the box together, and threw it into the mill-pond. Now he was happy that he had undone the prophecy of the astrologers, but he traveled any way once more to the capital to ask their counsel, and he received the same answer as before—that his daughter was to marry the miller's son. Per the Rich Merchant said again that this was impossible and returned home.

There he was told, however, that the miller still had a little boy in his house, because the day after he had sold his son to Per the Rich Merchant the miller had found a box which was caught in the waterwheel at the mill, and when he opened the box it turned out to contain a little boy who looked a great deal like the one they had sold. And now Per the Rich Merchant came once more and wanted to buy the boy, but the miller didn't want to sell him, because he looked so much like their first little boy. Per the Rich Merchant then promised them that in addition to all the rest he would give them the mill if he could only have the boy. The miller

Translated from *Sveriges Samtliga Folksagor* by Waldemar Liungman. Used by permission.

found this good pay, since he would become rich at once. So Per the Rich Merchant got the boy, but now he could stay in the home of Per the Rich Merchant where he grew up to be a tall and handsome lad.

Nonetheless, Per the Rich Merchant tried to figure out how to get rid of him. He came to think of the big forest which was close by and which was full of outlaws. They had not as yet let a human being through alive. He therefore sent the youth with a letter through the forest by the hideout of the outlaws.

When the boy had been wandering there for a whole day, he came to a hut in one of the forest clearings. Since nobody was home he walked in, and since he felt tired after the long walk he put the letter in his cap so that he wouldn't lose it, lay down, and fell asleep. Soon the outlaws came home. They took the letter from the cap and read it. Then they understood that Per the Rich Merchant had sent the boy through the forest for them to murder him so that in that way he wouldn't have him as his son-in-law. But this time Per the Rich Merchant was mistaken. The outlaws wrote a letter to his wife, woke up the youth and forced him to go home with it.

When he came home, Per the Rich Merchant was not there, as the outlaws knew all along, and his wife took the letter and read it. In it Per the Rich Merchant ordered his daughter and the miller's boy to get married immediately. Moreover, they were to have a house near his own and a carriage with two horses.

"You must have done Per the Rich Merchant a great service, haven't you?" said the wife.

When Per the Rich Merchant came home he wondered who had moved into the house next to his own. His wife told him that she had received a letter from him in which he himself had ordered what had taken place. Per the Rich Merchant was outraged and then he understood that it was the outlaws who had played this trick on him.

After some time he called the youth to him and told him that if he could travel to the dragon in the northern mountain and pick three scales from his tail and bring them home he would approve of him as his son-in-law.

"I'll try," said the youth, and set out wandering. First he came to a king's castle and asked the way to the dragon in the northern mountain.

"Oh dear, so many go there but nobody ever returns, but if you get there would you ask the dragon why the water in the well of the castle is so foul?"

"Yes, I'll do that," said the youth. Then he wandered to the next king's castle and asked there too for the road to the dragon in the northern mountain and received the same answer:

"Oh dear, so many go there but nobody ever returns, but if you get there would you ask the dragon why we never have any fruit in our garden?"

"Yes, I'll do that," said the youth. Then he continued on his way and came to one more royal castle and asked for the road to the dragon in the northern mountain. Here the same reply was repeated:

"Oh dear, so many go there but nobody ever returns, but if you get there would you ask the dragon what has become of our princess?"

"Yes, I'll do that," said the youth.

He continued on his way until he got to a big river and down at the shore a man sat in a boat. He asked him for the road to the dragon in the northern mountain and the man answered:

"Yes, he lives on the other side of that big mountain. But what do you want to go there for? I have been sitting here for a hundred years and ferried people over to the dragon, but no one has ever returned, but if you get there would you ask the dragon how long I am supposed to sit here ferrying people across?"

"Yes, I'll do that," said the youth. He was then ferried across to the other side and set out up the mountain. There he reached a big door and knocked, but nobody answered, so he opened it himself and stepped inside. He came to a large hall, but saw nobody. Then he heard the lovely voice of a girl singing in the next room. He walked up to the door and knocked on it and received a friendly "Come in, please" as an answer. When he opened the door he saw a beautiful princess sitting there. She asked him how he had dared to come there to the big dragon, and he told her that he intended to pick three scales from the dragon's tail and what he had promised the three royal castles and the ferryman to do.

"I don't think that will work," said the princess, "because he will kill you as soon as he comes home."

"Oh no, I am not afraid of the dragon," said the youth. When the princess heard that he was so brave, she said that she wanted to help him.

"If you take a drink from the horn that hangs here on the wall then you will be able to manage the big sword that hangs on its side. He walked up and took a drink and he became so strong that he could cut and swing with the sword as much as he liked.

Then they heard terrific thunder and a crash, so that the entire mountain was shaking.

"Now the dragon is coming," said the princess. "You can hide under my bed." When the dragon entered he said:

"I smell the blood of a Christian man!"

"A raven flew over the chimney and dropped a bone which I threw out. That's probably what smells," said the princess.

"I guess that's what it is," said the dragon, "but now let's go to bed, for I am tired." When they had been lying for a while the princess woke up and said that she had dreamed about a royal castle which had foul water in its well and nobody knew how that came about.

"If they had sense enough to take away a sour log which is lying on the bottom, they would have fresh water," said the dragon.

In a little while the princess woke up again and said that she had dreamed about a royal castle which never had any fruit.

"If they had sense enough to take away the golden chain which is buried around the garden they would probably have fruit," said the dragon.

When they had been sleeping for a while she woke up again and said that she had dreamed about a royal castle from which the princess had been spirited away into a mountain but nobody knew where.

"Yes, that's you all right, but now be quiet."

In a while she woke up again and said that she had dreamed that there was a ferryman who had been ferrying people across a river for one hundred years and he wondered when he would be relieved. But now the dragon was angry and jumped up and said:

"If he had sense enough to say: Now you must relieve me, he would be free, but if you are not quiet now I'll kill you."

"Yes, I'll sleep and won't ask any more," said the princess.

And when the dragon had fallen asleep the boy sneaked up, took a drink from the horn, seized the sword, and walked up and cut his head off. Then he took three scales from the dragon's tail while the monster was in his death-throes, and after that he and

the princess hurried out, and when the dragon died the mountain collapsed with a dreadful crash.

The ferryman ferried them across and when they had landed on the other side he asked what he would have to do to be free.

"Well," said the youth, "you just have to say: Now you must relieve me, then the other one has to sit there."

"Why didn't you tell me that before?"

"Because then I would have had to relieve you."

In the royal castle the happiness was great when they received the princess back. The king suggested that the youth marry her but he said that he was already married. He then received a wagon loaded with gold and silver and pulled by two horses, and the princess saw him on his way.

When he came to that royal castle which had no fruit, he asked if he could have what was buried around the garden.

"Yes, you could if there will only be apples and pears in the garden." He then dug up the golden chain and got wagons with many horses up front to pull it, and the happiness was great in the royal castle when it got fruit in the garden again. When he came to the royal castle with the bad water, he said that they should remove a log which was on the bottom of the well and then they would have fresh water as before. Also here there was great happiness and he received wagons loaded with gold and silver and beautiful horses before them. He was now many times richer than Per the Rich Merchant, and when he came home his father-in-law was struck with amazement over his wealth. Then he delivered the three scales and Per the Rich Merchant now had to acknowledge him as his son-in-law but wondered if there was nothing more to be had in the mountain.

"Sure, there must be more, because I didn't take everything," said the youth.

Per the Rich Merchant then made ready a horse and a carriage and took off, but he never returned. Probably he is sitting to this day on the ferry as a ferryman.

*Thirty-three*

# The Animal Wife

*Greek*

It chanced there was once a fisherman, unmarried. He used to go
fishing regularly with his rod and line. If he could catch one or
two okes of fish, he would sell them and so could manage. This he
did every day. After living like this for a long time, one morning
he rose up very early and went let us say to the beach of Xinída.
He baited his line and cast it. Then he drew it in and pulled out a
sea tortoise. "Anyhow I will take this," said he, "and put it into
my cottage to eat the fleas; living alone I am eaten up with them."
Besides the tortoise he caught some two okes of fish and brought
them all home. He left the tortoise there and some small quantity
of fish for himself and took the rest off to sell.

When he had gone out, lo! from the shell of the tortoise there
came a girl: there was not her like in the world. She tucked up
her sleeves and took and scraped the fish; she cooked them, some
stewed and some grilled, and set them aside in the cupboard.
Then she went again into the shell of the tortoise. The fisherman
came and opened the cupboard to take the fish and cook them. He
found them all cooked and well cooked too; of a good savor. He
said to himself: "Some neighbor, I suppose, saw that I came back
tired and cooked them for me; I wish I knew her to take her a
couple of fish." Well, he ate and lay down to sleep. In the morning he woke up and again went fishing: this was his business. He
brought his fish home; left the share for himself and went again to
sell the rest. The girl came out again and cooked the fish even
better and again hid herself. The fisherman came back; again he
found the fish cooked. Then he thought "Oh, I wish I knew who
this is; anyhow I could give her two or three fish." To cut the
story short, the tortoise did this for him several times. Then he
thought of a cunning device: "I must keep watch and catch her
and see who it is." So he went out fishing again, brought back the
fish, left those he wanted to eat, and pretending to go away he hid

From *Modern Greek Folktales*, edited by R. M. Dawkins. Reprinted by permission of the Clarendon Press, Oxford.

himself to keep watch. The girl again came out of her shell to cook the fish. He saw her and opened the door and went and looked for the shell to try to burn it. She said: "Do not burn it; if you do you will suffer much trouble." He wanted to burn it but she stood in his way. Well, what would you expect? He threw it on the fire and it was burned up. With no longer a shell to hide in she stood revealed. She went on serving him and was as his wife.

Let us now leave them and look at the king. He wanted to marry and sent out everywhere to find the most beautiful girl and to bring her to him to be his wife. They traveled over all the world but found no woman as fair as the fisherman's wife. This they went and told the king. So the king called together his council to consider and see how they could get the fisherman's wife for him. They said: "There is no way but this. We must order him to overlay the whole palace with gold; that he cannot do and on this pretext we may do away with him and take his wife." So they sent for the fisherman: the king wanted him. He said: "And what does the king want of me? I am a poor man; what use can I be to him?" He went and the king said: "You must take and overlay the whole palace with gold outside and inside, and do this by Sunday. If you don't, I shall cut off your head." Said he: "But, my lord king, where shall I find all that gold; I am but a poor man." Thrown out of the palace, he went home weeping and sighing. His wife questioned him and he told her. She said: "You see now? Did not I tell you not to burn my shell unless you would have much trouble? But sit down and eat and don't be troubled." But could he even swallow his food? When he had finished, she said: "You must go to the place where you used to fish and call for my mother and tell her to give you the little box on the hearth. She must give you the little box; not the big one: do you understand?" Her husband went to the place and cried out: "Ho! mother of the tortoise!" At once she made answer: "At your orders, my son." He said: "You must give me, so says your daughter, the little box which is, she says, on the hearth." Behold, she brought it at once and gave it to him. He said to himself: "And what is this? Can it be some trick? What," said he, "can be the use of this?" Well, he took it to his wife and she said "Now you must go and tell the king to let you have men for the work." Then the men started with brooms and brushes and gilded all the whole palace outside and inside with the stairs and the courts as well. Seeing all this the king said in astonishment: "I say, this is a marvellously cunning fellow." He summoned his council and after consideration they again sent for the fisherman and said: "Tomorrow you must invite to dinner the whole army." Said the fisherman: "But, my lord king, how can I find food to entertain so many men? I am a poor man." The king said: "Do what I say; otherwise, off with your head." Once more the fisherman was kicked out and thrown down the stairs. He went home weeping and beating his breast. His wife questioned him and he told her about it. She said: "Did not I tell you not to burn my shell, or much trouble would come to you? Now come and sit down to eat and do not be troubled." He sat down to eat but he could not swallow the food. His wife said: "Once more you must go to the rock where you caught me and call upon my mother; she will answer you, and you must tell her to give you the little pot on the hearth; bring it here; that is all." In the morning the poor fisherman rose and went to the rock and cried: "Ho, mother of the tortoise." At once she answered: "At your orders, my son. What is it you want?" He said: "Your daughter says you must give me the tiny little pot on the hearth." She brought it and gave it to him. He took it and went off, saying to himself: "But of what good can this be? It seems to me all nonsense: how can all those men be fed out of this tiny little pot?" However he brought it to his wife, and she said: "You must now go to the king and tell him to send you plenty of men as servants and set the little pot on the hearth. Light a fire and call upon the pot and it will provide you with everything you need." The king gave him servants in plenty. He went to the field, a big field, and there he built a hearth and lit a fire and set the little pot on it. Then he said: "Bring me straw mats, bring me spoons, forks, knives, napkins, bread, and so on." The little pot produced them all and the servants set the tables and the army was assembled and there they all sat down to eat; thousands of men. Then said he to the little pot: "Bring out soup, boiled meats, food, this that and the other." Then the pot brought out food of every possible kind and they all ate and were filled to bursting. The king saw this and was near to death.

Again the king assembled his council. They sent for the fisherman and said: "You must get us a man, two spans high and his beard three spans." The fisherman felt ready to die; weeping and bewailing himself he went off to his wife. She said: "What is the matter?" He said: "The other demands I have fulfilled, but look at this one; it is a thing which can never be done. Now for sure I shall perish. They will bring me to my death and when I leave you our wicked enemy will take you." She said: "But tell me what it is that the king said to you." He said: "He wants me to go and get him a man two spans high and his beard three spans." She said: "And does that trouble you? The man who keeps my hens, he is the man." He said: "Tell me then, my wife." She said: "Now sit down and eat and tomorrow you must go again to my mother and tell her to tell my hen-man that he must come here for we have need of him." At dawn he rose and again went to the rock and cried: "Ho! mother of the tortoise." "At your orders, my son: what is it you wish?" He said: "Your daughter says you must tell her hen-man to come to her for she has need of him." She said: "The man is her brother: I will tell him and then if he is willing, . . ." He said: "For sure he must come; the need is great." She went off and said to the hen-man: "You must go there, for your sister wants you and the need is great." The man at once said: "I will go, and I will take her a big basket full of eggs." He filled a big linen basket with eggs; he put it on his head and went off. The poor fisherman saw him with amazement. They went off in procession one after another. On their way the little man was lost in the brushwood. He could see him here and then he saw him there; he could not be sure where he was. He shouted out to him: "Come here." The little man answered. Then he found him underneath a shrub, and tied him with his belt not to lose him again. Thus they came to the house. His sister received them. "Let me see you, brother. You know where you must go? To the palace. Don't leave any breath in any of them; clear them right out."

Next day the hen-man took a club and with the fisherman he went off to the king. The fisherman had sent a message so they were expecting them. The whole world ran there to see. The hen-man ran up the stairs of the palace and everybody was laughing at him. When he came before the king—the councilors too were there—they all laughed, ha ha ha. The hen-man made as though he were angry and said: "But why are you laughing? Do you take me for a buffoon?" He smote with the club this way and he smote that way and cleared them all out and didn't leave alive either the king or anyone else.

Then he crowned his brother-in-law as king and his sister as queen.

They ate and drank their fill;
They died when they had no food.
Children they had at their will;
The land was full of their brood.


*Thirty-four*

# Friends in Life and Death

*Norwegian*

Once on a time there were two young men who were such great friends that they swore to one another they would never part, either in life or death. One of them died before he was at all old, and a little while after the other wooed a farmer's daughter, and was to be married to her. So when they were bidding guests to the wedding, the bridegroom went himself to the churchyard where his friend lay, and knocked at his grave and called him by name. No! he neither answered nor came. He knocked again, and he called again, but no one came. A third time he knocked louder and called louder to him, to come that he might talk to him. So, after a long, long time, he heard a rustling, and at last the dead man came up out of the grave.

"It was well you came at last," said the bridegroom, "for I have been standing here ever so long, knocking and calling for you."

"I was a long way off," said the dead man, "so that I did not quite hear you till the last time you called."

"All right!" said the bridegroom; "but I am going to stand bridegroom today, and you mind well, I dare say, what we used to talk about, and how we were to stand by each other at our weddings as best man."

"I mind it well," said the dead man, "but you must wait a bit till I have made myself a little smart; and, after all, no one can say I have on a wedding garment."

The lad was hard put to it for time, for he was overdue at home to meet the guests, and it was all but time to go to church; but still he had to wait awhile and let the dead man go into a room by himself, as he begged, so that he might brush himself up a bit, and come smart to church like the rest; for, of course, he was to go with the bridal train to church.

Yes! the dead man went with him both to church and from church, but when they had got so far on with the wedding that they had taken off the bride's crown, he said he must go. So, for old friendship's sake, the bridegroom said he would go with him to the grave again. And as they walked to the churchyard the bridegroom asked his friend if he had seen much that was wonderful, or heard anything that was pleasant to know.

"Yes! that I have," said the dead man. "I have seen much, and heard many strange things."

"That must be fine to see," said the bridegroom. "Do you know, I have a mind to go along with you, and see all that with my own eyes."

"You are quite welcome," said the dead man; "but it may chance that you may be away some time."

"So it might," said the bridegroom; but for all that he would go down into the grave.

But before they went down the dead man took and cut a turf out of the graveyard and put it on the young man's head. Down and down they went, far and far away, through dark, silent wastes, across wood, and moor, and bog, till they came to a great, heavy gate, which opened to them as soon as the dead man touched it. Inside it began to grow lighter, first as though it were moonshine, and the farther they went the lighter it got. At last they got to a spot where there were such green hills, knee-deep in grass, and on them fed a large herd of kine, who grazed as they went; but for all they ate those kine looked poor, and thin, and wretched.

"What's all this?" said the lad who had been bridegroom; "why are they so thin and in such bad case, though they eat, every one of them, as though they were well paid to eat?"

"This is a likeness of those who never can have enough, though they rake and scrape it together ever so much," said the dead man.

So they journeyed on far and farther than far, till they came to some hill pastures, where there was naught but bare rocks and stones, with here and there a blade of grass. Here was grazing another herd of kine, which were so sleek, and fat, and smooth that their coats shone again.

"What are these," asked the bridegroom, "who have so little to live on, and yet are in such good plight? I wonder what they can be."

"This," said the dead man, "is a likeness of those who are content with the little they have, however poor it be."

So they went farther and farther on till they came to a great lake, and it and all about it was so bright and shining that the bridegroom could scarce bear to look at it—it was so dazzling.

"Now, you must sit down here," said the dead man, "till I come back. I shall be away a little while."

With that he set off, and the bridegroom sat down, and as he sat sleep fell on him, and he forgot everything in sweet deep slumber. After a while the dead man came back.

"It was good of you to sit still here, so that I could find you again."

But when the bridegroom tried to get up, he was all overgrown with moss and bushes, so that he found himself sitting in a thicket of thorns and brambles.

So when he had made his way out of it, they journeyed back again, and the dead man led him by the same way to the brink of the grave. There they parted and said farewell, and as soon as the bridegroom got out of the grave he went straight home to the house where the wedding was.

But when he got where he thought the house stood, he could not find his way. Then he looked about on all sides, and asked every one he met, but he could neither hear nor learn anything of the bride, or the wedding, or his kindred, or his father and mother; nay, he could not so much as find any one whom he knew. And all he met wondered at the strange shape, who went about and looked for all the world like a scarecrow.

Well! as he could find no one he knew, he made his way to the priest, and told him of his kinsmen and all that had happened up to the time he stood bridegroom, and how he had gone away in the midst of his wedding. But the priest knew nothing at all about it at first; but when he had hunted in his old registers, he found out that the marriage he spoke of had happened a long, long time ago, and that all the folk he talked of had lived four hundred years before.

In that time there had grown up a great stout oak in the priest's yard, and when he saw it he clambered up into it, that he might look about him. But the greybeard who had sat in heaven and slumbered for four hundred years, and had now at last come back, did not come down from the oak as well as he went up. He was stiff and gouty, as was likely enough; and so when he was coming down he made a false step, fell down, broke his neck, and that was the end of him.

*Thirty-five*

# The Two Stepsisters

*Norwegian*

Once on a time there was a couple, and each of them had a daughter by a former marriage. The woman's daughter was dull and lazy, and could never turn her hand to anything, and the man's daughter was brisk and ready; but somehow or other she could never do anything to her stepmother's liking, and both the woman and her daughter would have been glad to be rid of her.

So it fell one day the two girls were to go out and spin by the side of the well, and the woman's daughter had flax to spin, but the man's daughter got nothing to spin but bristles.

"I don't know how it is," said the woman's daughter, "You're always so quick and sharp, but still I'm not afraid to spin a match with you."

Well, they agreed that she whose thread first snapped should go down the well. So they spun away; but just as they were hard at it, the man's daughter's thread broke, and she had to go down the well. But when she got to the bottom, she saw far and wide around her a fair green mead, and she hadn't hurt herself at all.

So she walked on a bit, till she came to a hedge which she had to cross.

"Ah! don't tread hard on me, pray don't, and I'll help you another time, that I will," said the hedge.

Then the lassie made herself as light as she could, and trode so carefully she scarce touched a twig.

So she went on a bit farther, till she came to a brindled cow, which walked there with a milking-pail on her horns. 'Twas a large pretty cow, and her udder was so full and round.

"Ah! be so good as to milk me, pray," said the cow; "I'm so full of milk. Drink as much as you please, and throw the rest over my hoofs, and see if I don't help you some day."

So the man's daughter did as the cow begged. As soon as she touched the teats, the milk spouted out into the pail. Then she drank till her thirst was slaked; and the rest she threw over the cow's hoofs, and the milking pail she hung on her horns again.

So when she had gone a bit farther, a big wether met her, which had such thick long wool, it hung down and draggled after him on the ground, and on one of his horns hung a great pair of shears.

"Ah! please clip off my wool," said the sheep, "for here I go about with all this wool, and catch up everything I meet, and besides, it's so warm, I'm almost choked. Take as much of the fleece as you please, and twist the rest round my neck, and see if I don't help you some day."

Yes; she was willing enough, and the sheep lay down of himself on her lap, and kept quite still, and she clipped him so neatly, there wasn't a scratch on his skin. Then she took as much of the wool as she chose, and the rest she twisted round the neck of the sheep.

A little farther on, she came to an apple-tree, which was loaded with apples; all its branches were bowed to the ground, and leaning against the stem was a slender pole.

"Ah! do be so good as to pluck my apples off me," said the Tree, "so that my branches may straighten themselves again, for it's bad work to stand so crooked; but when you beat them down, don't strike me too hard. Then eat as many as you please, lay the rest round my root, and see if I don't help you some day or other."

Yes; she plucked all she could reach with her hands, and then she took the pole and knocked down the rest, and afterwards she ate her fill, and the rest she laid neatly round the root.

So she walked on a long, long way, and then she came to a great farm-house, where an old hag of the trolls lived with her daughter. There she turned in to ask if she could get a place.

"Oh!" said the old hag; "it's no use your trying. We've had ever so many maids, but none of them was worth her salt."

But she begged so prettily that they would just take her on trial, that at last they let her stay. So the old hag gave her a sieve, and bade her go and fetch water in it. She thought it strange to fetch water in a sieve, but still she went, and when she came to the well, the little birds began to sing:

> "Daub in clay,
> Stuff in straw;
> Daub in clay,
> Stuff in straw."

Yes, she did so, and found she could carry water in a sieve well enough; but when she got home with the water, and the old witch saw the sieve, she cried out:

"This you haven't sucked out of your own breast."

So the old witch said, now she might go into the byre to pitch out dung and milk kine; but when she got there she found a pitchfork so long and heavy she couldn't stir it, much less work with it. She didn't know at all what to do, or what to make of it; but the little birds sang again that she should take the broomstick and toss out a little with that, and all the rest of the dung would fly after it. So she did that, and as soon as ever she began with the broomstick, the byre was as clean as if it had been swept and washed.

Now she had to milk the kine, but they were so restless that they kicked and frisked; there was no getting near them to milk them.

But the little birds sang outside:

"A little drop, a tiny sup,
    For the little birds to drink it up."

Yes, she did that; she just milked a tiny drop, 'twas as much as she could, for the little birds outside; and then all the cows stood still and let her milk them. They neither kicked nor frisked; they didn't even lift a leg.

So when the old witch saw her coming in with the milk, she cried out:

"This you haven't sucked out of your own breast. But now just take this black wool and wash it white."

This the lassie was at her wit's end to know how to do, for she had never seen or heard of any one who could wash black wool white. Still she said nothing, but took the wool and went down with it to the well. There the little birds sang again, and told her to take the wool and dip it into the great butt that stood there; and she did so, and out it came as white as snow.

"Well, I never!" said the old witch, when she came in with the wool, "it's no good keeping you. You can do everything, and at last you'll be the plague of my life. We'd best part, so take your wages and be off."

Then the old hag drew out three caskets, one red, one green, and one blue, and of these the lassie was to choose one as wages for her service. Now she didn't know at all which to choose, but the little birds sang:

> "Don't take the red, don't take the green,
> But take the blue, where may be seen
> Three little crosses all in a row;
> We saw the marks, and so we know."

So she took the blue casket, as the birds sang.

"Bad luck to you, then," said the old witch; "see if I don't make you pay for this!"

So when the man's daughter was just setting off, the old witch shot a red-hot bar of iron after her, but she sprang behind the door and hid herself, so that it missed her, for her friends, the little birds, had told her beforehand how to behave. Then she walked on and on as fast as ever she could; but when she got to the apple-tree, she heard an awful clatter behind her on the road, and that was the old witch and her daughter coming after her.

So the lassie was so frightened and scared, she didn't know what to do.

"Come hither to me, lassie, do you hear," said the apple-tree, "I'll help you; get under my branches and hide, for if they catch you they'll tear you to death, and take the casket from you."

Yes; she did so, and she had hardly hidden herself before up came the old witch and her daughter.

"Have you seen any lassie pass this way, you apple-tree?" said the old hag.

"Yes, yes," said the apple-tree; "one ran by here an hour ago; but now she's got so far ahead you'll never catch her up."

So the old witch turned back and went home again.

Then the lassie walked on a bit, but when she came just about where the sheep was, she heard an awful clatter beginning on the road behind her, and she didn't know what to do, she was so scared and frightened; for she knew well enough it was the old witch, who had thought better of it.

"Come hither to me, lassie," said the wether, "and I'll help you. Hide yourself under my fleece, and then they'll not see you; else they'll take away the casket, and tear you to death."

Just then up came the old witch, tearing along.

"Have you seen any lassie pass here, you sheep?" she cried to the wether.

"Oh yes," said the wether, "I saw one an hour ago, but she ran so fast you'll never catch her."

So the old witch turned round and went home.

But when the lassie had come to where she met the cow, she heard another awful clatter behind her.

"Come hither to me, lassie," said the cow, "and I'll help you to hide yourself under my udder, else the old hag will come and take away your casket, and tear you to death."

True enough, it wasn't long before she came up.

"Have you seen any lassie pass here, you cow?" said the old hag.

"Yes, I saw one an hour ago," said the cow, "but she's far away now, for she ran so fast I don't think you'll ever catch her up."

So the old hag turned round, and went back home again.

When the lassie had walked a long, long way farther on, and was not far from the hedge, she heard again that awful clatter on the road behind her, and she got scared and frightened, for she knew well enough it was the old hag and her daughter, who had changed their minds.

"Come hither to me, lassie," said the hedge, "and I'll help you. Creep under my twigs, so that they can't see you; else they'll take the casket from you, and tear you to death."

Yes; she made all the haste she could to get under the twigs of the hedge.

"Have you seen any lassie pass this way, you hedge?" said the old hag to the hedge.

"No, I haven't seen any lassie," answered the hedge, and was as smooth-tongued as if he had got melted butter in his mouth; but all the while he spread himself out, and made himself so big and tall, one had to think twice before crossing him. And so the old witch had no help for it but to turn round and go home again.

So when the man's daughter got home, her stepmother and her stepsister were more spiteful against her than ever; for now she was much neater, and so smart, it was a joy to look at her. Still she couldn't get leave to live with them, but they drove her out into a pig-sty. That was to be her house. So she scrubbed it out so neat and clean, and then she opened her casket, just to see what she had got for her wages. But as soon as ever she unlocked it, she saw inside so much gold and silver, and lovely things, which came streaming out till all the walls were hung with them, and at last the pig-sty was far grander than the grandest king's palace.

And when the stepmother and her daughter came to see this, they almost jumped out of their skin, and began to ask what kind of a place she had down there?

"Oh," said the lassie, "can't you see, when I have got such good wages. 'Twas such a family and such a mistress to serve, you couldn't find their like anywhere."

Yes; the woman's daughter made up her mind to go out to serve too, that she might get just such another gold casket. So they sat down to spin again, and now the woman's daughter was to spin bristles, and the man's daughter flax, and she whose thread first snapped was to go down the well. It wasn't long, as you may fancy, before the woman's daughter's thread snapped, and so they threw her down the well.

So the same thing happened. She fell to the bottom, but met with no harm, and found herself on a lovely green meadow. When she had walked a bit she came to the hedge.

"Don't tread hard on me, pray, lassie, and I'll help you again," said the hedge.

"Oh!" said she, "what should I care for a bundle of twigs!" and tramped and stamped over the hedge till it cracked and groaned again.

A little farther on she came to the cow, which walked about ready to burst for want of milking.

"Be so good as to milk me, lassie," said the cow, "and I'll help you again. Drink as much as you please, but throw the rest over my hoofs."

Yes, she did that; she milked the cow, and drank till she could drink no more; but when she left off, there was none left to throw over the cow's hoofs, and as for the pail, she tossed it down the hill and walked on.

When she had gone a bit farther, she came to the sheep, which walked along with his wool dragging after him.

"Oh, be so good as to clip me, lassie," said the sheep, "and I'll serve you again. Take as much of the wool as you will, but twist the rest round my neck."

Well, she did that; but she went so carelessly to work, that she cut great pieces out of the poor sheep, and as for the wool, she carried it all away with her.

A little while after she came to the apple-tree, which stood there quite crooked with fruit again.

"Be so good as to pluck the apples off me that my limbs may

grow straight, for it's weary work to stand all awry," said the apple-tree. "But please take care not to beat me too hard. Eat as many as you will, but lay the rest neatly round my root, and I'll help you again."

Well, she plucked those nearest to her, and thrashed down those she couldn't reach with the pole; but she didn't care how she did it, and broke off and tore down great boughs, and ate till she was as full as full could be, and then she threw down the rest under the tree.

So when she had gone a good bit farther, she came to the farm where the old witch lived. There she asked for a place, but the old hag said she wouldn't have any more maids, for they were either worth nothing, or were too clever, and cheated her out of her goods. But the woman's daughter was not to be put off, she *would* have a place, so the old witch said she'd give her a trial, if she was fit for anything.

The first thing she had to do was to fetch water in a sieve. Well, off she went to the well, and drew water in a sieve, but as fast as she got it in it ran out again. So the little birds sang,

> "Daub in clay,
> Put in straw;
> Daub in clay,
> Put in straw."

But she didn't care to listen to the birds' song, and pelted them with clay, till they flew off far away. And so she had to go home with the empty sieve, and got well scolded by the old witch.

Then she was to go into the byre to clean it, and milk the kine. But she was too good for such dirty work, she thought. Still, she went out into the byre, but when she got there, she couldn't get on at all with the pitchfork, it was so big. The birds said the same to her as they had said to her stepsister, and told her to take the broomstick, and toss out a little dung, and then all the rest would fly after it; but all she did with the broomstick was to throw it at the birds. When she came to milk, the kine were so unruly, they kicked and pushed, and every time she got a little milk in the pail, over they kicked it. Then the birds sang again:

> "A little drop, and a tiny sup,
> For the little birds to drink it up."

But she beat and banged the cows about, and threw and pelted at the birds everything she could lay hold of, and made such a to do, 'twas awful to see. So she didn't make much either of her pitching or milking, and when she came indoors she got blows as well as hard words from the old witch, who sent her off to wash the black wool white; but that, too, she did no better.

Then the old witch thought this really too bad, so she set out the three caskets, one red, one green, and one blue, and said she'd no longer any need of her services, for she wasn't worth keeping, but for wages she should have leave to choose whichever casket she pleased.

Then sang the little birds:

> "Don't take the red, don't take the green,
> But choose the blue, where may be seen
> Three little crosses all in a row;
> We saw the marks, and so we know."

She didn't care a pin for what the birds sang, but took the red, which caught her eye most. And so she set out on her road home, and she went along quietly and easily enough; there was no one who came after *her*.

So when she got home, her mother was ready to jump with joy, and the two went at once into the ingle, and put the casket up there, for they made up their minds there could be nothing in it but pure silver and gold, and they thought to have all the walls and roof gilded like the pig-sty. But lo! when they opened the casket there came tumbling out nothing but toads, and frogs, and snakes; and worse than that, whenever the woman's daughter opened her mouth, out popped a toad or a snake, and all the vermin one ever thought of, so that at last there was no living in the house with her.

That was all the wages *she* got for going out to service with the old witch.

*Thirty-six*

# Tom Tit Tot

*English*

Once upon a time there was a woman, and she baked five pies. And when they came out of the oven, they were that overbaked the crusts were too hard to eat. So she says to her daughter:

"Darter," says she, "put you them there pies on the shelf, and leave 'em there a little, and they'll come again."—She meant, you know, the crust would get soft.

But the girl, she says to herself: "Well, if they'll come again, I'll eat 'em now." And she set to work and ate 'em all, first and last.

Well, come supper-time the woman said: "Go you, and get one o' them there pies. I dare say they've come again now."

The girl went and she looked, and there was nothing but the dishes. So back she came and says she: "Noo, they ain't come again."

"Not one of 'em?" says the mother.

"Not one of 'em," says she.

"Well, come again, or not come again," said the woman, "I'll have one for supper."

"But you can't, if they ain't come," said the girl.

"But I can," says she. "Go you, and bring the best of 'em."

"Best or worst," says the girl, "I've ate 'em all, and you can't have one till that's come again."

Well, the woman she was done, and she took her spinning to the door to spin, and as she span she sang:

> "My darter ha' ate five, five pies to-day.
> My darter ha' ate five, five pies to-day."

The king was coming down the street, and he heard her sing, but what she sang he couldn't hear, so he stopped and said:

"What was that you were singing, my good woman?"

The woman was ashamed to let him hear what her daughter had been doing, so she sang, instead of that:

> "My darter ha' spun five, five skeins to-day.
> My darter ha' spun five, five skeins to-day."

"Stars o' mine!" said the king, "I never heard tell of any one that could do that."

Then he said: "Look you here, I want a wife, and I'll marry your daughter. But look you here," says he, "eleven months out of the year she shall have all she likes to eat, and all the gowns she likes to get, and all the company she likes to keep; but the last month of the year she'll have to spin five skeins every day, and if she don't I shall kill her."

"All right," says the woman; for she thought what a grand marriage that was. And as for the five skeins, when the time came, there'd be plenty of ways of getting out of it, and likeliest, he'd have forgotten all about it.

Well, so they were married. And for eleven months the girl had all she liked to eat, and all the gowns she like to get, and all the company she liked to keep.

But when the time was getting over, she began to think about the skeins and to wonder if he had 'em in mind. But not one word did he say about 'em, and she thought he'd wholly forgotten 'em.

However, the last day of the last month he takes her to a room she'd never set eyes on before. There was nothing in it but a spinning-wheel and a stool. And says he: "Now, my dear, here you'll be shut in to-morrow with some victuals and some flax, and if you haven't spun five skeins by the night, your head'll go off."

And away he went about his business.

Well, she was that frightened, she'd always been such a gatless girl, that she didn't so much as know how to spin, and what was she to do to-morrow with no one to come nigh her to help her? She sat down on a stool in the kitchen, and law! how she did cry!

However, all of a sudden she heard a sort of a knocking low down on the door. She upped and oped it, and what should she see but a small little black thing with a long tail. That looked up at her right curious, and that said:

"What are you a-crying for?"

"What's that to you?" says she.

"Never you mind," that said, "but tell me what you're a-crying for."

"That won't do me no good if I do," says she.

"You don't know that," that said, and twirled that's tail round.

"Well," says she, "that won't do no harm, if that don't do no good," and she upped and told about the pies, and the skeins, and everything.

"This is what I'll do," says the little black thing, 'I'll come to your window every morning and take the flax and bring it spun at night."

"What's your pay?" says she.

That looked out of the corner of that's eyes, and that said: "I'll give you three guesses every night to guess my name, and if you have n't guessed it before the month's up you shall be mine."

Well, she thought she'd be sure to guess that's name before the month was up. "All right," says she, "I agree."

"All right," that says, and law! how that twirled that's tail.

Well, the next day, her husband took her into the room, and there was the flax and the day's food.

"Now, there's the flax," says he, "and if that ain't spun up this night, off goes your head." And then he went out and locked the door.

He'd hardly gone, when there was a knocking against the window.

She upped and she oped it, and there sure enough was the little old thing sitting on the ledge.

"Where's the flax?" says he.

"Here it be," says she. And she gave it to him.

Well, come the evening a knocking came again to the window. She upped and she oped it, and there was the little old thing with five skeins of flax on his arm.

"Here it be," says he, and he gave it to her.

"Now, what's my name?" says he.

"What, is that Bill?" says she.

"Noo, that ain't, says he, and he twirled his tail.

"Is that Ned?" says she.

"Noo, that ain't," says he, and he twirled his tail.

"Well, is that Mark?" says she.

"Noo, that ain't," says he, and he twirled his tail harder, and away he flew.

Well, when her husband came in, there were the five skeins ready for him. "I see I shan't have to kill you to-night, my dear," says he; "you'll have your food and your flax in the morning," says he, and away he goes.

Well, every day the flax and the food were brought, and every day that there little black impet used to come mornings and evenings. And all the day the girl sat trying to think of names to say to it when it came at night. But she never hit on the right one. And as it got towards the end of the month, the impet began to look so maliceful, and that twirled that's tail faster and faster each time she gave a guess.

At last it came to the last day but one. The impet came at night along with the five skeins, and that said:

"What, ain't you got my name yet?"

"Is that Nicodemus?" says she.

"Noo, 't ain't," that says.

"Is that Sammle?" says she.

"Noo, 't ain't," that says.

"A-well, is that Methusalem?" says she.

"Noo, 't ain't that neither," that says.

Then that looks at her with that's eyes like a coal o' fire, and that says: "Woman, there's only to-morrow night, and then you'll be mine!" And away it flew.

Well, she felt that horrid. However, she heard the king coming along the passage. In he came, and when he sees the five skeins, he says, says he:

"Well, my dear," says he. "I don't see but what you'll have your skeins ready to-morrow night as well, and as I reckon I shan't have to kill you, I'll have supper in here to-night." So they brought supper, and another stool for him, and down the two sat.

Well, he hadn't eaten but a mouthful or so, when he stops and begins to laugh.

"What is it?" says she.

"A-why," says he, "I was out a-hunting to-day, and I got away to a place in the wood I'd never seen before. And there was an old chalk-pit. And I heard a kind of a sort of humming. So I got off my hobby, and I went right quiet to the pit, and I looked down. Well, what should there be but the funniest little black thing you ever set eyes on. And what was that doing, but that had a little spinning-wheel, and that was spinning wonderful fast, and twirling that's tail. And as that span that sang:

" 'Nimmy nimmy not
My name's Tom Tit Tot.' "

Well, when the girl heard this, she felt as if she could have jumped out of her skin for joy, but she didn't say a word.

Next day that there little thing looked so maliceful when he came for the flax. And when night came, she heard that knocking against the window panes. She oped the window, and that come right in on the ledge. That was grinning from ear to ear, and Oo! that's tail was twirling round so fast.

"What's my name?" that says, as that gave her the skeins.

"Is that Solomon?" she says, pretending to be afeard.

"Noo, 'tain't," that says, and that came further into the room.

"Well, is that Zebedee?" says she again.

"Noo, 'tain't," says the impet. And then that laughed and twirled that's tail till you couldn't hardly see it.

"Take time, woman," that says; "next guess, and you're mine." And that stretched out that's black hands at her.

Well, she backed a step or two, and she looked at it, and then she laughed out, and says she, pointing her finger at it:

> "Nimmy nimmy not
> Your name's Tom Tit Tot."

Well, when that heard her, that gave an awful shriek and away that flew into the dark, and she never saw it any more.

# The Three Aunts

*Norwegian*

Once on a time there was a poor man who lived in a hut far away in the wood, and got his living by shooting. He had an only daughter, who was very pretty, and as she had lost her mother when she was a child, and was now half grown up, she said she would go out into the world and earn her bread.

"Well, lassie!" said the father, "true enough you have learned nothing here but how to pluck birds and roast them, but still you may as well try to earn your bread."

So the girl went off to seek a place, and when she had gone a little while, she came to a palace. There she stayed and got a place, and the queen liked her so well that all the other maids got envious of her. So they made up their minds to tell the queen how the lassie said she was good to spin a pound of flax in four-and-twenty hours, for you must know the queen was a great housewife, and thought much of good work.

"Have you said this? then you shall do it," said the queen; "but you may have a little longer time if you choose."

Now, the poor lassie dared not say she had never spun in all her life, but she only begged for a room to herself. That she got, and the wheel and the flax were brought up to her. There she sat sad and weeping, and knew not how to help herself. She pulled the wheel this way and that, and twisted and turned it about, but she made a poor hand of it, for she had never even seen a spinning-wheel in her life.

But all at once, as she sat there, in came an old woman to her.

"What ails you, child?" she said.

"Ah!" said the lassie, with a deep sigh, "it's no good to tell you, for you'll never be able to help me."

"Who knows?" said the old wife. "Maybe I know how to help you after all."

Well, thought the lassie to herself, I may as well tell her, and so she told her how her fellow servants had given out that she was good to spin a pound of flax in four-and-twenty hours.

"And here am I, wretch that I am, shut up to spin all that heap in a day and a night, when I have never even seen a spinning-wheel in all my born days."

"Well, never mind, child," said the old woman, "If you'll call me Aunt on the happiest day of your life, I'll spin this flax for you, and so you may just go away and lie down to sleep."

Yes, the lassie was willing enough, and off she went and lay down to sleep.

Next morning when she awoke, there lay all the flax spun on the table, and that so clean and fine, no one had ever seen such even and pretty yarn. The queen was very glad to get such nice yarn, and she set greater store by the lassie than ever. But the rest were still more envious, and agreed to tell the queen how the lassie had said she was good to weave the yarn she had spun in four-and-twenty hours. So the queen said again, as she had said it she must do it; but if she couldn't quite finish it in four-and-twenty hours, she wouldn't be too hard upon her, she might have a little more time. This time, too, the lassie dared not say No, but begged for a room to herself, and then she would try. There she sat again, sobbing and crying, and not knowing which way to turn, when another old woman came in and asked:

"What ails you, child?"

At first the lassie wouldn't say, but at last she told her the whole story of her grief.

"Well, well!" said the old wife, "never mind. If you'll call me Aunt on the happiest day of your life, I'll weave this yarn for you, and so you may just be off, and lie down to sleep."

Yes, the lassie was willing enough; so she went away and lay down to sleep. When she awoke, there lay the piece of linen on the table, woven so neat and close, no woof could be better. So the lassie took the piece and ran down to the queen, who was very glad to get such beautiful linen, and set greater store than ever by the lassie. But as for the others, they grew still more bitter against her, and thought of nothing but how to find out something to tell about her.

At last they told the queen the lassie had said she was good to make up the piece of linen into shirts in four-and-twenty hours. Well, all happened as before; the lassie dared not say she couldn't sew; so she was shut up again in a room by herself, and there she sat in tears and grief. But then another old wife came, who said she would sew the shirts for her if she would call her Aunt on the happiest day of her life. The lassie was only too glad to do this, and then she did as the old wife told her, and went and lay down to sleep.

Next morning when she woke she found the piece of linen made up into shirts, which lay on the table—and such beautiful work no one had ever set eyes on; and more than that, the shirts were all marked and ready for wear. So, when the queen saw the work, she was so glad at the way in which it was sewn, that she clapped her hands, and said:

"Such sewing I never had, nor even saw, in all my born days"; and after that she was as fond of the lassie as of her own children; and she said to her:

"Now, if you like to have the prince for your husband, you shall have him; for you will never need to hire work-women. You can sew, and spin, and weave all yourself."

So as the lassie was pretty, and the prince was glad to have her, the wedding soon came on. But just as the prince was going to sit down with the bride to the bridal feast, in came an ugly old hag with a long nose—I'm sure it was three ells long.

So up got the bride and made a curtsey, and said:

"Good-day, Auntie."

"*That* Auntie to my bride?" said the prince.

"Yes, she was!"

"Well, then, she'd better sit down with us to the feast," said the Prince; but to tell you the truth, both he and the rest thought she was a loathsome woman to have next you.

But just then in came another ugly old hag. She had a back so humped and broad, she had hard work to get through the door. Up jumped the bride in a trice, and greeted her with "Good-day, Auntie!"

And the prince asked again if that were his bride's aunt. They both said, Yes; so the prince said, if that were so, she too had better sit down with them to the feast.

But they had scarce taken their seats before another ugly old hag came in, with eyes as large as saucers, and so red and bleared, 't was gruesome to look at her. But up jumped the bride again, with her "Good-day, Auntie," and her, too, the prince asked to sit down; but I can't say he was very glad, for he thought to himself:

"Heaven shield me from such aunties as my bride has!" So when he had sat a while, he could not keep his thoughts to himself any longer, but asked:

"But how, in all the world can my bride, who is such a lovely lassie, have such loathsome misshapen aunts?"

"I'll soon tell you how it is," said the first. "I was just as good-looking when I was her age; but the reason why I've got this long nose is, because I was always kept sitting, and poking, and nodding over my spinning, and so my nose got stretched and stretched, until it got as long as you now see it."

"And I," said the second, "ever since I was young, I have sat and scuttled backwards and forwards over my loom, and that's how my back has got so broad and humped as you now see it."

"And I," said the third, "ever since I was little, I have sat, and stared and sewn, and sewn and stared, night and day; and that's why my eyes have got so ugly and red, and now there's no help for them."

"So, so!" said the prince, " 't was lucky I came to know this; for if folk can get so ugly and loathsome by all this, then my bride shall neither spin, nor weave, nor sew all her life long."

*Thirty-eight*

# The Hunchback's Gift

*Irish*

There was once a poor man who lived in the fertile glen of Aherlow, at the foot of the gloomy Galtee mountains, and he had a great hump on his back: he looked just as if his body had been rolled up and placed upon his shoulders; and his head was pressed down with the weight so much that his chin, when he was sitting, used to rest upon his knees for support. The country people were rather shy of meeting him in any lonesome place, for though, poor creature, he was as harmless and as inoffensive as a new-born infant, yet his deformity was so great that he scarcely appeared to be a human creature, and some ill-minded persons had set strange stories about him afloat. He was said to have a great knowledge of herbs and charms; but certain it was that he had a mighty skillful hand in plaiting straw and rushes into hats and baskets, which was the way he made his livelihood.

Lusmore, for that was the nickname put upon him by reason of his always wearing a sprig of the fairy cap, or lusmore (the foxglove), in his little straw hat, would ever get a higher penny for his plaited work than any one else, and perhaps that was the reason why some one, out of envy, had circulated the strange stories about him. Be that as it may, it happened that he was returning one evening from the pretty town of Cahir towards Cappagh, and as little Lusmore walked very slowly, on account of the great hump upon his back, it was quite dark when he came to the old moat of Knockgrafton, which stood on the right-hand side of his road. Tired and weary was he, and noways comfortable in his own mind at thinking how much farther he had to travel, and that he should be walking all the night; so he sat down under the moat to rest himself, and began looking mournfully enough upon the moon.

Presently there rose a wild strain of unearthly melody upon the ear of little Lusmore; he listened, and he thought that he had never heard such ravishing music before. It was like the sound of many voices, each mingling and blending with the other so strangely that they seemed to be one, though all singing different strains, and the words of the song were these:

*Da Luan,*[1] *Da Mort, Da Luan, Da Mort, Da Luan, Da Mort;*

when there would be a moment's pause, and then the round of melody went on again.

Lusmore listened attentively, scarcely drawing his breath lest he might lose the slightest note. He now plainly perceived that the singing was within the moat; and though at first it had charmed him so much, he began to get tired of hearing the same round sung over and over so often without any change; so availing himself of the pause when the *Da Luan, Da Mort,* had been sung three times, he took up the tune, and raised it with the words *augus Da Cadine,* and then went on singing with the voices inside of the moat, *Da Luan, Da Mort,* finishing the melody, when the pause again came, with *augus Da Cadine.*

The fairies within Knockgrafton, for the song was a fairy melody, when they heard this addition to the tune, were so much delighted that, with instant resolve, it was determined to bring the mortal among them, whose musical skill so far exceeded theirs, and little Lusmore was conveyed into their company with the eddying speed of a whirlwind.

Glorious to behold was the sight that burst upon him as he came down through the moat, twirling round and round, with the lightness of a straw, to the sweetest music that kept time to his motion. The greatest honor was then paid him, for he was put above all the musicians, and he had servants tending upon him, and everything to his heart's content, and a hearty welcome to all; and, in short, he was made as much of as if he had been the first man in the land.

Presently Lusmore saw a great consultation going forward among the fairies, and, notwithstanding all their civility, he felt very much frightened, until one stepping out from the rest came up to him and said:

> "Lusmore! Lusmore!
> Doubt not, nor deplore,
> For the hump which you bore
> On your back is no more;
> Look down on the floor,
> And view it, Lusmore!"

[1] The names of the days of the week.

When these words were said, poor little Lusmore felt himself so light, and so happy, that he thought he could have bounded at one jump over the moon, like the cow in the history of the cat and the fiddle; and he saw, with inexpressible pleasure, his hump tumble down upon the ground from his shoulders. He then tried to lift up his head, and he did so with becoming caution, fearing that he might knock it against the ceiling of the grand hall, where he was; he looked round and round again with greatest wonder and delight upon everything, which appeared more and more beautiful; and, overpowered at beholding such a resplendent scene, his head grew dizzy, and his eyesight became dim. At last he fell into a sound sleep, and when he awoke he found that it was broad daylight, the sun shining brightly, and the birds singing sweetly; and that he was lying just at the foot of the moat of Knockgrafton, with the cows and sheep grazing peacefully round about him. The first thing Lusmore did, after saying his prayers, was to put his hand behind to feel for his hump, but no sign of one was there on his back, and he looked at himself with great pride, for he had now become a well-shaped dapper little fellow, and more than that, found himself in a full suit of new clothes, which he concluded the fairies had made for him.

Towards Cappagh he went, stepping out as lightly, and springing up at every step as if he had been all his life a dancing-master. Not a creature who met Lusmore knew him without his hump, and he had a great work to persuade every one that he was the same man—in truth he was not, so far as outward appearance went.

Of course it was not long before the story of Lusmore's hump got about, and a great wonder was made of it. Through the country, for miles round, it was the talk of every one, high and low.

One morning, as Lusmore was sitting contented enough, at his cabin door, up came an old woman to him, and asked him if he could direct her to Cappagh.

"I need give you no directions, my good woman," said Lusmore, "for this is Cappagh; and whom may you want here?"

"I have come," said the woman, "out of Decie's country, in the county of Waterford looking after one Lusmore, who, I have heard tell, had his hump taken off by the fairies; for there is a son of a gossip of mine who has got a hump on him that will be his death; and maybe if he could use the same charm as Lusmore, the hump may be taken off him. And now I have told you the reason of my coming so far: 'tis to find out about this charm, if I can."

Lusmore, who was ever a good-natured little fellow, told the woman all the particulars, how he had raised the tune for the fairies at Knockgrafton, how his hump had been removed from his shoulders, and how he had got a new suit of clothes into the bargain.

The woman thanked him very much, and then went away quite happy and easy in her own mind. When she came back to her gossip's house, in the county of Waterford, she told her everything that Lusmore had said, and they put the little hump-backed man, who was a peevish and cunning creature from his birth, upon a car, and took him all the way across the country. It was a long journey, but they did not care for that, so the hump was taken from off him; and they brought him, just at nightfall, and left him under the old moat of Knockgrafton.

Jack Madden, for that was the humpy man's name, had not been sitting there long when he heard the tune going on within the moat much sweeter than before; for the fairies were singing it the way Lusmore had settled their music for them, and the song was going on; *Da Luan, Da Mort, Da Luan, Da Mort, Da Luan, Da Mort, augus Da Cadine*, without ever stopping. Jack Madden, who was in a great hurry to get quit of his hump, never thought of waiting until the fairies had done, or watching for a fit opportunity to raise the tune higher again than Lusmore had; so having heard them sing it over seven times without stopping, out he bawls, never minding the time or the humor of the tune, or how he could bring his words in properly *augus Da Cadine, augus Da Hena*, thinking that if one day was good, two were better; and that if Lusmore had one new suit of clothes given him, he should have two.

No sooner had the words passed his lips than he was taken up and whisked into the moat with prodigious force; and the fairies came crowding round about him with great anger, screeching, and screaming, and roaring out, "Who spoiled our tune? who spoiled our tune?" and one stepped up to him, above all the rest and said:

"Jack Madden! Jack Madden!
Your words came so bad in
The tune we felt glad in;

> This castle you're had in,
> That your life we may sadden;
> Here's two humps for Jack Madden!"

And twenty of the strongest fairies brought Lusmore's hump and put it down upon poor Jack's back, over his own, where it became fixed as firmly as if it was nailed on with twelve-penny nails, by the best carpenter that ever drove one. Out of their castle they then kicked him; and, in the morning, when Jack Madden's mother and her gossip came to look after their little man, they found him half dead, lying at the foot of the moat, with the other hump upon his back. Well to be sure, how they did look at each other! but they were afraid to say anything, lest a hump might be put upon their own shoulders. Home they brought the unlucky Jack Madden with them, as downcast in their hearts and their looks as ever two gossips were; and what through the weight of his other hump, and the long journey, he died soon after, leaving they say his heavy curse to any one who would go to listen to fairy tunes again.

*Thirty-nine*

# The Princess Who Was Rescued from Slavery

*Swedish*

Once upon a time there was a merchant who had a son, and he was not suited for anything but life at sea. For that reason the father bought him a ship, loaded it up, and let him sail for foreign countries. When he had reached his destination and unloaded his cargo he met a captain who asked if he would go with him to see the slave market. He saw a slave there that he liked very much and wanted to buy immediately. When he asked what the price was he was told, "He costs as much as your cargo." He bought the slave but when they were at sea again the slave fell ill and died. So there the captain was empty-handed.

Translated from *Sveriges Samtliga Folksagor* by Waldemar Liungman. Used by permission.

The father was so kind that he loaded up the ship for him once more. Safely in harbor again he was asked if he wanted to go and look at the slave girls. At the slave market he noticed a very beautiful girl, and when he asked her price the answer was: "She costs as much as your cargo." He bought the slave girl and returned home to his own country. There he married her and they moved into a small house near the seashore.

But soon the man went to sea again while the wife sat at home and embroidered flags. One time when he came home the wife said that he could take the flags along on his trip; but he must not hoist them until he had reached Rumania.

He sailed off again and reached a city in Rumania, where he hoisted all of his pretty flags. The king sent down a messenger to ask who had been so brave as to give him permission to hoist his flags.

"Nobody," answered the captain, "but my wife has made them for me." When the king received that answer he sent word that the captain should come and talk to him. At the palace the captain had to explain first how he had gotten the flags and then how he had got his wife. From this the king concluded that the captain's wife must be his daughter who had been stolen and was never heard of since.

The king now sent out a warship to fetch home his daughter. The captain had to go along to show where they lived.

On the voyage home the commander of the warship ordered the crew to draw their swords and force the princess to tell the king that he was the one who had saved her. She had to promise this if she wanted to keep her life, while the real rescuer, her husband, would be killed. Her husband pleaded that instead of killing him they tie him to a door and throw him into the sea; this wish was granted.

The poor captain drifted on the sea till evening came. He then landed on a deserted island, loosened his ropes and lay down to rest under a tree. When he had been lying there for a while he heard a loud noise and a terrible commotion. A cold hand was stroking his forehead.

"What is this commotion about," he asked, "can a person not be allowed to sleep in peace?"

The ghost replied: "I am a poor mate who happened to owe a friend six shillings at the time of my death. And therefore he chases me from my grave each night."

The captain gave the mate six shillings, which was all he had left. In return for this the mate said: "If you need my help I am ready and willing."

The captain answered with a sneering laugh: "And what could you do to help me, you miserable worm?"

"Oh," said the mate, "I can do many things."

The captain then said: "Take me to the capital of Rumania before the ship with the princess aboard arrives."

The mate lifted him on his shoulders and carried him through the air at great speed. Before the cock had crowed the dead mate was standing with his load in the streets of the capital. The captain wandered around in the dark until he found a shoemaker, with whom he sought employment. It happened to be the royal shoemaker, who was just about to make wedding slippers for the princess.

"Very well," said the shoemaker, "I am in need of a helper just now, for the princess is expected home at any time." The assistant was allowed to make her shoes, but he requested permission to work during the night.

In the evening he called the mate, who during the night made a pair of the very prettiest slippers for the princess. They were so pretty that the assistant who had supposedly made them was sent for. When he got to the palace the princess, who had just returned, sent him some money as a reward, but he returned the coins in a purse that the princess had once crocheted for him from her own hair. She immediately recognized the purse, but kept quiet.

A few days later the castle was to be painted. Now the shoemaker's assistant took the position as painter and again made the request that he be permitted to work during the night, and the mate again helped him. By morning the palace was decorated with many paintings which depicted the life of the princess both as a slave girl and as the wife of the captain in the simple home by the seashore.

The king was very much surprised when he saw the pictures and he sent for the princess, who interpreted them for him and said that the painter was none other than her husband and rescuer. They then agreed to keep this a secret till the wedding day.

The day of the wedding arrived and the guests gathered. On one side of the princess was the commander of the warship, who had pretended to be the rescuer of the princess and was going to be her bridegroom. On the other side was the real rescuer of the princess, her husband. They then got to talking about what punishment should fall on a person who had acted in the same way as the commander.

"He should be burned alive in oil," said the commander.

"You have just sentenced yourself," said the king, "for you have acted in that manner."

The commander now fell to his knees and prayed for mercy and they decided only to sentence him to exile; but the princess lived happily with her rescuer until her death.

# The Hearth-Cat

*Portuguese*

There was once a schoolmistress who was a widow, and had a daughter who was very plain. This mistress had a pupil who was very pretty, and the daughter of a traveler. The mistress was very attached to the pupil's father, and every day would beg the girl to ask him to marry her, promising to give the girl porridge made with honey. The girl went home to ask her father to marry her schoolmistress, as she would then give her porridge made with honey. To this request the father replied that he would not marry her, for he well knew that though she said now that she would give her porridge made with honey, later on she would give her porridge with gall. Yet, as the child began to cry, begging her father to consent, the father, who loved his child very much, in order to comfort her, replied that he would order a pair of boots to be made of iron, and hang them up until the boots would rust to pieces with age, when he would marry the mistress.

The little girl, very pleased to hear this, went immediately to tell the mistress, who then instructed her pupil to wet the boots every day. The little girl did so, and after a while the boots fell to pieces, and she went and told her father of it. He then said that he would marry the mistress, and on the following day married her.

So long as the father was at home the child was treated with kindness and affection, but the moment he went out the mistress was very unkind to her, and treated her badly. She one day sent her to graze a cow, and gave her a loaf, which she desired her to bring back whole, and an earthen pot with water, out of which she expected her to drink, and yet was to bring back full. One day the mistress told the girl that she wished her to employ herself in winding some skeins of thread until the evening. The little girl went away crying and bewailing her lot; but the cow comforted her, and told her not to be distressed—to fix the skein on her horns and unravel the thread. The good cow after that took out all the crumb from the loaf by making a small hole with one of her horns, and then stopped the aperture, and gave the girl the loaf back again entire. In the evening the girl returned home.

When her stepmother saw that she had finished her task, and brought all the thread ready wound, she was very vexed and wanted to beat her, saying that she was sure the cow had had something to do with it, and next day ordered the animal to be killed. At this the girl began to cry very bitterly, but the stepmother told her that she would have to clean and wash the cow's entrails in a tank they had, however grieved she might feel for the loss of the animal. The cow, however, again told the girl not to be troubled, but to go and wash her entrails, but to be careful to save whatever she saw come out of them.

The girl did so, and when she was cleaning them she saw a ball of gold come out and fall into the water. The girl went into the tank to search for it, and there she saw a house with everything in it in disorder, and she began to arrange and make the house look tidy. She suddenly heard footsteps, and in her hurry she hid herself behind the door. The fairies entered and began to look about, and a dog came in also with them, and went up to where she was and began to bark, saying: "Bow, bow, bow, behind the door hides somebody who did us good, and will yet render us more services. Bow, bow, bow, behind the door hides somebody who has done us good, and will yet render us more services." The fairies, as they searched about, hearing the dog bark, discovered where the girl was hiding, and began to say to her, "We endow you by the power we possess with the gift of beauty, making you the most lovely maiden ever seen." The next fairy then said, "I cast a sweet spell over you, so that when you open your mouth to speak, pearls and gold shall drop from your lips." The third fairy coming forward said, "I endow you with every blessing, making you the happiest maiden in the world. Take this wand, it will grant you whatever you may ask."

The girl then left the enchanted region, and returned home, and as soon as the mistress's daughter saw her approach she commenced to cry out to her mother to come quickly and see the hearth-cat, who had come back at last. The mistress ran to greet her, and asked her where and what she had been doing all that time. The girl related the contrary of what she had seen, as the fairies had instructed her to do—that she had found a tidy house, and that she had disarranged everything in it, to make it look untidy.

The mistress sent her own daughter there, and she had hardly arrived at the house when she began at once to do as her half-sister had told her; she disarranged everything, to make the house look untidy and uncared for. And when she heard the fairies coming in she hid behind the door. The little dog saw her, and barking at her said, "Behind the door stands one who has done us much harm, and will still continue to molest us. Bow, bow, bow, behind the door stands one who has done us much harm, and will continue to molest us on the first opportunity." The fairies hearing this approached her, and one began to say, "I throw a spell over you which will render you the ugliest maid that can be found." The next one took up the word and said, "I bewitch you, so that when you attempt to speak all manner of filth shall fall out of your mouth." And the third fairy said, "I also bewitch you, and you shall become the poorest and most wretched maid in existence."

The mistress's daughter returned home, thinking she was looking quite a beauty; but when she came up close to her mother, and began to speak, the mother burst out crying on seeing her own daughter so disfigured and wretched. Full of rage, she sent her stepdaughter to the kitchen, saying, that she was the hearth-cat, and that she should take care that she kept there, as the only place which was fit for her.

On a certain day the mistress and her daughter repaired to some races which were then taking place, but when the girl saw that they had left the house, she asked her divining rod to give her a very handsome dress, boots, a hat, and everything complete. She dressed and adorned herself with all she had, and went to the races, and stood in front of the royal stand. The mistress's daughter instantly saw her, and began to exclaim and cry out at the top of her voice, in the midst of all the people present, saying, "Oh! mother, mother, that beautiful maiden over there is our very hearth-cat." The mother, to quiet her, told her to be calm; that the maiden was not her stepsister, as she had remained at home under lock and key.

The races were hardly over when the girl departed home; but the king, who had seen her, was in love with her. The moment the mother reached home she asked the hearth-cat whether she had been out. She replied, that she had not; and showed her face besmeared with smut.

Next day the girl asked the wand to strike and give her another dress which would be more splendid than the previous one. She put on her things and repaired to the races. The moment the king perceived her he felt very pleased indeed; but the races were hardly concluded than she retired in haste, and went into her carriage and drove home, leaving the king more in love than ever with her.

The third day the girl asked the divining rod to give her a garment which should surpass the other two in richness and beauty, and other shoes; and she went and attended the races. When the king saw her, he was delighted, but was again disappointed to see her depart before the races were concluded. In her hurry to enter her carriage quickly, she let fall one of her slippers. The king picked it up and returned to the palace, and fell lovesick. The slipper had some letters upon it which said, "This shoe will only fit its owner."

The whole kingdom was searched to find the lady whose foot would be found to fit the slipper exactly, yet no one was found. The schoolmistress went to the palace to try the slipper on, but all her efforts were in vain. After her, her daughter followed, and endeavored her best to fit the slipper on, but with no better success. There only remained the hearth-cat.

The king inquired who was the next to try on the slipper, and asked the mistress if there was any other lady left in her house who could fit on the slipper. The schoolmistress then said that there only remained a hearth-cat in her house, but that she had never worn such a slipper. The king ordered the girl to be brought to the palace, and the mistress had no alternative but to do so. The king himself insisted on trying the slipper on the girl's foot, and the moment she put her little foot into the slipper and drew it on, it fitted exactly. The king then arranged that she should remain in the palace and married her. And he ordered the mistress and her daughter to be put to death.

*Forty-one*

# Katie Woodencloak

*Norwegian*

Once on a time there was a king who had become a widower. By his queen he had one daughter, who was so clever and lovely, there wasn't a cleverer or lovelier princess in all the world. So the king went on a long time sorrowing for the queen, whom he had loved so much, but at last he got weary of living alone, and married another queen, who was a widow, and had, too, an only daughter; but this daughter was just as bad and ugly as the other was kind, and clever, and lovely. The stepmother and her daughter were jealous of the princess, because she was so lovely; but so long as the king was at home they daren't do her any harm, he was so fond of her.

Well, after a time he fell into war with another king, and went out to battle with his host, and then the stepmother thought she might do as she pleased; and so she both starved and beat the princess, and was after her in every hole and corner of the house. At last she thought everything too good for her, and turned her out to herd cattle. So there she went about with the cattle, and herded them in the woods and on the fells. As for food, she got little or none, and she grew thin and wan, and was always sobbing and sorrowful. Now in the herd there was a great dun bull, which always kept himself so neat and sleek, and often and often he came up to the princess, and let her pat him. So one day when she sat there, sad, and sobbing, and sorrowful, he came up to her and asked her outright why she was always in such grief. She answered nothing, but went on weeping.

"Ah!" said the bull, "I know all about it quite well, though you won't tell me; you weep because the queen is bad to you, and because she is ready to starve you to death. But food you've no need to fret about, for in my left ear lies a cloth, and when you take and spread it out, you may have as many dishes as you please."

So she did that, took the cloth and spread it out on the grass, and lo! it served up the nicest dishes one could wish to have; there was wine too, and mead, and sweet cake. Well, she soon got up her flesh again, and grew so plump, and rosey, and white, that the queen and her scrawny chip of a daughter turned blue and yellow for spite. The queen couldn't at all make out how her stepdaughter got to look so well on such bad fare, so she told one of her maids to go after her in the wood, and watch and see how it all was, for she thought some of the servants in the house must give her food. So the maid went after her, and watched in the wood, and then she saw how the stepdaughter took the cloth out of the bull's ear, and spread it out, and how it served up the nicest dishes, which the stepdaughter ate and made good cheer over. All this the maid told the queen when she went home.

And now the king came home from war, and had won the fight against the other king with whom he went out to battle. So there was great joy throughout the palace, and no one was gladder than the king's daughter. But the queen shammed sick, and took to her bed, and paid the doctor a great fee to get him to say she could never be well again unless she had some of the dun bull's flesh to eat. Both the king's daughter and the folk in the palace asked the doctor if nothing else would help her, and prayed hard for the bull, for every one was fond of him, and they all said there wasn't that bull's match in all the land. But no; he must and should be slaughtered, nothing else would do. When the king's daughter heard that, she got very sorrowful, and went down into the byre to the bull. There, too, he stood and hung down his head, and looked so downcast that she began to weep over him.

"What are you weeping for?" asked the bull.

So she told him how the king had come home again, and how the queen had shammed sick and got the doctor to say she could never be well and sound again unless she got some of the dun bull's flesh to eat, and so now he was to be slaughtered.

"If they get me killed first," said the bull, "they'll soon take your life too. Now, if you're of my mind, we'll just start off, and go away tonight."

Well, the princess thought it bad, you may be sure, to go and leave her father, but she thought it still worse to be in the house with the queen; and so she gave her word to the bull to come to him.

At night, when all had gone to bed, the princess stole down to the byre to the bull, and so he took her on his back, and set off from the homestead as fast as ever he could. And when the folk got up at cockcrow next morning to slaughter the bull, why, he was gone; and when the king got up and asked for his daughter, she was gone too. He sent out messengers on all sides to hunt for them, and gave them out in all the parish churches; but there was no one who had caught a glimpse of them. Meanwhile, the bull went through many lands with the king's daughter on his back, and so one day they came to a great copper wood, where both the trees, and branches, and leaves, and flowers, and everything, were nothing but copper.

But before they went into the wood, the bull said to the king's daughter:

"Now, when we get into this wood, mind you take care not to touch even a leaf of it, else it's all over both with me and you, for here dwells a troll with three heads who owns this wood."

No, bless her, she'd be sure to take care not to touch anything. Well, she was very careful, and leaned this way and that to miss the boughs, and put them gently aside with her hands; but it was such a thick wood, 'twas scarce possible to get through; and so, with all her pains, somehow or other she tore off a leaf, which she held in her hand.

"AU! AU! what have you done now?" said the bull; "there's nothing for it now but to fight for life or death; but mind you keep the leaf safe."

Soon after they got to the end of the wood, and a troll with three heads came running up:

"Who is this that touches my wood?" said the troll.

"It's just as much mine as yours," said the bull.

"Ah!" roared the troll, "we'll try a fall about that."

"As you choose," said the bull.

So they rushed at one another, and fought; and the bull he butted, and gored, and kicked with all his might and main; but the troll gave him as good as he brought, and it lasted the whole day before the bull got the mastery; and then he was so full of wounds, and so worn out, he could scarce lift a leg. Then they were forced to stay there a day to rest, and then the bull bade the king's daughter to take the horn of ointment which hung at the troll's belt, and rub him with it. Then he came to himself again, and the day after they trudged on again. So they traveled many, many days, until, after a long long time, they came to a silver wood, where both the trees, and branches, and leaves, and flowers, and everything, were silver.

Before the bull went into the wood, he said to the king's daughter:

"Now, when we get into this wood, for heaven's sake mind you take good care; you mustn't touch anything, and not pluck off so much as one leaf, else it is all over both with me and you; for here is a troll with six heads who owns it, and him I don't think I should be able to master."

"No," said the king's daughter; "I'll take good care and not touch anything you don't wish me to touch.

But when they got into the wood, it was so close and thick, they could scarce get along. She was as careful as careful could be, and leaned to this side and that to miss the boughs, and put them on one side with her hands, but every minute the branches struck her across the eyes, and, in spite of all her pains, it so happened she tore off a leaf.

"AU! AU! what have you done now?" said the bull. "There's nothing for it now but to fight for life and death, for this troll has six heads, and is twice as strong as the other, but mind you keep the leaf safe, and don't lose it."

Just as he said that, up came the troll.

"Who is this," he said, "that touches my wood?"

"It's as much mine as yours," said the bull.

"That we'll try a fall about," roared the troll.

"As you choose," said the bull, and rushed at the troll, and gored out his eyes, and drove his horns right through his body, so that the entrails gushed out but the troll was almost a match for him, and it lasted three whole days before the bull got the life gored out of him. But then he, too, was so weak and wretched, it was as much as he could do to stir a limb, and so full of wounds, that the blood streamed from him. So he said to the king's daughter she must take the horn of ointment that hung at the troll's belt, and rub him with it. Then she did that, and he came to himself; but they were forced to stay there a week to rest before the bull had strength enough to go on.

At last they set off again, but the bull was still poorly, and they went rather slow at first. So to save time the king's daughter said as she was young and light of foot, she could very well walk, but she couldn't get leave to do that. No; she must seat herself up on his back again. So on they traveled through many lands a long time, and the king's daughter did not know in the least whither they went; but after a long, long time they came to a gold wood. It was so grand, the gold dropped from every twig, and all the trees, and boughs, and flowers, and leaves, were of pure gold. Here, too, the same thing happened as had happened in the silver wood and copper wood. The bull told the king's daughter she mustn't touch it for anything, for there was a troll with nine heads who owned it, and he was much bigger and stouter than both the others put together, and he didn't think he could get the better of him. No; she'd be sure to take heed not to touch it; that he might know very well. But when they got into the wood, it was far thicker and closer than the silver wood, and the deeper they went into it the worse it got. The wood went on getting thicker and thicker, and closer and closer and at last she thought there was no way at all to get through it. She was in such an awful fright of plucking off anything, that she sat, and twisted and turned herself this way and that, and hither and thither, to keep clear of the boughs, and she put them on one side with her hands but every moment the branches struck her across the eyes, so that she couldn't see what she was clutching at; and lo! before she knew how it came about, she had a gold apple in her hand. Then she was so bitterly sorry she burst into tears and wanted to throw it away but the bull said she must keep it safe and watch it well, and comforted her as well as he could but he thought it would be a hard tussle, and he doubted how it would go.

Just then up came the troll with the nine heads, and he was so ugly, the king's daughter scarcely dared to look at him.

"Who is this that touches my wood?" he roared.

"It's just as much mine as yours," said the bull.

"That we'll try a fall about," roared the troll again.

"Just as you choose," said the bull; and so they rushed at one another, and fought, and it was such a dreadful sight the king's daughter was ready to swoon away. The bull gored out the troll's eyes, and drove his horns through and through his body, till the entrails came tumbling out; but the troll fought bravely; and when the bull got one head gored to death, the rest breathed life into it again, and so it lasted a whole week before the bull was able to get the life out of them all. But then he was utterly worn out and wretched. He couldn't stir a foot, and his body was all one wound. He couldn't so much as ask the king's daughter to take the horn of ointment which hung at the troll's belt, and rub it over him. But she did it all the same, and then he came to himself by little and little; but they had to lie there and rest three weeks before he was fit to go on again.

Then they set off at a snail's pace, for the bull said they had still a little farther to go, and so they crossed over many high hills and thick woods. So after a while they got upon the fells.

"Do you see anything?" asked the bull.

"No, I see nothing but the sky and the wild fell," said the king's daughter.

So when they climbed higher up, the fell got smoother, and they could see farther off.

"Do you see anything now?" asked the bull.

"Yes, I see a little castle far, far away," said the Princess.

"That's not so little though," said the bull.

After a long, long time, they came to a great cairn, where there was a spur of the fell that stood sheer across the way.

"Do you see anything now?" asked the bull.

"Yes, now I see the castle close by," said the king's daughter, "and now it is much, much bigger."

"Thither you're to go," said the bull. "Right underneath the castle is a pig-sty, where you are to dwell. When you come thither you'll find a wooden cloak, all made of strips of lath; that you must put on, and go up to the castle and say your name is 'Katie Woodencloak,' and ask for a place. But before you go, you must take your penknife and cut my head off, and then you must flay me, and roll up the hide, and lay it under the wall of rock yonder, and under the hide you must lay the copper leaf, and the silver leaf, and the golden apple. Yonder, up against the rock, stands a stick; and when you want anything, you've only got to knock on the wall of rock with that stick."

At first she wouldn't do anything of the kind; but when the bull said it was the only thanks he would have for what he had done for her, she couldn't help herself. So, however much it grieved her heart, she hacked and cut away with her knife at the big beast till she got both his head and his hide off, and then she laid the hide up under the wall of rock, and put the copper leaf, and the silver leaf, and the golden apple inside it.

So when she had done that, she went over to the pig-sty, but all the while she went she sobbed and wept. There she put on the wooden cloak, and so went up to the palace. When she came into the kitchen she begged for a place, and told them her name was Katie Woodencloak. Yes, the cook said she might have a place— she might have leave to be there in the scullery, and wash up, for the lassie who did that work before had just gone away.

"But as soon as you get weary of being here, you'll go your way too, I'll be bound."

No; she was sure she wouldn't do that.

So there she was, behaving so well, and washing up so handily. The Sunday after there were to be strange guests at the palace, so Katie asked if she might have leave to carry up water for the prince's bath; but all the rest laughed at her, and said:

"What should you do there? Do you think the prince will care to look at you, you who are such a fright?"

But she wouldn't give it up, and kept on begging and praying; and at last she got leave. So when she went up the stairs, her wooden cloak made such a clatter, the prince came out and asked:

"Pray, who are you?"

"Oh, I was just going to bring up water for your Royal Highness's bath," said Katie.

"Do you think now," said the prince, "I'd have anything to do with the water you bring?" and with that he threw the water over her.

So she had to put up with that, but then she asked leave to go to church; well, she got that leave too, for the church lay close by. But first of all she went to the rock, and knocked on its face with the stick which stood there, just as the bull had said. And straightway out came a man, who said:

"What's your will?"

So the princess said she had got leave to go to church and hear the priest preach, but she had no clothes to go in. So he brought out a kirtle, which was as bright as the copper wood, and she got a horse and saddle beside. Now, when she got to the church, she was so lovely and grand, all wondered who she could be, and scarce one of them listened to what the priest said, for they looked too much at her. As for the prince, he fell so deep in love with her, he didn't take his eyes off her for a single moment.

So, as she went out of church, the prince ran after her, and held the church door open for her; and so he got hold of one of her gloves, which was caught in the door. When she went away and mounted her horse, the prince went up to her again, and asked whence she came.

"Oh, I'm from Bath," said Katie; and while the prince took out the glove to give it to her, she said:

"Bright before and dark behind,
Clouds come rolling on the wind;
That this prince may never see
Where my good steed goes with me."

The prince had never seen the like of that glove, and went about far and wide asking after the land whence the proud lady, who rode off without her glove, said she came; but there was no one who could tell where "Bath" lay.

Next Sunday some one had to go up to the prince with a towel.

"Oh, may I have leave to go up with it?" said Katie.

"What's the good of your going?" said the others; "you saw how it fared with you last time."

But Katie wouldn't give in; she kept on begging and praying, till she got leave; and then she ran up the stairs, so that her wooden cloak made a great clatter. Out came the Prince, and when he saw it was Katie, he tore the towel out of her hand, and threw it into her face.

"Pack yourself off, you ugly troll," he cried; "do you think I'd have a towel which you have touched with your smutty fingers?"

After that the prince set off to church, and Katie begged for leave to go too. They all asked what business she had at church —she who had nothing to put on but that wooden cloak, which was so black and ugly. But Katie said the priest was such a brave man to preach, what he said did her so much good; and so at last she got leave. Now she went again to the rock and knocked, and so out came the man, and gave her a kirtle far finer than the first one; it was all covered with silver, and it shone like the silver wood; and she got besides a noble steed, with a saddle-cloth broidered with silver, and a silver bit.

So when the king's daughter got to the church, the folk were still standing about in the churchyard. And all wondered and wondered who she could be, and the prince was soon on the spot, and came and wished to hold her horse for her while she got off. But she jumped down, and said there was no need, for her horse was so well broken, it stood still when she bade it, and came when she called it. So they all went into church, but there was scarce a soul that listened to what the priest said, for they looked at her a deal too much; and the prince fell still deeper in love than the first time.

When the sermon was over, and she went out of church, and was going to mount her horse, up came the prince again and asked her whence she came.

"Oh, I'm from Towelland," said the king's daughter; and as she said that, she dropped her riding-whip, and when the prince stooped to pick it up, she said:

> "Bright before and dark behind,
> Clouds come rolling on the wind;
> That this prince may never see
> Where my good steed goes with me."

So away she was again; and the prince couldn't tell what had become of her. He went about far and wide, asking after the land whence she said she came, but there was no one who could tell him where it lay; and so the prince had to make the best he could of it.

Next Sunday some one had to go up to the prince with a comb. Katie begged for leave to go up with it, but the others put her in mind how she had fared the last time, and scolded her for wishing to go before the prince—such a black and ugly fright as she was in her wooden cloak. But she wouldn't leave off asking till they let her go up to the prince with his comb. So, when she came clattering up the stairs again, out came the prince, and took the comb, and threw it at her, and bade her be off as fast as she could. After that the prince went to church, and Katie begged for leave to go too. They asked again what business she had there, she who was so foul and black, and who had no clothes to show herself in. Might be the prince or some one else would see her, and then both she and all the others would smart for it; but Katie said they had something else to do than to look at her; and she wouldn't leave off begging and praying till they gave her leave to go.

So the same thing happened now as had happened twice before. She went to the rock and knocked with the stick, and then the man came out and gave her a kirtle which was far grander than either of the others. It was almost all pure gold, and studded with diamonds; and she got besides a noble steed, with a gold broidered saddle-cloth and a golden bit.

Now when the king's daughter got to the church, there stood the priest and all the people in the churchyard waiting for her. Up came the prince running, and wanted to hold her horse, but she jumped off, and said:

"No; thanks—there's no need, for my horse is so well broken, he stands still when I bid him."

So they all hastened into church, and the priest got into the pulpit, but no one listened to a word he said; for they all looked too much at her, and wondered whence she came; and the prince, he was far deeper in love than either of the former times. He had no eyes, or ears, or sense for anything, but just to sit and stare at her.

So when the sermon was over, and the king's daughter was to go out of the church, the prince had got a firkin of pitch poured out in the porch, that he might come and help her over it; but she didn't care a bit—she just put her foot right down into the midst of the pitch, and jumped across it; but then one of her golden shoes stuck fast in it, and as she got on her horse, up came the prince running out of the church, and asked whence she came.

"I'm from Combland," said Katie. But when the prince wanted to reach her the gold shoe, she said:

"Bright before and dark behind,
Clouds come rolling on the wind;
That this prince may never see
Where my good steed goes with me."

So the prince couldn't tell still what had become of her, and he went about a weary time all over the world asking for "Combland"; but when no one could tell him where it lay, he ordered it to be given out everywhere that he would wed the woman whose foot could fit the gold shoe.

So many came of all sorts from all sides, fair and ugly alike; but there was no one who had so small a foot as to be able to get on the gold shoe. And after a long, long time, who should come but Katie's wicked stepmother, and her daughter, too, and her the gold shoe fitted; but ugly she was, and so loathly she looked, the prince only kept his word sore against his will. Still they got ready the wedding-feast, and she was dressed up and decked out as a bride; but as they rode to church, a little bird sat upon a tree and sang:

"A bit off her heel,
And a bit off her toe;
Katie Woodencloak's tiny shoe
Is full of blood—that's all I know."

And, sure enough, when they looked at it, the bird told the truth, for blood gushed out of the shoe.

Then all the maids and women who were about the palace had to go up to try on the shoe, but there was none of them whom it would fit at all.

"But where's Katie Woodencloak?" asked the prince, when all the rest had tried the shoe, for he understood the song of birds very well, and bore in mind what the little bird had said.

"Oh, she! think of that!" said the rest; it's no good her coming forward. "Why, she's got legs like a horse."

"Very true, I daresay," said the prince; "but since all the others have tried, Katie may as well try too."

"Katie!" he bawled out through the door; and Katie came trampling upstairs, and her wooden cloak clattered as if a whole regiment of dragoons were charging up.

"Now, you must try the shoe on, and be a princess, you too," said the other maids, and laughed and made game of her.

So Katie took up the shoe, and put her foot into it like nothing, and threw off her wooden cloak; and so there she stood in her gold kirtle, and it shone so that the sunbeams glistened from her; and, lo! on her other foot she had the fellow to the gold shoe.

So when the prince knew her again, he grew so glad, he ran up to her and threw his arms round her, and gave her a kiss; and when he heard she was a king's daughter, he got gladder still, and then came the wedding-feast; and so

Snip, snip, snover,
This story's over.

*Forty-two*

# One-Eye, Two-Eyes, and Three-Eyes

*German*

There was a woman who had three daughters. The eldest was called One-Eye because she only had a single eye in the middle of her forehead, the middle daughter was called Two-Eyes because she had two eyes like other human beings, and the youngest was called Three-Eyes because she had three eyes; in her case, too, the third eye was right in the middle of her forehead. But because Two-Eyes didn't look any different from other people, her sisters and her mother couldn't abide her. "You with your two eyes!" they'd say to her. "You're no better than the common run of people. You don't belong to us." They pushed her about, threw her poor cast-off clothes, only gave her their left-overs to eat, and hurt her in every way they could.

Once Two-Eyes had to go out in the fields and tend the goat, but she was still very hungry because her sisters had given her so little to eat. She sat down on a log and began to weep and wept so hard that two little brooks flowed from her eyes. When once in her distress she looked up, a woman was standing beside her, who asked, "Two-Eyes, why are you weeping?" Two-Eyes answered, "I have good reason to weep. Because I have two eyes like other people, my sisters and my mother can't abide me, push me from corner to corner, throw me old cast-off clothes, and only give me their left-overs to eat. Today they gave me so little that I'm still very hungry." The wise woman said, "Two-Eyes, dry your face. I'll tell you something so you won't be hungry any more. Just say to your goat,

'Goat, bleat!
Table, be set.'

Then a nicely set table will be standing before you with the finest food upon it, so that you can eat to your heart's content. When you've eaten your fill and don't need the table any longer, just say,

'Goat, bleat!
Table, be gone!'

Then it will disappear again before your eyes."

Thereupon the wise woman went away. Now Two-Eyes thought, "I must try at once and see if what she said is true, for I'm far too hungry," and said,

"Goat, bleat!
Table, be set!"

Scarcely had she uttered the words when a table was standing there, covered with a white cloth, on it a plate and knife and fork and silver spoon. On it were the finest dishes, steaming and still warm, as if they'd just come from the kitchen. Then Two-Eyes repeated the shortest grace she knew, "Lord God, be our guest at all times. Amen," helped herself and enjoyed it greatly. And when she'd had her fill, she said, as the wise woman had taught her,

"Goat, bleat!
Table, be gone!"

Immediately the table and everything on it vanished again. "That's a fine way to keep house," thought Two-Eyes and was very happy and in good spirits. In the evening when she came home with the goat, she found an earthenware bowl with food that her sisters had put out for her. She didn't touch it, however. The next day she again went out with her goat and left untouched the few scraps that had been offered her. The first time and the second time the sisters didn't notice it at all, but when it happened every time, they did take notice and said, "Things aren't right with Two-Eyes. She leaves the food untouched every time, and yet she used to eat up everything that was offered her. She must have found other ways and means."

To get at the truth of the matter, when Two-Eyes drove the goat to pasture, One-Eye was to go along and see what she did out there, and whether anyone brought her any food or drink. Now when Two-Eyes set out again, One-Eye went to her and said, "I'm going along into the fields to see that the goat is properly tended and driven to where the grass is good." Two-Eyes saw, however, what One-Eye had in mind and, driving the goat out to the tall grass, said, "Come, One-Eye, let's sit down. I'll sing you something." One-Eye sat down and was tired from the unaccustomed walk and the heat of the sun, and Two-Eyes kept singing,

> "One-Eye, are you awake?
> One-Eye, are you asleep?"

Then One-Eye shut her one eye and fell asleep. When Two-Eyes saw that One-Eye was fast asleep and couldn't reveal anything, she said,

> "Goat, bleat!
> Table, be set!"

sat down at her table, and ate and drank her fill. Then again she called out,

> "Goat, bleat!
> Table, be gone!"

and everything at once vanished. Two-Eyes now woke One-Eye up and said, "One-Eye, you want to tend the goat and fall asleep doing it! Come, let's go home." They went home, and Two-Eyes again left her bowl untouched, and One-Eye was unable to reveal to her mother why she wouldn't eat, saying by way of excuse, "I fell asleep out there."

The next day the mother said to Three-Eyes, "This time you're to go and find out whether Two-Eyes eats out there, and if anybody brings her food and drink, because she must be eating and drinking on the sly." Then Three-Eyes went to Two-Eyes and said, "I'm going along to see whether the goat's properly tended and driven to where the grass is good." But Two-Eyes saw what Three-Eyes had in mind and, driving the goat out to the tall grass, said, "Let's sit down here, Three-Eyes. I'll sing you something." Three-Eyes sat down and was tired from the walk and the heat of the sun, and Two-Eyes again began the song she'd sung before and sang,

> "Three-Eyes, are you awake?"

but instead of now singing, as she should have done,

> "Three-Eyes, are you asleep?"

she inadvertently sang,

> "*Two*-Eyes, are you asleep?

and kept singing,

> "Three-Eyes, are you awake?
> *Two*-Eyes, are you asleep?"

Then two of Three-Eyes' eyes closed and went to sleep, but the third eye, because it wasn't addressed by the little rhyme, didn't go to sleep. To be sure, Three-Eyes closed it, but only as a trick, just as if it had gone to sleep with the others. Nevertheless, it blinked and could see everything very well indeed. When Two-Eyes thought that Three-Eyes was fast asleep, she said her little rhyme,

> "Goat, bleat!
> Table, be set!"

ate and drank to her heart's content and then bade the table be gone again, saying,

> "Goat, bleat!
> Table, be gone!"

Three-Eyes had seen everything. Then Two-Eyes went to her, woke her up and said, "My, Three-Eyes! Did you fall asleep? You're a good goatherd! Come, let's go home." When they got home, again Two-Eyes ate nothing, and Three-Eyes said to her mother, "Now I know why the proud creature doesn't eat. When she says to the goat out there,

> 'Goat, bleat!
> Table, be set!'

then a table stands before her set with the best food, much better than what we have here. And when she's eaten her fill, she says,

> 'Goat, bleat!
> Table, be gone!'

and everything vanishes. I saw it all quite clearly. She put two of my eyes to sleep with a little rhyme, but the one in my forehead luckily stayed awake." Then the envious mother cried, "Do you think you're going to live better than we? You'll lose your taste for that!" fetched a butcher's knife and stuck it into the goat's heart so that it dropped dead.

When Two-Eyes saw that, she went sadly out, sat down on a log in the field, and wept bitter tears. Suddenly the wise woman was again standing beside her and said, "Two-Eyes, why are you weeping?" "I have good reason to weep," she answered. "My mother stabbed to death the goat which set my table so beautifully every day when I recited your little rhyme. Now I'll have to suffer from hunger and sorrow again." "Two-Eyes," said the wise woman, "I'll give you a good piece of advice: ask your sisters to give you the entrails of the slaughtered goat and bury them in the earth outside the front door. It will bring you luck." She disappeared, and Two-Eyes went home and said to her sisters, "Dear sisters, please give me some part of my goat. I don't ask for anything that's any good; just give me the entrails." Then they laughed and said, "You may have them if that's all you want." Two-Eyes took the entrails and in the evening, according to the wise woman's instructions, buried them secretly outside the front door.

The next morning when they were all awake and stepped outside the front door, there stood a wonderful and splendid tree with leaves of silver, and hanging among them fruit of gold more beautiful and more delicious than anything in the whole wide world. They didn't know how the tree had got there in the night, but Two-Eyes saw that it had grown out of the goat's entrails, for it was standing on the exact spot where she'd buried them in the earth. Then the mother said to One-Eye, "Climb up, my child, and pick the fruit for us." One-Eye climbed up, but as she was about to take hold of one of the gold apples, the branch flew out of her hands. That happened every time, so that she wasn't able to pick a single apple, no matter how she stood. Then the mother said, "Three-Eyes, you climb up. With your three eyes you can look about better than One-Eye." One-Eye slid down and Three-Eyes climbed up, but she was no more skilful, and watch as sharp as she might, the gold apples always drew away. Finally the mother grew impatient and herself climbed up but could get hold of the fruit no better than One-Eye and Three-Eyes and just kept reaching into space. Then Two-Eyes said, "I'll go up. Perhaps I'll be more successful." "You with your two eyes!" cried the sisters. "What do you think you can do?" Nevertheless, Two-Eyes climbed up, and the gold apples didn't draw away from her but of their own accord lowered themselves into her hand so that she was able to pick one after another, and brought down a whole apron full. Her mother took them away from her, and instead of treating poor Two-Eyes any better on this account, as they should have done, her mother and One-Eye and Three-Eyes were merely jealous that she alone was able to get the fruit and were only the harsher with her.

Once when they were standing together by the tree, a young knight happened to come by. "Quick, Two-Eyes! creep under there, so we won't have to be ashamed of you," and in all haste tipped an empty cask that was right by the tree over poor Two-Eyes and also shoved under it the gold apples which she had picked. When the knight got nearer, he turned out to be a handsome gentleman who stopped, admired the splendid gold and silver tree, and said to the two sisters, "Who does this beautiful tree belong to? Whoever will give me a branch from it may in return ask for what they want." Then One-Eye and Three-Eyes answered that the tree was theirs and that, of course, they'd break off a branch for him. They both worked hard at it but couldn't do it, for every time the branches and fruit drew away from them. Then the knight said, "It's certainly strange that the tree belongs to you and yet you haven't got the power to break anything off it." They insisted that the tree was theirs. While they were talking thus, Two-Eyes pushed a few gold apples out from under the cask so that they rolled to the feet of the knight, for Two-Eyes was angry that One-Eye and Three-Eyes weren't telling the truth. When the knight saw the apples, he was astonished and asked where they came from. One-Eye and Three-Eyes answered that they had another sister who wasn't, however, allowed to appear because she had only two eyes like other ordinary people. But the knight demanded to see her and cried, "Two-Eyes, come out!" Then Two-Eyes came quite happily out from under the cask, and the knight marveled at her great beauty and said, "You, Two-Eyes, can surely break off a branch of the tree for me." "Yes," answered Two-Eyes, "of course I can do that, for the tree belongs to me." She climbed up and with next to no trouble broke off a branch with fine silver leaves and gold fruit and handed it to the knight. Then the knight said, "Two-Eyes, what shall I give you in return?" "Alas," answered Two-Eyes, "from early morning till late at night I suffer from hunger and thirst, trouble and distress. If you'll take me with you and free me, I'd be happy." Then the knight lifted her onto his horse and took her to his father's mansion. There he gave her fine clothes, food and drink to her heart's

content, and because he loved her so, he had the marriage bene-
diction said over them, and the wedding was celebrated amid
great rejoicing.

When Two-Eyes was carried off this way by the handsome
knight, the two sisters at first very much envied her her luck.
"However, the wonderful tree remains in our hands," they
thought. "Even if we can't pick any fruit from it, just the same
everybody will stop in front of it, come to us, and praise it. Who
knows where our luck may yet lie!" But the next morning the tree
had vanished and with it their hopes, and when Two-Eyes looked
out of her chamber, there to her great joy it was standing outside
and thus had followed her.

Two-Eyes lived happily for a long time. Once two poor women
came to her at the mansion and begged for alms. Two-Eyes
looked at them closely and recognized her sisters One-Eye and
Three-Eyes, who had got so poor that they were wandering about
and had to beg for bread from door to door. Two-Eyes bade them
welcome, however, was kind to them and looked after them, so
that both regretted deeply the wrong they had done to their sister
in their youth.

*Forty-three*

# The Self-Propelled Carriage

*French*

Once upon a time long, long ago—it was in the time of the feudal
lords—a poor woman whose name was Marguerite lived at Mon-
teil-au-Vicomte. She had three sons; the two oldest were big,
strong, strapping youngsters, but this was not so of the youngest.
Not that he was less intelligent than the others, nor that he was
sickly. But when he walked he always looked down at the ground
or at one side or the other, and he was so timid that he wouldn't
even have dared crush an ant.

In those times the king announced that he would give his
daughter in marriage to the one who could build a carriage that
would go by itself.

From *The Borzoi Book of French Folk Tales*, by Paul Delarue and translated
by Austin Fife. © Copyright 1956 by Alfred A. Knopf, Inc. Reprinted by
permission of Alfred A. Knopf, Inc.

The eldest, when he heard of it, said to his mother: "Tomorrow you will prepare me a basket. I will go to the forest of Garenne to try to make that carriage."

He got up very early in the morning and departed. As he passed by the fountain of *Collation* he found a little old woman who was soaking a very dry crust of bread in the water in order to be able to eat it.

"Well, hello, my good old woman," he said. "What are you doing here so early in the morning?"

"Ah, young man, I am soaking my crust of bread in the fountain. It will go down better. And where are you going?"

"I am going to the Garenne forest to make some forks and rakes."

"Forks it shall be, rakes it shall be!"

When he was in the wood the strokes that his knife made carved out either a fork or a rake. In the evening when he came back he was loaded with them, but no carriage.

The second son said: "I'm going to go in my turn."

And the next day he took his basket and departed for the forest of Garenne. He also met the little old woman who was soaking her bread in the fountain, and she asked him where he was going. He replied that he was going to the forest of Garenne to make goads and clubs.

And the old woman said: "Goads and clubs it shall be!"

And all the strokes of his knife made nothing but goads or clubs, and in the evening he came back loaded with them; but there was still no carriage.

When the youngest saw this he said: "Both of you have gone; I want to go in my turn; perhaps I shall have more luck."

Marguerite and her two other sons replied: "Where do you intend to go? You're certainly too stupid. You couldn't even cut a club."

And he answered: "Prepare me a basket; it won't put you to much trouble. I want to try."

The next morning he departed early as the others had done. And he also saw the old woman who was soaking her crust of bread in the water. As soon as he saw her he said to her:

"Oh, my good lady, why don't you take my white bread and my cheese? Also, please take my little bottle of wine to warm your stomach. I am young; I can eat your dry bread."

"Thank you, my good boy," she replied. "You are very good to poor people. Where are you going?"

"Good woman, the king's trumpeters have announced that he will give his daughter in marriage to the one who will make a self-propelled carriage; my two brothers have tried but they didn't succeed; I am going to try in my turn."

"Well, a carriage it shall be, my good boy. May you make a carriage that will go all by itself!"

When he was in the woods all the ax blows that he gave produced parts of the carriage, and in the evening it was finished; when he climbed back up the slope, it traveled like mad. He met the old woman again, and she said to him:

"Well, my fine young man, so you have succeeded! You shall marry the king's daughter. But to do that you will have to hire all those whom you meet on your road as you take the carriage to the king, and you must set out at once without going back home."

So he set out immediately with his self-propelled carriage; and he had already gone a considerable distance when he met a poor devil who was licking the door of an old oven where bread had not been cooked for a hundred years at least.

"Well, my friend, what are you doing there?" he asked.

"Oh, I am licking the doors to this oven. I like bread so much that it makes me feel as if I were eating some."

"Well, come with me and you shall eat bread at your leisure. Do you want to be hired?"

"I ask for nothing better."

"What wages do you want?"

"A hundred francs a year."

"A hundred francs? All right. Get in my carriage."

A little farther he met another man who was licking a barrel stave, and he hired him for another hundred francs. Farther on he saw a man running with big stones tied to his feet; he asked him why he put them on his feet, and the man answered:

"Those are millstones; when I run I go so fast that if I have nothing tied to my feet and I want to catch rabbits I pass right over them."

He was hired for a hundred francs too.

Farther on he found another man who was hurling stones in the air, and he said to him: "What are you doing, throwing stones in the air like that? Aren't you afraid of putting someone's eyes out?"

The man replied: "Don't be afraid. I throw them so far that I have already killed half a dozen partridges on the other side of the Red Sea."

And he got in the carriage, having been hired for a hundred francs.

The carriage kept going, and farther on our young man saw another man who was bent half over toward the earth and seemed to be listening to something.

"What are you listening to?" he asked.

"I can hear wool being spun in the center of the earth," came the answer.

For another hundred francs he got in the carriage.

After having passed Orléans he saw another great big fellow who had his legs spread apart, his feet on two little mountains, and his body bent double with his behind in the air. He said to him: "What are you doing in this fine posture?"

The other straightened up and replied: "Can't you see that with the wind from my behind I make thirty-six windmills turn in that little valley, and I could make that many more turn if I wanted to!"

After bargaining, he hired him for a hundred francs, and he got in the carriage, and finally they came to Paris.

The king, who had been advised that the carriage that went by itself was arriving, was in the midst of his court on the balcony of his palace, and when he saw all of these friends dressed in trousers and coats full of holes, he didn't like it and he was sorry for his bargain.

He said: "You do have the self-propelled carriage, it's true, but to win my daughter more is required. Among your associates is there one capable of eating a hundred bread rolls at one sitting?"

Marguerite's son turned toward the man who had licked the doors of the oven and said to him: "You like bread so much, can you do that?"

And the man replied: "Just bring them; I'll eat twice as many if necessary!"

And, as a matter of fact, the hundred rolls were eaten as if it were nothing at all.

The king watched him eat, quite astonished, and said: "You do have a companion who has a fine appetite. It will cost a lot of money to feed him. But do you have one who could drink a hundred barrels of wine?"

Then the boy turned toward the man who had licked the barrel stave. "Could you do it?" he said.

And the other replied: "To drink a hundred barrels of wine is nothing; afterwards I am still thirsty."

The hundred barrels disappeared just like the hundred rolls.

The king, more and more astonished, said: "As for eating and drinking, you have satisfied me. But have you got one who could go from Paris to Bordeaux and back as fast as the mail coach?"

"You, young man," the boy said to the man whom he had found with millstones tied to his feet, "can certainly do that!"

"Of course I can; even if I remove only one millstone, still I shall get back ahead of time."

And the man let the mail coach leave, then he took one of the millstones off his feet, and he departed as if the devil were carrying him. And he had soon caught up with and passed the mail coach and arrived in Bordeaux far ahead of it.

As he was ahead of time he said: "I have plenty of time before I must leave once more. I'm thirsty and hungry. I'm going to go break crust and have a drink."

He ate, but instead of having one drink he had two, then three, and he drank so much that he fell asleep at the table. The mail coach had arrived and departed once more, and the man was still sleeping. It was only five leagues from Paris when Marguerite's son, worried, said to the man who could hear wool being spun:

"Can you tell me what my employee is doing, if he is ahead of the mail coach, or if he is still behind it?"

The man listened a moment and replied:

"Our companion is snoring in an inn in Bordeaux, and the mail coach is no more than five leagues from Paris."

"Never will he arrive!" said the boy. "But you who throw stones so well, can't you wake him up!"

"Of course I can," said the other.

And he took a flat stone from his pocket, wound up, and threw it. The stone passed through a windowpane of the inn where the runner was sleeping, fell on his shoulder, and he woke up, rubbed his eyes, looked at the time, and said:

"I certainly am late! Yet there's still nothing lost. But I must remove the other millstone."

When he had removed it, he departed at such a fast clip that he arrived fifteen minutes ahead of the mail coach.

The king remained calm, and his daughter, who was beside the carriage, laughed behind his back. The boy, who was afraid the king might make further demands, took her in his arms, put her in the carriage, and departed with all his associates. The king, in anger, had cannon aimed at the carriage, and the artillerymen were going to set the weapons off, when the man who caused windmills to turn bent over and let go with such a gust that the cannons and the cannoneers were hurled into the air so high that they still haven't fallen back to the earth. They may have been blown all the way to the moon.

The king was obliged to give his daughter in marriage to Marguerite's son, and that was the first time that the self-propelled carriage was used at a marriage.


*Forty-four*

# Faithful John

*German*

There was once an old king. He was ill and thought, "I'm probably on my deathbed." Then he said, "Have Faithful John come to me." Faithful John was his favorite servant and was so named because he'd been faithful to him all his life. When he now came to the bedside, the king said to him: "Most faithful John, I feel that my end is drawing near and I'm worried about nothing but my son. He is still young in years and not always able to look out for himself; unless you promise me to instruct him in everything he ought to know and be his foster father, I shan't be able to shut my eyes in peace." Then Faithful John replied, "I shan't leave him and I'll serve him faithfully, even if it costs me my life." Then the old king said: "Now I will die consoled and in peace," and added, "After my death you're to show him the whole palace, all the chambers, halls, and vaults, and all the treasures that are in them, but you're not to show him the last chamber in the long passageway, in which is hidden the portrait of the daughter of the king of the Golden Roof. If he sees the portrait, he'll fall violently in love with her and will fall down in a faint and because of her

From *German Folk Tales*, collected and edited by Grimm Brothers. Translated by Francis P. Magoun, Jr. and Alexander H. Krappe. Copyright © 1960, by Southern Illinois University Press. Reprinted by permission of the Southern Illinois University Press.

will run great dangers. You're to guard him against that." When Faithful John had again given the old king his hand on it, the latter grew quiet, laid his head on his pillow, and died.

When the old king had been carried to his grave, Faithful John told the young king what he had promised his father on his deathbed and said, "I shall certainly keep this promise and be as loyal to you as I was to him, even if it costs me my life." The period of mourning passed; then Faithful John said to him, "Now it's time for you to see your heritage; I'll show you your ancestral palace." Then he led him all about, up and down, and showed him all the treasures and the sumptuous chambers; but there was the one chamber that he didn't open: that is, the one with the dangerous portrait. The picture was placed in such a way that, on opening the door, one looked straight at it, and it was so beautifully done that one might think it was real flesh and blood and alive and that there couldn't be anything lovelier and more beautiful in the whole world. The young king was well aware that Faithful John always passed one particular door by and said, "Why don't you ever open it for me?" "There's something in there," he answered, "that will frighten you." But the king replied, "I've seen the whole palace; now I want to know what's in there." He stepped forward and was about to force the door open when Faithful John held him back, saying, "I promised your father before his death that you shouldn't see what's in that chamber; it might bring you and me great misfortune." "Oh no," answered the young king, "if I don't get in, it'll certainly be my ruin. I shouldn't rest day or night till I'd seen it with my own eyes. I shan't move from the spot till you've unlocked it."

Then Faithful John saw there was nothing further to do about it, and with heavy heart and many sighs picked out the key from the big bunch. When he'd opened the door, he went in first, thinking he'd cover the picture so the king, who was standing behind him, mightn't see it. But what good did that do? The king stood on tiptoe and looked over his shoulder, and when he beheld the portrait of the girl who was so beautiful, sparkling with gold and jewels, he fell down in a faint. Faithful John lifted him up, carried him to his bed, and thought sorrowfully, "The mishap's occurred. Lord God! what will come of it all?" Then he strengthened him with wine until he regained consciousness. The first words he said were, "What beautiful person is that a portrait of?" "It's the daughter of the king of the Golden Roof," Faithful John replied. Then the king went on to say, "My love for her is so great that if all the leaves on the trees were tongues, they couldn't express it. I'll risk my life to win her. You're my most faithful John and must help me."

The faithful servant reflected for a long time on how to accomplish this, for it was difficult even to get into the presence of the princess. Finally he hit upon a plan and said to the king, "Everything she has about her is of gold: tables, chairs, dishes, cups, bowls, and all household utensils. There are five tons of gold in your treasury. Have one ton of it wrought by the goldsmiths of your kingdom into all sorts of vessels and utensils, into all kinds of birds, game, and strange animals. She'll like that, and we'll travel to her with these things and try our luck. The king summoned all his goldsmiths. They had to work day and night, till finally the most magnificent things were ready. When everything had been loaded on a ship, Faithful John put on merchant's clothes, and the king had to do the same and disguise himself completely. Then they journeyed overseas and traveled until they came to the city where the daughter of the king of the Golden Roof dwelt.

Faithful John bade the king stay on the ship and wait for him. "Perhaps," he said, "I'll bring the princess with me. Therefore see to it that everything is ready; have the golden vessels put on display and the entire ship decked out." Then he gathered up a number of gold trinkets in his apron, went ashore and straight to the royal palace. When he reached the palace courtyard, a pretty girl was standing by the well; she had two golden pails in her hands and was drawing water, and as she was about to carry away the bright water and had turned around, she saw the stranger and asked who he was. He replied, "I'm a merchant," opened his apron, and let her look in. Then she cried out, "Oh, what beautiful goldware!" set the pails down, and looked at the things one after the other. Then the girl said, "The king's daughter must see this; she's so fond of gold trinkets that she'll buy them all from you." She took him by the hand and led him upstairs, for she was the chambermaid. When the king's daughter saw the goldware, she was most happy and said, "It's so beautifully wrought that I'll buy it all from you." But Faithful John said, "I'm only a rich merchant's servant. What I have here is nothing to what my master has down on board his ship, yes, the most artfully and wonderfully wrought objects ever made of gold." Then she wanted to have everything brought up to her, but he said, "That would take many days, there's so much of it, and it would take so many halls to display it in that there's not enough room in your dwelling." This roused her curiosity and desire more and more, so she finally said, "Take me down to the ship; I'll go there in person and view your master's treasures."

Then Faithful John brought her to the ship and was very happy. On beholding her, the king saw that her beauty was even greater than her portrait had shown, and he thought that his heart would burst with joy. Now she went aboard, and the king escorted her in. But Faithful John stayed behind near the helmsman and ordered the ship to put off: "Set all sail, so that she'll fly like a bird in the air!" Inside the ship, however, the king showed her the gold service, every single piece: dishes, cups, bowls, the birds, game, and strange animals. Many hours passed while she looked at everything, and in her joy she didn't notice that the ship was moving along. After she had looked at the last object, she thanked the merchant and wanted to go home, but when she came to the ship's side, she saw that it was far from land and on the high seas, speeding forward under full sail. "Oh," she cried in fright, "I've been tricked; I'm being abducted and have fallen into the power of a merchant. I'd rather die." But the king took her by the hand and said, "I'm not a merchant; I'm a king and not inferior to you in birth. I've abducted you by guile because of my great, great love for you: the first time I saw your portrait, I fell to the ground in a faint." When the daughter of the king of the Golden Roof heard this, she was consoled, and her heart inclined toward him so that she willingly consented to become his wife.

But it so happened that while they were on the high seas Faithful John, as he was sitting near the bow of the ship and playing some music, saw three ravens flying through the air. Then he stopped playing and listened to what they were saying to one another, for he understood it well. One of them cried, "Well, there he's bringing home the daughter of the king of the Golden Roof." "Yes, indeed," answered the second, "but he hasn't got her yet." Then the third rejoined, "Yes, he has got her; she's sitting beside him in the ship." Then the first spoke again and cried, "What good will that do him? When they reach shore, a horse as red as a fox will come galloping up; he'll want to mount it, and if he does so, it'll run away with him into the air, so that he'll never see the maiden again." Then the second said, "Is there no way of saving him?" "Oh, yes. If someone else quickly mounts the horse, takes out the gun that's surely in the holster, and shoots the horse dead, then the young king will be saved. But who knows that? And if anybody does know it and tells the king, he'll be turned to stone from his toes to his knees." Then the second raven said, "I know still more. Even if the horse is killed, the young king still won't keep his bride. When they enter the palace together, they'll find a perfectly made bridal shirt lying in a bowl, looking as if it were woven of gold and silver, though it's nothing but sulphur and pitch. If he puts it on, it'll burn him to the quick and to the marrow." Then the third said, "Is there absolutely no way of saving him?" "Oh, yes," replied the second. "If someone takes hold of the shirt with gloves on and throws it into the fire so that it burns up, the young king will be saved. But what good's that? Whoever knows this and tells him will turn to stone from his knees to his heart." Then the third said, "I know still more. Even if the bridal shirt is burned up, still the young king won't have his bride. After the wedding, when the ball opens and the young queen dances, she'll suddenly turn pale and fall down as if dead, and unless someone lifts her up and draws three drops of blood from her right breast and spits them out again, she'll die. But if anybody who knows it tells the secret, his whole body will be turned to stone from top to toe." Having thus spoken, the ravens continued their flight, but Faithful John had understood everything and from that time on was quiet and sad. For if he kept from his master what he'd heard, misfortune would befall the latter, and if he told him, he himself would have to sacrifice his life. Finally, however, he said to himself, "I shall save my master, even if I perish in the attempt."

When they went ashore, it happened as the raven had predicted: a superb horse, red as a fox, came galloping up. "Well," said the king, "it shall carry me to my palace," and was about to mount it. But Faithful John got ahead of him, swung quickly onto it himself, drew the gun from the holster, and shot the horse dead. Then the other servants of the king, who were not very fond of Faithful John, cried, "What a shame to kill the fine animal that was to carry the king to his palace." The king, however, said: "Be still and leave him alone; he's my most faithful John. Who knows to what good purpose he did it!" Now they entered the palace, and there in the hall was a bowl with a perfectly made bridal shirt lying in it, looking as if it were made of gold and silver. The young king stepped up and was about to take hold of it, but Faithful John pushed him aside, seized it with his gloves on, carried it quickly to the fireplace, and let it burn up. The other servants again began to murmur, "Look! Now he's burning even the king's bridal shirt." But the young king said, "Who knows to what good purpose he did it! Leave him alone; he's my most faithful John." Now the wedding was celebrated; the ball began, and the bride, too, entered the hall. Then Faithful John paid close attention and watched her face. Suddenly she turned pale and fell to the ground as if dead. He rushed quickly up, lifted her, and carried her into a chamber; there he laid her down, knelt, and sucked three drops of blood from her right breast and spat them out. At once she began to breathe again and recovered. The young king, however, had been looking on and didn't know why Faithful John had done it. He got angry and shouted, "Throw him into prison!" The next morning Faithful John was condemned to death and led to the gallows. When he stood up there and was about to be executed, he said: "Everyone condemned to die is allowed to say one last word before his end. Am I to have this right, too?" "Yes," answered the king, "it will not be refused you." Then Faithful John said, "I was condemned unjustly and have always been faithful to you," and then told how at sea he'd heard the ravens' conversation and how he'd been forced to do all this to save his master. Then the king cried out, "Oh, my most faithful John, mercy, mercy! Bring him down from the gallows!" But with the last word he uttered, Faithful John had fallen down dead and was a piece of stone.

The king and queen were greatly grieved by this, and the king said, "How ill I rewarded such great loyalty," and had the stone image picked up and placed in his bedchamber next to his bed. Whenever he looked at it he'd weep and say, "If only I could bring you back to life, my most faithful John!" Some time passed, and the queen gave birth to twins, two boys; they grew up and were her joy. Once when the queen was at church and the two children were sitting beside their father and playing, the latter again looked sadly at the stone image and, sighing, said, "Oh, if only I could bring you back to life, my most faithful John!" Then the stone began to speak and said, "Yes, you can bring me back to life if to do so you're willing to sacrifice what you most love." Then the king exclaimed, "I'm willing to sacrifice everything I have in this world for you." Then the stone went on, "If with your own hand you'll cut off the heads of your two children and anoint me with their blood, I'll come back to life." The king was frightened when he heard he'd have to kill his dear children with his own hand, but he thought of Faithful John's great loyalty and how he'd died for him, and drew his sword and with his own hand cut off his children's heads. And when he'd anointed the stone with their blood, it came to life, and Faithful John stood before him hale and hearty. He said to the king, "Your loyalty to me shall not remain unrewarded," took the children's heads, put them in place, and anointed the wounds with their blood. In an instant they were whole again, skipped about, and continued their play as if nothing had happened. Now the king rejoiced greatly, and when he saw the queen coming, hid Faithful John and the two children in a big cupboard. When she came in, he said to her, "Did you pray at church?" "Yes," she answered, "but I was thinking all the time about Faithful John and that he fell into such misfortune on our account." Then he said, "Dear wife, we can bring him back to life, but it will cost us our two children; we'll have to sacrifice them." The queen turned pale and in her heart was frightened, but said, "We owe it to him because of his great loyalty." Then the king was glad that she thought as he'd thought, stepped to the cupboard and, unlocking it, brought out the children and Faithful John, saying, "God be praised! He is disenchanted, and our two children, too, have been given back to us," and told her how it all happened.

Then they lived happily together until their death.

*Forty-five*

# The Princess on the Glass Hill

*Norwegian*

Once on a time there was a man who had a meadow, which lay high up on the hillside, and in the meadow was a barn, which he had built to keep his hay in. Now, I must tell you, there hadn't been much in the barn for the last year or two, for every St. John's night, when the grass stood greenest and deepest, the meadow was eaten down to the very ground the next morning, just as if a whole drove of sheep had been there feeding on it over night. This happened once, and it happened twice. So at last the man grew weary of losing his crop of hay, and said to his sons—for he had three of them, and the youngest was nicknamed Boots, of course—that now one of them must just go and sleep in the barn in the outlying field when St. John's night came, for it was too bad a joke that his grass should be eaten, root and blade, this year, as it had been the last two years. So whichever of them went must keep a sharp lookout; that was what their father said.

Well, the eldest son was ready to go and watch the meadow; trust him for looking after the grass! It shouldn't be his fault if man or beast, or the fiend himself, got a blade of grass. So, when evening came, he set off to the barn, and lay down to sleep; but a little on in the night came such a clatter, and such an earthquake, that walls and roof shook, and groaned, and creaked. Then up jumped the lad, and took to his heels as fast as ever he could; nor dared he once look round till he reached home; and as for the hay, why it was eaten up this year just as it had been twice before.

The next St. John's night, the man said again it would never do to lose all the grass in the outlying field year after year in this way, so one of his sons must just trudge off to watch it, and watch it well too. Well, the next oldest son was ready to try his luck, so he set off, and lay down to sleep in the barn as his brother had done before him; but as night wore on there came on a rumbling and quaking of the earth, worse even than on the last St. John's night, and when the lad heard it he got frightened, and took to his heels as though he were running a race.

Next year the turn came to Boots; but when he made ready to go, the other two began to laugh, and to make game of him, saying, "You're just the man to watch the hay, that you are; you who have done nothing all your life but sit in the ashes and toast yourself by the fire."

But Boots did not care a pin for their chattering, and stumped away, as evening drew on, up the hillside to the outlying field. There he went inside the barn and lay down; but in about an hour's time the barn began to groan and creak, so that it was dreadful to hear.

"Well," said Boots to himself, "if it isn't worse than this, I can stand it well enough."

A little while after came another creak and an earthquake, so that the litter in the barn flew about the lad's ears.

"Oh!" said Boots to himself, "if it isn't worse than this, I daresay I can stand it out."

But just then came a third rumbling, and a third earthquake, so that the lad thought walls and roof were coming down on his head; but it passed off, and all was still as death about him.

"It'll come again, I'll be bound," thought Boots; but no, it did not come again; still it was and still it stayed. But after he had lain a little while he heard a noise as if a horse were standing just outside the barn-door, and cropping the grass. He stole to the door, and peeped through a chink, and there stood a horse feeding away. So big, and fat, and grand a horse Boots had never set eyes on; by his side on the grass lay a saddle and bridle, and a full set of armor for a knight, all of brass, so bright that the light gleamed from it.

"Ho, ho!" thought the lad; "it's you, is it, that eats up our hay? I'll soon put a spoke in your wheel; just see if I don't."

So he lost no time, but took the steel out of his tinderbox, and threw it over the horse; then it had no power to stir from the spot, and became so tame that the lad could do what he liked with it. So he got on its back, and rode off with it to a place which no one knew of, and there he put up the horse. When he got home his brothers laughed, and asked how he had fared?

"You didn't lie long in the barn, even if you had the heart to go so far as the field."

"Well," said Boots, "all I can say is, I lay in the barn till the sun rose, and neither saw nor heard anything; I can't think what there was in the barn to make you both so afraid."

"A pretty story!" said his brothers; "but we'll soon see how you have watched the meadow." So they set off; but when they reached it, there stood the grass as deep and thick as it had been over night.

Well, the next St. John's eve it was the same story over again; neither of the elder brothers dared to go out to the outlying field to watch the crop; but Boots had the heart to go, and everything happened just as it had happened the year before. First a clatter and an earthquake, then a greater clatter and another earthquake, and so on a third time; only this year the earthquakes were far worse than the year before. Then all at once everything was as still as death, and the lad heard how something was cropping the grass outside the barn-door, so he stole to the door, and peeped through a chink; and what do you think he saw? why, another horse standing right up against the wall, and chewing and champing with might and main. It was far finer and fatter than that which came the year before, and it had a saddle on its back, and a bridle on its neck, and a full suit of mail for a knight lay by its side, all of silver, and as grand as you would wish to see.

"Ho, ho!" said Boots to himself; "it's you that gobbles up our hay, is it? I'll soon put a spoke in your wheel." And with that he took the steel out of his tinderbox, and threw it over the horse's crest, which stood as still as a lamb. Well, the lad rode this horse, too, to the hiding-place where he kept the other one, and after that he went home.

"I suppose you'll tell us," said one of his brothers, "there's a fine crop this year too, up in the hayfield."

"Well, so there is," said Boots; and off ran the others to see, and there stood the grass thick and deep, as it was the year before. But they didn't give Boots softer words for all that.

Now, when the third St. John's eve came, the two elder brothers still hadn't the heart to lie out in the barn and watch the grass, for they had got so scared at heart the night they lay there before, that they couldn't get over the fright; but Boots, he dared to go; and, to make a long story short, the very same thing happened this time as had happened twice before. Three earthquakes came, one after the other, each worse than the one which went before, and when the last came, the lad danced about with the shock from one barn wall to the other; and after that, all at once, it was still as death. Now when he had lain a little while he heard something tugging away at the grass outside the barn, so he stole again to the door-chink, and peeped out, and there stood a horse close outside—far, far bigger and fatter than the two he had taken before.

"Ho, ho!" said the lad to himself, "it's you, is it, that comes here eating up our hay? I'll soon stop that—I'll soon put a spoke in your wheel." So he caught up his steel and threw it over the horse's neck, and in a trice it stood as if it were nailed to the ground, and Boots could do as he pleased with it. Then he rode off with it to the hiding-place where he kept the other two, and then went home. When he got home his two brothers made game of him as they had done before, saying they could see he had watched the grass well, for he looked for all the world as if he were walking in his sleep, and many other spiteful things they said, but Boots gave no heed to them, only asking them to go and see for themselves; and when they went, there stood the grass as fine and deep this time as it had been twice before.

Now, you must know that the king of the country where Boots lived had a daughter, whom he would only give to the man who could ride up over the hill of glass, for there was a high, high hill, all of glass, as smooth and slippery as ice, close by the king's palace. Upon the tip-top of the hill the king's daughter was to sit, with three golden apples in her lap, and the man who could ride up and carry off the three golden apples was to have half the kingdom, and the princess to wife. This the king had stuck up on all the church-doors in his realm, and had given it out in many other kingdoms besides. Now, this princess was so lovely that all who set eyes on her fell over head and ears in love with her whether they would or no. So I needn't tell you how all the princes and knights who heard of her were eager to win her to wife, and half the kingdom beside; and how they came riding from all parts of the world on high prancing horses, and clad in the grandest clothes, for there wasn't one of them who hadn't made up his mind that he, and he alone, was to win the princess.

So when the day of trial came, which the king had fixed, there was such a crowd of princes and knights under the glass hill, that it made one's head whirl to look at them; and every one in the country who could even crawl along was off to the hill, for they all were eager to see the man who was to win the princess. So the two elder brothers set off with the rest; but as for Boots, they said outright he shouldn't go with them, for if they were seen with such a dirty changeling, all begrimed with smut from cleaning their shoes and sifting cinders in the dust-hole, they said folk would make game of them.

"Very well," said Boots, "it's all one to me. I can go alone, and stand or fall by myself."

Now when the two brothers came to the hill of glass the knights and princes were hard at it, riding their horses till they were all in a foam; but it was no good, by my troth; for as soon as ever the horses set foot on the hill, down they slipped, and there wasn't one who could get a yard or two up. And no wonder, for the hill was as smooth as a sheet of glass, and as steep as a house-wall. But all were eager to have the princess and half the kingdom. So they rode and slipped, and slipped and rode, and still it was the same story over again.

At last all their horses were so weary that they could scarce lift a leg, and in such a sweat that the lather dripped from them, and so the knights had to give up trying any more. So the king was just thinking that he would proclaim a new trial for the next day, to see if they would have better luck, when all at once a knight came riding up on so brave a steed that no one had ever seen the like of it in his born days, and the knight had mail of brass, and the horse a brass bit in his mouth, so bright that the sunbeams shone from it. Then all the others called out to him he might just as well spare himself the trouble of riding at the hill, for it would lead to no good; but he gave no heed to them, and put his horse at the hill, and went up it like nothing for a good way, about a third of the height; and when he had got so far, he turned his horse round and rode down again. So lovely a knight the Princess thought she had never yet seen; and while he was riding, she sat and thought to herself:

"Would to heaven he might only come up, and down the other side."

And when she saw him turning back, she threw down one of the golden apples after him, and it rolled down into his shoes. But when he got to the bottom of the hill he rode off so fast that no one could tell what had become of him. That evening all the knights and princes were to go before the king, that he who had ridden so far up the hill might show the apple which the princess had thrown, but there was no one who had anything to show. One after the other they all came, but not a man of them could show the apple.

In the evening the brothers of Boots came home too, and had such a long story to tell about the riding up the hill.

"First of all," they said, "there was not one of the whole lot who could get so much as a stride up; but at last came one who had a suit of brass mail, and a brass bridle and saddle, all so bright that the sun shone from them a mile off. He was a chap to ride, just! He rode a third of the way up the hill of glass, and he could easily have ridden the whole way up, if he chose; but he turned around and rode down, thinking, maybe, that was enough for once."

"Oh! I should so like to have seen him, that I should," said Boots, who sat by the fireside, and stuck his feet into the cinders as was his wont.

"Oh!" said his brothers, "you would, would you? You look fit to keep company with such high lords, nasty beast that you are, sitting there among the ashes."

Next day the brothers were all for setting off again, and Boots begged them this time, too, to let him go with them and see the riding; but no, they wouldn't have him at any price, he was too ugly and nasty, they said.

"Well, well!" said Boots; "if I go at all, I must go by myself. I'm not afraid."

So when the brothers got to the hill of glass, all the princes and knights began to ride again, and you may fancy they had taken care to shoe their horses sharp; but it was no good—they rode and slipped, and slipped and rode, just as they had done the day before, and there was not one who could get so far as a yard up the hill. And when they had worn out their horses, so that they could not stir a leg, they were all forced to give it up as a bad job. So the king thought he might as well proclaim that the riding should take place the day after for the last time, just to give them one chance more; but all at once it came across his mind that he might as well wait a little longer, to see if the knight in brass mail would come this day too. Well, they saw nothing of him; but all at once came one riding on a steed, far, far braver and finer than that on which the knight in brass had ridden, and he had silver mail, and a silver saddle and bridle, all so bright that the sunbeams gleamed and glanced from them far away. Then the others shouted out to him again, saying he might as well hold hard, and not try to ride up the hill, for all his trouble would be thrown away. But the knight paid no heed to them, and rode straight at the hill, and right up it, till he had gone two-thirds of the way, and then he wheeled his horse round and rode down again. To tell the truth, the Princess liked him still better than the knight in brass, and she sat and wished he might only be able to come right up to the top, and down the other side; but when she saw him turning back, she threw the second apple after him, and it rolled down and fell into his shoe. But as soon as ever he had come down from the hill of glass, he rode off so fast that no one could see what became of him.

At even, when all were to go in before the king and the princess, that he who had the golden apple might show it; in they went, one after the other, but there was no one who had any apple to show, and the two brothers, as they had done on the former day, went home and told how things had gone, and how all had ridden at the hill and none got up.

"But, last of all," they said, "came one in a silver suit, and his horse had a silver saddle and a silver bridle. He was just a chap to ride; and he got two-thirds up the hill, and then turned back. He was a fine fellow and no mistake; and the princess threw the second gold apple to him."

"Oh!" said Boots, "I should so like to have seen him too, that I should."

"A pretty story!" they said. "Perhaps you think his coat of mail was as bright as the ashes you are always poking about, and sifting, you nasty dirty beast."

The third day everything happened as it had happened the two days before. Boots begged to go and see the sight, but the two wouldn't hear of his going with them. When they got to the hill there was no one who could get so much as a yard up it; and now all waited for the knight in silver mail, but they neither saw nor heard of him. At last came one riding on a steed, so brave that no one had ever seen his match; and the knight had a suit of golden mail, and a golden saddle and bridle, so wondrous bright that the sunbeams gleamed from them a mile off. The other knights and princes could not find time to call out to him not to try his luck, for they were amazed to see how grand he was. So he rode right at the hill, and up it like nothing, so that the princess hadn't even time to wish that he might get up the whole way. As soon as ever he reached the top, he took the third golden apple from the princess' lap, and then turned his horse and rode down again. As soon as he got down, he rode off at full speed, and was out of sight in no time.

Now, when the brothers got home at even, you may fancy what long stories they told, how the riding had gone off that day; and among other things, they had a deal to say about the knight in golden mail.

"He just was a chap to ride!" they said; "so grand a knight isn't to be found in the wide world."

"Oh!" said Boots, "I should so like to have seen him; that I should."

"Ah!" said his brothers, "his mail shone a deal brighter than the glowing coals which you are always poking and digging at; nasty dirty beast that you are."

Next day all the knights and princes were to pass before the

king and the Princess—it was too late to do so the night before, I suppose—that he who had the gold apple might bring it forth; but one came after another, first the princes, and then the knights, and still no one could show the gold apple.

"Well," said the king, "some one must have it, for it was something that we all saw with our own eyes, how a man came and rode up and bore it off."

So he commanded that every one who was in the kingdom should come up to the palace and see if they could show the apple. Well, they all came, one after another, but no one had the golden apple, and after a long time the two brothers of Boots came. They were the last of all, so the king asked them if there was no one else in the kingdom who hadn't come.

"Oh, yes," said they; "we have a brother, but he never carried off the golden apple. He hasn't stirred out of the dust-hole on any of the three days."

"Never mind that," said the king; "he may as well come up to the palace like the rest."

So Boots had to go up to the palace.

"How, now," said the king; "have you got the golden apple? Speak out!"

"Yes, I have," said Boots; "here is the first, and here is the second, and here is the third too"; and with that he pulled all three golden apples out of his pocket, and at the same time threw off his sooty rags, and stood before them in his gleaming golden mail.

"Yes!" said the king; "you shall have my daughter, and half my kingdom, for you well deserve both her and it."

So they got ready for the wedding, and Boots got the princess to wife, and there was great merry-making at the bridal-feast, you may fancy, for they could all be merry though they couldn't ride up the hill of glass; and all I can say is, if they haven't left off their merry-making yet, why, they're still at it.

*Forty-six*

# The Servant Who Took the
# Place of His Master

*Greek*

There was once a prince who wanted to make a journey somewhere to see the world a little; so he spoke to his father, the king,
and begged him to give him a ship with all its necessary fittings.
In her he embarked with all the men for the service of the ship to
keep him company. So they journeyed for many days until they
came to land. There in that country, his head being dizzy with so
much sailing, the prince chose to go ashore. So he disembarked
and found it a desert place where there was neither beast nor
man. After he had been going for a long time far into that land he
saw a shepherd. The man led the prince to his sheepfold and gave
him of what he had, as is the custom with shepherds.

It happened, on that very evening when the prince was lodging
at the sheepfold, that the shepherd's wife had a baby, and the
prince became his godfather and gave him the name of Johnnie.
And when the time came for the prince to go away to his father's
kingdom, he told the shepherd to guard the child well, and when
he was big to send him to school to learn letters; when he got a
little bigger, he should send him to his kingdom. And in order to
be able to recognize him he left him a locket, saying: "This locket
you must hang on his neck so that I can recognize the boy when
he comes to my kingdom, that he is my godson, the boy whom I
held at the font."

When the boy was a little grown, his father made him ready
and hung the locket on him, and bade him farewell, telling him to
be obedient and well-behaved; and so the boy went off.

As he was going on his way there met him a man with no
beard, and the man asked him where he was going. The boy told
him the truth, that he was going to find his godfather; in order
that he might recognize him, his godfather had left him a locket,

From *Modern Greek Folktales*, edited by R. M. Dawkins. Reprinted by permission of the Clarendon Press, Oxford.

and he had it hung on his neck that he might not lose it.

Like the cunning fellow he was, from that moment the beardless man thought out all sorts of tunes to play to Johnnie, and he told him that he too was going to the same place. As they were going on the way they became thirsty and they came upon a well. The man proposed to the boy that as the younger he should go down the well to fill the jar which the beardless man had with him, and then he would draw him up again. Then Johnnie, who had no cunning about him, went down. The beardless man then told him that he would leave him down there to die, and the boy began to beseech him to pull him up. After he had for a long time treated him thus cruelly, the beardless man asked him to give him the locket so that he himself could pass as the boy, the prince's godson; Johnnie, being only a young boy, consented to this. And again the beardless man made a proposal, that Johnnie as the younger, should let himself appear to be the servant and should so present himself before the prince. Also he was to swear that only if he should die and come to life again would he reveal what the beardless man had done to him.

Poor Johnnie was in a sad fix and consented to all the demands of the beardless man, and he took an oath to God: "Only if I die and come to life again will I reveal what you have done to me." And on these terms the beardless man drew him up out of the well.

So the two of them went on together and came to the city where the prince was. They appeared before him, and the beardless man gave the locket into his hand and said that he was the boy to whom he had been godfather. But the eye of the prince was on the boy and he asked the beardless man who the boy was whom he had with him. He replied that he had taken him for company on the way. The prince kept him there because he had a liking for him.

One day in summer at midday the swallows, birds that never tire, were flying in and out of the men's room; it was there they had their nests. One swallow was late in coming and her mate scolded her and hit her with his wing. The son of the shepherd, who had learned the language of birds, began to smile at what they were saying. Then the beardless man, who had been seeking a cause to drive the boy away, gave him a buffet. The king was sorely vexed at his conduct and asked the beardless man why he had hit the boy. He answered that Johnnie had smiled to mock him. The king asked Johnnie if this were true, and he said that his laughter had been about the birds—the pair of swallows—because the cock bird with his wing had struck at his mate and had scolded her because she was so late, and she had told him that she had been tarrying to collect the hair combings of a beautiful girl. These were all of gold, and she wanted to bring them for their nest, for they would be very soft for their chicks. The girl, said the swallow, was called the Girl with Golden Hair.

When the beardless man heard this, he told the prince to order Johnnie to go and fetch the Girl with Golden Hair because for the prince she would be the most beautiful wife who could ever be found. So the boy was ordered to go to fetch her. Then the boy, who held by his father's counsel not to be disobedient although the command might cost him much, took a fine strong horse and went off to look for the Girl with Golden Hair.

As he was going on his way, he met an ogress, a Lamia, and greeted her in a way that pleased her, and she told him in answer that she would not devour him, for he was the godson of a prince, and she asked him what he had come out to seek. He answered that he had come to seek the Girl with Golden Hair. Then she said: "And have you come out with empty hands?" And she gave him this counsel—to go back and get forty sheep killed and flayed and forty skins of honey, for on the way he would come to a place crowded and black with ants, and farther on to a great swarm of bees; to be able to get by he must throw the sheep to the ants and the honey to the bees, and the ants would betake themselves to the sheep and the bees to the honey.

So the boy turned back and went and asked for everything the Lamia had said, and when he had been given them he started on his way. Then from a long way off he saw a little hill which, to his amazement, was black all over. When he came closer he perceived that it was the ant-hill, and the horse laid back his ears and was reluctant to pass it. The boy went forward and at some distance away threw down the sheep, and when the ants had the smell of them they all ran to that place and so the boy had a chance to get past. And as he went by, the king of the ants called upon him to stop, and in his little voice he told him that the great ones among them had held a council and because of the good he had done them in bringing them food they had resolved that they too would do him some benefit. Then the king gave him a wing and told him that if he had any need of them he must singe it in the fire and they would go to him wherever he was. The boy took the wing and put it away safely, and then he went on his way. Going farther he came upon a great swarm of bees so that he could not pass by. So he poured out the honey near them. At once the swarm broke up and made for the honey and thus he got past there also without the horse taking fright. But the bees also called a council just like the ants, and they resolved to do him a kindness. The king of the bees flew out and caught up with Johnnie and gave him a wing, telling him to put it away as a treasure to be guarded, because all their great ones had resolved to do him a benefit. If he were in need, he had nothing to do but to singe the wing a little in the fire. Saying this to him, the bee went away. And thus the boy was again able to pass, and he reached the place of the Girl with Golden Hair. And when the people saw him, they asked him where he had come from and where he was going, and he told them he had come there with the intention to fetch away the Girl with Golden Hair.

Then they told him that, as for the Girl with Golden Hair, it was only by performing certain tasks that a man could win her, and that if he were willing to wager on these tasks, she would propound them to him, and that if he could not succeed in them his head would be cut off. Then they pointed out to him a tower built of the heads of young men of every sort—men who had undertaken the wagers and had failed—and now only one head was lacking for the tower to be complete: "Well, think it over and make up your mind." Johnnie heard all this paying very good heed, yet for all that he consented to engage in the test. They showed him a very big granary, full of wheat, barley, oats, and other grains, but all the sorts were mixed up together, and they told him that if he could in one night empty that store and not a grain escape him and then set each sort apart, then the Girl with Golden Hair should be his.

Well, when he heard of this test he began to think how he could succeed in it, and he remembered what the ant had said. He took out the wing and singed it and before you could say "Amen," the ant appeared and asked him what were his orders. "I want you to empty this granary in one night and this very evening, and each kind must be put separate and you must not miss even one grain." At once all the ants came, going in and going out like an army when in full array it is exercising on the field, and by the morning they had shifted all the grain just as he had said. One of the ants who was lame was late in coming out of the granary, and they went to see what had happened, because they were uneasy about her, and when they went in the ant was coming out carrying a grain of wild barley, which had rolled down into a crack, and she had been working at it all night before she could get it out. For all that the others had done, it was only the lame ant who had saved the head of the poor lad. When men rose up in the morning and saw the granary all cleared, swept out, and washed, and every grain set in its separate place, they were all amazed and could not imagine how this had happened.

The Girl with Golden Hair also heard of this, to her great displeasure, and she set before him yet another test. She sent word to him that she would come down with her serving women, and they would all be wearing clothes of one cut and pattern, and all of them would be veiled; if he could recognize her, she swore that she would follow him wherever he took her and he should have her for his wife. When he heard this he fell into deep thought and great confusion. Dizzy with care and trouble, it came into his mind what the bee had said. He brought out the wing and singed it, and at once the bee appeared before him. "What are your orders, master?" So he told her what was happening to him. Then the bee told him that she would go to the place where the girls were to be dressing themselves, and she would put a mark on the Girl with Golden Hair, and that when the girls went downstairs she would follow her. When they reached the place where the girls would be brought for him to pick her out, then she would come round to her and alight on her head and on the covering of her head she would lay some honey. He must be careful in his excitement not to be confused and pick upon another girl.

So when the time came for the girls to dress the bee was there and she made a clear mark on the Girl with Golden Hair, and when the girls were dressed and had gone down from the palace to the place where the king was and with him all the first men of the palace and of the realm, there was Johnnie with his eyes cast down. When the bee saw him she went and buzzed and tickled him, and at once he came to himself and lifted up his eyes. He kept them alert and watched the bee to see where she went and alighted, going and coming back again, and on the head of which girl she left some honey. The girls all passed in front of him three times, and at the third time he took one of them by the hand: it was the Girl with Golden Hair. She at once showed her face and by her beauty bright as the sun he saw who it was.

Now when he had succeeded in the second test, fireworks and illuminations of all sorts were prepared so that the night was as bright as the day. Everybody was delighted, for by then they had had too much of seeing so many young men brought to death and the tower built of their heads.

Next day the two of them were sent off on their way with all good wishes. The boy took her and they went off to the country of the prince who had been Johnnie's godfather. The prince marveled at her, but the beardless man was jealous of the boy's bravery and at his fine achievements, and he wanted to kill him, so he gave him a drink which brought him to his death. When the Girl with Golden Hair saw him fallen down dead, she gave him a draught of the Water of Immortality and raised him up again. Johnnie uttered a sigh and said: "Ah, how sweetly I was sleeping; why did you awaken me?" Then the girl told him the story of how the beardless man had poisoned him and how she with the Water of Immortality had raised him up again.

The youth remembered the oath that he had sworn, and that now that he had been dead and was alive again the bond was loosed, because he had sworn: "I will reveal what this man has done to me only if I die and come to life again." So now was the time and now he had a right to reveal to his godfather the hidden secret. Therefore very fully and point by point he told all that we have narrated from the beginning to the end. And when she heard it the girl told what Johnnie had endured for her sake, and how if he had not been able to find how to pass the tests she set him he would have lost his head, and how she had sworn to him to take him for her husband and to be married to him. The young man too said that to her he owed his life and he was hers.

When the king and the prince heard all this, in order to show the world that they were just judges they gave orders that the beardless man should be hanged, and Johnnie they married to the Girl with Golden Hair, and the wedding was celebrated with joy and with many fair diversions.

*Forty-seven*

# The Goose-Girl

*German*

There was once an old queen whose husband had long since been dead and who had a beautiful daughter. As the latter grew up, she was betrothed to a king's son far away. When the time came for them to be married and the girl had to set out for the foreign country, the old queen packed up for her ever so many valuables and ornaments, gold and silver, tumblers and jewels, everything that belonged in a royal dowry, for she loved her child with all her heart. She also gave her a maid-in-waiting who was to ride with her and deliver her into the hands of the bridegroom. Each of them was given a horse for the journey; the princess' horse was named Falada and could talk. When the hour of departure was at hand, the old queen went to her bedroom, took a little knife and cut her fingers with it so that they bled. Then she put a piece of white cloth underneath and let three drops of blood fall upon it and, giving them to her daughter, said, "Dear child, keep them safely; you'll need them on the journey."

Thus they took sad farewell of one another. The king's daughter put the white cloth in her bosom, mounted her horse, and rode off to meet her bridegroom. When they'd been riding for an hour, she felt very thirsty and said to her maid-in-waiting, "Dismount and fill the tumbler you brought along for me with water from the brook; I'd very much like a drink." "If you're thirsty," said the maid-in-waiting, "get off yourself, lie down by the water, and drink. I don't care to be your servant." Then, because she was very thirsty, the king's daughter dismounted, stooped over the brook and drank, and wasn't allowed to drink out of the gold tumbler. As she exclaimed "Dear Lord!" the three drops of blood answered, "If your mother knew this, her heart within her would break." But the royal bride was meek, said nothing, and got on

From *German Folk Tales*, collected and edited by Grimm Brothers. Translated by Francis P. Magoun, Jr. and Alexander H. Krappe. Copyright © 1960, by Southern Illinois University Press. Reprinted by permission of the Southern Illinois University Press.

her horse again. Thus they rode on for some miles, but the day was warm, the sun scorching hot, and she soon got thirsty again. When they came to a stream, again she called out to her maid-in-waiting, "Dismount and give me a drink in my gold tumbler," for she'd long since forgotten all the unkind words. But the maid spoke even more haughtily, "If you want a drink, drink by yourself; I don't care to be your servant." Then being very thirsty, the king's daughter again dismounted, lay down by the running water, wept and said, "Dear Lord!" and the drops of blood again answered, "If your mother knew this, her heart within her would break." As she was drinking in this way and leaning way over, the piece of cloth with the three drops of blood fell out of her bosom and floated away with the current, and in her great anguish she didn't notice it. The maid-in-waiting had, however, been watching and rejoiced to gain control over the bride, for in losing the drops of blood she had become weak and helpless. Now when she was once again about to mount her horse, whose name was Falada, the maid said, "My place is on Falada and yours on my nag," and she had to put up with it. Then the maid brusquely ordered her to take off her royal garments and put on her poor clothes, and finally she had to swear most solemnly under the open sky that she'd say nothing about it to anybody at the royal court. Had she not sworn this oath, she'd have been killed on the spot. Falada saw all this and took good notice of it.

The maid now mounted Falada and the true bride got on the nag, and thus they continued until they finally reached the royal seat. There was great rejoicing there over their arrival, and the king's son hastened to meet them, lifted the maid-in-waiting down from her horse, and thought she was his spouse. She was escorted upstairs, while the true king's daughter had to stay downstairs. The old king was looking out the window and saw her stop in the courtyard and noticed how fair she was, and slender and really beautiful; he went at once to the royal apartment and asked the bride about the girl she had with her and who was standing below in the courtyard, and who she was. "I brought her along with me for company; give the girl some work to do so that she won't stand about idle." But the old king had no work for her and could only say, "I've a very little boy who tends the geese; she may help him." The boy's name was Conrad, and the true bride had to help him tend the geese.

Soon, however, the false bride said to the young king, "Dearest spouse, do me a favor, I beg you." "That I'll do gladly," he answered. "Then summon the skinner and have him cut off the neck of the horse I rode coming here, for it annoyed me on the way." As a matter of fact, she was afraid the horse might tell how she'd treated the king's daughter. When the plan was about to be carried out and faithful Falada was to die, word reached the ears of the true king's daughter, and she secretly promised to pay the skinner some money if he'd render her a small service. In the town was a big dark gateway through which morning and evening she had to pass with the geese, and "would he please nail up Falada's head under the dark gateway where she might see it a few times more." The skinner promised to do so, cut off the head, and nailed it fast under the dark gateway.

Early in the morning when she and Conrad were driving the geese out through the gateway, she said as she passed.

> "O Falada, there you hang!"

Then the head answered,

> "O young queen, there you go!
> And if your mother knew it,
> her heart would break."

In silence she went on out of the town, and they drove the geese into the country. When she came to the pasture, she sat down and undid her hair; it was pure gold, and Conrad saw it and liked the way it shone and was about to pull out a few hairs. Then she said,

> "Blow, blow, wind,
> carry off Conrad's cap
> and make him chase after it
> until I've braided it and fixed it
> and put it up again."

Then such a strong wind came up that it blew Conrad's cap far away, and he had to run after it. By the time he got back, she'd finished combing and putting it up, and he couldn't get hold of a single hair. Then Conrad was angry and didn't speak to her, and thus they tended the geese until evening came. Then they went home.

The next morning as they were driving the geese out through the dark gateway, the girl said,

"O Falada, there you hang!"

Falada answered,

"O young queen, there you go!
And if your mother knew it,
her heart would break."

Out in the country she sat down again in the pasture and began to comb out her hair, and Conrad ran up and was about to grab at it. Then she quickly said,

"Blow, blow, wind,
carry off Conrad's cap
and make him chase after it
until I've braided it and fixed it
and put it up again."

Then the wind blew, and it blew the cap off his head and blew it so far that Conrad had to run after it. And when he came back, she'd long since fixed her hair, and he couldn't get hold of a single strand. Thus they tended the geese until evening came.

In the evening, however, after they'd got home, Conrad went before the old king and said, "I don't want to tend geese with the girl any longer." "Why not?" asked the old king. "Oh, my! she aggravates me all day long." Then the old king ordered him to tell how he got on with her. Then Conrad said, "In the morning when we pass out with the flock through the dark gateway, there's a nag's head there on the wall, and she says to it,

"O Falada, there you hang!"

Then the head answers,

"O young queen, there you go!
And if your mother knew it,
her heart would break.' "

Thus Conrad went on and told what happened out in the pasture and how he had to run after his cap in the wind.

The old king ordered him to drive the geese out again the next day, and when it was morning, he himself took up a position behind the dark gateway and there heard her talking to Falada's head. Then he also followed her into the country and hid in some bushes in the pasture. There he soon saw with his own eyes how the goose girl and the goose boy drove the flock and how after a while she sat down and unbraided her hair, which shone brilliantly. Straightway she again said,

"Blow, blow, wind,
carry off Conrad's cap
and make him chase after it
until I've braided it and fixed it
and put it up again."

Then a gust of wind came and went off with Conrad's cap, so that he had to run a long way, while the girl kept on quietly combing and braiding her locks.

All this the old king observed. Then he went back without being noticed and in the evening, when the goose girl came home, he called her aside and asked her why she did all that. "That I may not tell you nor may I confide my sorrow to anyone, for I swore this most solemnly under the open sky; otherwise I should have lost my life." He pressed her and gave her no peace but could get nothing out of her. Then he said, "If you won't tell me anything, then confide your grief to the iron stove there," and went away. Then she crept into the iron stove, began to lament and weep, and poured out her heart, saying, "Here I sit abandoned by everyone and yet I'm a king's daughter; a false maid-in-waiting forced me to take off my royal clothes and has taken my place at the side of my betrothed, while as a goose-girl I must do menial work. If my mother knew it, her heart within her would break." The old king was, however, standing outside by the stovepipe, was listening to her, and heard what she said. Then he came back in and bade her come out of the stove. Then royal clothes were put on her, and she was so beautiful that it seemed a miracle.

The old king called his son and revealed to him the fact that he had a false bride who was nothing but a maid-in-waiting, and that the true bride was standing here, the former goose-girl. The young king was exceedingly happy on seeing her beauty and goodness, and a great feast was prepared to which everybody, all their good friends, were bidden. At the head of the table sat the bridegroom, with the king's daughter on one side, the maid-in-waiting on the other. But the maid-in-waiting was as if bedazzled and no longer recognized the former in her glittering jewels. When they had eaten and drunk and were in high spirits, the old king propounded a riddle to the maid-in-waiting: what punishment would a woman deserve who tricked her lord in such and such a way? At the same time he told the whole story and asked, "What verdict does she deserve?" Then the false bride said, "She deserves nothing better than to be stripped stark naked and put in a barrel studded inside with sharp nails; furthermore, two white horses must be hitched to it and drag her through street after street until she is dead." "You're the person," said the old king, "and you've pronounced your own sentence, and that's what will happen to you." When the verdict was carried out, the young king married the true bride, and both ruled their kingdom in peace and bliss.

*Forty-eight*

# Lord Peter

*Norwegian*

Once on a time there was a poor couple, and they had nothing in the world but three sons. What the names the two elder had I can't say, but the youngest he was called Peter. So when their father and mother died, the sons were to share what was left, but there was nothing but a porridge-pot, a griddle, and a cat.

The eldest, who was to have first choice, he took the pot; "for," said he, "whenever I lend the pot to any one to boil porridge, I can always get leave to scrape it."

The second took the griddle; "for," said he, "whenever I lend it to any one, I'll always get a morsel of dough to make a bannock."

But the youngest, he had no choice left him; if he was to choose anything it must be the cat.

"Well," said he, "if I lend the cat to any one I shan't get much by that; for if pussy gets a drop of milk, she'll want it all herself. Still, I'd best take her along with me; I shouldn't like her to go about here and starve."

So the brothers went out into the world to try their luck, and each took his own way; but when the youngest had gone a while, the cat said:

"Now you shall have a good turn, because you wouldn't let me stay behind in the old cottage and starve. Now, I'm off to the wood to lay hold of a fine fat head of game, and then you must go up to the king's palace that you see yonder, and say you are come with a little present for the king; and when he asks who sends it, you must say, 'Why, who should it be from but Lord Peter?' "

Well, Peter hadn't waited long before back came the cat with a reindeer from the wood; she had jumped up on the reindeer's head, between his horns, and said, "If you don't go straight to the king's palace I'll claw your eyes out."

So the reindeer had to go whether he liked it or no.

And when Peter got to the palace he went into the kitchen with the deer, and said: "Here I'm come with a little present for the king, if he won't despise it."

Then the king went out into the kitchen, and when he saw the fine plump reindeer, he was very glad.

"But, my dear friend," he said, "who in the world is it that sends me such a fine gift?"

"Oh!" said Peter, "who should send it but Lord Peter?"

"Lord Peter! Lord Peter!" said the king. "Pray tell me where he lives"; for he thought it a shame not to know so great a man. But that was just what the lad wouldn't tell him; he daren't do it, he said, because his master had forbidden him.

So the king gave him a good bit of money to drink his health, and bade him be sure and say all kind of pretty things, and many thanks for the present to his master when he got home.

Next day the cat went again into the wood, and jumped up on a red deer's head, and sat between his horns, and forced him to go to the palace. Then Peter went again into the kitchen, and said he was come with a little present for the king, if he would be pleased to take it. And the king was still more glad to get the red deer than he had been to get the reindeer, and asked again who it was that sent so fine a present.

"Why, it's Lord Peter, of course," said the lad; but when the king wanted to know where Lord Peter lived, he got the same answer as the day before; and this day, too, he gave Peter a good lump of money to drink his health with.

The third day the cat came with an elk. And so when Peter got into the palace-kitchen, and said he had a little present for the king, if he'd be pleased to take it, the king came out at once into the kitchen; and when he saw the grand big elk, he was so glad he scarce knew which leg to stand on; and this day, too, he gave Peter many many more dollars—at least a hundred. He wished now, once for all, to know where this Lord Peter lived, and asked and asked about this thing and that, but the lad said he daren't say, for his master's sake, who had strictly forbidden him to tell.

"Well, then," said the king, "beg Lord Peter to come and see me."

Yes, the lad would take that message; but when Peter got out into the yard again, and met the cat, he said:

"A pretty scrape you've got me into now, for here's the king, who wants me to come and see him, and you know I've nothing to go in but these rags I stand and walk in."

"Oh, don't be afraid about that," said the cat; "in three days you shall have coach and horses, and fine clothes, so fine that the gold falls from them, and then you may go and see the king very well. But mind, whatever you see in the king's palace, you must say you have far finer and grander things of your own. Don't forget that."

No, no, Peter would bear that in mind, never fear.

So when three days were over, the cat came with a coach and horses, and clothes, and all that Peter wanted, and altogether it was as grand as anything you ever set eyes on; so off he set, and the cat ran alongside the coach. The king met him well and graciously; but whatever the king offered him, and whatever he showed him, Peter said, 'twas all very well, but he had far finer and better things in his own house. The king seemed not quite to believe this, but Peter stuck to what he said, and at last the king got so angry, he couldn't bear it any longer.

"Now I'll go home with you," he said, "and see if it be true what you've been telling me, that you have far finer and better things of your own. But if you've been telling a pack of lies, Heaven help you, that's all I say."

"Now, you've got me into a fine scrape," said Peter to the cat, "for here's the king coming home with me; but my home, that's not so easy to find, I think."

"Oh! never mind," said the cat; "only do you drive after me as I run before."

So off they set; first Peter, who drove after his cat, and then the king and all his court.

But when they had driven a good bit, they came to a great flock of fine sheep, that had wool so long it almost touched the ground.

"If you'll only say," said the cat to the shepherd, "this flock of sheep belongs to Lord Peter, when the king asks you, I'll give you this silver spoon," which she had taken with her from the king's palace.

Yes, he was willing enough to do that. So when the king came up, he said to the lad who watched the sheep:

"Well, I never saw so large and fine a flock of sheep in my life! Whose is it, my little lad?"

"Why," said the lad, "whose should it be but Lord Peter's?"

A little while after they came to a great, great herd of fine brindled kine, who were all so sleek the sun shone from them.

"If you'll only say," said the cat to the neat-herd, "this herd is Lord Peter's, when the king asks you, I'll give you this silver ladle"; and the ladle too she had taken from the king's palace.

"Yes, with all my heart," said the neat-herd.

So when the king came up, he was quite amazed at the fine fat herd, for such a herd he had never seen before, and so he asked the neat-herd who owned those brindled kine.

"Why, who should own them but Lord Peter?" said the neat-herd.

So they went on a little farther, and came to a great, great drove of horses, the finest you ever saw, six of each color, bay, and black, and brown, and chestnut.

"If you'll only say this drove of horses is Lord Peter's when the king asks you," said the cat, "I'll give you this silver goblet"; and the goblet too she had taken from the palace.

Yes, the lad was willing enough; and so when the king came up, he was quite amazed at the grand drove of horses, for the matches of such horses he had never yet set eyes on, he said.

So he asked the lad who watched them, whose all these blacks, and bays, and browns, and chestnuts were.

"Whose should they be," said the lad, "but Lord Peter's?"

So when they had gone a good bit farther, they came to a castle; first there was a gate of tin, and next a gate of silver, and next a gate of gold. The castle itself was of silver, and so dazzling white, that it quite hurt one's eyes to look at in the sunbeams which fell on it just as they reached it.

So they went into it, and the cat told Peter to say this was his house. As for the castle inside, it was far finer than it looked outside, for everything was pure gold—chairs, and tables, and benches, and all. And when the king had gone all over it, and seen everything high and low, he got quite shameful and downcast.

"Yes," he said at last; "Lord Peter has everything far finer than I have, there's no gainsaying that," and so he wanted to be off home again.

But Peter begged him to stay to supper, and the king stayed, but he was sour and surly the whole time.

So as they sat at supper, back came the troll who owned the castle, and gave such a great knock at the door.

"WHO'S THIS EATING MY MEAT AND DRINKING MY MEAD LIKE SWINE IN HERE?" roared out the troll.

As soon as the cat heard that, she ran down to the gate.

"Stop a bit," she said, "and I'll tell you how the farmer sets to work to get in his winter rye."

And so she told him such a long story about the winter rye.

"First of all, you see, he plows his field, and then he dungs it, and then he plows it again, and then he harrows it"; and so she went on till the sun rose.

"Oh, do look behind you, and there you'll see such a lovely lady," said the cat to the troll.

So the troll turned round, and, of course, as soon as he saw the sun he burst.

"Now all this is yours," said the cat to Lord Peter. "Now, you must cut off my head; that's all I ask for what I have done for you."

"Nay, nay," said Lord Peter, "I'll never do any such thing, that's flat."

"If you don't," said the cat, "see if I don't claw your eyes out."

Well, so Lord Peter had to do it, though it was sore against his will. He cut off the cat's head, but there and then she became the loveliest princess you ever set eyes on, and Lord Peter fell in love with her at once.

"Yes, all this greatness was mine first," said the princess, "but a troll bewitched me to be a cat in your father's and mother's cottage. Now you may do as you please, whether you take me as your queen or not, for you are now king over all this realm."

Well, well, there was little doubt Lord Peter would be willing enough to have her as his queen, and so there was a wedding that lasted eight whole days, and a feast besides, and after it was over I stayed no longer with Lord Peter and his lovely queen, and so I can't say anything more about them.

*Forty-nine*

# The Gold Bird

*German*

In olden times there was a king who had beautiful grounds behind his palace. In the grounds stood a tree which bore gold apples. When the apples got ripe, they were counted, but the very next morning one was missing. This was reported to the king, and he ordered that watch be kept under the tree every night. The king had three sons, and as night came on, he sent the eldest to the garden. When it was midnight he couldn't fight off sleep, and the following morning another apple was again missing. The next night the second son had to mount watch but fared no better. When it struck twelve, he fell asleep, and in the morning an apple was missing. Now it was the third son's turn to stand watch. He, too, was quite willing, but the king didn't have much confidence in him, thinking that he'd accomplish even less than his brothers. Finally, however, he gave his permission, so the youth lay down under the tree, kept watch, and didn't let sleep overpower him. When it struck twelve, something rustled in the air, and in the light of the moon he saw a bird flying along whose feathers shone with solid gold. The bird lighted on the tree and had just pecked off an apple when the youth shot an arrow at it. The bird flew away, but the arrow had struck its plumage, and one of its gold feathers dropped down. The youth picked it up, took it next morning to the king, and told him what he'd seen in the night. The king assembled his council, and everyone declared that a feather like this was worth more than the whole kingdom. "If the feather is so precious," said the king, "I shan't be satisfied with just one but will and must have the whole bird."

The eldest son set out, trusting to his cleverness, and thought he'd surely find the gold bird. When he'd gone some distance, he saw a fox sitting by the edge of the forest and, leveling his gun,

From *German Folk Tales*, collected and edited by Grimm Brothers. Translated by Francis P. Magoun, Jr. and Alexander H. Krappe. Copyright © 1960, by Southern Illinois University Press. Reprinted by permission of the Southern Illinois University Press.

took aim at it. "If you don't shoot me," cried the fox, "I'll give you a good piece of advice in return. You're on your way to the gold bird and this evening you'll come to a village where two inns face one another. One will be brightly lighted and fun will be going on there. Don't turn in there but go into the other, even though it's of mean appearance." "How can such a silly creature be giving me sensible advice?" thought the king's son, and pulled the trigger. But he missed the fox, which, straightening out its tail, ran quickly into the forest. Then he continued on his way and in the evening came to the village with the two inns. In one there was singing and dancing, while the other had a poor and sorry appearance. "I'd certainly be a fool," he thought, "if I went into the shabby inn and avoided the fine one." So he entered the gay inn, led a merry life there, and forgot the bird, his father, and all good advice.

When some time had passed and the eldest son didn't come home and didn't come home, the second son set out to look for the gold bird. Like the eldest he met the fox, who gave him the good advice, which he didn't heed. He came to the two inns, at the window of one of which his brother was standing and from which the noise of revelry resounded. His brother called out to him, and he couldn't resist the temptation, went in, and did nothing but gratify his desires.

Again some time passed. Then the king's youngest son wanted to set out and try his luck. But his father wouldn't allow it, saying, "It's useless; he's even less likely to find the gold bird than his brothers, and if he meets with an accident, he won't know what to do. He hasn't got it in him." Finally, however, when the boy left him no peace, he let him set out. Again the fox was sitting outside the forest, begged for its life, and gave the good piece of advice. The youth was goodhearted and said, "Don't worry, little fox, I won't hurt you." "You won't regret it," answered the fox, "and, to get on faster, climb onto my tail." No sooner had he sat down than the fox began to race at full speed, so that the wind whistled through his hair. When they came to the village, the youth got off, acted on the good advice, and without looking about, went into the mean inn, where he quietly spent the night.

Next morning when he came out into the field, the fox was already sitting there and said, "I'm going to tell you what else you've got to do. Keep going straight on; finally you'll reach a palace before which a whole troop of soldiers will be lying. However, pay no attention to them, for they will all be sleeping and snoring. Walk right through them and straight into the palace. Go through all the rooms, and finally you'll reach a chamber where there's a gold bird in a wooden cage. Beside it is an empty gold cage just there as an ornament, but be careful not to take the bird out of its poor cage and put it in the splendid cage, otherwise you'll come to grief." After these words the fox again straightened out its tail and the king's son sat down on it; then they raced at full speed, so that the wind whistled through his hair. Arriving at the palace, he found everything as the fox had said. The king's son came to the chamber where the gold bird was in the wooden cage while a gold cage stood beside it, and three golden apples were lying about in the room. He thought it would be ridiculous to leave the beautiful bird in the mean and ugly cage, opened the cage door, took hold of it, and put it in the gold cage. At that very moment, however, the bird uttered a piercing cry. The soldiers awoke, rushed in, and took him off to prison. Next morning he was brought to trial and, since he confessed to everything, was sentenced to death. But the king said he'd grant him his life on the condition that he'd fetch him the gold horse which was swifter than the wind; in that case he should receive as a reward the gold bird in addition to his life.

The king's son set out, but he sighed and was sad, for where would he find the gold horse? All of a sudden he saw his old friend the fox sitting by the wayside. "You see," said the fox, "it happened that way because you didn't listen to me. But take heart, I'll champion your cause and tell you how to get to the gold horse. You must go straight ahead and you'll come to a palace where the horse is stabled. The grooms will be lying outside the stable but will be sleeping and snoring, and you may take the gold horse right out. But you must be careful about one thing: put the mean wood and leather saddle on it, not the gold saddle which is hanging near by, otherwise you'll get into trouble." Then the fox straightened out its tail, the king's son sat down on it, and off they raced at full speed, so that the wind whistled through his hair. Everything happened as the fox had said: he went into the stable where the gold horse was standing, but when he was about to put the mean saddle on it, he thought, "A beautiful animal like that will be insulted if I don't put on the fine saddle to which it's entitled." But scarcely had the gold saddle touched the horse than it began to neigh loudly. The grooms woke up, seized the youth, and threw him into prison. Next morning he was sentenced to death by the court, but the king promised to grant him his life and the gold horse in the bargain if he could fetch the beautiful princess from the gold palace.

With heavy heart the youth set out but by good luck soon found the faithful fox. "I should now abandon you to your misfortune," said the fox, "but I'm sorry for you and once more will help you out of your difficulty. Your way leads straight to the gold palace. You'll arrive there in the evening, and at night when all is still, the beautiful princess will go to the bathhouse to take her bath there. When she goes in, rush at her and give her a kiss; then she'll follow you, and you'll be able to take her away with you. But don't think of letting her first take leave of her parents, otherwise you'll get into trouble." Then the fox straightened out its tail, the king's son sat down on it, and off they raced at full speed, so that the wind whistled through his hair. When he got to the gold palace, it was as the fox had said. He waited till about midnight when everybody was fast asleep and the fair damsel went to the bathhouse; then he rushed out and gave her a kiss. She said she'd gladly go with him but implored him with tears in her eyes to permit her first to take leave of her parents. At first he resisted her request, but when she kept on weeping and fell at his feet, he finally gave in. No sooner had the damsel stepped up to her father's bedside than the latter and everybody else in the palace woke up, and the youth was arrested and put in prison.

Next morning the king said to him, "Your life is forfeit, and you'll be pardoned only if you remove the mountain which is before my windows and blocks my view, and that you must accomplish within eight days. If you succeed, you shall have my daughter as a reward." The king's son set to work, dug and shoveled unceasingly, but when after seven days he saw how little he'd accomplished and that all his labor amounted to so much as nothing, he fell into a state of great depression and gave up all hope. In the evening of the seventh day, however, the fox appeared and said, "You don't deserve my championing your cause; all the same, just go over there and go to sleep. I'll do the work for you." Next morning when he woke up and looked out the window, the mountain had disappeared. Joyfully the youth went to the king and reported that his condition had been fulfilled, and whether he would or no, the king had to keep his word and give him his daughter.

The two set out together, and before long the faithful fox joined them. "True enough, you've got the best thing," it said, "but with the damsel from the gold castle goes the gold horse, too." "How am I to get that?" asked the youth, "I'll tell you," answered the fox, "first of all take the fair damsel to the king who sent you to the gold castle. There'll be tremendous rejoicing; they'll gladly give you the gold horse and will lead it out to you. Mount it at once and shake everybody's hand good-bye, last of all the fair damsel's. When you've got hold of her, pull her up in one motion and race away. No one will be able to overtake you, for the horse is swifter than the wind."

Everything was accomplished successfully, and the king's son took the fair damsel away on the gold horse. The fox didn't stay behind but said to the youth, "Now I'll help you get the gold bird, too. When you're close to the palace where the bird is, have the damsel dismount, and I'll take her under my protection. Then ride the gold horse into the palace yard. On seeing this there will be great rejoicing, and they'll bring you out the gold bird. When you have the cage in your hand, race back to us and take the damsel away with you again." When the plan had succeeded and the king's son was about to ride home with his treasures, the fox said, "Now you are to reward me for my help." "What do you demand for that?" said the youth. "When we reach the forest over there, shoot me dead and cut off my head and my paws." "That would be a fine expression of gratitude," said the king's son, "I can't possibly grant you that." "If you won't do it," said the fox, "then I must leave you. But before I go, I'll give you a good piece of advice. Beware of two things: don't ransom anybody from the gallows and don't sit down on the edge of any well." With that it ran into the forest.

The youth thought, "That's a queer animal with strange notions. Who'd ransom a man from the gallows! And I've never had the slightest desire to sit down on the edge of a well." He rode on with the fair damsel, and his way again led him through the village where his two brothers had stayed. There was a great noise and uproar there, and when he asked what the matter was, they said that two people were to be hanged. On coming nearer he saw that they were his two brothers who had been up to all sorts of bad tricks and had squandered all their possessions. He asked if there wasn't some way to ransom them. "If you're willing to pay for them," answered the people, "but why should you want to waste your money on these evil-doers and ransom them?" However, he didn't hesitate, bought them off, and when they'd been released, they continued their journey in company.

They came to a forest where they'd first met the fox, and since it was cool and pleasant there and the sun very hot, the two brothers said, "Let's rest here a bit by the well and eat and drink." He agreed and in the course of the conversation forgot himself and sat down on the edge of the well, suspecting no harm. But the two brothers pushed him backward into the well, took the damsel, the horse, and the bird, and rode home to their father. "Here we're bringing not only the gold bird," they said, "but we've also got the gold horse and the damsel from the gold palace." There was great rejoicing, but the horse didn't eat, the bird didn't sing, and the damsel sat and wept.

The youngest brother had not perished, however. Fortunately the well was dry, and he landed on soft moss without being hurt, though he couldn't get out again. Even in this predicament the faithful fox didn't desert him but jumped down to where he was and scolded him for having forgotten his advice. "Nevertheless, I can't leave it at that," it said, "I'll help you to the light of day again." It told him to take hold of its tail and to hold onto it tight, and then it pulled him out. "Even now you're not altogether out of danger," said the fox. "Your brothers weren't certain of your death and all around the forest have mounted guards who are to kill you if you show yourself." A poor man was sitting by the wayside, with whom the youth changed clothes and thus reached the king's court. No one recognized him, but the bird began to sing, the horse to eat, and the fair damsel stopped weeping. Astonished, the king asked, "What can that mean?" The damsel said, "I don't know, but I was so sad and now I'm so happy. I feel as though my true bridegroom had come." She told him all that had happened, though the other brothers had threatened her with death should she give anything away. The king ordered all the people in the palace to be brought into his presence, and the youth, too, came in his ragged clothes in the guise of a poor beggar. The damsel, however, recognized him at once and fell on his neck. The wicked brothers were seized and executed, while he was married to the fair damsel and named the king's heir.

But what happened to the poor fox? A long time afterward the king's son once again went into the forest where he met the fox, who said, "Now you have everything you can wish for, but to my misfortune there's no end, and yet it's in your power to unspell me." Once again it implored him to shoot it and to cut off its head and its paws. Accordingly he did so, and no sooner was it done than the fox turned into a man and was none other than the brother of the fair princess, freed at last from the spell under which he'd lain. And now there was no limit to their happiness as long as they lived.

*Fifty*

# The Well at the World's End

*Irish*

Once there was a king that had three sons, and he was so sick that no one thought he'd ever recover. They went to consult a wise old hermit that lived in a wood near, and he said that nothing would cure the king but a draught from the World's-End water. So the eldest son thought to himself: "I'll set out to bring this drink, and then I'll be sure to get all the kingdom from my father when he's about to die." So he got leave from his father and set out. He went first to the hermit, and asked him whereabouts was the "End of the World," and the hermit gave him directions how he'd go to it. He was to cross seven seas, and seven lakes, and seven rivers, and seven mountains, and seven hills, and seven commons, and then he'd see before him a castle of brass, and all he knew farther was that the Well of the World's-End water was in the garden of that castle.

So the prince set out, and one day he sat down by the way side to eat some bread and cold meat. Up came a poor, ragged, withered old woman, and asked him to give her a bit to keep the life in her. "Go away, you old hag, out of that!" said he, "I have nothing for you." "Well, well," said she; "God help the poor! But would your Majesty tell a poor body where you're going?" "What's that to you, you old witch?" said he again; "go about your business, and don't be bothering me!" "Well, prince," said she, "your birth is better than your manners anyhow. Still, for sake of the king and queen that owns you, I'll give you an advice. Never blow your bugle till you first draw your sword, and when you're on duty resist temptation." "Thank you for nothing," said he. "I've got enough of you." So she went away, muttering.

Well, when he passed the remaining hills and commons and lakes and rivers, he saw far off the castle of brass, and in good time he arrived at it. There was a bugle horn hanging by the door, and, without minding the old woman's advice, he put it to his mouth and blew it without thinking of his sword. Open flew the door, and out on him rushed two lions roaring like thunder. He thought to pull out his sword, but they kept on biting and scratching and tearing him till he thought he was done for. "Go then," says one of them. "You are a bad prince, but you are on a good business, and we'll give you your life." Well, he stumbled in, and there he was in a long hall, and at each side were standing fifty knights in armor, holding up their spears, and all dead asleep. His heart beat, but he passed on, and in the next hall there was a beautiful princess with a crown on her head, and she sitting on a throne. He approached her, and made all sorts of nice speeches to her, but she reminded him of the business he was on, and told him there was no time to be lost. "After passing through the next hall," said she, "you will be in the garden where the well of the World's-End water springs. If you are not out of the castle with your bottle full before the clock strikes twelve, there's a heavy doom hanging over you."

In the next hall there was a table laid out with the finest food and drink the prince ever saw, and he was so tired with walking, and so spent in his struggle with the lions, that he fell to. The clock still wanted a quarter; he'd have time enough. When it was two minutes before the hour he went into the garden, and he was so hot, and it was so delightful in the shade, for the well was under a tree, that he sat down on a garden seat, and felt that it would be as much as his life was worth to be obliged to leave it. While he was half dozing, the clock began to strike. Oh, murder! he began to fill the bottle as fast as he could, but it was on the seventh stroke before he had it filled. Seven, eight, nine, ten—he was in the dining room, and in the lady's room. It was eleven when he was running into the knight's hall, but he was only in the middle of it when bang went twelve, and the knights struck the ends of their spears on the ground, and came round him in a ring. What could his single sword do against so many? He hadn't even power to draw it. A rough fellow with a bush of red hair on his head came in, and tied him hand and foot, and threw him into a dungeon.

Well, his place was empty at home for half a year, and then his next brother set out; and to make a long story short, he behaved the same way and got the same treatment. Last of all the youngest set off, and very differently he behaved to the poor old woman, and she gave him when they were parting two cakes, and told him what to do with them.

When he reached the castle he drew the sword, and then blew the bugle horn. Open flew the doors, and out rushed the lions. But he held out a cake to each beast, and down they sat like two lambs to eat them. He went through the first hall, and went on one knee before the lady in the second. There was pleasure on her face at the sight of him, but she told him there was no delay to be made. So he passed through the next room without taking bit or sup, though he felt as hungry and thirsty as he could be. The greatest temptation was on him when he went into the garden—he was so hot and faint—to sit on the seat and enjoy the cool, but he didn't give way. He filled his bottle and returned through the dining hall without sitting down to refresh himself. He would have stopped to speak to the lady, but she warned him away, and he had no temptation to stop between the two rows of men in the iron armor. He passed the lions who were still eating their cakes, and when he closed the door after him he blew the bugle with all his force. The sound came out like thunder where the rocks are on every side, and before it ceased, down came the castle as if the sky was falling. The stones never sunk into the earth, they vanished after seeming to fall a little, though the noise they made was frightful. When all was cleared, there was neither lions, nor armed men, nor loaded tables to be seen. The princess was sitting on a grassy ridge, and the two brothers lying unbound in a furrow.

There was great joy among the four, for the princess was released from enchantment as well as the brothers from their chains. They set out for the palace, but they were met on the road by a coach and horses, which the princess said were sent by a powerful friend she had. The elder brothers saw that either of them had little chance to be her husband: so at times they plotted together, and when they were near home, at the very spot where the old woman met with them all, they fell on their youngest brother, tied him neck and heels, and left him inside the wood to die of pain and hunger. The princess gave one cry when she saw her prince seized, but never opened her mouth after till they reached the palace. The brothers then made her swear that she would never reveal who got the water, or what became of the youngest prince, and she did so without the smallest objection.

Well, there was great joy in the palace when the princes and the beautiful lady arrived, and when they told that they returned with the water. They said they knew nothing of their youngest brother, and that made the king sad. However, the eldest son called for a cup of gold, and poured in some of the water, and handed it to his father. He drank some of it, but laid down the cup in a moment. He said he was seized with a colic, and cried out with the pain. "Let me give the drink," said the second eldest, "you know it was I that got it." He took up the cup and handed it to the king; but as bad as he was before, he was twice worse now; and how the brothers looked at one another! They begged the princess to hand the cup next, but she didn't seem to hear them. Well, all were at their wits' end, when in walked a tall beggarwoman and her son, and both in rags. "Will your Majesty allow this young man to hand you the cup?" "Oh, if it is of any use, let him do so; but if not, he'll be torn between wild horses." "Oh, very well." The young man went forward, and presented the cup, but the king turned all manner of colors, and twisted his face into a dozen of forms before he'd let it to his lips again. The moment he swallowed one sup his late pains left him, and his old sickness was gone, and he stood up in perfect health. He was about opening his mouth to thank the boy and his mother, but she touched him with a rod she had in her hands, and his rags were gone, and there was the youngest prince in his own dress, and as handsome as the May!

A fine looking woman was where the beggar stood a minute since, and she wasn't long about explaining the whole wickedness of the brothers. They looked for all the world like two dogs that had lost their tails, and seemed to wish to sink into the ground. They were banished the same day from the court, and the next day came on the marriage of the youngest son with the enchanted lady.

*Fifty-one*

# The Goldfish

*Russian*

Near the shore of an island in the ocean stood a small, dilapidated hut; in this hut lived an old man and his wife. They lived in dire poverty. The old man made himself a net and began to catch fish in the sea, for that was his only means of livelihood. One day the old man cast his net and began to pull on it; it seemed to him heavier than it had ever been before—he could barely drag it out. He looked, and the net was empty; there was only one fish in it. It was not an ordinary fish, but a goldfish. The goldfish implored him in a human voice: "Do not take me, old man. Let me go back into the blue sea; I will return your kindness by doing whatever you wish." The old man thought and thought and said: "I do not want anything of you; go back to the sea!" He threw the goldfish into the water and returned home. His wife asked him: "Did you get a big catch, old man?" "Only one little goldfish," the old man replied, "and even that I threw back into the sea—it implored me so earnestly, saying, 'Let me go back into the blue sea, and I will return your kindness by doing whatever you wish.' I took pity on the little fish, I did not demand anything of it but let it go free, for nothing." "Ah, you old devil!" said his wife. "You had a great chance but did not know how to take advantage of it."

The old woman became full of spite, abused her husband from dawn to dark, and did not give him a minute's rest. "At least you should have asked for some bread! Soon we won't even have a dry crust. What will you eat then?" The old man could not bear it any longer and went to the goldfish to ask for bread. He came to the sea and cried in a loud voice: "Goldfish, goldfish, stand with your tail to the sea, and your head to me!" The goldfish came to the shore. "What do you want, old man?" he asked. "My wife is furious at me, she sent me to you to get some bread." "Go home, you will find plenty of bread." The old man returned. "Well, wife, do we have plenty of bread?" he asked her. "We have plenty of bread, but we have this trouble: our trough broke, I have nothing to do my washing in. Go to the goldfish and ask him to give us a new trough." The old man went to the sea, and said: "Goldfish, goldfish, stand with your tail to the sea, and your head to me!" The goldfish came, saying: "What do you want, old man?" "My wife sent me to ask you for a new trough." "Very well, you will have a new trough." The old man returned and as soon as he crossed the threshold his wife again beset him. "Go to the goldfish," she said, "ask him to build us a new house; it is impossible to live in this one—any minute, it may fall apart."

The old man went to the sea. "Goldfish, goldfish," he said, "stand with your tail to the sea, and your head to me!" The fish came, stood with his head to the old man, and his tail to the sea, and asked: "What do you want, old man?" "Build us a new house. My wife scolds me and does not give me any rest. 'I don't want to live in this old hut,' she says, 'it may fall apart any minute.'" "Grieve not, old man, go home and pray to God; everything will be done." The old man returned, and on his plot stood a new oaken house, richly carved. His wife ran out to meet him; she was even angrier than before and abused him roundly. "You old dog, you don't know how to take advantage of your luck. Just because you have got a new house, you think you have accomplished something! Now, go back to the goldfish and say to it that I don't want to be a peasant—I want to be a governor, so that law-abiding men will obey me and bow from their waists when they meet me."

The old man went to the sea and in a loud voice: "Goldfish, goldfish, stand with your tail to the sea, and your head to me!" The goldfish came, stood with its tail to the sea, and its head to him. "What do you want, old man?" he asked. The old man answered: "My wife gives me no peace, she has become quite foolish; she does not want to be a peasant woman, she wants to be a governor." "Very well, grieve not, go home and pray to God: everything will be done." The old man returned, and instead of a wooden house there was a stone house of three stories; servants ran about in the courtyard, cooks bustled in the kitchen, and the old woman, dressed in rich brocade, sat on a high-backed chair and gave orders. "Good day, wife," said the old man. "You boor, how dare you call me, the governor, your wife? Hey there, you servants! Take this peasant to the stable and whip him as hard as you can!"

The servants ran up, seized the old man by his collar, and dragged him to the stable, and there the stable boys began to thrash him with whips; they thrashed him so hard that he could barely stand on his feet. Then the old woman appointed the old man to be her janitor; she ordered a broom to be given him to sweep the yard, and he had to eat and drink in the kitchen. The old man led a miserable life. All day long he had to clean the yard; if any dirt was discovered, he was led to the stable. "What a witch!" thought the old man. "She has found a comfortable hole and dug herself in like a sow; she does not even consider me her husband any longer."

Some time passed; the old woman became weary of being governor, summoned the old man before her, and ordered: "Go to the goldfish, old devil, and tell him that I don't want to be a governor, I want to be a queen." The old man went to the sea and said: "Goldfish, goldfish, stand with your tail to the sea, and your head to me!" The goldfish came. "What do you want, old man?" he asked. "My wife has become even more foolish," the old man answered. "She no longer wants to be a governor, she wants to be a queen." "Grieve not, go home and pray to God: everything will be done." The old man returned, and instead of the house he found a lofty castle with a golden roof; around it sentries walked and presented arms. Behind the castle was a large garden, and in front of it was a green meadow; in the meadow troops were gathered. The old woman was dressed like a queen; she came out on the balcony with generals and boyars and began to review the troops. The drums thundered, the band played, the soldiers cried "Hurrah!"

After some time the old woman became weary of being a queen; she ordered the old man to be found and brought into her august presence. A tumult arose, the generals bustled about, the boyars ran everywhere. "What old man?" they asked. At long last he was found in the backyard and led before the queen. "Listen, you old devil," she said to him. "Go to the goldfish and say to him that I don't want to be a queen. I want to be the ruler of the sea, so that all the seas and all the fishes will obey me." The old man tried to refuse, but in vain. "If you do not go," she said, "your head will roll."

Taking his courage in his hands the old man went to the sea. When he came there he said: "Goldfish, goldfish, stand with your tail to the sea, and your head to me!" The goldfish did not come. The old man called a second time—still the goldfish did not come. He called a third time, and suddenly the sea began to roll and roar; it had been bright and clear a moment before but now it grew quite black. The fish came to the shore. "What do you want, old man?" he asked. "My wife has become even more foolish. She no longer wants to be a queen, she wants to be the ruler of the sea, to rule over all the waters and command all the fishes." The goldfish did not say anything to the old man but turned around and went down to the depths of the sea. The old man returned home, and when he looked, he could not believe his eyes. The castle was gone as though it had never been there, and in its place stood a small, dilapidated hut, and in the hut sat his wife in a ragged dress. They began to live as before. The old man again took to catching fish; but no matter how often he cast his net into the sea, he never could catch the goldfish again.

*Fifty-two*

# The Grateful Animals and the Talisman

*Greek*

Once there was a woman, and she had an only child, a little boy. This boy never came out of the house at all, but sat on the dusty floor close by the ashes; so his mother called him Cinderello.

One day his mother said to him: "Come, my little lad, go out for a while." Cinderello said: "Give me a farthing and I will." His mother gave him a farthing; he took it and out he went. As soon as he came out into the road he came upon some children, who were about to kill a puppy. He said to them: "Come, children, give the puppy to me and I will give you a farthing." He gave them the farthing and took the puppy and brought it home.

Another day his mother again said: "Come, my little lad, go

From *Modern Greek Folktales*, edited by R. M. Dawkins. Reprinted by permission of the Clarendon Press, Oxford.

out for a while." Cinderello said: "Give me another farthing and I will." She gave him a farthing; Cinderello took it and went out. As he was passing along the road again he met some children about to kill a kitten. He said: "Give the kitten to me and I will give you this farthing." He took the kitten and paid over the farthing. The kitten he took home and there again he sat down in the dust.

One day his mother again said to him: "Come, my little lad; you go out for a while." Cinderello said: "Give me another farthing and I will go." His mother gave him a farthing and Cinderello went out. As he was walking he again met some children about to kill a snake. He said: "Give the snake to me and I will give you this farthing." He gave them the farthing and took the snake also to his house.

So he reared the three animals, and when they had grown big, one day the snake said to him: "Come now, take me to my own country." Cinderello rose up and followed the snake, and off they went. On the way the snake turned around and said: "I have a father, and he is the king of the snakes. Now when we go there, all the snakes will throw themselves upon you, but you must not be afraid. I will call out to them and they will leave you alone. Then when you go into my father's house he will want to give you many gifts because you rescued me, but you must refuse to accept any of them and ask only for the ring which he has underneath his tongue."

They went there, and the little snake gave one hiss and snakes started to come to them, more and more; the whole place was full of snakes. Among them was a big snake which was their king. When the snakes saw Cinderello they rushed upon him to devour him. He cried out to the little snake and they fell back. Then the snake went to his father and said: "This boy, my father, saved me from death; by now I would have been dead and forgotten. So today I have brought him here for you to give him whatever he may ask of you." The great snake took him to his house and said: "What favor do you want from me for saving my little son?" Cinderello said: "I do not want anything, except this: I would like the ring which you keep underneath your tongue." Then said the king of the snakes: "This is a great thing you ask, yet to please my son you may have it." Cinderello took the ring and went off.

On the way he was thirsty. "The snake," said he, "offered me all those things and I took nothing except only this ring, and now here I am dying of thirst." In anger he dashed the ring down and ran on. As he did this there jumped out from the ring a black man, who said: "What are your commands, master?" "What commands?" said the boy. "I want something to eat." Quickly the black man set a table and served food and wine; all you could wish. When Cinderello had done eating, the black man cleared everything away and went back again into the ring. The boy took up the ring and went to his village. He set his mother to go and make a proposal for his marriage to the king's daughter.

The king said: "If in a certain place your son can satisfy with food all the men in my realm, then I will accept him as my daughter's husband. I grant him a term of forty days. If within the forty days he does not do this, I will have his head." The mother went and told him. Now the days were passing by; Cinderello sat at ease paying no heed to the matter. At the end of the thirty-ninth day the king sent him a notice that the days were coming to an end and he must not pretend that he had forgotten about it. The boy sent a message back that he knew all about it and that the king was not to be uneasy. When the forty days were up, he took the ring and went to the place where he was to provide food for the multitude. He dashed down the ring; out came the black man and said: "What are your commands, master?" "I want you," said he, "to set out food to eat, everywhere." The people went and ate and there was even food left over.

Then again the king said to Cinderello's mother: "If," said he, "your son can cover with gold coins a straight path all the way from your door to my door, again within a term of forty days, then I will accept him as my son-in-law." Again when the forty days were over the boy dashed the ring down and ordered the black man quickly to make a path laid with gold coin from their door all the way to the palace, and this to be done before the king rose up in the morning. The black man fell to the work and before you could count three he had done it. The king rose up and opened his window; lo his eyes were dazzled by the brightness of the path.

Once more the king sent for the boy's mother and said: "One more thing your son must do and then I will make him my son-in-law. I want him to make a tower finer than my own. Again I grant him a term of forty days. If he cannot do this, I will have his head." Not to make a long story of it, at the end of the forty days the boy once more dashed down the ring; the black man came out and built a tower very much finer than the king's. In the morning the king opened his window and saw it; it was all made of gold. Then the king went and took Cinderello and married him to his daughter. In the tower he set a blackamoor to guard them.

In order not to lose the ring Cinderello kept it always in his mouth. Then the blackamoor who was their guard and Cinderello's wife made a pact between them. The blackamoor said to the wife: "Can you," said he, "take the ring from his mouth and bring it here to me?" The wife went off and when her husband was asleep contrived to get the ring out of his mouth. Then she gave it to the guard. As soon as he had it in his hand he dashed it down, and the black man came out of it and said: "What are your commands, master?" "When he is asleep," said the blackamoor, "you must take this man up, bed and all, and put him out in the road without his being aware of it. Then you must pull down this tower and set it up in the midst of the sea and in it there must be no one but me and my wife." The black man of the ring pulled down the tower, threw poor Cinderello out into the road, and set up the tower in the midst of the sea, putting in it the blackamoor guard and Cinderello's wife. In the morning Cinderello woke up and found that he had been sleeping in the road and that he no longer had with him either his wife or the ring. At once he rose up and with tears went to the king and made his complaints. Then the poor fellow went home lamenting.

Some days passed. "This," said Cinderello, "I can endure no longer. I must go off and find what fate has in store for me." He took the puppy and the little cat and went off. As he was passing by the shore of the sea, the cat saw a great wave in the midst of the sea. She said to Cinderello: "Will you give us leave to go and see what this is in the sea?" Cinderello gave them leave. The dog with the cat on his back swam over the sea and came to the tower. The cat climbed up to the roof. On that very evening the mice were celebrating a wedding. The cat made a dash at them and caught the bridegroom. He said: "Let me go and whatever you want I will do." "Can you," said the cat, "get me the ring from out of the master's mouth?" "I can," said the mouse. So he went and dipped his tail into the honey and then went and rolled it about in the pepper. Then he went and stuck it into the blackamoor's nose as he lay asleep. The blackamoor sneezed; out flew the ring. The mouse carried it off to the cat, and the cat took it and went down from the roof and told the dog of her success.

Then the cat mounted on the dog's back, and he plunged in to swim; thus they would take the ring back to Cinderello. When they were nearly there, the dog said: "Let me hold the ring too; I want to see it." The cat would not and the dog threatened to let her fall into the sea. The cat was frightened and let him have it. How did they do then? Well, they let the ring slip and it fell into the sea. When they came to land, Cinderello asked them how they had fared. The cat said: "We found the ring but by the fault of the dog here we lost it in the sea." The dog said not a word. Again Cinderello began to weep. As he was weeping the cat saw men rowing a fishing boat that way; cats you know are fond of fish. She went near the fishermen and cried out, "miaou, miaou." The fishermen were sorry for her and threw her some fish. As she was eating the fish, inside one of them she found the ring. With delight she took it and brought it to Cinderello.

Cinderello took the ring and went to the king and said: "Do you want me," said he, "to bring you the blackamoor and your daughter in the tower so that they may be close by here?" "Well, if you can," said the king, "will you not stay here and do this?" Then Cinderello dashed down the ring and the black man came out and said: "What are your commands, master?" "The tower," he said, "which is now in the sea you must take and bring here just as it is and set it where it was at first." The black man of the ring went off and took the tower and set it down outside the palace in the same place as it had been before. The king took his sword and went up to the tower, and slew his daughter and the blackamoor. The king had another daughter and afterwards he gave her to Cinderello as his wife. In the tower Cinderello kept the cat and the puppy and they all lived together happily.

*Fifty-three*

# The Ass That Lays Money

*Italian*

There was once a poor widow with an only son, whose brother-in-law was a steward. One day she said to her child: "Go to your uncle and ask him to give you something to keep you from starving." The boy went to the farm and asked his uncle to help him a little. "We are dying of hunger, uncle. My mother earns a little by weaving, and I am too small to find anything. Be charitable to us, for we are your relatives." The steward answered: "Why not? You should have come sooner and I would have helped you the sooner. But now I will give you something to support you always, without need of anything more. I will give you this little ass that lays money. You have only to put a cloth under him, and he will fill it for you with handsome coins. But take care! Don't tell it, and don't leave this animal with any one."

The youth departed in joy, and after he had traveled a long way, he stopped at an inn to sleep, for his house was distant. He said to the landlord: "Give me a lodging, but look! my ass spends the night with me." "What!" said the landlord, "what are you thinking about! It cannot be." The youth replied: "Yes, it can be, because my ass does not leave my side." They disputed a while, but the landlord finally consented; but he had some suspicions; and when the boy and his beast were shut in the room, he looked through the keyhole, and saw that wonder of an ass that laid money in abundance. "Bless me!" cried the host. "I should be a fool, indeed, if I let this piece of good fortune escape my hands!" He at once looked for another ass of the same color and size, and while the lad was asleep, exchanged them. In the morning the boy paid his bill and departed, but on the way, the ass no longer laid any money. The stupefied child did not know what to think at first, but afterwards examining it more closely, it appeared to him that the ass was not his, and straightway he returned to the innkeeper, to complain of his deception. The landlord cried out: "I wonder at your saying such a thing! We are all honest people here, and don't steal anything from anybody. Go away, blockhead, or you will find something to remember a while."

The child, weeping, had to depart with his ass, and he went back to his uncle's farm, and told him what had happened. The uncle said: "If you had not stopped at the innkeeper's, you could not have met with this misfortune. However, I have another present to help you and your mother. But take care! Do not mention it to any one, and take good care of it. Here it is. I give you a tablecloth, and whenever you say: 'Tablecloth, make ready,' after having spread it out, you will see a fine repast at your pleasure."

The youth took the tablecloth in delight, thanked his uncle, and departed; but like the fool he was, he stopped again at the same inn. He said to the landlord: "Give me a room and you need not prepare anything to eat. I have all I want with me." The crafty innkeeper suspected that there was something beneath this, and when the lad was in his room, he looked through the key-hole, and saw the tablecloth preparing the supper. The host exclaimed: "What good luck for my inn! I will not let it escape me." He quickly looked for another tablecloth like this one, with the same embroidery and fringe, and while the child was sleeping, he exchanged it for the magic one, so that in the morning the lad did not perceive the knavery. Not until he had reached a forest, where he was hungry, did he want to make use of the tablecloth. But it was in vain that he spread it out and cried: "Tablecloth, make ready." The tablecloth was not the same one, and made nothing ready for him.

In despair the boy went back to the innkeeper to complain, and the landlord would have thrashed him if he had not run away, and he ran until he reached his uncle's. His uncle, when he saw him in such a plight said: "Oh! what is the matter?" "Uncle!" said the boy, "the same innkeeper has changed the tablecloth, too, for me." The uncle was on the point of giving the dunce a good thrashing; but afterwards, seeing that it was a child, he calmed his anger, and said: "I understand; but I will give you a remedy by which you can get back everything from that thief of a landlord. Here it is! It is a stick. Hide it under your bolster; and if any one comes to rob you of it, say to it, in a low voice: 'Beat, beat!' and it will continue to do so until you say to it, 'Stop.' "

Imagine how joyfully the boy took the stick! It was a handsome polished stick, with a gold handle, and delighted one only to see it. So the boy thanked his uncle for his kindness, and after he had journeyed a while, he came to the same inn. He said: "Landlord, I wish to lodge here tonight." The landlord at once drew his conclusions about the stick, which the boy carried openly in his hands, and at night when the lad appeared to be sound asleep, but really was on the watch, the landlord felt softly under the bolster and drew out the stick. The boy, although it was dark, perceived the theft and said in a low voice: "Beat, beat, beat!" Suddenly blows were rained down without mercy; everything broken to pieces, the chest of drawers, the looking-glass, all the chairs, the glass in the windows; and the landlord, and those that came at the noise, beaten nearly to death. The landlord screamed to split his throat:

"Save me, boy, I am dead!" The boy answered: "What! I will not deliver you, if you do not give me back my property,—the ass that lays gold, and the tablecloth that prepares dinner." And if the landlord did not want to die of the blows, he had to consent to the boy's wishes.

When he had his things back, the boy went home to his mother and told her what had happened to him, and then said: "Now, we do not need anything more. I have an ass that lays money, a tablecloth that prepares food at my will, and a stick to defend me from whoever annoys me." So that woman and her son, who from want had become rich enough to cause every one envy, wished from pride to invite their relatives to a banquet, to make them acquainted with their wealth. On the appointed day the relatives came to the woman's new house; but noon strikes, one o'clock strikes, it is almost two, and in the kitchen the fire is seen extinguished, and there were no provisions anywhere. "Are you playing a joke on us?" said the relatives. "We shall have to depart with dry teeth." At that moment, however, the clock struck two, and the lad, after spreading the cloth on the table, commanded: "Tablecloth, prepare a grand banquet." In short, those people had a fine dinner and many presents in money, and the boy and his mother remained in triumph and joy.

*Fifty-four*

# Two Out of the Sack

*Russian*

Once there was an old man who lived with his wife. The wife constantly abused her husband; not a day passed on which she did not beat him with a broomstick or oven fork; he had no peace with her at all! He went into the field with some traps and set them. He caught a crane and said to him: "Be like a son to me! I will take you to my home and perhaps she won't scold me so much." The crane answered: "Little father! Come home with me!" So they set out for the crane's house. When they arrived the crane took a sack from the wall and said: "Two out of the sack!" At once two strong fellows climbed out of the sack, set oaken tables, spread silken cloths, and served food and drink of various kinds. The old man beheld delicacies such as he had never seen in his life, and rejoiced greatly. The crane said to him: "Take this sack and bring it to your wife."

The old man took the sack and went home; he went the long way, and stopped to spend the night with his godmother, who had three daughters. They made a supper for him, out of whatever they had on hand. The old man tasted it and said to his godmother: "Your fare is poor!" "It is all we have," answered the godmother. So he said: "Remove your fare!" And he spoke to the sack as the crane had bidden him to: "Two out of the sack!" At once two men jumped out of the sack, set up oaken tables, spread silken cloths, and served food and drink of various kinds.

The godmother and her daughters were amazed and decided to rob the old man of his sack. The godmother said to her daughters: "Go, heat up a bath; perhaps my godson will steam himself a little." As soon as he went to the bath, the godmother commanded her daughters to sew up a sack exactly like the old man's; they sewed it, put it in the place of the old man's, and took his own for themselves. The old man came out of the bath, took the new sack, and cheerfully went home to his wife. While still in the yard he called in a loud voice: "Old woman, old woman, come to meet me and my son the crane!" The old woman cast a quick glance at him and muttered between her teeth: "Just wait, old dog, till I get after you with this oven fork." But the old man kept repeating: "Old woman, come to meet me with my son, the crane!" He entered the hut, hung the sack on a hook, and cried: "Two out of the sack!" No one came out. He cried again: "Two out of the sack!" Again no one came out. The old woman thought he was raving, seized a wet broom, and began to belabor him.

The old man became frightened, wept, and went back into the field. Out of nowhere the crane appeared, saw his misfortune, and said: "Come, little father, come again to my house." So they went. Another sack just like the first one hung on the wall. "Two out of the sack!" said the crane. Two men climbed out of the sack and served a magnificent dinner, just as the other men had done. "Take this sack," the crane said to the old man. He took it and went home; he walked and walked along the road, got hungry, and, as the crane had told him to, said: "Two out of the sack!"

Two strong men with big sticks climbed out of the sack and began to thrash him, saying: "Go not to the godmother, steam not in the bath!" They thrashed and thrashed him until he managed to say: "Two into the sack!" The moment he said this the two men went back into the sack.

The old man took the sack and went on; he came to the same godmother, hung his sack on a hook, and said: "Heat a bath for me." She did. He went to the bath, steaming himself a little, but mainly passing the time away. The godmother called her daughters and told them to sit down, for she was hungry. "Two out of the sack!" said she. Two strong men with big sticks climbed out of the sack and began to thrash the godmother, saying: "Return the old man's sack!" They thrashed and thrashed her. Then she said to her eldest daughter: "Go and call my godson from the bath; tell him that the two men have beaten me up!" "I have not steamed myself yet," answered the old man. And they thrashed her with more blows, saying: "Return the old man's sack!" The godmother sent her second daughter, saying: "Hurry, bring my godson back into the room." He answered: "I have not yet washed my head!" The godmother could not bear it any longer; she ordered her daughter to bring back the stolen sack. Then the old man came out of the bathroom, saw his old sack, and said: "Two into the sack!" The two men with the sticks went back into it.

The old man took both sacks, the punishing one and the kindly one, and went home. While he was still in the yard he called to his wife: "Come, meet me and my son the crane!" She cast a quick glance at him and said: "Just wait till you come into the hut, I'll thrash you!" The old man came into the room and called to his wife: "Sit down!" Then he said: "Two out of the sack!" The two men climbed out of the sack and served food and drink. The old woman ate and drank her fill and praised her husband: "Well, old man, now I won't thrash you!" The old man, having eaten, went into the yard, put the kindly sack into the larder, hung the punishing one on a hook, and walked about in the yard, not so much to walk as to pass the time.

The old woman wanted to drink some more, so she repeated the words she had heard her husband say: "Two out of the sack!" Two men with big sticks climbed out of the sack and began to thrash the old woman; and they thrashed her so hard that she could bear it no longer. She called her husband: "Old man, old man, come into the hut, the two men are beating me up!" But he walked around, laughing and saying: "They'll show you how it's done!" The two men thrashed the old woman even harder, repeating: "Don't thrash your husband! Don't thrash your husband!" At last the old man took pity on her, came in, and said: "Two into the sack!" And the two men disappeared into the sack. From that time on the old man and his wife lived in such peace and friendship that he always boasted of her goodness, and that is the end of the story.

*Fifty-five*

# Horns

*Russian*

Once there was a laborer to whom God had given great strength. He learned that a dragon was haunting the king's daughter, and he boasted that he alone could destroy this terrible beast. The king's men heard his boasts and they pressed him: "Go, laborer, heal the princess." If the ale is drawn it must be drunk; so the laborer went to the king and said: "I can heal the princess; what will I receive for my trouble?" The king was overjoyed and said: "I will give you the princess in marriage." The laborer asked for seven oxhides, iron nuts, iron claws, and an iron hammer. He donned the seven oxhides and the iron claws, filled his pocket with nuts, real ones and iron ones, took the big hammer in his hands, and went to the princess' room.

The dragon flew to the princess. Upon seeing the laborer he gnashed his teeth and said: "Why have you come here?" "For the same purpose as you," said the laborer, and remained sitting where he was, cracking nuts. The dragon saw that he could accomplish nothing by force, so he came over to the laborer and asked for some nuts; the laborer gave him the iron ones. The dragon tried to crack them with his teeth and then spat them out: "Brother, your nuts are no good. Let us play a game of cards instead." "With pleasure, but for what stakes?" They agreed that he who lost would get a thrashing. They began to play and the

From *Russian Fairy Tales*, edited and translated by Norbert Guterman. Copyright 1945 by Pantheon Books, Inc. Reprinted by permission of Pantheon Books, a Division of Random House, Inc.

dragon lost. The laborer took his hammer and gave the dragon such a thrashing that he was almost stunned. "Now," said the dragon, "let us play for our skins; whoever loses will have his skin torn off." The laborer lost; the dragon tore one oxhide off him. "Let us play another game," the dragon said. This time the dragon lost; the laborer immediately plunged his iron claws into the dragon's skin and tore it off. The dragon died on the spot.

When the king heard of this he was overjoyed and married his daughter to the laborer. But the princess grew tired of living with a simple peasant; she ordered him to be taken to the woods and slain there. Her servants seized him, led him to the woods, but pitied him and did not kill him. The laborer wandered through the woods weeping. He met three men who were engaged in a dispute. The moment they came up to him they began to implore him: "Please, good man, settle our dispute. We have found a pair of boots that walk, a flying carpet, and a magic tablecloth. How shall we divide them?" "This way: whoever climbs up that oak first shall have them all." They foolishly consented and rushed to the tree. As soon as they had climbed up the laborer donned the walking boots, sat on the flying carpet, took the magic tablecloth, and said: "I want to be near the king's city."

And in a trice he was there. He pitched a tent, ordered his tablecloth to spread a dinner, and invited the king and his daughter to visit him. They came to him but they did not recognize him. He feasted them, gave them meat and drink, then led the princess to the flying carpet, quietly took the tablecloth, pushed the princess onto the carpet, and ordered it to fly into a dark forest. In the forest the laborer told the princess who he was; she began to caress and cajole him, and succeeded in beguiling him. As soon as he fell asleep, the princess seized the magic tablecloth, sat on the flying carpet, and was gone.

The laborer awoke and saw that the princess, the flying carpet, and the magic tablecloth were gone; only his walking boots remained. He wandered and wandered through the woods; he felt hungry, spied two apple trees, plucked an apple from one of them, and began to eat it. He ate one apple and a horn grew on his head; he ate another apple and another horn grew on his head. He tried the apples of the other tree; at once his horns vanished and he turned into a handsome youth. He filled his pocket with apples from both trees and went to the king's city. He walked by the palace and saw a scullery maid, one of the princess' servants, who was very ugly. "Don't you want an apple, little dove?" She took one and ate it, and turned into such a beauty as no tongue can tell of nor pen describe. The scullery maid went to the princess and the princess gasped. "Buy some for me," she said, "buy them without fail." The maid went out and bought some; but when the princess ate of them, horns grew on her head.

Next day the laborer came to the princess and told her that he could turn her back into a beauty. She implored him to do so. He told her to go into the bath chamber; there he undressed her and belabored her so severely with iron rods that he was sure that she would remember it for a long time. Then he told her that he was her lawful husband. The princess repented, gave him back his flying carpet and his magic tablecloth, and the laborer gave her some of the good apples to eat. And they began to live happily and to prosper.

*Fifty-six*

# The Magic Bird

*Greek*

Once upon a time there were in a village a man and his wife; they had three children and one hen, and this hen laid golden eggs. The man went away on a journey and his wife fell in love with a Jew. The Jew said: "I mean to come and live with you, but you must kill your children because they are now big and will tell your husband and he will kill me. You must also kill the hen and keep for me the head, the liver, and the heart." So the woman killed the hen and put its head, liver, and heart into the cupboard for him to eat when he came in the evening. At midday when the children were let out of school they had nothing to eat. They opened the cupboard and saw the pieces, and thought that their mother had put them there for them, and so they ate them. The child who ate the head became wiser than all men; the one who ate the liver, gold coins fell from his mouth; the one who ate the heart had the power of reading men's hearts.

When in the evening their mother came with the Jew she went

From *Modern Greek Folktales*, edited by R. M. Dawkins. Reprinted by permission of the Clarendon Press, Oxford.

to take the plate from the cupboard to give it to him; she found
that it was not there. Then the Jew perceived that the children
had eaten it all and he told their mother to kill them at once. So in
front of the door they dug out a pit, so that the children should
fall into it when they came back from school. The boy, who could
read men's hearts, was aware of all this and he told his brothers
what had been done: "When you come into the house you must
press always to one side." The children went off and came to the
house; they ate and drank and went to sleep. In the morning they
rose up and went to school. Then the Jew came again and he told
their mother that she must put poison into their food: and this she
did. The reader of hearts saw what had happened and he told his
brothers what was afoot: "And you must not eat the food." They
they again escaped. Then a plot was made to kill them, but the
reader of hearts again was aware of it and he would not let them
go to the house at all, but they started off to go to another village.

As they were on the way they came upon a beautiful girl
playing cards. The one from whose mouth gold coins fell stayed
awhile to play with her. She saw him spitting out gold coins, so
she made him drunk: he threw up the liver and she ate it. The
boy wandered off at random and as he was passing by he saw a
fig-tree—the season was winter and the tree had on it black figs.
He ate two figs and two horns grew on his head. Then he gathered two more figs and put them into his pouch. Going farther he
found another fig-tree and this one had white figs. He ate two of
the figs and his horns disappeared. He picked two more and put
them into his pouch. He walked below the house of the card-play-
ing girl and cried: 'Figs for sale!' When she heard him cry figs
for sale and in winter, she went down and bought. As soon as she
ate the figs two horns grew on her head. Well, she sent for all the
doctors but no one could put her right. Then the boy passed again
by her house crying: "Good doctor here!" She called for him and
he went up to her. When he saw her he said: "A great sin you
have committed and you must confess it to me." She began to tell
him: "I used to play cards and won much money from people.
Then a man came who could spit gold from his mouth. I made
him drunk and he threw up a liver and I ate it, and now I too can
spit coins." Then the doctor said to her: "This is the sin you have
done. You must give me the liver and I will make you well." Then
the girl let the boy have the liver, and he gave her the white figs
and the horns fell from off her head.

Then the boy went and found his brothers: one was a vizier and one was a head man; this third one had become a chief elder. One evening as they were at supper the reader of hearts said: "Tomorrow our parents will come here and we must in no way let it be seen that we are their sons. We can pretend to be playing ball with apples, and when the apples fall to the ground and we stoop as though to pick them up, then we shall be bowing down before them as it is fitting we should, but they will not be aware that we are." So in the morning their parents came and under this pretext the children paid their due obeisance without the parents being aware that they were receiving the homage of their sons.

They went to the government house and there the father said: "Two months ago I went away from my home and I left with my wife three sons and a hen which laid golden eggs; now I have returned and can find none of them." Then he asked his wife where they were and she said: "We had, my master, these three sons and they are dead; also we had a hen and she has been stolen. And what was I to do? Am I God to save my sons from dying?" Then her sons said to her: "Did you now tell us that you had three sons and they are dead? Behold, we are your sons." Then they tied her to horses and started them off and she was torn to pieces and the sons lived with their father.

# The King's Hares

*Norwegian*

There was once upon a time a man who gave up his farm to his eldest son and heir, but he had still three sons, and they were called Peter, Paul, and Ashiepattle. They stayed at home and would do no work of any kind, for they had had too good a time of it in their young days, and now they thought they were too good for everything and that nothing was good enough for them.

At last Peter heard that the king wanted a youngster to watch his hares, and so he told his father that he would go and try for this situation, which he thought would just suit him, for he would serve no less a man than the king, he said. His father thought that there was no doubt some more suitable work to be found for him, for he who should watch hares ought to be light and smart, and no lazybones, and when the hares began to run and fly about, there would be quite another dance than hanging about the house all day doing nothing. Well, there was no help for it, Peter would try it, and go he must; so he took his bag on his back and trudged down the hill. When he had gone a good long distance, he met an old woman who stood fixed with her nose in a big block, and when he saw how she pulled and tugged to get loose he began laughing with all his might.

"Don't stand there and grin," said the woman, "but come and help an old woman; I was going to chop up a little wood and then I got my nose stuck in this block, and so I have been standing and tugging and pulling away, and never tasted a mouthful for a hundred years," she said.

But Peter only laughed more and more; he thought it was great fun, and said that since she had been standing thus a hundred years, she might hold out for another hundred years.

When he came to the king's palace, he got the place to look after the hares at once. It was not a bad place to serve in there; he was to have good food and good wages, and the princess into the bargain. But if even one of the king's hares were lost, they were to cut three red stripes out of his back, and throw him into the snake-pit.

As long as Peter was in the fields near the palace, he managed to keep all the hares in one flock, but as the day wore on and the hares came into the wood, they began to scamper and fly about the hills in all directions. Peter ran after them as fast as his legs would carry him, but at last he had only one of the hares left, and when this was gone, he was very nearly burst with running. And so he saw no more of the hares.

Towards evening he began strolling homewards; when he came to the gate, he stopped there gaping and staring about for them, but no hares came. When he came into the palace yard in the evening the king was waiting for him with his knife ready, and cut three red stripes out of his back, put pepper and salt into them, and cast him into the snake-pit.

After some time Paul wanted to go to the king's palace and watch the king's hares. His father told him what he had said to his elder brother and more besides, but there was no help for it; he must and would go. It fared, however, no better with him than with Peter. The old woman stood there and tugged and pulled away at her nose, which stuck in the block, but Paul only laughed and thought it was great fun, and left her standing there. He got the place at once; there was no difficulty about that. But the hares ran away from him among the hills, although he ran and rushed about after them till he blew and panted like a sheepdog in the sunshine. When he came back to the palace in the evening without the hares, the king was waiting on the steps with the knife in his hand, and cut three broad red stripes out of his back, put pepper and salt into them, and then took him away to the snake-pit with him.

Well, when some time had passed, Ashiepattle wanted to set out for the king's palace and watch his hares. He told his father that it would be just suitable work for him to run about fields and woods among the strawberry hills after a flock of hares, and now and then lie down and take a nap on some sunny hill.

The old man thought he no doubt could fine some more suitable work to do, but if he did not fare better, he could not fare worse than his brothers. He that would watch the king's hares must not drag himself along as if he were a lazybones with soles of lead to his boots, or like a fly on a tar-brush, for when the hares began to scamper about on the hillsides it was quite another dance than lying at home and catching fleas with mittens on. He that wanted to get away from that work with a whole back would have to be smart and light on his legs; in fact he ought to fly about faster than a piece of dried skin or a bird's wing.

Well, that might be, said Ashiepattle, but for all that he would go to the palace and serve the king; he couldn't think of serving any man less than a king. He would look after the hares, he said; they couldn't be much worse than the goat and the calf he had to mind at home. So Ashiepattle took his bag on his back and trudged down the hill.

When he had gone a good bit of the way, he began to feel very hungry, but just then he came up to the old woman, who was standing with her nose in the block, tugging and pulling away at it to get loose.

"Good day, old mother," said Ashiepattle; "are you standing there sharpening your nose, you poor old soul?"

"I haven't heard anybody call me mother for a hundred years," said the old woman; "come and help me out of this, and give me something to eat; I haven't had food in my mouth all this time. I'll be as good as a mother to you, if you do!"

Well yes, he thought she would want both meat and drink in that case, said Ashiepattle. So he took the axe and split the block for her, and then she got her nose out of the cleft. He sat down to eat and shared his food with her, but the old woman had a splendid appetite, as you may guess, and finished the best part of it.

When they had done, she gave Ashiepattle a whistle, and told him how to use it. If he blew into one end of it, everything which he wished far away would be scattered to all sides, but if he blew into the other end it would all come together again; and if the whistle were lost or taken from him, he had only to wish for it and it would come back to him. That is quite a whistle, thought Ashiepattle.

When he came to the king's palace, he was taken into service at once, as they made little or no difficulty about that. He was to have both food and wages, and if he could look after the king's hares, so none were lost, he should have the princess as well, but if any got away, if it only were one of the youngest hares, they would cut three red stripes out of his back; and the king seemed to be so sure of this, that he went and sharpened his knife there and then.

"Well, it's a small matter to look after these hares," thought Ashiepattle, for when they were let out they were as tame as a flock of sheep, and as long as they were in the fields about the place they were all in a flock and followed him; but when they came up in the wood it was close upon noon, and the sun shone at his best, and off went the hares scampering about the hills.

"Halloa!" cried Ashiepattle, and blew into the one end of the whistle; "off you go!" and away the hares ran to all sides; not one was to be seen. But when he came to an open place in the wood, where they had been burning charcoal, he took his whistle and blew into the other end of it, and before he could say a word there were the hares, all in a row, just as if they had been a regiment of soldiers on a drill-ground. Well, that is quite a whistle, thought Ashiepattle. And so he went to take a nap over on a sunny hillside, while the hares scampered about and looked after themselves till the evening came. He then blew them together again, and came back to the palace with them just like a flock of sheep.

The king and the queen and the princess too stood in the door and wondered what sort of youngster this was who could look after the hares so well and bring them home with him again. The king counted them backwards and forwards, pointing to each with his finger, but no, not so much as one of the young hares was missing.

"That is quite a lad," said the princess.

The next day he set out again for the wood with the hares, but as he lay and took a rest among the strawberries, the housemaid in the palace came up to him. They had sent her after him to find out how it was that he managed to look after the king's hares so well.

He took out his whistle and showed it to her; he blew into the one end of it and away flew the hares like the wind between the hills, and when he blew into the other end, they came scampering down the hill and stood in a row before him.

"What a pretty whistle," said the housemaid; she would willingly give a hundred dollars for it, if he would sell it.

"Well, yes," said Ashiepattle, "it is quite a whistle." It was not to be bought for money, but if she beside the hundred dollars would give him a kiss for every dollar, she should have it.

Yes, that she would do willingly; she would not mind giving him two for every dollar and thank him for it besides.

So she got the whistle, but when she came back to the palace, the whistle was gone, for Ashiepattle had wished for it back again; and when the evening set in, he came home with his hares just like a flock of sheep. For all the king counted and pointed and reckoned, he could not find as much as a hair of them missing.

The third day when he was out with the hares, they sent the princess after him to try and get the whistle from him. She made herself as blithesome as a lark, and at last she offered him two hundred dollars if he would sell her the whistle, and tell her how she should manage to get it safe home with her.

"Well, yes, it is quite a whistle," said Ashiepattle. It was not for sale, he said, but for all that, he would do it for her sake, if she would give him a hundred dollars and a kiss for each dollar in the bargain. On those terms she could have the whistle, and if she wanted to keep it, she must look well after it; that was her business.

"That was a very high price for a hare-whistle," thought the princess, and she was rather shy about giving him the kisses, but since they were out in the wood, where no one could see or hear it, she would not mind giving him the kisses; for the whistle she must and would have, she said.

When Ashiepattle had got what he was to have, she got the whistle, and so she went holding it tight and fingering it all the way, but when she came to the palace and was about to show it to the king, it disappeared between her fingers.

The next day the queen would go herself and try to get the whistle from him; she thought she would be sure to bring it back with her. She was rather close-fisted in money matters and offered him only fifty dollars, but she had to raise her price till it rose to three hundred. Ashiepattle said it was quite a whistle, and it was really no bid at all for it, but for her sake he wouldn't mind selling it to her, if she would give him three hundred dollars and a smacking kiss for each dollar in the bargain. He got that, and much more, for she was not so stingy in that respect.

When she had got the whistle, she tied it up well and put it in a safe place; but she fared no better than the others, for when she was going to pull the whistle out it was gone, and in the evening Ashiepattle came home driving the king's hares before him like a tame flock of sheep.

"This is all stuff and nonsense," said the king; "I shall have to go myself, if we are to get this confounded whistle from him. I see no other way out of it." So when Ashiepattle next day had got into the wood with the hares, the king set out after him, and found him on the same sunny hillside where the women folk had met him, and made the bargain with him.

Well, the king and Ashiepattle became good friends and got on very well together, and Ashiepattle showed him the whistle and blew both in the one and the other end. The king thought it was a funny whistle, and would buy it by all means, even if he should pay a thousand dollars for it.

"Yes, it is quite a pipe," said Ashiepattle, and it was not to be had for money; "but do you see that white horse down yonder?" he said, and pointed over in the wood.

"Yes, that's my own mare, Snowflake," said the king. He knew that himself without anybody telling him.

"Well, if you will give me a thousand dollars and will kiss that white mare down in the bog behind that big fir-tree you shall have the whistle."

"Is it not to be had at any other price?" said the king.

"No, it is not," said Ashiepattle.

"But I suppose I may put my silk handkerchief between?" said the king.

Yes, he might do that. And so the king got the whistle, and put it into his purse, and this he put into his pocket and buttoned it well up, and set off on his way home. But when he came to the palace, and was going to pull out the whistle, he was no better off than the women folk; he had not the whistle any more than they. Ashiepattle came home driving the flock of hares and there was not a hare missing.

The king was in a great rage at the way in which Ashiepattle had made a fool of them all. There was no question about it; Ashiepattle must lose his life. The queen said the same; it was best to punish such a scamp right off. But Ashiepattle thought it was neither right nor fair, for he had done nothing but what they had told him to do, and besides, he had only tried to save his back and life as well as he could. So the king said he would pardon him if he could tell so many lies that they filled the large brewing-vat and flowed over. If he could do that he might keep his life.

Well, that was neither a long nor a difficult piece of work, said Ashiepattle; he thought he could master that job. So he began telling them how he had fared from the very first; he told them about the old woman with her nose in the block and then he would say: "I must get on faster with telling lies if the vat is to be full." So he told them about the whistle he had got, and about the housemaid who came to him, and wanted to buy it for a hundred dollars, and about all the kisses she had to give him in the bargain. Then he told them of the princess, how she came to him, and how much she had to kiss him to get the whistle, when nobody saw or heard it over in the wood—"I must get on with these lies if the vat is to be full," said Ashiepattle—so he told them about the queen, how stingy she was with the money and how liberal she was with kisses, that one could hear the smacks all over the wood—"I must really get on with my lies if the vat is to be full," said Ashiepattle.

"Well, I think it's pretty full," said the queen.

"Not at all," said the king.

At last Ashiepattle began to tell about the king, who came to him, and about the white mare down in the bog, and if the king wanted the whistle he—he would have—he would have to—"I beg your Majesty's pardon, but I must put some lies together if the vat is to be full—and—"

"Stop, lad, stop! It is full!" cried the king. "Don't you see the vat is flowing over?"

So the king and queen thought they could not do any better than give him the princess and half the kingdom; there was no help for it.

"That was quite a whistle," said Ashiepattle.

*Fifty-eight*

# The Lamb With the Golden Fleece

*Hungarian*

There was once a poor man who had a son, and as the son grew up his father sent him out to look for work. The son traveled about looking for a place, and at last met with a man who arranged to take him as a shepherd. Next day his master gave him a flute, and sent him out with the sheep to see whether he was fit for his work. The lad never lay down all day, very unlike many lazy fellows. He drove his sheep from place to place and played his flute all day long. There was among the sheep a lamb with golden fleece, which, whenever he played his flute, began to dance. The lad became very fond of this lamb, and made up his mind not to ask any wages of his master, but only this little lamb. In the evening he returned home; his master waited at the gate; and, when he saw the sheep all there and all well-fed, he was very pleased, and began to bargain with the lad, who said he wished for nothing but the lamb with the golden fleece. The farmer was very fond of the lamb himself, and it was with great unwillingness he promised it; but he gave in afterwards when he saw what a good servant the lad made.

The year passed away; the lad received the lamb for his wages, and set off home with it. As they journeyed night set in just as he reached a village, so he went to a farmhouse to ask for a night's lodging. There was a daughter in the house who when she saw the lamb with the golden fleece determined to steal it. About midnight she arose, and lo! the moment she touched the lamb she stuck hard-and-fast to its fleece, so that when the lad got up he found her stuck to the lamb. He could not separate them, and as he could not leave his lamb he took them both.

As he passed the third door from the house where he had spent the night he took out his flute and began to play. Then the lamb began to dance, and on the wool the girl. Round the corner a woman was putting bread into the oven; looking up she saw the lamb dancing, and on its wool the girl. Seizing the baking shovel in order to frighten the girl, she rushed out and shouted, "Get away home with you, don't make such a fool of yourself." As the girl continued dancing the woman called out, "What, won't you obey?" and gave her a blow on her back with the shovel, which at once stuck to the girl, and the woman to the shovel, and the lamb carried them all off.

As they went they came to the church. Here the lad began to play again, the lamb began to dance, and on the lamb's fleece the girl, and on the girl's back the shovel, and at the end of the shovel the woman. Just then the priest was coming out from matins, and seeing what was going on began to scold them, and bid them go home and not be so foolish. As words were of no avail, he hit the woman a sound whack on her back with his cane, when to his surprise the cane stuck to the woman, and he to the end of his cane.

With this nice company the lad went on; and towards dark reached the royal borough and took lodgings at the end of the town for the night with an old woman. "What news is there?" said he. The old woman told him they were in very great sorrow, for the king's daughter was very ill, and no physician could heal her, but if she could but be made to laugh she would be better at once; no one had as yet been able to make her smile; and moreover the king had issued that very day a proclamation stating that whoever made her laugh should have her for his wife, and share the royal power.

The lad with the lamb could scarcely wait till daylight, so anxious was he to try his fortune. In the morning he presented himself to the king and stated his business and was very graciously received. The daughter stood in the hall at the front of the house; the lad then began to play the flute, the lamb to dance, on the lamb's fleece the girl, on the girl's back the shovel, at the end of the shovel the woman, on the woman's back the cane, and at the end of the cane the priest. When the princess saw this sight she burst out laughing, which made the lamb so glad that it shook everything off its back, and the lamb, the girl, the woman, and the priest each danced by themselves for joy.

The king married his daughter to the shepherd; the priest was made court-chaplain; the woman court bakeress; and the girl lady-in-waiting to the princess.

The wedding lasted from one Monday to the other Tuesday, and the whole land was in great joy, and if the strings of the fiddle hadn't broken they would have been dancing yet!

*Fifty-nine*

# The Blue Belt

*Norwegian*

Once on a time there was an old beggar-woman, who had gone out to beg. She had a little lad with her, and when she had got her bag full, she struck across the hills towards her own home. So when they had gone a bit up the hillside they came upon a little blue belt, which lay where two paths met, and the lad asked his mother's leave to pick it up.

"No," said she, "may be there's witchcraft in it"; and so with threats she forced him to follow her. But when they had gone a bit farther, the lad said he must turn aside a moment out of the road, and meanwhile his mother sat down on a tree-stump. But the lad was a long time gone, for as soon as he got so far into the wood that the old dame could not see him, he ran off to where the belt lay, took it up, tied it round his waist, and lo! he felt as strong as if he could lift the whole hill. When he got back, the old dame was in a great rage, and wanted to know what he had been doing all that while. "You don't care how much time you waste, and yet you know the night is drawing on, and we must cross the hill before it is dark!" So on they tramped, but when they had got about half-way, the old dame grew weary, and said she must rest under a bush.

"Dear mother, "said the lad, mayn't I just go up to the top of this high crag while you rest, and try if I can't see some sign of folk hereabouts?"

Yes, he might do that; so when he had got to the top he saw a light shining from the north. So he ran down and told his mother.

"We must get on, mother; we are near a house, for I see a bright light shining quite close to us in the north." Then she rose and shouldered her bag, and set off to see; but they hadn't gone far, before there stood a steep spur of the hill, right across their path.

"Just as I thought!" said the old dame; "now we can't go a step farther; a pretty bed we shall have here!"

But the lad took the bag under one arm, and his mother under the other, and ran straight up the steep crag with them.

"Now, don't you see! don't you see that we are close to a house! don't you see the bright light?

But the old dame said those were no Christian folk, but trolls, for she was at home in all that forest far and near, and knew there was not a living soul in it until you were well over the ridge and had come down on the other side. But they went on, and in a little while they came to a great house which was all painted red.

"What's the good?" said the old dame, "we daren't go in, for here the trolls live."

"Don't say so; we must go in. There must be men where the lights shine so," said the lad. So in he went, and his mother after him, but he had scarce opened the door before she swooned away, for there she saw a great stout man, at least twenty feet high, sitting on the bench.

"Good evening, grandfather!" said the lad.

"Well, here I've sat three hundred years," said the man who sat on the bench, "and no one has ever come and called me grandfather before." Then the lad sat down by the man's side, and began to talk to him as if they had been old friends.

"But what's come over your mother?" said the man, after they had chattered a while. "I think she swooned away; you had better look after her."

So the lad went and took hold of the old dame; and dragged her up the hall along the floor. That brought her to herself, and she kicked and scratched, and flung herself about, and at last sat down upon a heap of firewood in the corner; but she was so frightened that she scarce dared to look one in the face.

After a while, the lad asked if they could spend the night there.

"Yes, to be sure," said the man.

So they went on talking again, but the lad soon got hungry, and wanted to know if they could get food as well as lodging.

"Of course," said the man, "That might be got too." And after he had sat a while longer, he rose up and threw six loads of dry pitch-pine on the fire. This made the old hag still more afraid.

"Oh! now he's going to roast us alive," she said, in the corner where she sat.

And when the wood had burned down to glowing embers, up got the man and strode out of his house.

"Heaven bless and help us! what a stout heart you have got," said the old dame; "don't you see we have got among trolls?"

"Stuff and nonsense!" said the lad; "no harm if we have."

In a little while back came the man with an ox so fat and big, the lad had never seen its like, and he gave it one blow with his fist under the ear, and down it fell dead on the floor. When that was done, he took it up by all the four legs, and laid it on the glowing embers, and turned it and twisted it about till it was burned brown outside. After that, he went to a cupboard and took out a great silver dish and laid the ox on it; and the dish was so big that none of the ox hung over on any side. This he put on the table, and then he went down into the cellar, and fetched a cask of wine, knocked out the head, and put the cask on the table, together with two knives, which were each six feet long. When this was done, he bade them go and sit down to supper and eat.

So they went, the lad first and the old dame after, but she began to whimper and wail, and to wonder how she should ever use such knives. But her son seized one, and began to cut slices out of the thigh of the ox, which he placed before his mother. And when they had eaten a bit, he took up the cask with both hands, and lifted it down to the floor; then he told his mother to come and drink, but it was still so high she couldn't reach up to it; so he caught her up, and held her up to the edge of the cask while she drank; as for himself he clambered up and hung down like a cat inside the cask while he drank. So when he had quenched his thirst, he took up the cask and put it back on the table, and thanked the man for the good meal, and told his mother to come and thank him too, and afeared though she was, she dared do nothing else but thank the man. Then the lad sat down again alongside the man and began to gossip, and after they had sat a while, the man said:

"Well, I must just go and get a bit of supper too"; and so he went to the table and ate up the whole ox—hoofs, and horns, and all—and drained the cask to the last drop, and then went back and sat on the bench.

"As for beds," he said, "I don't know what's to be done. I've only got one bed and a cradle; but we could get on pretty well if you would sleep in the cradle, and then your mother might lie in the bed yonder."

"Thank you kindly, that'll do nicely," said the lad; and with that he pulled off his clothes and lay down in the cradle; but to tell you the truth, it was quite as big as a four-poster. As for the old dame, she had to follow the man, who showed her to bed, though she was out of her wits for fear.

"Well," thought the lad to himself, " 'twill never do to go to sleep yet. I'd best lie awake and listen how things go as the night wears on."

So after a while the man began to talk to the old dame, and at last he said:

"We two might live here so happily together, could we only be rid of this son of yours."

"But do you know how to settle him? Is that what you're thinking of?" said she.

"Nothing easier," said he; at any rate he would try. He would just say he wished the old dame would stay and keep house for him a day or two, and then he would take the lad out with him up the hill to quarry corner-stones, and roll down a great rock on him. All this the lad lay and listened to.

Next day the troll—for it was a troll as clear as day—asked if the old dame would stay and keep house for him a few days; and as the day went on he took a great iron crowbar, and asked the lad if he had a mind to go with him up the hill and quarry a few corner-stones. With all his heart, he said, and went with him; and so, after they had split a few stones, the troll wanted him to go down below and look after cracks in the rock; and while he was doing this, the troll worked away, and wearied himself with his crowbar till he moved a whole crag out of its bed, which came rolling right down on the place where the lad was; but he held it up till he could get on one side, and then let it roll on.

"Oh!" said the lad to the troll, "now I see what you mean to do with me. You want to crush me to death; so just go down yourself and look after the cracks and refts in the rock, and I'll stand up above."

The troll did not dare to do otherwise than the lad bade him, and the end of it was that the lad rolled down a great rock, which fell upon the troll, and broke one of his thighs.

"Well! you *are* in a sad plight," said the lad, as he strode down, lifted up the rock, and set the man free. After that he had to put him on his back and carry him home; so he ran with him as fast as a horse, and shook him so that the troll screamed and screeched as if a knife were run into him. And when he got home, they had to put the troll to bed, and there he lay in a sad pickle.

When the night wore on the troll began to talk to the old dame again, and to wonder however they could be rid of the lad.

"Well," said the old dame, "if you can't hit on a plan to get rid of him, I'm sure I can't."

"Let me see," said the troll; "I've got twelve lions in a garden; if they could only get hold of the lad they'd soon tear him to pieces."

So the old dame said it would be easy enough to get him there. She would sham sick, and say she felt so poorly, nothing would do her any good but lion's milk. All that the lad lay and listened to; and when he got up in the morning his mother said she was worse than she looked, and she thought she should never be right again unless she could get some lion's milk.

"Then I'm afraid you'll be poorly a long time, mother," said the lad, "for I'm sure I don't know where any is to be got."

"Oh! if that be all," said the troll, "there's no lack of lion's milk, if we only had the man to fetch it"; and then he went on to say how his brother had a garden with twelve lions in it, and how the lad might have the key if he had a mind to milk the lions. So the lad took the key and a milking pail, and strode off; and when he unlocked the gate and got into the garden, there stood all the twelve lions on their hind-paws, rampant and roaring at him. But the lad laid hold of the biggest, and led him about by the fore-paws, and dashed him against stocks and stones, till there wasn't a bit of him left but the two paws. So when the rest saw that, they were so afraid that they crept up and lay at his feet like so many curs. After that they followed him about wherever he went, and when he got home they laid down outside the house, with their fore-paws on the door sill.

"Now, mother, you'll soon be well," said the lad, when he went in, "for here is the lion's milk."

He had just milked a drop in the pail.

But the troll, as he lay in bed, swore it was all a lie. He was sure the lad was not the man to milk lions.

When the lad heard that, he forced the troll to get out of bed, threw open the door, and all the lions rose up and seized the troll, and at last the lad had to make them leave their hold.

That night the troll began to talk to the old dame again. "I'm sure I can't tell how to put this lad out of the way—he is so awfully strong; can't you think of some way?"

"No," said the old dame; "if you can't tell, I'm sure I can't."

"Well," said the troll, "I have two brothers in a castle; they are twelve times as strong as I am, and that's why I was turned out and had to put up with this farm. They hold that castle, and round it there is an orchard with apples in it, and whoever eats those apples sleeps for three days and three nights. If we could only get the lad to go for the fruit, he wouldn't be able to keep from tasting the apples, and as soon as ever he fell asleep my brothers would tear him in pieces."

The old dame said she would sham sick, and say she could never be herself again unless she tasted those apples; for she had set her heart on them.

All this the lad lay and listened to.

When the morning came the old dame was so poorly that she couldn't utter a word but groans and sighs. She was sure she should never be well again, unless she had some of those apples that grew in the orchard near the castle where the man's brothers lived; only she had no one to send for them.

Oh! the lad was ready to go that instant; but the eleven lions went with him. So when he came to the orchard, he climbed up into the apple-tree and ate as many apples as he could, and he had scarce got down before he fell into a deep sleep; but the lions all lay round him in a ring. The third day came the troll's brothers, but they did not come in man's shape. The came snorting like man-eating steeds, and wondered who it was that dared to be there, and said they would tear him to pieces so small that there should not be a bit of him left. But up rose the lions and tore the trolls into small pieces, so that the place looked as if a dungheap had been tossed about it; and when they had finished the trolls they lay down again. The lad did not wake till late in the afternoon, and when he got on his knees and rubbed the sleep out of his eyes, he began to wonder what had been going on, when he saw the marks of hoofs. But when he went towards the castle, a maiden looked out of a window who had seen all that had happened, and she said:

"You may thank your stars you weren't in that tussle, else you must have lost your life."

"What! I lose my life! No fear of that, I think," said the lad.

So she begged him to come in, that she might talk with him, for she hadn't seen a Christian soul ever since she came there. But when she opened the door the lions wanted to go in too, but she got so frightened that she began to scream, and so the lad let them lie outside. Then the two talked and talked, and the lad asked how it came that she, who was so lovely, could put up with those ugly trolls. She never wished it, she said; 'twas quite against her will. They had seized her by force, and she was the king of Arabia's daughter. So they talked on, and at last she asked him what he would do; whether she should go back home, or whether he would have her to wife. Of course he would have her, and she shouldn't go home.

After that they went round the castle, and at last they came to a great hall, where the trolls' two great swords hung high up on the wall.

"I wonder if you are man enough to wield one of these," said the princess.

"Who?—I?" said the lad. " 'Twould be a pretty thing if I couldn't wield one of these."

With that he put two or three chairs one atop of the other, jumped up, and touched the biggest sword with his finger tips, tossed it up in the air, and caught it again by the hilt leaped down, and at the same time dealt such a blow with it on the floor, that the whole hall shook. After he had thus got down he thrust the sword under his arm and carried it about with him.

So when they had lived a little while in the castle, the princess thought she ought to go home to her parents, and let them know what had become of her; so they loaded a ship, and she set sail from the castle.

After she had gone, and the lad had wandered about a little, he called to mind that he had been sent on an errand thither, and had come to fetch something for his mother's health; and though he said to himself:

"After all, the old dame was not so bad but she's all right by this time"—still he thought he ought to go and just see how she was. So he went and found both the man and his mother quite fresh and hearty.

"What wretches you are to live in this beggarly hut," said the lad. "Come with me up to my castle, and you shall see what a fine fellow I am."

Well! they were both ready to go, and on the way his mother

talked to him, and asked, "How it was he had got so strong?"

"If you must know, it came of that blue belt which lay on the hillside that time when you and I were out begging," said the lad.

"Have you got it still?" asked she.

Yes, he had. It was tied round his waist.

"Might she see it?"

Yes, she might; and with that he pulled open his waistcoat and shirt to show it her.

Then she seized it with both hands, tore it off, and twisted it round her fist.

"Now," she cried, "what shall I do with such a wretch as you? I'll just give you one blow, and dash your brains out!"

"Far too good a death for such a scamp," said the troll. "No! let's first burn out his eyes, and then turn him adrift in a little boat."

So they burned out his eyes and turned him adrift, in spite of his prayers and tears; but, as the boat drifted, the lions swam after, and at last they laid hold of it and dragged it ashore on an island, and placed the lad under a fir-tree. They caught game for him, and they plucked the birds and made him a bed of down; but he was forced to eat his meat raw, and he was blind. At last, one day the biggest lion was chasing a hare which was blind, for it ran straight over stock and stone, and the end was, it ran right up against a fir-stump and tumbled head over heels across the field right into a spring; but lo! when it came out of the spring it saw its way quite plain, and so saved its life.

"So, so!" thought the lion, and went and dragged the lad to the spring, and dipped him over head and ears in it. So, when he had got his sight again, he went down to the shore and made signs to the lions that they should all lie close together like a raft; then he stood upon their backs while they swam with him to the mainland. When he had reached the shore he went up into a birch copse, and made the lions lie quiet. Then he stole up to the castle, like a thief, to see if he couldn't lay hands on his belt; and when he got to the door, he peeped through the keyhole, and there he saw his belt hanging up over a door in the kitchen. So he crept softly in across the floor, for there was no one there; but as soon as he got hold of the belt, he began to kick and stamp about as though he were mad. Just then his mother came rushing out:

"Dear heart, my darling little boy! do give me the belt again," she said.

"Thank you kindly," said he. "Now you shall have the doom you passed on me," and he fulfilled it on the spot. When the old troll heard that, he came in and begged and prayed so prettily that he might not be smitten to death.

"Well, you may live," said the lad, "but you shall undergo the same punishment you gave me"; and so he burned out the troll's eyes, and turned him adrift on the sea in a little boat, but he had no lions to follow him.

Now the lad was all alone, and he went about longing and longing for the princess; at last he could bear it no longer; he must set out to seek her, his heart was so bent on having her. So he loaded four ships and set sail for Arabia. For some time they had fair wind and fine weather, but after that they lay windbound under a rocky island. So the sailors went ashore and strolled about to spend the time, and there they found a huge egg, almost as big as a little house. So they began to knock it about with large stones, but, after all, they couldn't crack the shell. Then the lad came up with his sword to see what all the noise was about, and when he saw the egg, he thought it a trifle to crack it; so he gave it one blow and the egg split, and out came a chicken as big as an elephant.

"Now we have done wrong," said the lad; "this can cost us all our lives," and then he asked his sailors if they were men enough to sail to Arabia in four-and-twenty hours, if they got a fine breeze. Yes, they were good to do that, they said, so they set sail with a fine breeze, and got to Arabia in three-and-twenty hours. As soon as they landed, the lad ordered all the sailors to go and bury themselves up to the eyes in a sandhill, so that they could barely see the ships. The lad and the captains climbed a high crag and sat down under a fir. In a little while came a great bird flying with an island in its claws, and let it fall down on the fleet, and sank every ship. After it had done that, it flew up to the sandhill and flapped its wings, so that the wind nearly took off the heads of the sailors, and it flew past the fir with such force that it turned the lad right about, but he was ready with his sword, and gave the bird one blow and brought it down dead.

After that he went to the town, where every one was glad because the king had got his daughter back; but now the king had hidden her away somewhere himself, and promised her hand as a reward to any one who could find her, and this though she was betrothed before. Now as the lad went along he met a man who had white bear-skins for sale, so he bought one of the hides and put it on; and one of the captains was to take an iron chain and lead him about, and so he went into the town and began to play pranks. At last the news came to the king's ears that there never had been such fun in the town before, for here was a white bear that danced and cut capers just as it was bid. So a messenger came to say the bear must come to the castle at once, for the king wanted to see its tricks. So when it got to the castle every one was afraid, for such a beast they had never seen before; but the captain said there was no danger unless they laughed at it. They mustn't do that, else it would tear them to pieces. When the king heard that, he warned all the court not to laugh. But while the fun was going on, in came one of the king's maids, and began to laugh and make game of the bear, and the bear flew at her and tore her, so that there was scarce a rag of her left. Then all the court began to bewail, and the captain most of all.

"Stuff and nonsense," said the king; "she's only a maid, besides it's more my affair than yours."

When the show was over, it was late at night. "It's no good your going away when it's so late," said the king. "The bear had best sleep here."

"Perhaps it might sleep in the ingle by the kitchen fire," said the captain.

"Nay," said the king, "it shall sleep up here, and it shall have pillows and cushions to sleep on." So a whole heap of pillows and cushions was brought, and the captain had a bed in a side-room.

But at midnight the king came with a lamp in his hand and a big bunch of keys, and carried off the white bear. He passed along gallery after gallery, through doors and rooms, upstairs and downstairs, till at last he came to a pier which ran out into the sea. Then the king began to pull and haul at posts and pins, this one up and that one down, till at last a little house floated up to the water's edge. There he kept his daughter, for she was so dear to him that he had hid her, so that no one could find her out. He left the white bear outside while he went in and told her how it had danced and played its pranks. She said she was afraid, and dared not look at it; but he talked her over, saying there was no danger, if she only wouldn't laugh. So they brought the bear in, and locked the door, and it danced and played its tricks; but just when the fun was at its height the princess's maid began to laugh. Then the lad flew at her and tore her to bits, and the princess began to cry and sob.

"Stuff and nonsense," cried the king; "all this fuss about a maid! I'll get you just as good a one again. But now I think the bear had best stay here till morning, for I don't care to have to go and lead it along all those galleries and stairs at this time of night."

"Well," said the princess, "if it sleeps here I'm sure I won't."

But just then the bear curled himself up and lay down by the stove; and it was settled at last that the princess should sleep there too, with a light burning. But as soon as the king was well gone, the white bear came and begged her to undo his collar. The princess was so scared she almost swooned away; but she felt about till she found the collar, and she had scarce undone it before the bear pulled his head off. Then she knew him again, and was so glad, there was no end to her joy, and she wanted to tell her father at once that her deliverer was come. But the lad would not hear of it; he would earn her once more, he said. So in the morning, when they heard the king rattling at the posts outside, the lad drew on the hide, and lay down by the stove.

"Well, has it lain still?" the king asked.

"I should think so," said the princess; "it hasn't so much as turned or stretched itself once."

When they got up to the castle again, the captain took the bear and led it away, and then the lad threw off the hide, and went to a tailor and ordered clothes fit for a prince; and when they were fitted on he went to the king, and said he wanted to find the princess.

"You're not the first who has wished the same thing," said the king, "but they have all lost their lives; for if any one who tries can't find her in four-and-twenty hours his life is forfeited."

Yes; the lad knew all that. Still he wished to try, and if he couldn't find her, 'twas his lookout. Now in the castle there was a band that played sweet tunes, and there were fair maids to dance with, and so the lad danced away. When twelve hours were gone, the king said:

"I pity you with all my heart. You're so poor a hand at seeking; you will surely lose your life."

"Stuff!" said the lad; "while there's life there's hope. So long as there's breath in the body there's no fear; we have lots of time";

and so he went on dancing till there was only one hour left.

Then he said he would begin to search.

"It's no use now," said the king; "time's up."

"Light your lamp; out with your big bunch of keys," said the lad, "and follow me whither I wish to go. There is still a whole hour left."

So the lad went the same way which the king had led him the night before, and he bade the king unlock door after door till they came down to the pier which ran out into the sea.

"It's all no use, I tell you," said the king; "time's up, and this will only lead you right out into the sea."

"Still five minutes more," said the lad, as he pulled and pushed ᴀt the posts and pins, and the house floated up.

"Now the time *is* up," bawled the king; "come hither, headsman, and take off his head."

"Nay, nay!" said the lad; "stop a bit, there are still three minutes. Out with the key, and let me get into this house."

But there stood the king and fumbled with his keys, to draw out the time. At last he said he hadn't any key.

"Well, if you haven't, I have," said the lad, as he gave the door such a kick that it flew to splinters inwards on the floor.

At the door the princess met him, and told her father this was her deliverer, on whom her heart was set. So she had him; and this was how the beggar boy came to marry the king's daughter of Arabia.


*Sixty*

# True and Untrue

*Norwegian*

Once on a time there were two brothers; one was called True, and the other Untrue. True was always upright and good towards all, but Untrue was bad and full of lies, so that no one could believe what he said. Their mother was a widow, and hadn't much to live on; so when her sons had grown up, she was forced to send them away, that they might earn their bread in the world. Each got a little scrip with some food in it, and then they went their way.

Now, when they had walked till evening, they sat down on a

windfall in the wood, and took out their scrips, for they were hungry after walking the whole day, and thought a morsel of food would be sweet enough.

"If you're of my mind," said Untrue, "I think we had better eat out of your scrip, so long as there is anything in it, and after that we can take to mine."

Yes! True was well pleased with this, so they fell to eating, but Untrue got all the best bits, and stuffed himself with them, while True got only the burned crusts and scraps.

Next morning they broke their fast off True's food, and they dined off it too, and then there was nothing left in his scrip. So when they had walked till late at night, and were ready to eat again, True wanted to eat out of his brother's scrip, but Untrue said "No," the food was his, and he had only enough for himself.

"Nay! but you know you ate out of my scrip so long as there was anything in it," said True.

"All very fine, I daresay," answered Untrue; "but if you are such a fool as to let others eat up your food before your face, you must make the best of it; for now all you have to do is to sit here and starve."

"Very well!" said True, "you're Untrue by name and untrue by nature; so you have been, and so you will be all your life long."

Now when Untrue heard this, he flew into a rage, and rushed at his brother, and plucked out both his eyes. "Now, try if you can see whether folk are untrue or not, you blind buzzard!" and so saying, he ran away and left him.

Poor True! there he went walking along and feeling his way through the thick wood. Blind and alone, he scarce knew which way to turn, when all at once he caught hold of the trunk of a great bushy lime-tree, so he thought he would climb up into it, and sit there till the night was over for fear of the wild beasts.

"When the birds begin to sing," he said to himself, "then I shall know it is day, and I can try to grope my way farther on." So he climbed up into the lime-tree. After he had sat there a little time, he heard how some one came and began to make a stir and clatter under the tree, and soon after others came; and when they began to greet one another, he found out it was Bruin the bear, and Greylegs the wolf, and Slyboots the fox, and Longears the hare, who had come to keep St. John's eve under the tree. So they began to eat and drink, and be merry; and when they had done eating, they fell to gossiping together. At last the fox said:

"Shan't we, each of us, tell a little story while we sit here?"

Well! the others had nothing against that. It would be good fun, they said, and the bear began; for you may fancy he was king of the company.

"The king of England," said Bruin, "has such bad eyesight, he can scarce see a yard before him; but if he only came to this lime-tree in the morning, while the dew is still on the leaves, and took and rubbed his eyes with the dew, he would get back his sight as good as ever."

"Very true!" said Greylegs. "The king of England has a deaf and dumb daughter too; but if he only knew what I know, he would soon cure her. Last year she went to the communion. She let a crumb of the bread fall out of her mouth, and a great toad came and swallowed it down; but if they only dug up the chancel floor, they would find the toad sitting right under the altar rails, with the bread still sticking in his throat. If they were to cut the toad open, and take and give the bread to the princess, she would be like other folk again as to her speech and hearing."

"That's all very well," said the fox; "but if the king of England knew what I know, he would not be so badly off for water in his palace; for under the great stone, in his palace-yard, is a spring of the clearest water one could wish for, if he only knew to dig for it there."

"Ah!" said the hare in a small voice; "the king of England has the finest orchard in the whole land, but it does not bear so much as a crab, for there lies a heavy gold chain in three turns round the orchard. If he got that dug up, there would not be a garden like it for bearing in all his kingdom."

"Very true, I dare say," said the fox; "but now it's getting very late, and we may as well go home."

So they all went away together.

After they were gone, True fell asleep as he sat up in the tree; but when the birds began to sing at dawn, he woke up, and took the dew from the leaves, and rubbed his eyes with it, and so got his sight back as good as it was before Untrue plucked his eyes out.

Then he went straight to the king of England's palace, and begged for work, and got it on the spot. So one day the king came out into the palace-yard, and when he had walked about a bit, he wanted to drink out of his pump; for you must know the day was hot, and the king very thirsty; but when they poured him out a glass, it was so muddy, and nasty, and foul, that the king got quite vexed.

"I don't think there's ever a man in my whole kingdom who has such bad water in his yard as I, and yet I bring it in pipes from far, over hill and dale," cried out the king.

"Like enough, your Majesty"; said True, "but if you would let me have some men to help me to dig up this great stone which lies here in the middle of your yard, you would soon see good water, and plenty of it."

Well! the king was willing enough; and they had scarcely got the stone well out, and dug under it a while, before a jet of water sprang out high up into the air, as clear and full as if it came out of a conduit, and clearer water was not to be found in all England.

A little while after the king was out in his palace-yard again, and there came a great hawk flying after his chickens, and all the king's men began to clap their hands and bawl out, "There he flies!" "There he flies!" The king caught up his gun and tried to shoot the hawk, but he couldn't see so far, so he fell into great grief.

"Would to Heaven," he said, "there was any one who could tell me a cure for my eyes; for I think I shall soon go quite blind!"

"I can tell you one soon enough," said True; and then he told the king what he had done to cure his own eyes, and the king set off that very afternoon to the lime-tree, as you may fancy, and his eyes were quite cured as soon as he rubbed them with the dew which was on the leaves in the morning. From that time forth there was no one whom the king held so dear as True, and he had to be with him wherever he went, both at home and abroad.

So one day, as they were walking together in the orchard, the king said, "I can't tell how it is, that I can't! there isn't a man in England who spends so much on his orchard as I, and yet I can't get one of the trees to bear so much as a crab."

"Well! well!" said True; "if I may have what lies three times twisted round your orchard, and men to dig it up, your orchard will bear well enough."

Yes! the king was quite willing, so True got men and began to dig, and at last he dug up the whole gold chain. Now True was a rich man, far richer indeed than the king himself, but still the king was well pleased, for his orchard bore so that the boughs of the trees hung down to the ground, and such sweet apples and pears nobody had ever tasted.

Another day too the king and True were walking about, and talking together, when the princess passed them, and the king was quite downcast when he saw her.

"Isn't it a pity, now, that so lovely a princess as mine should want speech and hearing?" he said to True.

"Ay, but there is a cure for that," said True.

When the king heard that, he was so glad that he promised him the princess to wife, and half his kingdom into the bargain, if he could get her right again. So True took a few men, and went into the church, and dug up the toad which sat under the altar-rails. Then he cut open the toad, and took out the bread and gave it to the king's daughter; and from that hour she got back her speech, and could talk like other people.

Now True was to have the princess, and they got ready for the bridal-feast, and such a feast had never been seen before; it was the talk of the whole land. Just as they were in the midst of dancing the bridal-dance, in came a beggar lad, and begged for a morsel of food, and he was so ragged and wretched that every one crossed themselves when they looked at him; but True knew him at once, and saw that it was Untrue, his brother.

"Do you know me again?" said True.

"Oh! where should such a one as I ever have seen so great a lord?" said Untrue.

"Still you *have* seen me before," said True. "It was I whose eyes you plucked out a year ago this very day. Untrue by name, and untrue by nature; so I said before, and so I say now; but you are still my brother, and so you shall have some food. After that, you may go to the lime-tree where I sat last year; if you hear anything that can do you good, you will be lucky."

So Untrue did not wait to be told twice. "If True has got so much good by sitting in the lime-tree, that in one year he has come to be king over half England, what good may not I get?" he thought. So he set off and climbed up into the lime-tree. He had not sat there long, before all the beasts came as before, and ate and drank, and kept St. John's eve under the tree. When they had left off eating, the fox wished that they should begin to tell stories, and Untrue got ready to listen with all his might, till his ears were almost fit to fall off. But Bruin the bear was surly, and growled and said:

"Some one has been chattering about what we said last year, and so now we will hold our tongues about what we know"; and with that the beasts bade one another "Good night," and parted, and Untrue was just as wise as he was before, and the reason was, that his name was Untrue, and his nature untrue too.

*Sixty-one*

# The Louse Skin

*Danish*

There was a man who had three sons whose names were Kristen, Jakob, and Jesper. The parents liked Jesper least, because he was always slovenly and dirty, and for that reason the brothers hated him too. Now, in the same town was a miller who owned a strange animal who was tethered in his farmyard. One day the king came driving past the mill, and when he saw the animal he asked the coachman to stop the horses.

The king then asked the miller what kind of strange animal he had come into possession of, and the miller said that it was a louse that the maid had once found in his bed. He had taken good care of it, but it was so large now that he had to tether it in the farmyard. The king wanted very much to buy it from him, and they agreed on a price, but since such a creature is a poor walker the king decided to put it in the back of the carriage. When he reached home the animal was dead, because it had not been able to stand all the shaking of the carriage.

The king was of course very sorry, but nothing could be done about it. He had the skin taken off and later on he had a fur made for his daughter from it. He then announced that whoever could guess the kind of skin his daughter's fur coat was made from should have her and half the kingdom for a dowry.

No sooner had Kristen and Jakob heard this than they decided to win the princess. They took plenty of food along as well as wine to quench their thirst, should they get thirsty. When they came close to the king's palace they met an ant, who asked them to give it something to eat from the food they had along, but they laughed and said that they had no time, for they were going to the king's palace to win the princess; and after that they hurried the best they could. But when they reached their destination and had to guess the kind of skin the coat was made from they were at a loss; they did not know in or out and had to leave without any success.

Now Jesper also took it into his head to try his luck, but the parents only laughed and said that a man as wise as he was really would be able to win the princess. The mother gave him some dry bread that she found in the innermost end of the table drawer, as well as some water in a bottle, and he was on his way. Outside the king's palace he too met the ant who asked for a little of the food he had brought along. Jesper opened his sack and shared his food with the ant. "Where are you going?" the ant asked. "I am going to the king's palace to win the princess" answered Jesper. "I will go along" answered the ant, and it crept up and settled down in Jesper's coat pocket.

It was evening when Jesper reached the king's palace, but the suitors were always allowed to sleep there. When the princess came into her room to undress and go to bed the ant crept quietly through the keyhole into her room. Now the princess took off her fur coat and flung it on a chair with the words: "Now, you lie there, you louse's fur." The ant immediately hurried to Jesper and told him that the princess's fur was made from a louse's skin.

The next day Jesper, together with a minister, was admitted into the presence of the king and the princess. The minister was very eager. You see, he wanted to win the beautiful princess at any price, but he looked at the fur coat and touched it and did not know in or out. Then Jesper said: "Is it not made of a louse's skin?" "Yes," said the king, but in the same instant the minister took the word and said that that was just what he was going to say, and the princess, who liked the minister the best, agreed with him and said that he deserved the prize. But Jesper was not happy with that, for he was the one who had guessed correctly.

Then the king said, "Now the three of you can sleep in one bed tonight, and the one of you my daughter turns to in the morning when I step in shall have her for his wife." But when they had gone to bed the ant settled down in the minister's beard and bit his nose so much that he had to sneeze all night, and that was not very comfortable for the princess. In the morning when the king stepped in, the princess was facing Jesper and so he won her.

When the wedding was over, Jesper, who was now a prince, asked her if she would like to visit his childhood home. If so, they would have to travel for some days. Yes, she would like that, but he wanted to leave a couple of days early and she was to follow later. Now Jesper left for his parents' house, and when he got there they immediately asked him whether he had won the princess. "How can you think that I, who am ordinarily so stupid, should win a princess?" answered Jesper. No, they could all see the good sense in that. But a couple of days after Jesper's arrival a fine lady came driving into the farm. The two oldest sons came immediately running to help her out of the carriage, but Jesper too came and said that he wanted to help her out, and before the brothers could stop him he opened the carriage door and lifted out the princess. He was, however, so clumsy that he dropped her while carrying her over a puddle, and her clothes were completely soiled. Jesper got no gratitude for his impertinence, but the princess made apologies on his behalf and said that she could put on some clean clothes and there was no more talk of that thing.

When the table had been set and the food was to be carried in Jesper asked for permission to wait on the princess. The father scolded him, but this day it appeared that Jesper wanted things his way, something that usually did not happen in the home. When he then put the soup tureen on the table, he set it down so hard that it broke in two pieces and the contents ran onto the princess' lap. The father took him by the scruff of his neck and flogged him so ruthlessly that the princess had to intercede for him and on her intercession he was set free. Then the father told at great length how bad Jesper had always been.

"But what if I now tell you that Jesper is my husband and king of my father's kingdom; what do you say then?" asked the princess. Now this was another tune. "Oh yes, Jesper has always been a clever fellow," said the father, "I always suspected that he would amount to something." Now the roast was carried in and the father invited Jesper to sit at the end of the table since he had become such a man, and he gave a speech praising him. But Jesper was through with his home; he told his father that this was to be the last visit, for now the princess had heard how they had treated him in the old days; and after that they returned to the king's palace. Jesper turned into a very capable king who governed the kingdom wisely, and if he has not died he is probably still alive.

# The Young Giant

*German*

A farmer had a son who was as big as your thumb and got no bigger, and in the course of some years didn't grow a hair's breadth. Once when the farmer was going to the fields to do some plowing, the little chap said, "Father, I want to come along with you." "You want to come along?" said the father; "You stay here. Out there you aren't any use; you might even get lost." Then Tom Thumb began to weep, and in order to have peace and quiet his father put him in his pocket and took him along. Out there in the country he took him out again and set him down in a new furrow. As he was sitting there, a big giant came walking over the mountain. "Do you see the big bogyman there?" said the father, wishing to frighten the little fellow into being good. "He's coming to get you." The giant had taken but a few steps with his long legs when he reached the furrow. He lifted little Tom Thumb up carefully with two fingers, looked at him, and without saying a word walked off with him. The father stood there speechless with fright and just supposed that his child was lost and that he'd never lay eyes on him again as long as he lived.

The giant carried the child home and let him nurse at his breast, and Tom Thumb grew and got big and strong after the manner of giants. Two years later the old giant went with him into the forest, and wanting to test him, "Pull out a rod." The boy was then already so strong that he tore a young tree, roots and all, out of the ground. But the giant thought, "It's got to be better than that," again took him along and suckled him for two years

From *German Folk Tales*, collected and edited by Grimm Brothers. Translated by Francis P. Magoun, Jr. and Alexander H. Krappe. Copyright © 1960 by Southern Illinois University Press. Reprinted by permission of the Southern Illinois University Press.

more. When next he tested him, his strength had so increased that he could pull an old tree out of the ground. Still the giant wasn't satisfied, suckled him for two years more, and when he went with him into the forest that time and said, "Now pull up a decent sized rod," the boy tore the biggest oak out of the ground so that it came crashing down. And for him that was the merest child's play. "That will do now," said the giant, "you've learned your trade," and led him back to the field where it had fetched him.

His father was standing there behind the plow. The young giant went up to him and said, "Look here, father, see what a man your son has grown to be!" The farmer was frightened and said, "No, you're not my son; I don't want you. Go away from me!" "Of course I'm your son; let me get to work; I can plow as well as you and better." "No no! you're not my son and you can't plow, either. Go away from me!" But because he was afraid of the big man, he let go of the plow, stepped back, and sat down on the ground near by. Then the boy took the implement and just pressed one hand on it, but the pressure was so tremendous that the plow went deep into the earth. The farmer couldn't sit there and look on, and called to him, "If you're going to plow, you mustn't press down so terribly hard; it makes for a poor job." But the boy unharnessed the horses, and pulling the plow himself, said, "Just go home, father, and have mother cook a big dish full of food; in the meantime I'll plow up the field easily enough." Then the farmer went home and ordered his wife to prepare the food. The boy plowed the field, two whole acres, all by himself, then harnessing himself to the harrow, harrowed it all with two harrows at once. When he'd finished, he went into the forest, tore up two oak trees, shouldered them, and on them laid one harrow in front and one behind, also one horse in front and one behind, and carried the whole load to his parents' house as if it were a bundle of straw. When he came into the farmyard, his mother didn't recognize him and asked, "Who is that dreadful big man?" The farmer said, "He's our son." "No, that certainly isn't our son," she said; "we didn't have one so big as that; ours was a tiny thing. Go away!" she called to him, "we don't want you."

The boy held his peace, led the horses into the stable, and gave them their oats and hay properly. When he had finished, he went into the living-room, sat down on the bench, and said, "Mother, now I'd like to eat. Is it almost ready?" "Yes," she said, and brought in two great big dishes full of food, enough to have satisfied herself and her husband for a week. The boy ate it all up himself and asked if she couldn't serve him more. "No," she said, "that's all we have." "That was really just a taste; I've got to have more." She didn't dare oppose him, went off and put a big slaughtering kettle full of food on the fire, and when it was ready, she brought it in. "At last a few more crumbs are coming along," he said, and ate it all up by himself. Still, even this wasn't enough to satisfy his hunger. Then he said, "Father, I see plainly that I won't get enough to eat here at home; if you'll get me an iron beam so strong that I can't break it across my knees, I'll go out into the world." The farmer was happy, hitched his two horses to the wagon, and from the blacksmith fetched a beam so big and thick that the two horses could just move it. The boy laid it across his knees, and snap! he broke it right in the middle like a bean pole and threw it away. The father hitched up four horses and fetched as big and thick a beam as the four horses could move. The boy broke this, too, across his knees and threw it away, saying, "Father, this is no good to me, you must hitch up a better team and fetch a stronger beam." Then his father hitched up eight horses and fetched as big and thick a beam as the eight horses could pull. When his son took hold of it, he broke a piece right off the top and said, "Father, I see that you can't get me the kind of beam I need; I'm not going to stay here any longer."

Then he went away and claimed to be journeyman blacksmith. He came to a village where a smith lived; he was a miser, begrudged everybody everything, and wanted everything for himself. The boy went into the smithy and asked if he didn't need a journeyman. "Yes," said the smith, looked at him, and thought, "he's an able fellow; he'll be good at leading off with the hammering and earn his keep." "What wages do you want?" he asked. "I don't want any at all," he answered, "only every fortnight when the other journeymen get paid off, I want to give you two blows which you must put up with." The miser was thoroughly satisfied with this, thinking he'd save a lot of money in that way. The next morning the new journeyman was to lead off with the hammering. When, however, the master brought the red-hot beam and the boy dealt the first blow, the iron flew to pieces and the anvil sank so deep into the ground that they simply couldn't get it out again. Then the miser got angry and said, "My goodness! I can't use you; you hammer altogether too roughly. What wages do you want for the one blow?" "I want to give you just a very light tap, nothing else," said the boy, raised up his foot and gave him such a kick that he flew off over four ricks of hay. Then he picked out for himself the thickest iron beam that was in the smithy, took it in his hand as a walking-stick, and went his way.

After going on a while, he came to an outlying estate and asked the superintendent if he didn't need a foreman. "Yes," said the superintendent, "I can use one. You look like an able fellow who can really do something. What do you want as a yearly wage?" Again he answered that he wasn't asking for any wages at all, but every year he wanted to deal him three blows which he'd have to put up with. This satisfied the superintendent, for he, too, was a miser. The next morning the farm servants were supposed to drive to the forest; the other servants were already up, but the boy was still in bed. Then one of them called to him, "It's time to get up; we're going to the forest and you've got to come along." "The deuce!" he said quite roughly and defiantly. "Just go along; as it is, I'll be back home before all the rest of you." Then the others went to the superintendent, told him that the foreman was still in bed and wouldn't drive with them to the forest. The superintendent said to wake him up once more and ask him to hitch up the horses. The foreman, however, replied as before: "Just go along; as it is, I'll be back home before all the rest of you." Then he lay there another two hours; finally he got out of his feather bed, but first fetched himself two bushels of peas from the loft, cooked himself a porridge, and ate it in all peace and quiet. Having done that, he went out, hitched up the horses, and drove to the forest.

Not far from the forest was a sunken road through which he had to drive; there he first drove the wagon ahead till the horses had to stop; then he went behind the wagon, took some trees and brush and built a big barricade there, so that no horse could get through. Now coming to the edge of the forest, the others were just driving out with their loaded carts and were going home. "Drive right along," he said to them. "As it is, I'll be home ahead of you." He didn't drive very far into the forest, but straightway tore two of the very biggest trees out of the ground, threw them on the wagon, and turned about. When he goes to the barricade, the others were still standing there, unable to get through. "You see," he said, "if you'd stayed with me, you'd have got home just as quickly and might have slept another hour." He wanted to drive on, but his horses couldn't get through the barricade, so he unhitched them, put them up on the wagon, himself took hold of the shaft, and "swish" pulled the whole thing through and as easily as if it were loaded with feathers. Once on the other side, he said to the others, "You see, I got through quicker than you," drove on, and the others had to stop. In the farmyard he took one of the trees in his hand, and showing it to the superintendent, said, "Isn't that a fine bit of cordwood?" Then the superintendent said to his wife, "The boy's good; even if he does sleep late, he's back home before the others."

He served the superintendent for a year. When it was up and the other servants got their wages, he said it was time for him to get his, too. The superintendent, however, was frightened at the thought of the blow he was due to receive, and begged him and begged him to let him off: he'd rather be foreman himself and let the boy be superintendent. "No," he said, "I don't want to be a superintendent. I'm a foreman and I want to stay a foreman; but I do want to deal out the blows agreed upon." The superintendent was willing to give him whatever he asked for, but it did no good; the foreman just said no to everything. Then the superintendent didn't know what to do and asked him for a fortnight's respite; he wanted to think up something. The foreman said he might have the fortnight.

The superintendent summoned all his clerks; they were to think it over and advise him. The clerks meditated for a long time, finally said that nobody's life was safe from the foreman: he could strike a man dead as easily as he could a midge. The superintendent should order him to go down the well and clean it, and when he was down there, they'd roll up one of the millstones that lay there and throw it on his head; then he'd never come to light again. The plan pleased the superintendent, and the foreman was willing to go down the well. When he was standing at the bottom, they rolled down the biggest millstone and thought his head was bashed in, but he called out, "Chase the chickens away from the well! They're scratching up there in the sand and throwing the grains into my eyes so that I can't see." Then the superintendent said "shoo! shoo!" and made believe he was scaring the chickens away. When the foreman had finished his job, he climbed up and said, "Just look! I really have a fine necklace on," meaning the millstone he was wearing around his neck.

Now the foreman wanted to receive his wages, but the superintendent again begged for a fortnight to think it over. The clerks assembled and advised him to send the foreman into an enchanted mill to grind rye there during the night; nobody had ever come out of it alive in the morning. The superintendent liked the proposal, summoned the foreman that very evening, and ordered him to drive a hundred and forty bushels of rye to the mill and grind it that very night; they wanted it badly. Then the foreman went up to the loft and put thirty-five bushels in his right pocket, thirty-five in his left, and took seventy in a long sack which hung half over his back, half over his chest. Loaded thus, he went to the enchanted mill.

The miller told him he could grind there quite all right in the daytime but not at night, since the mill was enchanted and whoever had gone in had been found dead there in the morning. "I'll come through, of course," he said; "just go along and have a good sleep." Then he went into the mill and poured the rye into the hopper. Toward eleven o'clock he went into the miller's room and sat down on the bench. After he'd been sitting there a little while, the door suddenly opened and in came a great big banqueting table, and on the table was placed wine and a roast and a lot of good food, all by itself, for there was nobody there to serve it. Afterward the chairs drew themselves up, but no people came, until suddenly he saw fingers busy with the knives and forks and putting food on the plates, though other than that he could see nothing. Since he was hungry and saw the food, he, too, sat down at the table, ate along with the rest, and enjoyed the meal. When he'd had enough and the others had quite cleaned their plates, too, the candles were suddenly all snuffed out, as he clearly heard, and as it was now pitch dark, he got something like a slap in the face. Then he said, "If anything like that happens again, I'll hit back," and since he got slapped a second time, he too, hit back, and so it went on all night. He took nothing without an argument and gave as good as he received, and wasn't slow in hitting out all about him. At daybreak, however, everything stopped.

When the miller got up, he wanted to see how he was and marveled that he was still alive. Then the foreman said, "I ate my fill, got slapped in the face but also slapped back." The miller was glad, said that the mill was now disenchanted, and would gladly have rewarded him with a lot of money. However, the foreman said, "I don't want any money, I have enough as it is." Then he took the flour on his back, went home, and told the superintendent that he'd done the job and now wanted his wages as agreed.

Hearing that, the superintendent got really frightened. He was beside himself, walked up and down the room, and drops of sweat ran down his forehead. To get some fresh air he opened the window, but before he could say Jack Robinson, the foreman had given him such a kick that he flew out the window into the air and on and on, until he was out of sight. Then the foreman said to the superintendent's wife, "If he doesn't come back, you'll have to take the other blow." "No! no!" she cried, "I can't stand it," and opened the other window because drops of sweat were running down her forehead. Then he gave her a kick so that she, too, flew out, and since she was lighter, she flew much higher than her husband. "Come to me," cried her husband, but she cried, "You come to me, I can't get to you," and there they soared in the air, and neither could get to the other, and whether they're still soaring, I don't know. The young giant, however, took his iron beam and went on his way.

*Sixty-three*

# The Miller's Four Sons

*French*

Once upon a time there was an old miller who had four sons and little with which to feed them. One morning when there remained in the mill only a piece of dry bread the size of a fist the miller called his sons and said to them:

"Come, my children, and listen to me; misfortune has come to the house and I no longer grind enough grain to feed five people. Divide between you the remainder of the bread, then go into the square field over there; each shall put himself in his corner and leave to go seek his fortune, walking straight forward."

The sons of the miller obeyed their father, and they went in different directions, after having promised to return to the square field in two years on the same day.

The eldest, after having walked some time, arrived in a town, and as he was tired, he stopped and began to amuse himself. He found himself in front of the house of a tailor, who came to his door and said to him:

"You are not from here, my boy; where are you going?"

"To seek my fortune and try to make a living," he answered.

"Come with me," said the tailor, "and I will teach you my trade."

The boy was indeed well off to find employment immediately, and he willingly followed the tailor.

The second son of the miller, feeling tired, had lain down upon the ground to rest. He saw passing a hunter who was swearing at his dogs; he was afraid and began to weep.

"Do not be afraid," said the hunter, approaching him, "I will not hurt you; just the opposite. Why are you weeping like this?"

"I am a poor boy, son of a miller," he answered, "and I have left my father's house because there was no more bread to feed us."

"If you wish to come with me," said the hunter, "I will teach you my profession."

The third boy was met by some robbers who asked him where he was going with so little baggage; he told them that distress had come to his father's mill and that he was going in search of his fortune.

"Come with us," said the robbers, "and we will teach you our profession."

"I do not wish to learn the trade of a thief," he answered; "I have always heard that it is a profession of rascals."

"No," they said, "thieves like us are honest folk, and though they sometimes trap fools and the credulous, at least they do not kill anyone."

The boy went off with them.

The fourth son of the miller had lain down on a high rock; he saw coming an astrologer who looked with his telescope to see what the weather was.

"Who are you, my child?" the astrologer asked him when he had noticed him.

"A poor boy who left his father's house because there was no more bread."

"Come with me," said the astrologer, "and I will teach you my profession."

At the end of two years, each of the brothers had finished his apprenticeship, and all wanted to return to their father's mill, just as they had agreed.

He who was with the tailor said to his employer: "Master, I am going to see my father."

"During the twenty-five years that I have been in the profession of tailoring, I have never seen anyone who worked better than you, my boy. I am satisfied with you, and I am going to give you a needle which will sew everywhere and will pass through iron as well as cloth."

The boy with the hunter said to him: "I am going to rejoin my father. During the two years that I have been with you I have given good service, haven't I?"

"Yes, my boy: I have been a hunter for twenty-five years, and I have never known anyone who could shoot like you. I am going to give you a rifle: with it you will get all you desire, you will kill all that you wish."

The one who had remained with the thieves said to his companions: "I am going to rejoin my father; during the two years I have been with you, you have had nothing to complain about concerning me, have you?"

"No," they answered, "but if you leave us, you will disclose to the gendarmes where we are hiding."

"Oh, no," he said, "never will I denounce the people whose bread I have eaten."

"You are such a good thief that in all the years we have practiced the profession we have never known any one who was more skilful than you. Here is a saber which we give you: within the hilt is a ladder which will permit you to climb where you wish."

The one who was with the astrologer said to his master: "Master, I am going to rejoin my father."

"Go ahead, my child," answered the astrologer, "I am satisfied with you; during the twenty-five years that I have practiced my profession, I have never seen anyone who knew better than you how to predict the weather. I am going to give you a field glass with which you may see as far as you wish."

The four brothers, each coming from a different direction, returned on the appointed day to the field they had left, and came together in the middle.

"We must," they said, "go immediately to the mill in order to see if our father is still alive; but we fear that he is dead, for the poor man was already old when we left him."

When they arrived in sight of the mill, they saw the wings turning in the wind: "Ah!" they cried, "our father is not yet dead, thank God!"

The miller was very happy to see his four children again, and he wanted to know what they had learned and what had happened to them.

The eldest said: "I learned the trade of tailoring, and my master said that during the twenty-five years he had been in the profession, he had never known anyone more skilful than I; he gave me a needle which sews iron as well as cloth."

"That is good," said the miller. "And you, what have you done?" he asked the second.

"I learned the profession of the hunter, and my master said that during twenty-five years he had hunted he had never seen a marksman more skilful than I. He gave me a rifle which hits whatever one wishes."

"The profession of hunting is a profession of the good-for-nothing," said the miller.

"No, for one receives money by selling his game."

"What profession have you learned?" the miller asked his third son.

"That of the robber."

"I do not like at all this profession of the murderer," cried the good man.

"Ah! my father, I have never killed anyone; but I have trapped more than one simpleton. Thieves are more honest people than you imagine; they have given me a saber with which I can climb where I wish."

"And you, little one, what trade have you learned?"

"That of the astrologer."

"Well and good, that's a fine profession."

"Yes," answered the son; "my employer told me that during the twenty-five years he has been an astrologer he has known no one who was as well informed upon the condition of the skies, and he has given me a field glass which lets me see all that I wish."

The miller said to them: "I must see if my children are as skilful and as cunning as they claim to be."

At some distance from the mill there was a tree in which there was the nest of a warbler so well hidden among the branches that one could not know where it was placed.

"What is there in this tree?" he asked.

The astrologer took his field glass, and after having put it to his eye, he said: "I see a nest of a warbler, and the bird has four eggs which she sits upon at this moment."

The thief unscrewed the hilt of his saber, and, climbing up his ladder, he took away the warbler from upon the nest so softly that she did not notice having left her nest; the hunter broke the eggs into more than fifty thousand pieces, the tailor resewed them with his needle, and the thief put them into the nest, put back the warbler and replaced the nest upon the tree, and all that was done so quickly that the bird had not even noticed anything.

"That is fine," said the miller to his sons, "I see that you are dexterous fellows. The daughter of the king has been carried away by a dragon who keeps her prisoner upon a rock in the middle of the sea. You must try to rescue her."

They took a boat and guided it in what they had been told was the direction of the rock. When they saw it, the astronomer looked with his field glass and said to his brothers:

"The dragon is sleeping now, and he keeps the daughter of the king between his paws."

The boat approached quietly, the thief unscrewed his ladder and noiselessly succeeded in rescuing the king's daughter, whom he took from the paws of the dragon without having awakened him; then, leading the princess, he descended into the boat which was quickly pushed away and was soon out of sight of the rock.

They believed themselves safe from all fear, when they heard in the air a voice which cried:

"Where is the daughter of the king? Where is the daughter of the king?"

The astrologer took his field glass and said: "I see the dragon who is coming after us."

The hunter put two balls into his rifle, and as soon as the monster was in sight, he adjusted it and killed him dead. But the enormous body of the dragon fell upon the boat and broke it into more than a thousand pieces. Then the tailor took his needle, sewing and resewing; in a moment the boat was put back again in the water, and one could not see where it had been broken.

The four brothers returned the princess to the palace of the king; since she was to marry her liberator, and as all the four had contributed to her deliverance, they drew straws to find out who should become the son-in-law of the king. Chance indicated the tailor, and after the wedding, which was very beautiful, the king gave to the miller's other three sons enough money to make them rich as lords.

*Sixty-four*

# The Speedy Messenger

*Russian*

In a certain land, in a certain kingdom, there were certain impass-
able swamps. A circuitous road went around them; it took three
years to travel fast on this road, and if one traveled slowly, even
five were not enough! Near the road lived a poor old man who had
three sons: the first was named Ivan, the second Vasily, and the
third was little Semyon. The old man determined to clear the
swamps, to lay a straight road for travelers on foot and travelers
on horseback, and to build white hazelwood bridges over the
streams, so that a man on foot could pass through the swamps in
three weeks and a rider on horseback in three days. He set to
work together with his sons, and after not a little time everything
was finished just as he had planned it: sturdy were the white
hazel bridges and cleared was the fine straight road.

The poor man returned to his hut and said to Ivan, his first-
born: "Go, my beloved son, sit under the first bridge and listen to
what folk say about us—whether it will be good or evil." Obedient to his father's command, Ivan hid himself under the bridge.

Two venerable hermits walked over the bridge and said to each
other: "To him who laid this bridge and cleared the road, whatever he asks of the Lord, the Lord will give it to him!" As
soon as Ivan heard these words, he came out from under the
hazelwood bridge, and said: "This bridge I laid with my father
and brothers." "And what do you wish of the Lord?" the holy
men asked him. "That the Lord make me rich for the rest of my
life!" "Very well, go to the open field. In the open field there is an
old oak. Under that oak is a deep vault, and in that vault are gold
and silver and precious stones galore. Take a shovel and dig—the
Lord will make you rich for life!" Ivan went to the open field, dug
up much gold and silver and many precious stones under the oak,
and took them home. "Well, little son," the poor man asked him,

From *Russian Fairy Tales*, edited and translated by Norbert Guterman. Copyright 1945 by Pantheon Books, Inc. Reprinted by permission of Pantheon
Books, a Division of Random House, Inc.

"have you seen anyone walking or driving over the bridge? And what do people say about us?" Ivan told his father that he had seen two venerable men and that they had rewarded him for life.

The next day the poor man sent Vasily, his middle son, to the bridge. Vasily sat under the hazel logs and listened. Two venerable men walked over the bridge, came to the spot above his hiding-place, and said: "He who laid this bridge, whatever he asks of the Lord, the Lord will give it to him." As soon as Vasily heard these words, he came out and said: "This bridge I laid with my father and brothers." "And what do you ask of the Lord?" "That the Lord give me bread for the rest of my life!" "Very well, go home, stake out a piece of fresh land, and sow it; the Lord will give you bread for all your life!" Vasily came home, told his father all that had happened, marked out a piece of fresh land, and sowed it with grain.

The third day the poor man sent his youngest son to the bridge. Little Semyon sat under the logs and listened. Two venerable men walked over the bridge, came to the spot above his hiding place, and said: "He who laid this bridge, whatever he asks of the Lord, the Lord will give it to him." Little Semyon heard these words, came out, and said: "This bridge I laid with my father and brothers." "And what do you ask of the Lord?" "I ask of him a favor—to serve as a soldier to the great sovereign!" "Ask for something else. A soldier's service is hard; if you become a soldier, you will fall captive to the Sea King, and many tears will you shed!" "Eh, you are venerable hermits and you know very well he who does not weep in this world will weep in the next!" "Well, since you will serve the king, we give you our blessing!" said the venerable old men. They put their hands on little Semyon and turned him into a fleetfooted stag.

The stag ran to his father's house. From the window his father and brothers saw him, jumped out of the hut, and wanted to catch him. The stag turned back. He came running to the two venerable old men, and they turned him into a hare. The hare darted back to the house; the father and brothers saw him, jumped out of the hut, and wanted to catch him, but he turned back again. He came running to the two venerable old men, who turned him into a little bird with a golden head. The bird flew to the house and sat on the window sill. The father and brothers saw him and jumped up to catch him, but he took wing and flew back. The bird came flying to the two venerable old men, who turned him into a human again and said: "Now, little Semyon, you can go into the king's service. If you ever need to run somewhere in a hurry, you can turn into a stag, a hare, and a bird with a golden head. We have taught you how."

Little Semyon went home and asked his father's permission to go into the king's service. "Why should you go?" answered the poor man. "You are still young and foolish." "No, father, let me go; it is God's will." The poor man gave permission, and little Semyon made his bundle, said farewell to his father and brothers, and set out on his way.

After some time, a long time or a short time, he came to the king's court, went straight to the king himself, and said: "Your Majesty, do not punish me, let me speak." "Speak, little Semyon." "Your Majesty, take me into your service." "Impossible! You are small and foolish; how could you serve?" "Although I am small and stupid, I will serve no worse than the others; God will help me." The king consented, took him as a soldier, and ordered him to stay near his person. Some time passed, and suddenly a certain king declared a terrible war against our king. He began to prepare himself to take the field; at the appointed hour his whole army assembled. Little Semyon asked permission to go to war; the king could not refuse him, so took him with him and set out to the field of battle.

For a long, long time the king marched with his troops. He left many, many lands behind him, and soon was close to the enemy —in about three days he would have to give battle. At that moment the king realized that he had neither his battle mace nor his sharp sword with him. He had forgotten them in his palace; he had nothing to defend himself with, to defeat the enemy forces with. He issued a call to all his troops: would someone undertake to go to the palace in a hurry and bring him his battle mace and sharp sword? To him who would do this service he promised his daughter, Princess Maria, in marriage, half his kingdom as a dowry, and the other half after his death. Volunteers presented themselves; some said that they could do the errand in three years; others, in two years; still others, in one year. But little Semyon said to the sovereign: "Your Majesty, I can go to the palace and bring the battle mace and the sharp sword in three days." The king was delighted, took him by the hand, kissed him on the mouth, and at once wrote a letter to Princess Maria telling her to trust this messenger and to give him the sword and the mace. Little Semyon took the letter from the king and set out on his way.

Having traveled about one verst, he turned into a fleet-footed stag and darted off like an arrow from a bow. He ran and ran until he got tired and turned from a stag into a hare; then he raced ahead at a hare's pace. He ran and ran until all his legs were weary and then turned from a hare into a little bird with a golden head; he flew even faster, flew and flew, and in a day and a half reached the kingdom where Princess Maria was. He turned back into a human, entered the palace, and gave the princess the letter. Princess Maria took it, unsealed it, read it, and said: "But how could you run across so many lands so speedily?" "This is how!" answered the messenger; he turned into a fleet-footed stag, ran once or twice across the princess' chamber, approached the princess, and put his head on her knees. She took her scissors and cut a tuft of fur from his head. The stag turned into a hare, the hare capered a little in the chamber and jumped on the princess' knees. She cut a tuft of fur from him then too. The hare turned into a little bird with a golden head, the bird flew about the room a little and perched on the princess' hand. Princess Maria cut a golden feather from his head, and wrapped all these—the stag's fur, the hare's fur, and the golden feather—into a handkerchief and hid them on her person. The bird with the golden head then turned back into a messenger.

The princess gave him meat and drink, helped him to get ready for his journey, and gave him the battle mace and the sharp sword; then they said good-by to each other, kissed heartily in farewell, and little Semyon went back to the king. Again he ran as a fleet-footed stag, bounded as a slant-eyed hare, flew as a little bird, and by the end of the third day saw the king's camp near by. At about three hundred paces from the army he lay down on the beach near a bayberry bush, to rest from his journey; he put the battle mace and the sharp sword by his side. From great weariness he fell asleep soon, and soundly. Just then a general happened to pass by the bayberry bush, saw the messenger, straightway pushed him into the sea, took the battle mace and the sharp sword, brought them to the king, and said: "Your Majesty, here are your battle mace and sharp sword, I fetched them myself— and that braggart, little Semyon, will surely take three years!" The king thanked the general, began to fight with the enemy, and in a short time won a brilliant victory over him.

As for little Semyon, we have seen that he fell into the sea. That very moment the Sea King seized him and carried him to the deepest depth. He lived with this king for a whole year, grew bored and sad, and wept bitterly. The Sea King came to him and said: "Well, little Semyon, are your bored here?" "I am bored, your Majesty!" "Would you fain go to the Russian world?" "I would, if such is your royal favor." The Sea King carried him out exactly at midnight, left him on the shore, and himself returned to the sea. Little Semyon prayed to God: "Lord, give me some sun!" Just before the rising of the red sun the Sea King came, again snatched him and carried him to the depths of the sea.

Little Semyon lived there for another whole year. He became bored, and wept very bitterly. The Sea King asked him: "What is the matter, are you bored?" "I am bored," said little Semyon. "Would you fain go to the Russian world?" "I would, your Majesty." The Sea King took him out to the shore at midnight, and himself returned to the sea. Little Semyon prayed to God with tears in his eyes: "My Lord, give me some sun!" Day had just begun to break when the Sea King came and snatched him and carried him once more to the depths of the sea. Little Semyon lived in the sea for a third year, became bored, and wept bitterly, inconsolably. "What is the matter, Semyon, are you bored?" the Sea King asked him. "Would you fain go to the Russian world?" "I would, your Majesty." The Sea King cast him out on the shore, and himself returned to the sea. Semyon, the little youth, prayed to God with tears in his eyes: "My Lord, give me some sun!" Suddenly the sun shone with his bright rays, and now the Sea King no longer could take him into captivity.

Little Semyon set out for his kingdom. He turned first into a stag, then into a hare, and then into a little bird with a golden head. After a short time he found himself near the king's palace. And while all this had been happening, the king had come back from the war and betrothed his daughter, Princess Maria, to the deceitful general. Little Semyon entered the chamber in which the bridegroom and the promised bride were sitting at table. Princess Maria saw him and said to the king: "Sovereign, my father! Do not punish me, let me speak." "Speak, my dear daughter! What do you wish?" "Sovereign, my father! My bridegroom is not the one who is sitting at the table, but the one who has just come! Now show us, little Semyon, how at that time you ran speedily for the battle mace and the sharp sword." Little

Semyon turned into a fleet-footed stag, ran once or twice across the chamber, and stopped near the princess. Princess Maria took from her kerchief the bit of fur she had cut from the stag, showed the king the spot at which she had clipped it, and said: "Look, father! Here are my proofs." The stag turned into a hare; the hare capered in the chamber and leapt to the princess' knee. Princess Maria took the bit of hare's fur from her kerchief. The hare turned into a little bird with a golden head; the bird flew a little in the chamber and perched on the princess' hand. Princess Maria untied the third knot in her kerchief and showed the golden feather. Then the king learned the real truth, ordered the general to be put to death, married Princess Maria to little Semyon, and made him his heir.

*Sixty-five*

# The Language of Animals

*Bulgarian*

A certain man had a shepherd, who served him faithfully and honestly for many years. This shepherd, when he was once upon a time following the sheep, heard a whistling on the hill, and, not knowing what it was, went off to see. When he got to the place, there was a conflagration, and in the middle of it a serpent was squeaking. When he saw this, he waited to see how the serpent would act, for all around it was burning, and the fire had almost come close to it. When the serpent saw him, it screamed: "Dear shepherd, do a good action: take me out of this fire." The shepherd took pity on its words, and reached it his crook, and it crawled out upon it. When it had crawled out, it coiled itself round his neck. When the shepherd saw this, he was frightened, and said: "Indeed you are a wretch! Is that the way you are going to thank me for rescuing you? So runs the proverb: 'Do good, and find evil.'" The serpent answered him: "Don't fear: I shall do you no harm; only carry me to my father; my father is the emperor of the serpents." The shepherd begged pardon, and excused himself: "I can't carry you to your father, because I have no one to leave in charge of my sheep." The serpent said to him: "Don't fear for your sheep; nothing will happen to them; only carry me to my father, and go quickly."

Then there was no help for it, so he started with it over the hill. When he came to a door, which was formed of nothing but serpents intertwined, and went up to it, the serpent which was coiled round his neck gave a whistle, and the serpents, which had twined themselves into the form of a door, immediately untwined, and made way for them to enter. As the shepherd and the serpent entered the palace, the serpent called to the shepherd: "Stop! let me tell you something: when you come into my father's palace, he will promise you what you desire, silver and gold; but don't you accept anything, only ask him to give you such a tongue that you will be able to understand all animals. He will not give you this readily, but at last grant it you he will." The shepherd went with it into its father's palace, and its father, on seeing it, shed tears, and asked it: "Hey, my son, where have you been till now?" It replied, and told him everything in order: what had taken place, and how it had taken place, and how the shepherd had rescued it.

Then the emperor of the serpents turned to the shepherd, and said to him: "Come, my son, what do you wish me to give you in recompense for rescuing my child?" The shepherd replied to him: "Nothing else, only give me such a tongue that I can understand all animals." The emperor of the serpents said to him: "That is not a proper gift for you, my son, because, if I give you anything of the kind, you will betray yourself in somebody's presence by boasting of it, and then you will die immediately; ask something else." The shepherd replied to him: "I wish for nothing else. If you will give it me, give it; if not, farewell!" He turned to go; but the emperor of the serpents cried out: "Stay! Return! If you ask this, come, that I may give it you. Open your mouth." The shepherd opened his mouth, and the emperor of the serpents spat into it, and told him to spit also into his mouth. And thus they spat thrice into each other's mouths. When this was done, the emperor of the serpents said to the shepherd: "Now you have the tongue which you desired; go, and farewell! But it is not permitted you to tell anybody, because, if you do, you will die. I am telling you the truth."

The shepherd then departed. As he went over the hill, he understood the conversation of the birds, and, so to speak, of everything in the world. When he came to his sheep, he found them correct in number, and sat down to rest. But scarcely had he lain down, when two crows flew up, perched on a tree hard by him, and began to converse in their language: "If that shepherd knew that just where that black lamb lies a vault full of silver and gold is buried in the ground, he would take its contents." When he heard this, he went and told his master, and he brought a cart, and they broke open the door of the vault, and took out its valuable contents. His master was a righteous man, and said to him: "Well, my son, this is all yours; the Lord has given it you. Go, provide a house, get married, and live comfortably." The shepherd took the property, went away, provided a house, got married, and lived very comfortably. This shepherd, after a little time, became so rich and prosperous that there was nobody richer than he in his own or the neighboring villages. He had shepherds, cowherds, swineherds, grooms, and everything on a handsome scale.

Once upon a time this shepherd ordered his wife on New Year's Eve to provide wine, brandy, and everything requisite, and to go the next morning to his cattle, to take the provisions to the herdsmen, that they, too, might enjoy themselves. His wife obeyed him, and did as her husband ordered her. The next day they got up, got ready, and went. When they arrived where the cattle were, the master said to his shepherds: "Lads, assemble together, and sit down to eat and drink your fill, and I will watch the cattle tonight." This was done; they assembled together, and he went out to sleep by the cattle. In the course of the night, after some time, the wolves began to howl and speak in their language, and the dogs to bark and speak in theirs. The wolves said: "Can we capture any young cattle?" The dogs answered in their language: "Come in, that we, too, may eat our fill of flesh." But among the dogs there was one old dog, who had only two teeth left. This dog spoke and answered the wolves: "In faith, as long as these two teeth of mine last, you shan't come near to do harm to my master." In the morning, when it dawned, the master called the herdsmen, and told them to kill all the dogs except that old one. His servants began to implore him: "Don't, master! Why? It's a sin." But he said to them: "Do just as I ordered you, and not otherwise."

Then he and his wife mounted their horses and went off. His wife rode a mare, and he a horse. As they went, the master's horse outstripped the wife's mare, and began to say to her in their language: "Go quicker; why do you hang back?" The mare's reply in defence of her lagging pace was so amusing that the man laughed out loud, turned his head, and looked behind him with a smile. His wife observed him smiling, whipped her mare to catch him up, and then asked him to tell her why he smiled. He said to her: "Well, suppose I did? Something came into my head." This answer did not satisfy her, but she began to worry him to tell her why he smiled. He said this and that to her to get out of it, but the more he said to get out of it, the more did she worry him. At length he said to her that, if he told her, he would die immediately. But she had no dread of her husband's dying, and went on worrying him: "There is no alternative, but tell me you must."

When they got home, they dismounted from their horses, and as soon as they had done so, her husband ordered a grave to be dug for him. It was dug, and he lay down in it, and said to his wife: "Did you not press me to tell you why I smiled? Come now, that I may tell you but I shall die immediately." On saying this, he gave one more look round him, and observed that the old dog had come from the cattle. Seeing this, he told his wife to give him a piece of bread. She gave it him, but the dog would not even look at it, but shed tears and wept; but the cock, seeing it, ran up and began to peck it. The dog was angry, and said: "As if *you'd* die hungry! Don't you see that our master is going to die?" "What a fool he is! Let him die! Whose fault is it? I have a hundred wives. When I find a grain of millet, I call them all to me, and finally eat it myself. If one of them gets cross at this, I give her one or two pecks, and she lowers her tail; but this man isn't equal to keeping one in order." When the man heard the cock say this, he jumped up at once out of the grave, seized a stick, chased his wife over hill and dale, and at last settled her completely, so that it never entered her head any more to ask him why he smiled.

*Sixty-six*

# The Three Languages

*Italian*

A father once had a son who spent ten years in school. At the end of that time, the teacher wrote the father to take away his son because he could not teach him anything more. The father took the boy home and gave a grand banquet in his honor, to which he invited the most noble gentlemen of the country. After many speeches by those gentlemen, one of the guests said to the host's son: "Just tell us some fine thing that you have learned." "I have learned the language of dogs, of frogs, and of birds." Everyone laughed on hearing this, and all went away ridiculing the pride of the father and the foolishness of the son. The former was so ashamed at his son's answer and so angry at him that he gave him up to two servants, with orders to take him into a wood and kill him and to bring back his heart. The two servants did not dare to obey this command, and instead of the lad they killed a dog, and carried its heart to their master.

The youth fled from the country and came to a castle a long way off, where lived the treasurer of the prince, who had immense treasures. There he asked for and obtained a lodging, but scarcely had he entered the house when a multitude of dogs collected about the castle. The treasurer asked the young man why so many dogs had come, and as the latter understood their language he answered that it meant that a hundred assassins would attack the castle that very evening, and that the treasurer should take his precautions. The castellan made two hundred soldiers place themselves in ambush about the castle and at night they arrested the assassins. The treasurer was so grateful to the youth that he wished to give him his daughter, but he replied that he could not remain now, but that he would return within a year and three days.

After he left that castle he arrived at a city where the king's daughter was very ill because the frogs which were in a fountain near the palace gave her no rest with their croaking. The lad perceived that the frogs croaked because the princess had thrown a cross into the fountain, and as soon as it was removed the girl recovered. The king, too, wished the lad to marry her, but he again said that he would return within a year and three days.

After leaving the king he set out for Rome, and on the way met three young men, who became his companions. One day it was very warm and all three lay down to sleep under an oak. Immediately a great flock of birds flew into the oak and awakened the pilgrims by their loud singing. One of them asked: "Why are these birds singing so joyfully?" The youth answered: "They are rejoicing with the new Pope, who is to be one of us."

And suddenly a dove alighted on his head, and in truth shortly after he was made Pope. Then he sent for his father, the treasurer, and the king. All presented themselves trembling, for they knew that they had committed some sin. But the Pope made them all relate their deeds, and then turned to his father and said: "I am the son whom you sent to be killed because I said I understood the language of birds, of dogs, and of frogs. You have treated me thus, and on the other hand a treasurer and a king have been very grateful for this knowledge of mine." The father, repenting his fault, wept bitterly, and his son pardoned him and kept him with him while he lived.

*Sixty-seven*

# The Lazy Boy

*Danish*

A woman had a son who was so unduly lazy that whenever his mother asked him to do something or to go somewhere he would say: "Yes, if I could only bring myself to do it!"

One day his mother asked him to fetch a bucket full of water. "Yes, if I could only bring myself to do it!" said the boy. But he finally went after all, and when he had pulled up the water a large toad was sitting in it. "Let me go!" pleaded the toad. "Yes, if I could only bring myself to do it!" said he. He finally let her go, and then she said that he could make as many wishes as he wanted and they would all come true. "Yes, if I could only bring myself to wish for something!" said he. He sat down astride the thrashing stool with the waterbucket in front of him, and when he had been sitting there for a while looking at it, he wished that it would walk home with him. The bucket and the stool walked softly off with him. The king's daughter was standing at the window when he came riding by in this fashion and when she saw that procession she could not help bursting into laughter. "I wish you would have a boy!" said he as he rode slowly on home with the water.

This went unnoticed; but some time later the princess gave birth to a boy. She was then asked who was the father of that boy, but she did not know. When the little one was a year old his grandfather gave him a gold apple, which he should give to the one that was his father. This was announced all over the country and all of the rich and noble people in the country came to court to see to whom the little boy would give the apple; and many people gathered for this occasion.

The lazy boy also came past and when he saw the many noble people he wanted to see what was going on. He walked to the door, got up on the tip of his toes and peeked in. As soon as the little one saw him he ran over and gave him the apple. When the king saw that such a boy was the father of his daughter's son he grew very angry and had his daughter, the child, and its father put in a boat which sailed over to a small island in the sea.

When they had been sailing on the water for some time the princess wished for something to eat. The boy wished for some too, and immediately food and wine were before them and they ate and drank. Afterwards they wished that they would soon be near land, and they were. The princess now asked the boy how it could have happened that he was the father of the child, and he told her. Later on they wished that they had a palace to live in and soon there was a wonderful palace for them. They also wished for a bridge from the island to the mainland, and it was not long before there was a bridge all the way. After that the princess— and the boy too, of course—wished that they would have a visit from her father, so that he could see how well established they were. And then one fine day the king and all of his courtiers came out to them. The boy then wished for many good things with which to entertain his guests. They ate and drank well, but after the meal the courtiers took the silverware and put it in their pockets. This annoyed the boy so much that he wished their noses would grow so long that they could hardly carry them. This wish too was granted: the noses of all the courtiers grew so long that they were stepping on them, and as they walked back across the bridge they stumbled over them and rolled into the sea.

*Sixty-eight*

# Tom Thumb

*German*

One evening a poor farmer was sitting by the hearth and poking the fire while his wife was spinning. Then he said, "How sad that we have no children! It's so quiet in our house, while in other houses there's so much noise and fun." "Yes," answered his wife with a sigh, "if we only had one single child and even if it were very tiny, only as big as a thumb, I'd be really content. And we'd love it with all our hearts." Now it happened that the wife got sickly and after seven months gave birth to a child which was, to be sure, perfect in all its parts but no taller than a thumb. Then they said, "It's as we wished and it shall be our darling child," and from its size they named it Tom Thumb. They gave him plenty to eat, but the child grew no bigger, just stayed as he was the first hour he was born. Nevertheless he had an intelligent look and soon turned out to be a clever and nimble little thing, lucky in everything he undertook.

One day the farmer was getting ready to go to the forest to cut wood and said to himself, "Now I wish there was somebody to come after me with the cart." "Oh, father," cried Tom Thumb, "of course I'll bring it; you can count on it, it'll be in the forest at the time you say." Then the man laughed, saying, "How can it? You're much too small to lead the horse by the bridle." "That doesn't matter, father. If mother will just hitch up the horse, I'll sit in its ear and call out to it how to go." "Well," answered the father, "we'll try it once."

When the time came, the mother hitched up the horse and put Tom Thumb in its ear, and then the little fellow called out to the horse how to go: "Hup! Whoa! Gee! Ree!" Then everything went as smooth as under a master coachman, and the cart took the right way toward the forest. Now it happened, just as the cart

From *German Folk Tales*, collected and edited by Grimm Brothers. Translated by Francis P. Magoun, Jr. and Alexander H. Krappe. Copyright © 1960, by Southern Illinois University Press. Reprinted by permission of the Southern Illinois University Press.

was turning a corner and the little chap was calling "Gee! gee!" that two strangers came along. "My!" said one, "what's that? There goes a cart, and a driver's calling to the horse, yet he isn't to be seen." "That's weird," said the other, "let's follow the cart and see where it stops." The cart went clear into the forest and straight to the spot where the wood was being cut. When Tom Thumb saw his father, he called to him, "You see, father, here I am with the cart. Now take me down." The father held the horse with his left hand and with his right took his little son out of the horse's ear. The boy sat down gaily on a straw.

When the two strangers saw Tom Thumb, they didn't know what to say from amazement. Then one took the other aside and said, "Listen, that little fellow might make our fortunes if we exhibited him for money in a big city. Let's buy him." So they approached the farmer, saying, "Sell us the little man; we'll treat him well." "No," answered the father, "he's the apple of my eye and I won't sell him for all the gold in the world." However, when he heard the proposal, Tom Thumb crept up on the pleat of his father's coat, got on his shoulder, and whispered in his ear, "Father, do give me away; I'll come back again all right." Then his father handed him over to the two men in return for a handsome sum of money. "Where do you want to sit?" they said to him. "Oh, just put me on the brim of your hat, then I can walk up and down and view the landscape and not fall off, either." They did as he asked, and when Tom Thumb had taken leave of his father, they set out with him. They went on till it got dusk. Then the little fellow said, "Take me down; you simply must." "Just stay up there," said the man on whose head he was sitting, "I shan't mind it. The birds, too, sometimes drop something on me." "No," said Tom Thumb, "I know what's proper. Just hurry up and lift me down." The man took off his hat and set the little chap in a plowed field by the roadside. Then he crawled and jumped a little here and there among the clods of earth, hunted out a mouse hole, and suddenly slipped into it. "Good evening, gentlemen," he called out laughing at them, "now go home without me." They came running up and poked in the mouse hole with sticks but in vain. Tom Thumb crawled farther and farther back, and since it soon got quite dark, they had to walk home again full of rage and with an empty purse.

When Tom Thumb saw that they were gone, he crept out again from the underground passage. "It's so dangerous walking in the dark," he said, "how easily one can break one's neck or leg!" Luckily he ran against an empty snail shell. "Thank goodness," he said, "here I can spend the night in safety," and sat down in it. Before long, as he was falling asleep, he heard two men passing; one of them said, "How shall we go about getting the rich parson's money and his silver?" "I could tell you that," Tom Thumb interrupted. "What's that!" said one of the thieves in a fright. "I heard somebody speak." They stopped and listened. Then Tom Thumb spoke again, "Take me along and I'll help you." "Where are you?" "Just search the ground and notice where the voice comes from," he replied. The thieves finally found him and lifted him up. "You little creature, how are you going to help us?" they said. "Look," he answered, "I'll creep between the iron bars into the parson's room and hand you whatever you want." "All right," they said, "we'll see what you can do."

When they got to the rectory, Tom Thumb crawled into the room, at the same time immediately shouted with all his might, "Do you want everything that's here?" The thieves were frightened and said, "Please do talk softly, so as not to wake anybody up." But Tom Thumb acted as though he hadn't understood them and again shouted, "What do you want? Do you want everything that's here?" The cook, who was sleeping in the next room, heard that, sat up in bed and listened. In their fright the thieves had, however, retreated a little; finally they plucked up courage again and thought, "The little chap's trying to tease us," so they came back and whispered to him, "Now be serious and hand us out something." Then Tom Thumb once more shouted out as loud as he could. "I'm quite willing to give you everything. Just put your hands in here." The maid, who was listening, heard this most distinctly, jumped out of bed, and stumbled in through the door. The thieves took to their heels and ran as if the Wild Huntsman were after them. When, however, the maid couldn't see anything, she went to light a candle. When she came along with it, Tom Thumb, without being seen, betook himself to the barn while the maid, having searched every nook and corner and finding nothing, went back to bed and thought she'd just been seeing and hearing things in her sleep.

Tom Thumb climbed about in the hay and found a nice place to sleep; he planned to rest up there until daybreak and then go back to his parents. But other experiences were in store for him.

Alas, the world is full of sorrow and misery! Already at the first crack of dawn the maid got up to feed the cattle. Her first trip was to the barn, where she picked up an armful of hay, the very hay in which poor Tom Thumb was lying asleep. He was sleeping so soundly, however, that he didn't notice anything and didn't wake up until he was in the mouth of a cow, which had gathered him in with the hay. "Good heavens," he cried, "how did I get into the fulling mill!" but soon saw where he was. He had to watch out not to get between the cow's teeth and be crushed, and anyway in the end he couldn't help slipping down into the stomach along with the hay. "They forgot the windows in this little room," he said, "and the sun doesn't get in, and no one's bringing a light." On the whole he thought the quarters bad, and, worst of all, more new hay kept coming in the door, and the place got more and more cramped. In his fright he finally shouted as loud as he could, "Don't bring me any more fodder! Don't bring me any more fodder!" The maid was just milking the cow, and when she heard talking without seeing anyone and heard the voice that was the same, too, that she'd heard in the night, she got so frightened that she slipped off her stool and spilled the milk. In all haste she ran to her master, crying, "Good heavens, parson, the cow's been talking!" "You're mad," answered the rector, but all the same he went into the stable himself to see what was up. Scarcely had he set foot there than Tom Thumb shouted, "Don't bring me any more fodder! Don't bring me any more fodder!" Then the rector himself got frightened, thought that an evil spirit had entered the cow, and ordered it killed.

It was slaughtered, but the stomach with Tom Thumb inside it was thrown on the dungheap. Tom Thumb had great difficulty in working himself through but managed to clear the way. Nevertheless, as he was about to stick his head out, a new misfortune occurred. A hungry wolf came along and swallowed the whole stomach in one gulp. Tom Thumb didn't lose courage. "Perhaps," he thought, "the wolf will listen to reason," and from its belly he called out, "Dear wolf, I know of a wonderful meal for you." "Where can I get it?" said the wolf. "In such and such a house: you'll have to crawl in through the drain, but you'll find all the cake, bacon, and sausage you want," and described his father's house to him in detail.

The wolf didn't have to be told twice, squeezed through the drain at night, and ate to its heart's content in the pantry. When it had eaten its fill, it wanted to go away again but it had got so fat that it couldn't go back out the same way. Tom Thumb had counted on this and now began to make a tremendous noise inside the wolf, roaring and yelling as loud as he could. "Will you be quiet," said the wolf, "you're waking the people up." "What do I care?" answered the little fellow. "You've eaten your fill; I want to have some fun, too," and began anew to yell with all his might.

This finally awakened his father and mother; they ran to the pantry and looked in through a crack. On seeing the wolf in there, they ran away; the man fetched an ax and his wife a scythe. "Stand back," said the man as they went into the pantry. "If I give it a blow and that doesn't kill it at once, you must go for it and cut it to pieces." Then Tom Thumb heard his father's voice and shouted, "Father dear, I'm here inside the wolf." Then his father said joyfully, "Thank God we've found our dear child again," and ordered his wife to lay the scythe aside so as not to hurt Tom Thumb. Then he hauled off and dealt the wolf such a blow on its head that it fell down dead. Then they got a knife and scissors, cut it open, and pulled the little fellow out again. "My," said the father, "how we've been worrying about you!" "Yes, father, I've been about in the world a lot. Thank heaven that I can breathe fresh air again." "Where all have you been?" "Oh, father, I was in a mouse hole, in a cow's stomach, and a wolf's belly, and now I'll stay with you and mother." "And we shan't sell you again for all the riches in the world," said the parents, hugging and kissing their darling Tom Thumb. They gave him food and drink and had new clothes made for him, for his own had been ruined on the journey.

*Sixty-nine*

# The Armless Maiden

*Russian*

In a certain kingdom, not in our land, there lived a wealthy merchant; he had two children, a son and a daughter. The father and mother died. The brother said to the sister: "Let us leave this

From *Russian Fairy Tales*, edited and translated by Norbert Guterman. Copyright 1945 by Pantheon Books, Inc. Reprinted by permission of Pantheon Books, a Division of Random House, Inc.

town, little sister; I will rent a shop and trade, and find lodgings for you; we will live together." They went to another province. When they came there, the brother inscribed himself in the merchant's guild, and rented a shop of woven cloths. The brother decided to marry and took a sorceress to wife. One day he went to trade in his shop and said to his sister: "Keep order in the house, sister." The wife felt offended because he said this to his sister. To revenge herself she broke all the furniture and when her husband came back she met him and said: "See what a sister you have; she has broken all the furniture in the house." "Too bad, but we can get some new things," said the husband.

The next day when leaving for his shop he said farewell to his wife and his sister and said to his sister: "Please, little sister, see to it that everything in the house is kept as well as possible." The wife bided her time, went to the stables, and cut off the head of her husband's favorite horse with a saber. She awaited him on the porch. "See what a sister you have," she said. "She has cut off the head of your favorite horse." "Ah, let the dogs eat what is theirs," answered the husband.

On the third day the husband again went to his shop, said farewell, and said to his sister: "Please look after my wife, so that she does not hurt herself or the baby, if by chance she gives birth to one." When the wife gave birth to her child, she cut off his head. When her husband came home he found her sitting and lamenting over her baby. "See what a sister you have! No sooner had I given birth to my baby than she cut off his head with a saber." The husband did not say anything; he wept bitter tears and turned away.

Night came. At the stroke of midnight he rose and said: "Little sister, make ready; we are going to mass." She said: "My beloved brother, I do not think it is a holiday today." "Yes, my sister, it is a holiday; let us go." "It is still too early to go, brother," she said. "No," he answered, "young maidens always take a long time to get ready." The sister began to dress; she was very slow and reluctant. Her brother said: "Hurry, sister, get dressed." "Please," she said, "it is still early, brother." "No, little sister, it is not early, it is high time to be gone."

When the sister was ready they sat in a carriage and set out for mass. They drove for a long time or a short time. Finally they came to a wood. The sister said: "What wood is this?" He answered: "This is the hedge around the church." The carriage caught in a bush. The brother said: "Get out, little sister, disentangle the carriage." "Ah, my beloved brother, I cannot do that, I will dirty my dress." "I will buy you a new dress, sister, a better one than this." She got down from the carriage, began to disentangle it, and her brother cut off her arms to the elbows, struck his horse with the whip, and drove away.

The little sister was left alone; she burst into tears and began to walk in the woods. She walked and walked, a long time or a short time; she was all scratched, but could not find a path leading out of the woods. Finally, after several years, she found a path. She came to a market town and stood beneath the window of the wealthiest merchant to beg for alms. This merchant had a son, an only one, who was the apple of his father's eye. He fell in love with the beggar woman and said: "Dear father and mother, marry me." "To whom shall we marry you?" "To this beggar woman." "Ah, my dear child, do not the merchants of our town have lovely daughters?" "Please marry me to her," he said. "If you do not, I will do something to myself." They were distressed, because he was their only son, their life's treasure. They gathered all the merchants and clerics and asked them to judge the matter: should they marry their son to the beggar woman or not? The priest said: "Such must be his fate, and God gives your son his sanction to marry the beggar woman."

So the son lived with her for a year and then another year. At the end of that time he went to another province, where her brother had his shop. When taking his leave he said: "Dear father and mother, do not abandon my wife; as soon as she gives birth to a child, write to me that very hour." Two or three months after the son left, his wife gave birth to a child; his arms were golden up to the elbows, his sides were studded with stars, there was a bright moon on his forehead and a radiant sun near his heart. The grandparents were overjoyed and at once wrote their beloved son a letter. They dispatched an old man with this note in all haste. Meanwhile the wicked sister-in-law had learned about all this and invited the old messenger into her house: "Come in, little father," she said, "and take a rest." "No, I have no time, I am bringing an urgent message." "Come in, little father; take a rest, have something to eat."

She sat him down to dinner, took his bag, found the letter in it, read it, tore it into little pieces, and wrote another letter instead: "Your wife," it said, "has given birth to a half dog and half bear

that she conceived with beasts in the woods." The old messenger
came to the merchant's son and handed him the letter; he read it
and burst into tears. He wrote in answer asking that his son be
not molested till he returned. "When I come back," he said, "I
will see what kind of baby it is." The sorceress again invited the
old messenger into her house. "Come in, sit down, take a rest,"
she said. Again she charmed him with talk, stole the letter he
carried, read it, tore it up, and instead ordered that her sister-in-
law be driven out the moment the letter was received. The old
messenger brought this letter; the father and mother read it and
were grieved. "Why does he cause us so much trouble?" they
said. "We married him to the girl, and now he does not want his
wife!" They pitied not so much the wife as the babe. So they gave
their blessing to her and the babe, tied the babe to her breast, and
sent her away.

She went, shedding bitter tears. She walked, for a long time or
a short time, all in the open field, and there was no wood or village
anywhere. She came to a dale and was very thirsty. She looked to
the right and saw a well. She wanted to drink from it but was
afraid to stoop, lest she drop her baby. Then she fancied that the
water came closer. She stooped to drink and her baby fell into the
well. She began to walk around the well, weeping, and wondering
how to get her child out of the well. An old man came up to her
and said: "Why are you weeping, you slave of God?" "How can I
help weeping? I stooped over the well to drink water and my baby
fell into it." "Bend down and take him out." "No, little father, I
cannot; I have no hands, only stumps." "Do as I tell you. Take
your baby." She went to the well, stretched out her arms, and God
helped, for suddenly she had her hands, all whole. She bent down,
pulled her baby out, and began to give thanks to God, bowing to
all four sides.

She said her prayers, went on farther, and came to the house
where her brother and husband were staying, and asked for
shelter. Her husband said: "Brother, let the beggar woman in;
beggar women can tell stories and recount real happenings." The
wicked sister-in-law said: "We have no room for visitors, we are
overcrowded." "Please, brother, let her come; there is nothing I
like better than to hear beggar women tell tales." They let her in.
She sat on the stove with her baby. Her husband said: "Now,
little dove, tell us a tale—any kind of story."

She said: "I do not know any tales or stories, but I can tell the

truth. Listen, here is a true happening that I can recount to you."
And she began: "In a certain kingdom, not in our land, lived a
wealthy merchant; he had two children, a son and a daughter.
The father and mother died. The brother said to the sister: 'Let
us leave this town, little sister.' And they came to another province. The brother inscribed himself in the merchant's guild and
took a shop of woven cloth. He decided to marry and took a
sorceress to wife." At this point the sister-in-law muttered: "Why
does she bore us with her stories, that hag?" But the husband
said: "Go on, go on, little mother, I love such stories more than
anything!"

"And so," the beggar woman went on, "the brother went to
trade in his shop and said to his sister: 'Keep order in the house,
sister.' The wife felt offended because he had said this to his sister
and out of spite broke all the furniture." And then she went on to
tell how her brother took her to mass and cut off her hands, how
she gave birth to a baby, how her sister-in-law lured the old
messenger—and again the sister-in-law interrupted her, crying:
"What gibberish she is telling!" But the husband said: "Brother,
order your wife to keep quiet; it is a wonderful story, is it not?"

She came to the point when her husband wrote to his parents
ordering that the baby be left in peace until his return, and the
sister-in-law mumbled: "What nonsense!" Then she reached
the point when she came to their house as a beggar woman, and
the sister-in-law mumbled: "What is this old bitch gibbering
about!" And the husband said: "Brother, order her to keep quiet;
why does she interrupt all the time?" Finally she came to the point
in the story when she was let in and began to tell the truth instead
of a story. And then she pointed at them and said: "This is my
husband, this is my brother, and this is my sister-in-law."

Then her husband jumped up to her on the stove and said:
"Now, my dear, show me the baby. Let me see whether my father
and mother wrote me the truth." They took the baby, removed its
swaddling clothes—and the whole room was illumined! "So it is
true that she did not tell us just a tale; here is my wife, and here is
my son—golden up to the elbows—his sides studded with stars, a
bright moon on his forehead, and a radiant sun near his heart!"

The brother took the best mare from his stable, tied his wife to
its tail, and let it run in the open field. The mare dragged her on
the ground until she brought back only her braid; the rest was
strewn on the field. Then they harnessed three horses and went

home to the young husband's father and mother; they began to live happily and to prosper. I was there and drank mead and wine; it ran down my mustache, but did not go into my mouth.

*Seventy*

# The Dancing Water, the Singing Apple, and the Speaking Bird

*Italian*

There was once an herb-gatherer who had three daughters who earned their living by spinning. One day their father died and left them all alone in the world. Now the king had a habit of going about the streets at night, and listening at the doors to hear what the people said of him. One night he listened at the door of the house where the three sisters lived, and heard them disputing about something. The oldest said: "If I were the wife of the royal butler, I would give the whole court to drink out of one glass of water, and there would be some left." The second said: "If I were the wife of the keeper of the royal wardrobe, with one piece of cloth I would clothe all the attendants, and have some left. The youngest said: "Were I the king's wife, I would bear him three children: two sons with apples in their hands, and a daughter with a star on her brow."

The king went back to his palace, and the next morning sent for the sisters, and said to them: "Do not be frightened, but tell me what you said last night." The oldest told him what she had said, and the king had a glass of water brought, and commanded her to prove her words. She took the glass, and gave all the attendants to drink, and there was some water left. "Bravo!" cried the king, and summoned the butler. "This is your husband. Now it is your turn," said the king to the next sister, and commanded a piece of cloth to be brought, and the young girl at once cut out garments for all the attendants, and had some cloth left. "Bravo!" cried the king again, and gave her the keeper of the wardrobe for her husband. "Now it is your turn," said the king to the youngest.

"Your Majesty, I said that were I the king's wife, I would bear him three children: two sons with apples in their hands, and a daughter with a star on her brow." The king replied: "If that is true, you shall be queen; if not, you shall die," and straightway he married her.

Very soon the two older sisters began to be envious of the youngest. "Look," said they: "She is going to be queen, and we must be servants!" and they began to hate her. A few months before the queen's children were to be born, the king declared war, and was obliged to depart; but he left word that if the queen had three children—two sons with apples in their hands and a girl with a star on her brow—the mother was to be respected as queen; if not, he was to be informed of it, and would tell his servants what to do. Then he departed for the war.

When the queen's children were born, as she had promised, the envious sisters bribed the nurse to put little dogs in the place of the queen's children, and sent word to the king that his wife had given birth to three puppies. He wrote back that she should be taken care of for two weeks, and then put into a treadmill.

Meanwhile the nurse took the little babies, and carried them out of doors, saying: "I will make the dogs eat them up," and she left them alone. While they were thus exposed, three fairies passed by and exclaimed: "Oh how beautiful these children are!" and one of the fairies said: "What present shall we make these children?" One answered: "I will give them a deer to nurse them." "And I a purse always full of money." "And I," said the third fairy, "will give them a ring which will change color when any misfortune happens to one of them."

The deer nursed and took care of the children until they grew up. Then the fairy who had given them the deer came and said: "Now that you have grown up, how can you stay here any longer?" "Very well," said one of the brothers, "I will go to the city and hire a house." "Take care," said the deer, "that you hire one opposite the royal palace." So they all went to the city and hired a palace as directed, and furnished it as if they had been royal personages. When the aunts saw these three youths, imagine their terror! "They are alive!" they said. They could not be mistaken, for there were the apples in their hands, and the star on the girl's brow. They called the nurse and said to her: "Nurse, what does this mean? are our nephews and niece alive?" The nurse watched at the window until she saw the two brothers go out, and then she went over as if to make a visit to the new house. She entered and said: "What is the matter, my daughter; how do you do? Are you perfectly happy? You lack nothing. But do you know what is necessary to make you really happy? It is the Dancing Water. If your brothers love you, they will get it for you!" She remained a moment longer and then departed.

When one of the brothers returned, his sister said to him: "Ah! my brother, if you love me go and get me the Dancing Water." He consented, and next morning saddled a fine horse, and departed. On his way he met a hermit, who asked him, "Where are you going, cavalier?" "I am going for the Dancing Water." "You are going to your death, my son; but keep on until you find a hermit older than I." He continued his journey until he met another hermit, who asked him the same question, and gave him the same direction. Finally he met a third hermit, older than the other two, with a white beard that came down to his feet, who gave him the following directions. "You must climb yonder mountain. On top of it you will find a great plain and a house with a beautiful gate. Before the gate you will see four giants with swords in their hands. Take heed; do not make a mistake; for if you do that is the end of you! When the giants have their eyes closed, do not enter; when they have their eyes open, enter. Then you will come to a door. If you find it open, do not enter; if you find it shut, push it open and enter. Then you will find four lions. When they have their eyes shut, do not enter; when their eyes are open, enter, and you will see the Dancing Water." The youth took leave of the hermit, and hastened on his way.

Meanwhile the sister kept looking at the ring constantly, to see whether the stone in it changed color; but as it did not, she remained undisturbed.

A few days after leaving the hermit the youth arrived at the top of the mountain, and saw the palace with the four giants before it. They had their eyes shut, and the door was open. "No," said the youth, "that won't do." And so he remained on the lookout a while. When the giants opened their eyes, and the door closed, he entered, waited until the lions opened their eyes, and passed in. There he found the Dancing Water, and filled his bottles with it, and escaped when the lions again opened their eyes.

The aunts, meanwhile, were delighted because their nephew did not return; but in a few days he appeared and embraced his sister. Then they had two golden basins made, and put into them the Dancing Water, which leaped from one basin to the other. When the aunts saw it they exclaimed: "Ah! how did he manage to get that water?" and called the nurse, who again waited until the sister was alone, and then visited her. "You see," said she, "how beautiful the Dancing Water is! But do you know what you want now? The Singing Apple." Then she departed. When the brother who had brought the Dancing Water returned, his sister said to him: "If you love me you must get for me the Singing Apple." "Yes, my sister, I will go and get it."

Next morning he mounted his horse, and set out. After a time he met the first hermit, who sent him to an older one. He asked the youth where he was going, and said: "It is a difficult task to get the Singing Apple, but hear what you must do: Climb the mountain; beware of the giants, the door, and the lions; then you will find a little door and a pair of shears in it. If the shears are open, enter; if closed, do not risk it." The youth continued his way, found the palace, entered, and found everything favorable. When he saw the shears open, he went into a room and saw a wonderful tree, on top of which was an apple. He climbed up and tried to pick the apple, but the top of the tree swayed now this way, now that. He waited until it was still a moment, seized the branch, and picked the apple. He succeeded in getting safely out of the palace, mounted his horse, and rode home, and all the time he was carrying the apple it kept making a sound.

The aunts were again delighted because their nephew was so long absent; but when they saw him return, they felt as though the house had fallen on them. Again they summoned the nurse, and again she visited the young girl, and said: "See how beautiful they are, the Dancing Water and the Singing Apple! But should you see the Speaking Bird, there would be nothing left for you to see." "Very well," said the young girl; "we will see whether my brother will get it for me."

When her brother came she asked him for the Speaking Bird, and he promised to get it for her. He met, as usual on his journey, the first hermit, who sent him to the second, who sent him on to a third one, who said to him: "Climb the mountain and enter the palace. You will find many statues. Then you will come to a garden, in the midst of which is a fountain, and on the basin is the Speaking Bird. If it should say anything to you, do not answer. Pick a feather from the bird's wing, dip it into a jar you will find there, and anoint all the statues. Keep your eyes open, and all will go well."

The youth already knew well the way, and soon was in the palace. He found the garden and the bird, which, as soon as it saw him, exclaimed: "What is the matter, noble sir; have you come for me? You have missed it. Your aunts have sent you to your death, and you must remain here. Your mother has been sent to the treadmill." "My mother in the treadmill?" cried the youth, and scarcely were the words out of his mouth when he became a statue like all the others.

When the sister looked at her ring she saw that it had changed its color to blue. "Ah!" she exclaimed, and sent her other brother after the first. Everything happened to him as to the first. He met the three hermits, received his instructions, and soon found himself in the palace, where he discovered the garden with the statues, the fountain, and the Speaking Bird.

Meanwhile the aunts, who saw that both their nephews were missing, were delighted; and the sister, on looking at her ring, saw that it had become clear again.

Now when the Speaking Bird saw the youth appear in the garden it said to him: "What has become of your brother? Your mother has been sent to the treadmill." "Alas, my mother in the treadmill!" And when he had spoken these words he became a statue.

The sister looked at her ring, and it had become black. Poor child! not having anything else to do, she dressed herself like a page and set out.

Like her brothers, she met the three hermits, and received their instructions. The third concluded thus: "Beware, for if you answer when the bird speaks you will lose your life." She continued her way, followed exactly the hermit's directions, and reached the garden in safety. When the bird saw her it exclaimed: "Ah! you here, too?" Now you will meet the same fate as your brothers. Do you see them? one, two, and you make three. Your father is at the war. Your mother is in the treadmill. Your aunts are rejoicing." She did not reply, but let the bird sing on. When it had nothing more to say it flew down, and the young girl caught it, pulled a feather from its wing, dipped it into the jar, and anointed her brothers' nostrils, and they at once came to life again. Then she did the same with all the other statues, with the lions and the giants, until all became alive again. Then she departed with her brothers, and all the noblemen, princes, barons, and kings' sons rejoiced greatly. Now when they had all come to life again the palace disappeared, and the hermits disappeared, for they were the three fairies.

The day after the brothers and sister reached the city where they lived, they summoned a goldsmith, and had him make a gold chain, and fasten the bird with it. The next time the aunts looked out they saw in the window of the palace opposite the Dancing Water, the Singing Apple, and the Speaking Bird. "Well," said they, "the real trouble is coming now!"

The bird directed the brothers and sister to procure a carriage finer than the king's, with twenty-four attendants, and to have the service of their palace, cooks and servants, more numerous and better than the king's. All of which the brothers did at once. And when the aunts saw these things they were ready to die of rage.

At last the king returned from the war, and his subjects told him all the news of the kingdom, and the thing they talked about the least was his wife and children. One day the king looked out of the window and saw the palace opposite furnished in a magnificent manner. "Who lives there?" he asked, but no one could answer him. He looked again and saw the brothers and sister, the former with the apples in their hands, and the latter with the star on her brow. "Gracious! if I did not know that my wife had given birth to three puppies, I should say that those were my children," exclaimed the king. Another day he stood by the window and enjoyed the Dancing Water and the Singing Apple, but the bird was silent. After the king had heard all the music, the bird said: "What does your Majesty think of it?" The king was astonished at hearing the Speaking Bird, and answered: "What should I think? It is marvelous." "There is something more marvelous," said the bird; "just wait." Then the bird told his mistress to call her brothers, and said: "There is the king; let us invite him to dinner on Sunday. Shall we not?" "Yes, yes," they all said. So the king was invited and accepted, and on Sunday the bird had a grand dinner prepared and the king came. When he saw the young people, he clapped his hands and said: "I cannot persuade myself; they seem my children."

He went over the palace and was astonished at its richness. Then they went to dinner, and while they were eating the king said: "Bird, every one is talking; you alone are silent." "Ah! your

Majesty, I am ill; but next Sunday I shall be well and able to talk, and will come and dine at your palace with this lady and these gentlemen." The next Sunday the bird directed his mistress and her brothers to put on their finest clothes; so they dressed in royal style and took the bird with them. The king showed them through his palace and treated them with the greatest ceremony: the aunts were nearly dead with fear. When they had seated themselves at the table, the king said: "Come, bird, you promised me you would speak; have you nothing to say?" Then the bird began and related all that had happened from the time the king had listened at the door until his poor wife had been sent to the treadmill; then the bird added: "These are your children, and your wife was sent to the mill, and is dying." When the king heard all this, he hastened to embrace his children, and then went to find his poor wife, who was reduced to skin and bones and was at the point of death. He knelt before her and begged her pardon, and then summoned her sisters and the nurse, and when they were in his presence he said to the bird: "Bird, you who have told me everything, now pronounce their sentence." Then the bird sentenced the nurse to be thrown out of the window, and the sisters to be cast into a cauldron of boiling oil. This was at once done. The king was never tired of embracing his wife. Then the bird departed and the king and his wife and children lived together in peace.

*Seventy-one*

# Snow-White

*German*

Once upon a time in the middle of winter when the snowflakes were falling from the sky like feathers, a queen was sitting by a window with a black ebony frame and was sewing. As she was thus sewing and looking at the snow, she stuck the needle in her finger, and three drops of blood fell into the snow. Because the

From *German Folk Tales*, collected and edited by Grimm Brothers. Translated by Francis P. Magoun, Jr. and Alexander H. Krappe. Copyright © 1960, by Southern Illinois University Press. Reprinted by permission of the Southern Illinois University Press.

red looked so pretty in the white snow, she thought to herself, "If only I had a child as white as snow, as red as blood, and as black as the wood of the window frame!" Soon thereafter she had a little daughter who was as white as snow, as red as blood, and whose hair was as black as ebony. Therefore she was called Snow-White, and when the child was born, the queen died.

A year later the king married a second wife. She was a beautiful woman but proud and haughty and couldn't bear being second in beauty to anyone. She had a marvelous mirror: when she stepped up to it and looked at herself in it, she'd say:

"Mirror, mirror on the wall,
Who is the fairest in all the land?"

The mirror would then reply:

"Lady Queen, you are the fairest in the land."

Then she'd be content, knowing that the mirror was telling the truth.

But Snow-White grew up and got more and more beautiful and, when she was seven, she was as beautiful as a bright day and fairer than the queen herself. Once when the queen asked her mirror:

"Mirror, mirror on the wall,
Who is the fairest in all the land,"

it replied:

"Lady Queen, you are the fairest here,
But Snow-White is a thousand times fairer than you."

Then the queen was frightened and got green and yellow with envy. From that hour, whenever she looked at Snow-White, she'd feel a turn, she hated the girl so. Envy and pride grew like a weed in her heart, higher and higher, so that day or night she no longer had any rest. Then she summoned a huntsman and said, "Take the child out into the forest; I don't want to lay eyes on her again. You're to kill her and bring me her lungs and her liver as a token." The huntsman obeyed and took her out, and when he'd drawn his hunting-knife and was about to pierce Snow-White's innocent heart, she began to weep and said, "Alas, dear huntsman, spare me my life. I'm willing to go into the wild forest and never come back home again," and because she was so beautiful, the huntsman took pity on her and said, "Just run away, poor child." "The wild animals will soon dovour you," he thought, feeling just the same as if a heavy load had been lifted from his heart because he didn't have to kill her. Since a young boar came running past, he killed it, took out its lungs and liver, and bought them as a token to the queen. The chef had to cook them in brine, and the wicked woman ate them up, thinking she'd eaten Snow-White's lungs and liver.

Now the poor child was all alone in the big forest and got so frightened that she even eyed all the leaves of the trees and didn't know what to do. She started running and ran over the sharp stones and through the thorn bushes, and the wild animals sprang past her but did her no harm. She ran as long as her legs would carry her till nearly nightfall. Then she saw a little cottage and went in to rest. In the cottage everything was tiny but indescribably pretty and neat. There was a little table there laid with a little white cloth with seven little plates, and each plate with its little spoon, furthermore seven little knives and forks, and seven little tumblers. Along the wall stood seven little beds side by side, spread with snow-white sheets. Because she was so hungry and thirsty, Snow-White ate some vegetables and bread off each plate and drank a drop of wine from each tumbler, for she didn't want to take everything away from any one of them. After that, since she was so tired, she lay down in one of the beds, but not one of them fitted her: one was too long, another too short, till finally the seventh was just right. She lay down in it, commended herself to God, and fell asleep.

When it had got quite dark, the masters of the cottage came home; they were the seven dwarfs who with pick and shovel mined for ore in the mountains. They lighted their seven little candles and, when it was light in the cottage, they saw that someone had been in there, for not everything was the way they'd left it. The first said, "Who's been sitting in my chair?" The second, "Who's been eating off my plate?" The third, "Who's been taking some of my roll?" The fourth, "Who's been eating some of my vegetables?" The fifth, "Who's been handling my fork?" The sixth, "Who's been cutting with my knife?" The seventh, "Who's been drinking out of my tumbler?" Then the first looked about and noticing a little wrinkle in his bed, said, "Who got into my bed?" The others came on the run, exclaiming, "Somebody's been lying in my bed, too!" The seventh, when he looked in his bed, saw Snow-White, who was lying there asleep. He called the others. They came running up and crying out in astonishment, fetched their seven candles and let the light shine on Snow-White. "My goodness, my goodness!" they exclaimed, "how beautiful the child is!" and were so happy that they didn't wake her up but let her go on sleeping in the bed. The seventh dwarf, however, slept with his companions, one hour with each till the night had passed.

When it was morning, Snow-White woke up, and seeing the seven dwarfs, was frightened. They were friendly, however, and asked, "What's your name?" "My name is Snow-White," she answered. "How did you get to our house?" continued the dwarfs. Then she told them that her stepmother had meant to have her slain, but that the huntsman had made her a present of her life, and that she'd walked all day until she finally found their cottage. "If you'll keep house for us," said the dwarfs, "cook, make the beds, wash, sew, and knit, and if you'll keep everything neat and clean, then you may stay with us and you shall lack nothing." "Yes, very gladly," said Snow-White, stayed on with them and kept their house in order. In the morning they'd go into the mountains to look for ore and gold, in the evening they'd come back, and then their food had to be ready. During the day the girl was alone, and the good little dwarfs warned her, saying, "Watch out for your stepmother. She'll soon know that you're here. Let absolutely nobody in."

The queen, after she thought she'd eaten Snow-White's lungs and liver, had no notion but that she was once more the fairest and most beautiful woman. She stepped up to her mirror and said:

> "Mirror, mirror on the wall,
> Who is the fairest in all the land?"

Then the mirror answered:

> "Lady Queen, you are the fairest here,
> But Snow-White over the mountains
> With the seven dwarfs
> Is a thousand times fairer than you."

Then she was frightened, for she knew that the mirror didn't lie and saw that the huntsman had deceived her and that Snow-White was still alive. Again she thought and thought how she might kill her, for so long as she was not the most beautiful woman in the whole land, her envy gave her no rest. When at last she'd thought up something, she stained her face, dressed herself up as an old peddler woman, and was quite unrecognizable. In this guise she crossed the seven mountains to the seven dwarfs, knocked at the door, and called, "Pretty wares for sale! pretty wares for sale!" Snow-White looked out the window and said, "How do you do, good woman, What have you got for sale?" "Good wares, pretty wares," she answered, "bodice laces of every color," and drew one out that was braided of silks of many colors. "I may safely let this good woman in," thought Snow-White. She unbolted the door and bought the pretty lace. "Child," said the old woman, "how you do look! Come, let me lace you up properly for once." Snow-White, suspecting no harm, stood in front of her and let herself be laced up with the new bodice lace. The old woman, however, laced her up so quickly and so tight that Snow-White lost her breath and fell down as if dead. "Well, you used to be the most beautiful!" she said and hurried out.

Not long after, the seven dwarfs came home in the evening, but how frightened they were to see their dear Snow-White lying on the floor, still and motionless as if dead. They lifted her up, and noticing that she was too tightly laced, cut the lace. Then she began to breathe a little and gradually revived. When the dwarfs heard what had happened, they said, "The old peddler woman was none other than the wicked queen. Watch out and don't let any person come in when we're not with you."

When the wicked woman got home she stepped up to the mirror and asked:

"Mirror, mirror on the wall,
Who is the fairest in all the land?"

Then as usual the mirror replied:

"Lady Queen, you are the fairest here,
But Snow-White beyond the mountains
With the seven dwarfs
Is a thousand times fairer than you."

When she heard this, all her blood went to her heart from fright, for she quite realized that Snow-White had come to life again. "But this time," she said, "I'll think up something that will be the death of you," and with witches' arts, in which she was expert, made a poisoned comb. Then disguising herself and assuming the appearance of a different old woman, she went on over the seven mountains to the seven dwarfs, knocked on the door and called, "Pretty wares for sale! pretty wares for sale!" Snow-White looked out and said, "Get right along! I mayn't let anybody in." "But surely you're allowed to look," said the old woman, took out the poisoned comb and held it up. The child liked it so well that she let herself be fooled and opened the door. When they'd agreed on the price, the old woman said, "Now I'll comb your hair properly for once." Poor Snow-White, suspecting no harm, let the old woman go ahead, but hardly had she put the comb in her hair than the poison in it worked, and the girl fell down unconscious. "You paragon of beauty!" said the wicked woman, "now you're done for!" and went away. Fortunately it was near evening, the time the seven dwarfs would be coming home. When they saw Snow-White lying on the floor as if dead, they at once suspected the stepmother, searched about, and found the poisoned comb. No sooner had they taken it out than Snow-White regained consciousness and told them what had happened. Once more they warned her to be on her guard and not to open the door for anyone.

At home the queen stood before her mirror and said:

> "Mirror, mirror on the wall,
> Who is the fairest in all the land?"

Then the mirror answered as before:

> "Lady Queen, you are the fairest here,
> But Snow-White beyond the mountains
> With the seven dwarfs
> Is a thousand times fairer than you."

On hearing the mirror talk thus, she trembled and shook with anger. "Snow-White shall die!" she cried, "even if it costs me my very life." Thereupon she went into a solitary chamber, quite hidden away, where no one ever went and there made a very poisonous apple. Outside it looked beautiful, white with red cheeks, so that everybody who saw it longed for it, but whoever ate even a tiny bit of it was doomed to die. When the apple was ready, she stained her face and disguised herself as a farmer's wife and went thus over the seven mountains to the seven dwarfs. She knocked at the door, and Snow-White put her head out the window, saying, "I mustn't let anybody in; the seven dwarfs have forbidden me to." "Quite all right," answered the farmer's wife, "but of course I'll get rid of my apples. There! I'll make you a present of one." "No," said Snow-White, "I mustn't accept anything." "Are you afraid of poison?" said the old woman. "Look, I'll cut the apple in half: you eat the red cheek and I'll eat the white." The apple had been so skillfully made that only the red cheek was poisonous. Snow-White looked greedily at the beautiful apple, and when she saw the farmer's wife eating some, she could no longer resist, put out her hand, and took the poisoned half. Scarcely, however, had she got a bite of it in her mouth than she fell dead to the floor. Then the queen gave her an awful look and burst out into loud laughter, saying, "White as snow, red as blood, black as ebony! This time the dwarfs can't wake you up again!" When she consulted the mirror at home:

> "Mirror, mirror on the wall,
> Who is the fairest in all the land?"

it finally replied:

> "Lady Queen, you are the fairest in the land."

Then her envious heart was at rest, at least as much as an envious heart can be.

When the dwarfs got home in the evening, they found Snow-White lying on the floor. No breath was coming out of her mouth, and she was dead. They lifted her up, looked to see if they might find something poisonous, unlaced her bodice, combed her hair, washed her with water and wine, but all to no purpose. The dear child was dead and remained dead. They laid her on a bier, and all seven sat down beside it and wept for three whole days. They were going to bury her, but she still looked as fresh as a living being and her pretty cheeks were still rosy. "We can't lower her into the dark ground," they said and had a transparent glass coffin made so that one could view her from all sides, put her in it, and on it wrote in letters of gold her name and that she was a king's daughter. Then they placed the coffin on the mountain, and one of them always stayed by it and guarded it, and the birds, too, came and wept over Snow-White, first an owl, then a raven, and finally a dove.

Snow-White lay in the coffin for a long, long time and didn't decay but looked rather as if she were asleep, for she was still as white as snow, as red as blood, and her hair was as black as ebony. A king's son happened to get into the forest and came to the dwarfs' cottage to spend the night. He saw the coffin on the mountain and beautiful Snow-White in it and read what was written on it in letters of gold. Then he said to the dwarfs, "Let me have the coffin; I'll give you whatever you want for it;" but the dwarfs answered, "We won't sell it for all the gold in the world." Then he said, "Make me a present of it then, for I can't live without seeing Snow-White. I'll honor her and esteem her as my most dearly beloved." Since he spoke thus, the good dwarfs took pity on him and gave him the coffin. The king's son now had his servants carry it off on their shoulders. Then by chance they stumbled over a shrub, and from the jolt the poisoned piece of apple which Snow-White had bitten off came out of her throat, and before long she opened her eyes, lifted the coffin lid, raised herself up, and was alive again. "Good heavens, where am I?" she cried. Joyfully the king's son said, "You're with me," and relating what had happened, said, "I love you more than everything on earth. Come with me to my father's palace. You shall be my wife." Then Snow-White fell in love with him and went with him, and their wedding was celebrated with great pomp and splendor.

Snow-White's wicked stepmother was also invited to the feast. Once she was all dressed in beautiful clothes, she stepped up to her mirror and said:

> "Mirror, mirror on the wall,
> Who is the fairest in all the land?"

The mirror answered:

> "Lady Queen, you are the fairest here,
> But the young queen is a thousand times fairer than you."

Then the wicked woman cursed and got so very frightened that she didn't know what to do. At first she didn't want to go to the wedding at all, but that gave her no peace; she had to go and see the young queen. When she came in, she recognized Snow-White and stood motionless from terror and fear. However, iron slippers had already been put over a charcoal fire and were now brought in with tongs and placed before her. Then she had to put the red-hot slippers on and dance until she dropped to the ground dead.

*Seventy-two*

# The Juniper

*German*

A long time ago, probably a good two thousand years, there lived
a rich man who had a beautiful and devout wife, and they loved
one another very much. They had no children but very much
wanted some. Day and night the wife prayed ever so much about
it, but they didn't have any and didn't have any. In front of the
house was a yard, and in it stood a juniper. Once in winter the
wife was standing under it, peeling herself an apple, and as she
was peeling the apple, she cut her finger, and the blood dropped
in the snow. "Alas," said the wife and heaved a deep sigh. Then
she looked at the blood in front of her and grew quite sad. "If only
I had a child as red as blood and as white as snow!" As she said
this, she became quite joyful of heart: she felt that something
would come of it. She went into the house, and a month passed
and the snow went away. After two months things got green.
After three months the flowers came up. After four months all the
trees in the forest burst into leaf and the green boughs were all
intertwined and the birds sang so that the whole forest resounded,
and the blossoms fell from the trees. The fifth month passed.
Then she stood under the juniper, and it was very fragrant. Her
heart leapt for joy, and she fell on her knees and was beside
herself. When the sixth month had passed, the fruit got full and
firm, and she became very quiet. In the seventh month she
reached for the juniper berries and ate them most greedily. Then
she grew sad and ill. The eighth month passed, and she called her
husband and, weeping, said, "If I die, bury me under the juniper." Then she became quite consoled and joyful, until the ninth
month passed. Then she had a child as white as snow and as red
as blood, and when she saw it, she was so happy that she died.

Her husband buried her under the juniper and began to weep

From *German Folk Tales*, collected and edited by Grimm Brothers. Translated
by Francis P. Magoun, Jr. and Alexander H. Krappe. Copyright © 1960, by
Southern Illinois University Press. Reprinted by permission of the Southern
Illinois University Press.

very hard. After a time he wept somewhat less and after weeping a little more, stopped. Some time after that he again took a wife.

By his second wife he had a daughter. The first wife's child was a little boy, and he was as red as blood and as white as snow. When the wife looked at her daughter, she loved her very dearly, but then she'd look at the little boy, and it pained her dreadfully, and he seemed to be always in the way. She kept thinking how she'd like to divert the whole inheritance to her daughter, and the Evil One inspired her with a grudge against the little boy. She shoved him about from pillar to post and buffeted him here and cuffed him there, so that the poor child was always in a state of fear. When he got out of school, he had no peace or quiet.

Once the wife went to her room, and her little daughter came up and said, "Mother, give me an apple." "Yes, my child," said the wife and gave her a nice apple from a chest. The chest had a big, heavy lid and a big, sharp iron lock. "Mother," said the little daughter, "isn't brother to have one, too?" That astonished the wife, but she said, "Yes, when he gets out of school." When she saw out the window that he was coming, the Evil One really seemed to possess her, and she made a grab and took her daughter's apple away from her, saying, "You shan't have one before your brother." Then she threw the apple into the chest and shut it. The little boy came in the door, and the Evil One suggested that she say to him in a friendly way, "Son, do you want an apple?" and looked at him angrily. "Mother," said the little boy, "how angry you look! Yes, give me an apple." Then she felt she ought to persuade him. "Come along," she said, opening the lid, "take out an apple for yourself," and as the little boy was bending over the chest, the Evil One whispered to her, and crash! she slammed down the lid, so that his head flew off and fell among the red apples. Then she was overcome with terror and thought, "How can I get out of this?" She went up to her room and took a white cloth from the top drawer of a dresser and put the boy's head back on the neck and tied the neckerchief around it so that nothing could be seen. She set him on a chair outside the front door and put the apple in his hand.

Afterward Marlene went to her mother in the kitchen; the latter was standing by the fire and had a pot of hot water in front of her which she kept stirring. "Mother," said Marlene, "brother's sitting outside the door looking quite pale, and has an apple in his hand. I asked him to give me the apple, but he didn't answer me.

Then I got quite frightened." "Go back," said the mother, "and if he won't answer you, box his ears." Then Marlene went back and said, "Brother, give me the apple," but he kept still. Then she boxed his ears, and his head fell off. At that she was frightened and began to weep and howl and, running to her mother, said, "Oh, mother, I've knocked my brother's head off." She kept on weeping and couldn't be comforted. "Marlene," said her mother, "What have you done! However, keep quiet about it, so that nobody will notice it. There's nothing to be done about it in any event. We'll cook him in vinegar." Then the mother took the little boy and chopped him up, put the pieces in a pot, and cooked him in vinegar. But Marlene stood by and wept and wept, and all her tears fell into the pot and they didn't need any salt.

The father came home and, sitting down to table, said, "Where's my son?" Then the mother served up a great big dish of marinated minced boy, and Marlene wept and couldn't stop. Again the father said, "Where's my son?" "Oh," said the mother, "he's gone across country to mother's great-uncle; he wanted to stay there for a while." "What's he doing there? He didn't even say good-bye to me." "Oh, he very much wanted to go and asked me if he might stay for six weeks. He'll be well looked out for there." "Oh," said the man, "I'm very sad. It isn't right; he should have said good-bye to me." Then he began to eat and said, "Marlene, why are you weeping? Of course brother will come back. Oh, wife," he went on to say, "how good the food tastes! Give me some more," and the more he ate, the more he wanted and said, "Give me some more. The rest of you shan't have any of this. I feel as if it were all mine." He went on eating and threw all the bones under the table until he had quite finished it. Then Marlene went to her dresser, took out her best piece of silk from the bottom drawer, collected all the bones, big and small, from under the table, tied them up in the silk cloth, carried them outside the door, and wept bitter tears. She laid them in the green grass under the juniper and, once she'd put them there, she suddenly felt light of heart and stopped weeping. Then the juniper began to stir, and the branches parted and joined again, just as when one rejoices and claps one's hands like that. At the same time a big mist issued from the tree, and right in the mist a fire seemed to burn, and from out of the fire flew such a beautiful bird that sang so magnificently and flew high up in the air. When it had gone, the juniper was as it had been before, but the cloth with the bones had vanished. Marlene was very happy and contented, just as when her brother was still alive. She went quite happily back into the house, sat down at table, and ate.

The bird, however, flew away and, lighting on a goldsmith's house, began to sing:

> "My mother, she killed me,
> My father, he ate me,
> My sister Marlene
> Collected all my bones,
> Tied them up in a silk cloth,
> Laid them under the juniper.
> Tweet, tweet, what a beautiful bird I am!"

The goldsmith was sitting in his workshop making a gold chain. He heard the bird that was perched on his roof and singing and thought it most beautiful. He got up and as he was walking across the threshold, lost a slipper, but he went right on up the middle of the street with only one slipper and one sock on. He had on his apron and was holding the gold chain in one hand and the tongs in the other, and the sun was shining bright on the street. He went and stopped and looked at the bird. "Bird," he said, "how beautifully you can sing. Sing me that piece again." "No," said the bird, "I don't sing twice for nothing. Give me the gold chain, and I'll sing it again for you." "There," said the goldsmith, "you have the gold chain. Now sing it for me again." Then the bird came, took the gold chain in its right claw, and perching in front of the goldsmith, sang:

> "My mother, she killed me,
> My father, he ate me,
> My sister Marlene
> Collected all my bones,
> Tied them up in a silk cloth,
> Laid them under the juniper.
> Tweet, tweet, what a beautiful bird I am!"

Then the bird flew away to a shoemaker and perching on his roof, sang:

> "My mother, she killed me,
> My father, he ate me,

> My sister Marlene
> Collected all my bones,
> Tied them up in a silk cloth,
> Laid them under the juniper.
> Tweet, tweet, what a beautiful bird I am!"

The shoemaker heard it and ran to the door in his shirt sleeves, looked towards the roof, and had to keep his hand before his eyes lest the sun blind him. "Bird," he said, "how beautifully you can sing." Then he called in though the door, "Wife, come out here, there's a bird. Just look at it; it certainly can sing beautifully." Then he called his daughter and her children and the journeyman, apprentice, and maid, and they all came out onto the street and, looking at the bird, saw how beautiful it was, that it had such bright red and green feathers, with something like pure gold around its neck, and that the eyes in its head twinkled like stars. "Bird," said the shoemaker, "now sing me that piece again." "No," said the bird, "I don't sing twice for nothing. You've got to make me a present of something." "Wife," said the husband, "go to the shop. There's a pair of red shoes on the top shelf; fetch them down." The wife went and fetched the shoes. "There, bird," said the man, "now sing me the piece once more." Then the bird came and taking the shoes in its left claw, flew back up on the roof and sang:

> "My mother, she killed me,
> My father, he ate me,
> My sister Marlene
> Collected all my bones,
> Tied them up in a silk cloth,
> Laid them under the juniper.
> Tweet, tweet, what a beautiful bird I am!"

When it finished, it flew away. It had the chain in its right claw and the shoes in its left and flew far away to a mill. The mill was going clickety-clack, clickety-clack, clickety-clack, and in the mill were sitting twenty miller's apprentices. They were holding a stone and cutting it chip-chip, chip-chip, chip-chip, and the mill was still going clickety-clack, clickety-clack, clickety-clack. The bird perched on a linden that stood outside the mill and sang:

> "My mother, she killed me."

Then one of the apprentices stopped.

"My father, he ate me."

Then two more stopped and heard:

"My sister Marlene."

Then four more stopped.

"Collected all my bones,
Tied them up in a silk cloth."

Now only eight were chipping.

"Laid them under . . ."

Now only five.

". . . the juniper."

Now only one.

"Tweet, tweet, what a beautiful bird I am!"

Then the last one, too, stopped and heard the last words. "Bird," he said, "how beautifully you sing." Let me hear that, too. Sing it for me once more." "No," said the bird, "I don't sing twice for nothing. Give me the millstone, then I'll sing it again." "Yes," he said, "if it belonged just to me, you should have it." "Yes," said the others, "if it sings once more, it'll have it." Then the bird came down, and all twenty millers took levers and raised the stone, "one, two, three, up!" Then the bird stuck its neck through the hole, putting it on like a collar, flew back up in the tree, and sang:

"My mother, she killed me,
My father, he ate me,
My sister Marlene
Collected all my bones,
Tied them up in a silk cloth,
Laid them under the juniper.
Tweet, tweet, what a beautiful bird I am!"

When it had finished, it spread its wings and in its right claw had the chain, in its left the shoes, and around its neck the millstone, and it flew far away to its father's house.

The father, the mother, and Marlene were sitting in the living room, and the father was saying, "How happy I feel; I'm in really good spirits." "Not I," said the mother, "I feel very frightened, just as if a storm were brewing." Marlene was sitting and weeping. Then the bird flew up, and as it lighted on the roof, the father said, "Oh, I feel so happy, and the sun's shining so bright outdoors. I feel as though I were going to see an old acquaintance again." "Not I," said the wife, "I'm frightened. My teeth are chattering and I feel as if fire were running through my veins." She tore open her bodice even more. Marlene was sitting in a corner weeping and had her handkerchief in front of her eyes and soaked it with her tears. Then the bird perched on the juniper and sang:

"My mother, she killed me."

The mother stopped up her ears and shut her eyes and didn't want to see anything or hear anything, but there was a roaring noise in her ears as in the wildest gale, and her eyes smarted and stung like lightning.

"My father, he ate me."

"Oh, mother," said the man, "there's a beautiful bird. It's singing so wonderfully, the sun's shining so warm, and it smells like pure cinnamon."

"My sister Marlene."

Then Marlene put her head on her knees and wept and wept, but the man said, "I'm going outdoors. I want to see the bird from close at hand." "Oh, don't go!" said the wife, "I feel as though the whole house was shaking and was in flames," but the man went out and looked at the bird.

"Collected all my bones,
   Tied them up in a silk cloth,
   Laid them under the juniper.
   Tweet, tweet, what a beautiful bird I am!"

At these words the bird dropped the gold chain, and it fell around the man's neck, so exactly around it that it fitted him perfectly. Then he went in and said, "See what a lovely bird it is! It made me a present of such a beautiful gold chain; it's so wonderful looking." The woman was very frightened and fell full length on the floor of the room, and her cap fell off her head. Then the bird again sang:

"My mother, she killed me."

"Oh that I were a thousand fathoms under the earth not to hear this!"

"My father, he ate me."

Then the wife fell down as if dead.

"My sister Marlene."

"Oh," said Marlene, "I'll go out, too, and see if the bird will give me something." So she went out.

"Collected all my bones,
Tied them up in a silk cloth."

Then it dropped the shoes down to her.

"Laid them under the juniper.
Tweet, tweet, what a beautiful bird I am!"

Then she felt so gay and happy, put on the new red shoes, and danced and skipped into the house. "Oh," she said, "I was so sad when I went out, and now I feel so gay. It's certainly a beautiful bird. It made me a present of a pair of shoes." "Not I," said the wife, jumping up and her hair standing on end like fiery flames, "I feel as if the world's coming to an end. I, too, want to go out and see whether it'll make me feel better." As she went out the door, crash! the bird threw the millstone on her head, so that she was squashed to death. The father and Marlene heard the noise and went out. Then steam and flames and fire rose from the spot, and when it was over, the little brother was standing there. He took his father and Marlene by the hand, and they were all three very happy and went into the house, sat down to table, and ate.

*Seventy-three*

# The Poor and the Rich

*German*

Once Our Lord went through the country as a poor man, thinking that he would like to find out how people were minded. He knocked at a stately house and asked for a night's lodging. The rich man looked at him and slammed the door shut without saying a word. Then he went to a poor man who lived in a thatched cottage. The people there asked him to come in and made some coffee and prepared a bed of straw. In the morning they made coffee again. After drinking it, Our Lord told the man to utter a wish. The poor man said, "I am content with what I have." Our Lord asked him if he would not like to have a fine house.

"Well," said the man, "that would be all right, if I can live there in peace." Then Our Lord left, and after a little while a fine new house was standing there.

The rich man saw it from his window and said, "What's this? Where there was a cottage yesterday, there is now a stately house!" His wife ran over to find out what was going on. The people told her what had happened. She told her husband.

"I could slap myself. The fellow was here, too!"

His wife said, "Ride after him. Perhaps he is still willing to do something for you." He mounted his horse and caught up with Our Lord. He made a great fuss and said that he had wanted to keep him and that he had left too soon! He should not bear him a grudge, but should rather do something for him as well. Our Lord told him to ride home. He would grant him three wishes.

It was very hot. The rich man was thinking aloud what he might wish and while doing so he slapped his horse, which started jumping. He said, "I wish you would break your neck!" With this the horse fell down and its neck was broken. Being very thrifty, he did not want to leave the saddle behind. So he put it on his shoulder. He was sweating a lot and became so angry

Reprinted from *Folktales of Germany* by Kurt Ranke by permission of The University of Chicago Press.

that he said, "Now my wife is sitting at home in a cool room. I wish she was sitting on this saddle and could not get off again." Immediately the saddle was gone. When he came home, his wife was sitting on the saddle in the middle of the room, and she was not able to get off. He told her what had happened and said that she might stay where she was. He was going to wish all the treasures the earth held. His wife said, "This won't help me any. You have wished me up here, and you are going to wish me down again!" He could do nothing; he had to do what his wife told him. So all this good luck brought him nothing but anger and a dead horse.

*Seventy-four*

# The Greater Sinner

*Greek*

Whoever dissuades a man who wants to get married by making unjust accusations against the bride, that man in the next world must abide burning in the pitch for ever. There was a man who killed nine and ninety men, and then he repented and went and confessed to the priest and begged for forgiveness. The confessor said: "If you have truly repented of what you have done, your sins shall be pardoned, but your pardon shall be even when this dry stick which you are to plant on the hill shall bring forth leaves."

The man went and planted the dry stick: every day he brought water to pour upon it; it produced no leaves. One day when he was in the field he saw a man passing by in a hurry: he asked him: "Where are you going that way?" The man made no answer. Again he asked him: "Where are you going that way?" Again he did not answer, and the man said to himself: "I shall kill that man; I speak to him and he will not speak to me." Then he killed him. Next day he went to water the stick, and what did he see? It had produced leaves. He went off and told the priest: "For all these many days I have been watering the dry twig and never did it produce leaves. Yesterday I killed yet another man: I had spoken to him and he would not speak to me. Then I went to

From *Modern Greek Folktales*, edited by R. M. Dawkins. Reprinted by permission of the Clarendon Press, Oxford.

water the twig and saw it all green leafage." "Ah," said the priest: "the man whom you killed was on his way to break up a betrothal and stop it, and therefore it has come about that your sins have been forgiven you."

# The Singing Bone

*Italian*

There was once a king who had three sons. His eyes were diseased, and he called in a physician who said that to cure them he needed a feather of the griffin. Then the king said to his sons: "He who finds this feather for me shall have my crown." The sons set out in search of it. The youngest met an old man, who asked him what he was doing. He replied: "Papa is ill. To cure him a feather of the griffin is necessary. And papa has said that whoever finds the feather shall have his crown." The old man said: "Well, here is some corn. When you reach a certain place, put it in your hat. The griffin will come and eat it. Seize him, pull out a feather, and carry it to papa."

The youth did so, and for fear that some one should steal it from him, he put it into his shoe, and started all joyful to carry it to his father. On his way he met his brothers, who asked him if he had found the feather. He said No; but his brothers did not believe him, and wanted to search him. They looked everywhere, but did not find it. Finally they looked in his shoe and got it. Then they killed the youngest brother and buried him, and took the feather to their father, saying that they had found it. The king healed his eyes with it.

A shepherd one day, while feeding his sheep, saw that his dog was always digging in the same place, and went to see what it was, and found a bone. He put it to his mouth, and saw that it sounded and said: "Shepherd, keep me in your mouth, hold me tight, and do not let me go! For a feather of the griffin, my brother has played the traitor, my brother has played the traitor."

One day the shepherd, with this whistle in his mouth, was passing by the king's palace, and the king heard him, and called him to see what it was. The shepherd told him the story, and how he had found it. The king put it to his mouth, and the whistle said: "Papa! papa! keep me in your mouth, hold me tight, and do not let me go. For a feather of the griffin, my brother has played the traitor, my brother has played the traitor." Then the king put it in the mouth of the brother who had killed the youngest, and the whistle said: "Brother! brother! keep me in your mouth, hold me fast, and do not let me go. For a feather of the griffin, you have played the traitor, you have played the traitor." Then the king understood the story and had his two sons put to death. And thus they killed their brother and afterwards were killed themselves.

*Seventy-six*

# The Princess Who Wanted to Solve Riddles

*Russian*

Once there was an old man who had three sons, of whom the third was called Ivan the Simpleton. At that time there was a certain tsar—for this was long ago—who had a daughter. She said to her father: "Permit me to solve riddles, father. If I solve a man's riddles, let his head be cut off; but him whose riddle I cannot solve, I will marry." Immediately they sent forth a call. Many men presented themselves and all of them were put to death, for the princess was able to solve their riddles. Ivan the Simpleton said to his father: "Give me your blessing, father! I want to go to the tsar's court and propound riddles." "What an absurd idea, you fool! Better men than you have been put to death!" "If you give me your blessing, I will go; if you do not, I will go anyway!" So the father gave him his blessing. Ivan the Simpleton set out. On his way he saw a field of grain, and in the field a horse. He drove the horse away with his whip to prevent him from trampling the grain, and said: "Here I have a riddle!" He went on farther, saw a snake, pierced it with his spear, and thought: "Here is another riddle!"

From *Russian Fairy Tales*, edited and translated by Norbert Guterman. Copyright 1945 by Pantheon Books, Inc. Reprinted by permission of Pantheon Books, a Division of Random House, Inc.

He came to the tsar's palace, was received by the princess, and was told to propound his riddles. He said: "On my way here, I saw a good thing, and in this good thing a good thing, and I took a good thing and drove out the good thing from the good thing; and the good thing ran away from the good thing out of the good thing." The princess rushed to look for this riddle in her book, but it was not there. She did not know how to solve it, so she said to her father: "Father, I have a headache today, my ideas are all confused, I will solve this riddle tomorrow." So the audience was postponed till the next day. Ivan the Simpleton was given a room and he sat there smoking his pipe. The princess chose a faithful chambermaid, and sent her to Ivan. "Go," she said, "ask him the answer to this riddle, promise him gold and silver, as much as he wants."

The chambermaid knocked at his door. Ivan the Simpleton opened it; the maid entered and asked the answer to the riddle, promising him mountains of gold and silver. Ivan the Simpleton answered: "What do I need money for! I have plenty of my own. Let the princess stand all night in my room without sleeping, then I will tell her the answer to my riddle." The chambermaid told the princess this answer; she accepted, and stood all night in Ivan's room without sleeping. In the morning Ivan the Simpleton told her that the answer to his riddle was that he had driven a horse out of the grain. So the princess was able to solve the riddle before the tsar and his court.

Then Ivan the Simpleton proposed another riddle: "On my way here I saw an evil thing, so I struck it with an evil thing, and the evil thing died from the evil thing." Again the princess looked in her book, but could not solve the riddle, and asked for a postponement till the next morning. At night she sent her chambermaid to get the answer from Ivan the Simpleton. "Promise him money," she said. "What do I need money for!" said Ivan. "I have plenty of my own. Let the princess stand all night in my room without sleeping, then I will tell her the answer." The princess agreed, did not sleep during the night, and was thus able to solve the riddle before the tsar and his court.

Ivan the Simpleton did not put his third riddle to the princess, but instead asked that all the senators be gathered together. In their presence he propounded a riddle about how the princess had been unable to solve the other riddles and had sent her chambermaid to bribe him with money. The princess could not solve this riddle either; again she questioned him, promising to give him silver and gold, as much as he wanted, and to send him home in a coach-and-four. But her efforts were in vain. Again she stood up all night without sleeping; and when Ivan the Simpleton told her what the riddle was about, she still could not tell the solution to the court, for then everyone would find out how she had obtained the answers to his first two riddles. She had to declare: "I cannot solve this riddle." So Ivan the Simpleton and the princess were married; they had a fine wedding and a gay feast and lived happily ever after.

*Seventy-seven*

# The Princess in the Earth Cave

*Swedish*

Once there were two kings who were neighbors. One of them had a son and the other a daughter. A certain wise man had foretold while they still were children that they were going to get married when they were grown. And as they grew up they liked each other more and more. Then the kings suddenly became enemies and the princess' father said to the prince's father:

"Your son shall never have my daughter."

Whereupon he rowed out with her to a tiny island far out in the lake and dug a cave for her deep down in the earth. And he brought her food, drink, and light to last for seven years. And she was to have a rooster and a cat for company. After the seven years had passed he would come to her with new supplies. However, she had managed to give to her fiancé a shirt which she had merely cut out and sewn a few stitches on and she had said that it would never be finished until she herself did it, and she had also given him a handkerchief with three drops of blood which would not be clean until she herself could wash it. The prince searched for her in vain, and finally open war broke out between the two kingdoms and the princess' father was killed and the castle pulled down.

When seven years had passed the food and the light were gone

Translated from *Sveriges Samtliga Folksagor* by Waldemar Liungman. Used by permission.

in the cave and the princess waited fruitlessly for her father. But the cat took to scratching and the rooster to clawing so that some light began to stream in. Then she began digging and finally they got out. There a wolf stood in front of her and said: "Get up on my back!" And then he swam ashore with her.

By and by she came to a cottage in which dwelt a poor, lonely, old man who burned charcoal for his living. She asked if she could stay with him and he agreed. The cottage wasn't far from the castle where the prince lived, and the prince was said to have promised to marry the girl who could finish sewing a shirt and wash a handkerchief clean. Many had tried but nobody had been able to. Once a young damsel came to the cottage where the princess and the charcoal burner lived. The charcoal burner told her that the girl who was staying with him was deft both at sewing and washing. Then the visitor asked her for help and it wasn't long before the shirt was ready and the handkerchief clean, because the princess didn't know that the prince had searched for her and she was sorrowing about her father's death. But the prince didn't understand that the girl who claimed that she had finished sewing the shirt and washed the handkerchief clean wasn't the one he was looking for. The wedding was therefore decided upon and when all the guests had arrived the young woman for whom the princess had been sewing suddenly sent for her and asked her to go in her place with the prince to the minister because she herself was about to have a baby any minute.

The princess now dressed in bridal array and a veil while the bride was hiding in the stable. When they set out to ride to church the substitute bride said to the prince:

> "Here horse-shoes resound in the hall
> But the mistress gives birth in the stall."

"What are you saying?" he asked. "I am just speaking to my horse."

Then they came to a bridge. There she said:

> "Be still, broad bridge, over brook so wide,
> For two royal children across shall ride."

He asked what she was saying and she answered: "I am just speaking to my horse."

When they rode past the ruin which once was her father's castle she said:

> "Charcoal lies smoldering here,
> Where ladies and knights once were.
> Here graze the black swine,
> Where once were beer and wine."

He asked what she was saying and she answered: "I am just talking to my horse."

When they had reached the church he happened to throw some snow at her by mistake and immediately he asked for forgiveness. But she laughed disdainfully and when he asked why she answered: "I can do nothing else. For a little snow you ask my forgiveness, but not for having killed my father."

The prince was then alarmed and took out a golden bracelet which he placed around her arm. It could be locked and he himself kept the key. Then he brought her to the altar and there they were regularly married.

When the bridal procession came back they sat down at the table. A guest who had been at the castle for a long time asked the princess if she didn't have anything to tell. She answered:

> "Seven years in the cave was my lot.
> Songs and riddles I thus forgot.
> Much suffering I bore,
> The wolf took me ashore,
> And charcoal I burned.
> Now as bride I appear
> For that damsel so fair."

Then she rose from the table and said:

"Now guess, gentlemen," and walked straight to the girl for whom she had been a substitute bride and said that she had done now what she had been asked to do. The young lady took back the bridal array, put it on, and then walked up to the bridal chamber. But since she couldn't take the bracelet off the princess, she asked her to sit down on a chair at the side of the bed in the darkness after the lights had been put out and if the prince asked for the bracelet to stretch out her arm, and she promised to do that. And when they had gone to bed the prince asked what all those things she had said on the way to church meant. Since she could neither answer nor knew what she had said, he finally asked to see the bracelet. Then the princess stuck out her arm as she had promised, but the prince pulled her to him and said: "To you I am married and you alone I want."

# The Clever Peasant Girl

*Italian*

Once upon a time there was a huntsman who had a wife and two children—a son and a daughter; and all lived together in a wood where no one ever came, and so they knew nothing about the world. The father alone sometimes went to the city and brought back the news. The king's son once went hunting and lost himself in that wood, and while he was seeking his way it became night. He was weary and hungry. Imagine how he felt! But all at once he saw a light shining at a distance. He followed it and reached the huntsman's house and asked for lodging and something to eat. The huntsman recognized him at once and said: "Highness, we have already supped on our best. But if we can find anything for you, you must be satisfied with it. What can we do? We are so far from the towns, that we cannot procure what we need every day." Meanwhile, he had a capon cooked for him. The prince did not wish to eat it alone, but called all the huntsman's family, and gave the head of the capon to the father, the back to the mother, the legs to the son, and the wings to the daughter, and ate the rest himself.

In the house there were only two beds, in the same room. In one the husband and wife slept, in the other the brother and sister. The old people went and slept in the stable, giving up their bed to the prince. When the girl saw that the prince was asleep, she said to her brother: "I will wager that you do not know why the prince divided the capon among us in the manner he did." "Do you know? Tell me why." "He gave the head to papa because he is the head of the family, the back to mamma because she has on her shoulders all the affairs of the house, the legs to you because you must be quick in performing the errands which are given you, and the wings to me to fly away and catch a husband." The prince pretended to be asleep but he was awake and heard these words, and perceived that the girl had much judgment; and as she was also pretty, he fell in love with her.

The next morning he left the huntsman's; and as soon as he reached the court, he sent him, by a servant, a purse of money. To the young girl he sent a cake in the form of a full moon, thirty patties, and a cooked capon, with three questions: "Whether it was the thirtieth of the month in the wood, whether the moon was full, and whether the capon crowed in the night." The servant, although a trusty one, was overcome by his gluttony and ate fifteen of the patties, and a good slice of the cake, and the capon. The young girl, who had understood it all, sent back word to the prince that the moon was not full but on the wane; that it was only the fifteenth of the month and that the capon had gone to the mill; and that she asked him to spare the pheasant for the sake of the partridge. The prince, too, understood the metaphor, and having summoned the servant, he cried: "Rogue! you have eaten the capon, fifteen patties, and a good slice of the cake. Thank that girl who has interceded for you; if she had not, I would have hanged you."

A few months after this, the huntsman found a gold mortar, and wished to present it to the prince. But his daughter said: "You will be laughed at for this present. You will see that the prince will say to you: 'The mortar is fine and good, but, peasant, where is the pestle?'" The father did not listen to his daughter; but when he carried the mortar to the prince, he was greeted as his daughter had foretold. "My daughter told me so," said the huntsman. "Ah! if I had only listened to her!" The prince heard these words and said to him: "Your daughter, who pretends to be so wise, must make me a hundred ells of cloth out of four ounces of flax; if she does not I will hang you and her."

The poor father returned home weeping, and sure that he and his daughter must die, for who could make a hundred ells of cloth with four ounces of flax? His daughter came out to meet him, and when she learned why he was weeping, said: "Is that all you are weeping for? Quick, get me the flax and I will manage it." She made four small cords of the flax and said to her father: "Take these cords and tell him that when he makes me a loom out of these cords I will weave the hundred ells of cloth." When the prince heard this answer he did not know what to say, and thought no more about condemning the father or the daughter.

The next day he went to the wood to visit the girl. Her mother was dead, and her father was out in the fields digging. The prince knocked, but no one opened. He knocked louder, but the same thing. The young girl was deaf to him. Finally, tired of waiting, he broke open the door and entered: "Rude girl! who taught you not to open to one of my rank? Where are your father and mother?" "Who knew it was you? My father is where he should be and my mother is weeping for her sins. You must leave, for I have something else to do than listen to you." The prince went away in anger and complained to the father of his daughter's rude manners, but the father excused her. The prince, at last seeing how wise and cunning she was, married her.

The wedding was celebrated with great splendor, but an event happened which came near plunging the princess into misfortune. One Sunday two peasants were passing a church; one of them had a hand-cart and the other was leading a she-ass ready to foal. The bell rang for mass and they both entered the church, one leaving his cart outside and the other tying the ass to the cart. While they were in the church the ass foaled, and the owner of the ass and the owner of the cart both claimed the colt. They appealed to the prince, and he decided that the colt belonged to the owner of the cart, because, he said, it was more likely that the owner of the ass would tie her to the cart in order to lay a false claim to the colt than that the owner of the cart would tie it to the ass. The owner of the ass had right on his side, and all the people were in his favor, but the prince had pronounced sentence and there was nothing to say. The poor man then applied to the princess, who advised him to cast a net in the square when the prince passed. When the prince saw the net, he said: "What are you doing, you fool? Do you expect to find fish in the square?" The peasant, who had been advised by the princess, answered: "It is easier for me to find fish in the square than for a cart to have foals."

The prince revoked the sentence, but when he returned to the palace, knowing that the princess had suggested the answer to the peasant, he said to her: "Prepare to return to your own home within an hour. Take with you what you like best and depart." She was not at all saddened by the prospect, but ate a better dinner than usual, and made the prince drink a bottle of wine in which she had put a sleeping potion and when he was sound asleep as a log, she had him put in a carriage and took him with her to her house in the wood. It was in January, and she had the roof of the house uncovered and it snowed on the prince, who awoke and called his servants. "What do you wish?" said the princess. "I command here. Did you not tell me to take from your house the thing I liked best? I have taken you, and now you are mine." The prince laughed and they made peace.

*Seventy-nine*

# The King Who Wanted a Beautiful Wife

*Italian*

There was once a king who wanted to marry. But his wife must be more beautiful than the sun, and no matter how many maidens he saw, none was beautiful enough to suit him. Then he called his trusty servant and commanded him to seek everywhere and see whether he could find a beautiful girl. The servant set out and wandered through the whole land, but found none who seemed handsome enough to him. One day, however, after he had run about a great deal and was very thirsty, he came to a little house. He knocked and asked for a drink of water. Now there dwelt in the house two very old women—one eighty and the other ninety years old—who supported themselves by spinning. When the servant asked for water, the one eighty years old rose, opened a little wicket in the shutter, and handed him out the water. From spinning so much, her hands were very white and delicate; and when the servant saw them he thought, "It must be a handsome maiden, for she has such a delicate white hand." So he hastened to the king, and said: "Your royal Majesty, I have found what you seek; so and so has happened to me." "Very well," answered the king, "go once more and try to see her."

The servant returned to the little house, knocked, and asked again for some water. The old woman did not open the window, but handed him the pitcher through the little opening in the shutter. "Do you live here all alone?" asked the servant. "No," she answered. "I live here with my sister; we are poor girls and support ourselves by the work of our hands." "How old are you, then?" "I am fifteen and my sister twenty." The servant went back to the king and told him all, and the king said: "I will take the one who is fifteen. Go and bring her to me." When the servant returned to the two old women, and told them that the king wished to elevate the younger to the position of his wife, she answered: "Tell the king I am ready to do his will. Since my birth no ray of the sun has ever struck me, and if a ray of the sun or a beam of light should strike me now, I would become perfectly black. Ask the king, therefore, to send a closed carriage for me at night, and I will come to his palace."

When the king heard this he sent royal apparel and a closed carriage, and at night the old woman covered her face with a thick veil and rode to the palace. The king received her joyfully, and begged her to lay aside the veil. She replied: "There are too many lighted candles here; their light would make me black." So the king married her without having seen her face. When they came into the king's chamber, however, and she removed her veil, the king saw for the first time what an ugly old woman he had married, and in his rage he opened the window and threw her out. Fortunately there was a nail in the wall, on which she caught by her clothes, and remained hanging between heaven and earth. Four fairies chanced to pass by, and when they saw the old woman hanging there, one of them cried: "See, sisters, there is the old woman who cheated the king; shall we wish her dress to tear and let her fall?" "Oh, no! let us not do that," cried the youngest and most beautiful of the fairies. "Let us rather wish her something good. I wish her youth." "And I, beauty." "And I, prudence." "And I, a good heart." Thus the fairies cried, and while they were yet speaking the old woman became a wondrous fair maiden.

The next morning, when the king looked out of the window and saw the beautiful girl hanging there, he was terrified, and thought: "Unhappy man! What have I done! Had I no eyes last night?" Then he had her carefully taken down with long ladders, and begged her pardon, saying: "Now we will have a great festival and be right happy." So they celebrated a splendid feast, and the young queen was the fairest in the whole city.

But one day the sister ninety years old came to the palace to visit the queen, her sister. "Who is this ugly creature?" asked the king. "An old neighbor of mine who is half-witted," replied the queen, quickly. The old woman kept looking at her rejuvenated sister, and asked: "What did you do to become so young and lovely? I, too, would like to be young and pretty again." She kept asking this the whole day, until the queen finally lost her patience, and said: "I had my old skin taken off, and this new, smooth skin came to light." The old woman went to a barber and said: "I will give you what you will to remove my old skin, so that I may become young and handsome again." "But good old woman, you will surely die if I skin you." The old woman would not listen to him, and at last he had to do her will. He took his knife and made a cut in her forehead. "Oh!" cried the old woman.

> "Who will look fair
> Must grief and pain bear,"

answered the barber. "Then skin away, master," said the old woman. The barber kept cutting on, until all at once the old woman fell down dead.

*Eighty*

# The Crumb in the Beard

*Italian*

There was once a king who had a daughter whose name was Stella. She was indescribably beautiful, but was so whimsical and hard to please that she drove her father to despair. There had been princes and kings who had sought her in marriage, but she had found defects in them all and would have none of them. She kept advancing in years, and her father began to despair of knowing to whom he should leave his crown. So he summoned his council and discussed the matter, and was advised to give a great banquet, to which he should invite all the princes and kings of the surrounding countries, for, as they said, there cannot fail to be among so many, some one who should please the princess, who was to hide behind a door, so that she could examine them all as she pleased.

When the king heard this advice, he gave the orders necessary for the banquet, and then called his daughter, and said: "Listen, my little Stella, I have thought to do so and so, to see if I can find any one to please you; behold, my daughter, my hair is white, and I must have some one to leave my crown to." Stella bowed her head, saying that she would take care to please him.

356

Princes and kings then began to arrive at the court, and when it was time for the banquet, they all seated themselves at the table. You can imagine what sort of a banquet that was, and how the hall was adorned: gold and silver shone from all their necks; in the four corners of the room were four fountains, which continually sent forth wine and the most exquisite perfumes. While the gentlemen were eating Stella was behind a door, as has been said, and one of her maids, who was near by, pointed out to her now this one, now that one. "See, your Majesty, what a handsome youth that is there." "Yes, but he has too large a nose." "And the one near your father?" "He has eyes that look like saucers." "And that other at the head of the table?" "He has too large a mouth; he looks as if he liked to eat." In short, she found fault with all but one, who, she said, pleased her, but he must be a very dirty fellow, for he had a crumb on his beard after eating.

The youth heard her say this, and swore vengeance. You must know that he was the son of the king of Green Hill, and the handsomest youth that could be seen. When the banquet was finished and the guests had departed, the king called Stella and asked: "What news have you, my child?" She replied that the only one who pleased her was the one with the crumb in his beard, but that she believed him to be a dirty fellow and did not want him. "Take care, my daughter, you will repent it," answered her father, and turned away.

You must know that Stella's chamber looked into a court-yard into which opened the shop of a baker. One night, while she was preparing to retire, she heard, in the room where they sifted the meal, some one singing so well and with so much grace that it went to her heart. She ran to the window and listened until he finished. Then she began to ask her maid who the person with the beautiful voice could be, saying she would like to know. "Leave it to me, your Majesty," said the maid; "I will inform you tomorrow." Stella could not wait for the next day; and, indeed, early the next day she learned that the one who sang was the sifter. That evening she heard him sing again, and stood by the window until everything became quiet. But that voice had so touched her heart that she told her maid that the next day she would try and see who had that fine voice. In the morning she placed herself by the window, and soon saw the youth come forth. She was enchanted by his beauty as soon as she saw him, and fell desperately in love with him.

Now you must know that this was none other than the prince who was at the banquet, and whom Stella had called "dirty." So he had disguised himself in such a way that she could not recognize him, and was meanwhile preparing his revenge. After he had seen her once or twice he began to take off his hat and salute her. She smiled at him, and appeared at the window every moment. Then they began to exchange words, and in the evening he sang under her window. In short, they began to make love in good earnest, and when he learned that she was free, he began to talk about marrying her. She consented at once, but asked him what he had to live on. "I haven't a penny," said he; "the little I earn is hardly enough to feed me." Stella encouraged him, saying that she would give him all the money and things he wanted.

To punish Stella for her pride, her father and the prince's father had an understanding, and pretended not to know about this love affair, and let her carry away from the palace all she owned. During the day Stella did nothing but make a great bundle of clothes, of silver, and of money, and at night the disguised prince came under the balcony, and she threw it down to him.

Things went on in this manner some time, and finally one evening he said to her: "Listen. The time has come to elope." Stella could not wait for the hour, and the next night she quietly tied a cord about her and let herself down from the window. The prince aided her to the ground, and then took her arm and hastened away. He led her a long ways to another city, where he turned down a street and opened the first door he met. They went down a long passage; finally they reached a little door, which he opened, and they found themselves in a hole of a place which had only one window, high up. The furniture consisted of a straw bed, a bench, and a dirty table. You can imagine that when Stella saw herself in this place she thought she would die. When the prince saw her so amazed, he said: "What is the matter? Does the house not please you? Do you not know that I am a poor man? Have you been deceived?" "What have you done with all the things I gave you?" "Oh, I had many debts, and I have paid them, and then I have done with the rest what seemed good to me. You must make up your mind to work and gain your bread as I have done. You must know that I am a porter of the king of this city, and I often go and work at the palace. Tomorrow, they have told me, the washing is to be done, so you must rise early and go with me there. I will set you to work with the other women, and when it is time for them to go home to dinner, you will say that you are not hungry, and while you are alone, steal two shirts, conceal them under your skirt, and carry them home to me."

Poor Stella wept bitterly, saying it was impossible for her to do that; but her husband replied: "Do what I say, or I shall beat you." The next morning her husband rose with the dawn, and made her get up, too. He had bought her a striped skirt and a pair of coarse shoes, which he made her put on, and then took her to the palace with him, conducted her to the laundry and left her, after he had introduced her as his wife, saying that she should remember what awaited her at home. Then the prince ran and dressed himself like a king, and waited at the gate of the palace until it was time for his wife to come.

Meanwhile poor Stella did as her husband had commanded, and stole the shirts. As she was leaving the palace, she met the king, who said: "Pretty girl, you are our porter's wife, are you not?" Then he asked her what she had under her skirt, and shook her until the shirts dropped out, and the king cried: "See there! the porter's wife is a thief; she has stolen some shirts." Poor Stella ran home in tears, and her husband followed her when he had put on his disguise again. When he reached home Stella told him all that had happened and begged him not to send her to the palace again; but he told her that the next day they were to bake, and she must go into the kitchen and help, and steal a piece of dough. Everything happened as on the previous day. Stella's theft was discovered, and when her husband returned he found her crying like a condemned soul, and swearing that she had rather be killed than go to the palace again.

He told her, however, that the king's son was to be married the next day, and that there was to be a great banquet, and she must go into the kitchen and wash the dishes. He added that when she had the chance she must steal a pot of broth and hide it about her so that no one should see it. She had to do as she was told, and had scarcely concealed the pot when the king's son came into the kitchen and told his wife she must come to the ball that had followed the banquet. She did not wish to go, but he took her by the arm and led her into the midst of the festival. Imagine how the poor woman felt at that ball, dressed as she was, and with the pot of broth! The king began to poke his sword at her in jest, until he hit the pot, and all the broth ran on the floor. Then all began to jeer her and laugh, until poor Stella fainted away from shame, and they had to go and get some vinegar to revive her.

At last the king's mother came forward and said: "Enough; you have revenged yourself sufficiently." Then turning to Stella: "Know that this is your mother, and that he has done this to correct your pride and to be avenged on you for calling him dirty." Then she took her by the arm and led her to another room, where her maids dressed her as a queen. Her father and mother then appeared and kissed and embraced her. Her husband begged her pardon for what he had done, and they made peace and always lived in harmony. From that day on she was never haughty, and had learned to her cost that pride is the greatest fault.

*Eighty-one*

# The Three Words of Advice

*Greek*

There was a tinsmith who was out of work. He saw that his family would go hungry, and so one day he said to his wife: "Wife, I can find no work here and we shall die of hunger. I must go abroad; it may be that there my luck will clear and we too shall behold turned towards us the face of God. As I wish to see you again, look well after our child. Now knead up a little maize flour and make me a few biscuits and let me go off with God's blessing." This his wife did and let her husband depart.

The man went off on his way and after ten days he came upon a great city. He looked here and he looked there; anyhow he found work on a farm. After fifteen years he said to his master: "I want to go back home again." His master took out two hundred gold pieces and gave them to him and sent him off on his way. The man was on the road when his master once more called after him: "Come," said he, "I want to say something to you. Give me ten pieces and I will give you a word of advice." The man took the ten pieces out of his pocket and handed them over: "Now tell me your word of advice." His master said: "Never mix yourself up in other

From *Modern Greek Folktales*, edited by R. M. Dawkins. Reprinted by permission of the Clarendon Press, Oxford.

people's affairs: you have seen nothing; you know nothing." "All good be with you, master," said the man and set out on the road.

"Hi, where are you? Stop, I want to tell you something else," his master shouted after him. "Give me ten more gold pieces and I will give you another word of advice." Again the man gave him the ten pieces and waited for the advice. "Never leave the king's highway." "All good be with you, master," said he and set out on the road.

"Hi, where are you? Stop, I want to tell you something else," his master shouted after him. "Give me another ten gold pieces and I will give you the last word of advice." The man grumbled: "This man with his words of advice will be taking back all the money he gave me. For all that I must hear the last advice." Saying this he gave his master the ten pieces, "First think and afterwards act." "All good be with you, master," said he and very quickly indeed was off on the road.

As he was on the road he met a young man and they went on together. They spent the evening at an inn. The innkeeper had no place to lodge them and he put them into the stable. To a manger there were tied three Persians horses munching their barley. The men lay down on the straw and went to sleep. At midnight they heard a little noise: both of them woke up and listened. They saw three men coming to make the horses ready; they were going to mount and ride away. With ten ears apiece the two companions listened to their talk. "There are three hours left before dawn," said one of them. "Let us get on the road quickly to be in time to cut in in front of them. At the big turn in the road we shall be in time to catch the guards with their load of treasure." The men at once mounted and set out on the road.

The young man rose and said to the tinsmith: "Let us go and tell the innkeeper." "Go to sleep," said the tinsmith: "Don't mix yourself up in other people's business. You have neither seen nor heard; this is no affair of ours." The youth would not listen to him and went and told the innkeeper. The innkeeper was a man in with the gang, and he was afraid that the youth might go and tell someone else. At once he seized the youth and hanged him on a poplar-tree. In the morning the tinsmith woke up and saw his companion hanged; he pretended to have seen nothing and went off. On the road he bethought him: "A piece of good luck those ten gold pieces I paid my master."

He went on and on, and on the road he met two camel-drivers

with ten camels loaded with Persian shawls and silk cloth. He joined company with them and they went on together. When they had gone some way they were hungry. What were they to do? The camel-drivers said to him: "Here we must leave the king's highway; here behind the hill there is a big inn; there we shall find something and have a meal and come back again." "For my part," said the tinsmith, "I will never leave the king's highway. If you like you may go and I will wait for you." The camel-drivers left their camels and went to the inn behind the hill. Before long the tinsmith heard a noise as of thunder; the ground shook. What had happened? The people of the inn had a store of powder and cartridges. A fire had been lit, and somehow it happened that sparks flew out and the place caught fire and everything there was burned up with the inn. So the camels were left with the tinsmith. Was there anything he could do? It was the will of God. So he took the camels and went off.

Ten days later he came to his house; the night was dark as pitch. He came close to the door and peering through a crack he saw: Oh, what did he see? His wife and a fine young man were sitting there by the side of the fire. He suspected something. In a rage he took up his gun to shoot and kill the youth. At that moment he remembered the third word of advice; he lowered his gun and bethought him who the lad might be. As he was thinking, he heard the youth saying: "Mother, in the morning I shall go to the field; you set the food by the fireside and go and fetch a load of wood." "Very well," said she, "I will go to fetch wood, my dear, but as for food, what am I to do? we have nothing here to cook. Your father, my darling, went off abroad; he is lost and has forgotten all about us." "What shall we do, Mother, do you ask? God is good and He will not forget us." At that moment his father opened the door and with tears rushed into the house and embraced them and kissed them, and from that time they lived happily.

362

*Eighty-two*

# The King and the Bishop

*Danish*

A bishop once had written over his gates and doors that he was the wisest man on earth. When the king heard of this he naturally got angry and sent word to the bishop that he should come to the castle, for the king wanted to speak to him. When the bishop came the king asked whether the bishop believed that he was the wisest person existing. The bishop answered yes to this, of course.

"Go home and come back in four days," said the king; "then I will ask you four more questions. If you can answer them you must be the wisest and if not, you must die."

The bishop came home and he did not feel very well about all this. Now, he had an old shepherd who noticed that the bishop was upset. He asked what he was so upset about, but the bishop did not want to tell him; but finally the shepherd made him tell. "That is not so bad," said the shepherd; "you can let me put on your clothes and have your silver-mounted pipe in my mouth and your silver-tipped stick in my hand."

He then traveled to the king, and the servant went in and announced that the bishop had arrived. The king then came in and walked back and forth over the floor. He said: "Can you tell me how fast I can travel around the world?" "If your Majesty has a horse that can follow the sun you can travel around the world in twenty-four hours." The king could not say that that was a lie. "Can you tell me how far it is from earth to heaven?" "If your Majesty is good at throwing stones, it is only a stone's throw." "Can you tell me how much I am worth?" "You are only worth twenty-eight pieces of silver; Jesus, our savior, was sold for thirty pieces of silver, and he should be worth two more pieces, I think." "Can you tell me what I am thinking?" said the king. "You think that I am the bishop, but I am really nothing but his shepherd."

This is how the king kept the shepherd and the bishop kept his head.

*Eighty-three*

# Intelligence and Luck

*Czech*

Once upon a time Luck met Intelligence on a garden-seat. "Make room for me!" said Luck. Intelligence was then as yet inexperienced, and didn't know who ought to make room for whom. He said: "Why should I make room for you? you're no better than I am." "He's the better man," answered Luck, "who performs most. See you there yon peasant's son who's plowing in the field? Enter into him, and if he gets on better through you than through me, I'll always submissively make way for you, whensoever and wheresoever we meet." Intelligence agreed, and entered at once into the plowboy's head.

As soon as the plowboy felt that he had intelligence in his head, he began to think: "Why must I follow the plow to the day of my death? I can go somewhere else and make my fortune more easily." He left off plowing, put up the plow, and drove home. "Daddy," says he, "I don't like this peasant's life; I'd rather learn to be a gardener." His father said: "What ails you, Vanek? have you lost your wits?" However, he bethought himself, and said: "Well, if you will, learn, and God be with you! Your brother will be heir to the cottage after me."

Vanek lost the cottage, but he didn't care for that, but went and put himself apprentice to the king's gardener. For every little that the gardener showed him, Vanek comprehended ever so much more. Ere long he didn't even obey the gardener's orders as to how he ought to do anything, but did everything his own way. At first the gardener was angry, but, seeing everything thus getting on better, he was content. "I see that you've more intelligence than I," said he, and henceforth let Vanek garden as he thought fit. In no long space of time Vanek made the garden so beautiful that the king took great delight in it, and frequently walked in it with the queen and with his only daughter.

The princess was a very beautiful damsel, but ever since she was twelve years old she had ceased speaking, and no one ever heard a single word from her. The king was much grieved, and caused proclamation to be made, that whoever should bring it to pass that she should speak again should be her husband. Many young kings, princes, and other great lords announced themselves one after the other, but all went away as they had come; no one succeeded in causing her to speak. "Why shouldn't I too try my luck?" thought Vanek; "who knows whether I mayn't succeed in bringing her to answer when I ask her a question?" He at once caused himself to be announced at the palace, and the king and his councilors conducted him into the room where the princess was.

The king's daughter had a pretty little dog, and was very fond of him because he was so clever, understanding everything that she wanted. When Vanek went into the room with the king and his councilors, he made as if he didn't even see the princess, but turned to the dog and said: "I have heard, doggie, that you are very clever, and I come to you for advice. We are three companions in travel, a sculptor, a tailor, and myself. Once upon a time we were going through a forest and were obliged to pass the night in it. To be safe from wolves, we made a fire, and agreed to keep watch one after the other. The sculptor kept watch first, and for amusement to kill time took a log and carved a damsel out of it. When it was finished he woke the tailor to keep watch in his turn. The tailor, seeing the wooden damsel, asked what it meant. 'As you see,' said the sculptor, 'I was weary, and didn't know what to do with myself, so I carved a damsel out of a log; if you find time hang heavy on your hands, you can dress her.' The tailor at once took out his scissors, needle, and thread, cut out the clothes, stitched away, and when they were ready, dressed the damsel in them. He then called me to come and keep watch. I, too, asked him what the meaning of all this was. 'As you see,' said the tailor, 'the sculptor found time hang heavy on his hands and carved a damsel out of a log, and I for the same reason clothed her; and if you find time hanging on your hands, you can teach her to speak.' And by morning dawn I had actually taught her to speak. But in the morning when my companions woke up, each wanted to possess the damsel. The sculptor said, 'I made her'; the tailor, 'I clothed her.' I, too, maintained my right. Tell me, therefore, doggie, to which of us the damsel belongs?"

The dog said nothing, but instead of the dog the princess replied: "To whom can she belong but to yourself? What's the good of the sculptor's damsel without life? What's the good of the tailor's dressing without speech? You gave her the best gift, life and speech, and therefore she by right belongs to you." "You have passed your own sentence," said Vanek; "I have given you speech again and a new life, and you therefore by right belong to me." Then said one of the king's councilors: "His Royal Grace will give you a plenteous reward for succeeding in unloosing his daughter's tongue; but you cannot have her to wife, as you are of mean lineage." The king said: "You are of mean lineage; I will give you a plenteous reward instead of our daughter."

But Vanek wouldn't hear of any other reward, and said: "The king promised without any exception, that whoever caused his daughter to speak again should be her husband. A king's word is a law; and if the king wants others to observe his laws, he must first keep them himself. Therefore the king *must* give me his daughter." "Seize and bind him!" shouted the councilor. "Whoever says the king *must* do anything, offers an insult to His Majesty, and is worthy of death. May it please your Majesty to order this malefactor to be executed with the sword?" The king said: "Let him be executed." Vanek was immediately bound and led to execution. When they came to the place of execution Luck was there waiting for him, and said secretly to Intelligence, "See how this man has got on through you, that he has to lose his head! Make way, and let me take your place!"

As soon as Luck entered Vanek, the executioner's sword broke against the scaffold, just as if someone had snapped it; and before they brought him another, up rode a trumpeter on horseback from the city, galloping as swift as a bird, trumpeted merrily, and waved a white flag, and after him came the royal carriage for Vanek. This is what had happened: The princess had told her father at home that Vanek had but spoken the truth, and the king's word ought not to be broken. If Vanek were of mean lineage the king could easily make him a prince. The king said: "You're right; let him be a prince!" The royal carriage was immediately sent for Vanek, and the councilor who had irritated the king against him was executed in his stead. Afterwards, when Vanek and the princess were going together in a carriage from the wedding, Intelligence happened to be somewhere on the road, and seeing that he couldn't help meeting Luck, bent his head and slipped on one side, just as if cold water had been thrown upon him. And from that time forth it is said that Intelligence has always given a wide berth to Luck whenever he has had to meet him.

*Eighty-four*

# The Treasure Chamber of Rhampsinitus

*Literary* (*Herodotus*, History, *Book II*)

King Rhampsinitus was possessed, they said, of great riches in silver—indeed to such an amount that none of the princes, his successors, surpassed or even equaled his wealth. For the better custody of this money, he proposed to build a vast chamber of hewn stone, one side of which was to form a part of the outer wall of his palace. The builder, therefore, having designs upon the treasures, contrived, as he was making the building, to insert in this wall a stone, which could easily be removed from its place by two men, or even by one. So the chamber was finished, and the king's money stored away in it. Time passed, and the builder fell sick, when finding his end approaching, he called for his two sons, and related to them the contrivance he had made in the king's treasure chamber, telling them it was for their sakes he had done it, that so they might always live in affluence. Then he gave them clear directions concerning the mode of removing the stone, and communicated the measurements, bidding them carefully keep the secret, whereby they would be Comptrollers of the Royal Exchequer so long as they lived. Then the father died, and the sons were not slow in setting to work: they went by night to the palace, found the stone in the wall of the building, and having removed it with ease, plundered the treasury of a round sum.

When the king next paid a visit to the apartment, he was astonished to see that the level of the treasure had fallen in some of the vessels wherein it was stored away. Whom to accuse, however, he knew not, as the seals were all perfect, and the fastenings of the room secure. Still each time that he repeated his visits, he found that more money was gone. The thieves in truth never stopped, but plundered the treasury ever more and more. At last the king determined to have some traps made, and set near the vessels which contained his wealth. This was done, and when the thieves came as usual to the treasure chamber, and one of them entered through the aperture and made straight for the jars, he suddenly found himself caught in one of the traps. Perceiving that he was lost, he instantly called his brother, and telling him what had happened, entreated him to enter as quickly as possible and cut off his head, that when his body should be discovered it might not be recognized, for that would bring ruin upon both. The other thief thought the advice good, and was persuaded to follow it; then, fitting the stone into its place, he went home, taking with him his brother's head.

When day dawned, the king came into the room, and marveled greatly to see the body of the thief in the trap without a head, while the building was still whole, and neither entrance nor exit was to be seen anywhere. In this perplexity he commanded the body of the dead man to be hung up outside the palace-wall, and set a guard to watch it, with orders that if any persons were seen weeping or lamenting near the place, they should be seized and brought before him. When the mother heard of this exposure of the corpse of her son, she took it sorely to heart, and spoke to her surviving child, bidding him devise some plan or other to get back the body, and threatening that if he did not exert himself, she would go herself to the king and denounce him as the robber.

The son said all he could to persuade her to let the matter rest, but in vain; she still continued to trouble him, until at last he yielded to her importunity, and contrived as follows: Filling some skins with wine, he loaded them on donkeys, which he drove before him till he came to the place where the guards were watching the dead body. Then pulling two or three of the skins towards him, he untied some of the necks which dangled by the asses' sides. The wine poured out freely, whereupon he began to beat his head and shout with all his might, seeming not to know which of the donkeys he should turn to first. When the guards saw the wine running, they were delighted to profit by the occasion and rushed one and all into the road, each with some vessel or other, and caught the liquor as it was spilling. The driver pretended anger, and loaded them with abuse; whereon they did their best to pacify him, until at last he appeared to soften and recover his good humor, drove his asses aside out of the road, and set to work to rearrange their burdens; meanwhile, as he talked and chatted with the guards, one of them began to rally him, and make him laugh, whereupon he gave them one of the skins as a gift. They now made up their minds to sit down and have a drinking-bout where they were, so they begged him to remain and drink with them. Then the man let himself be persuaded, and stayed. As the drinking went on, they grew very friendly together, so presently he gave them another skin, upon which they drank so copiously that they were all overcome with the liquor, and growing drowsy lay down, and fell asleep on the spot. The thief waited till it was the dead of the night, and then took down the body of his brother; after which, in mockery, he shaved off the right side of all the soldiers' beards, and so left them. Laying his brother's body upon the asses, he carried it home to his mother, having thus accomplished the thing that she had required of him.

When it came to the king's ears that the thief's body was stolen away, he was sorely vexed. Wishing, therefore, whatever it might cost, to catch the man who had contrived the trick, he had recourse (the priests said) to an expedient which I can scarcely credit. He sent his own daughter to the common stews, with orders to admit all comers, but to require every man to tell her what was the cleverest and wickedest thing he had done in the whole course of his life. If any one in reply told her the story of the thief, she was to lay hold of him and not allow him to get away. The daughter did as her father willed, whereon the thief, who was well aware of the king's motive, felt a desire to outdo him in craft and cunning. Accordingly he contrived the following plan: He procured the corpse of a man lately dead, and cutting off one of the arms at the shoulder, put it under his dress, and so went to the king's daughter. When she put the question to him as she had done to all the rest, he replied, that the wickedest thing he had ever done was cutting off the head of his brother when he was caught in a trap in the king's treasury, and the cleverest was making the guards drunk and carrying off the body. As he spoke, the princess caught at him but the thief took advantage of the darkness to hold out to her the hand of the corpse. Imagining it to be his own hand, she seized and held it fast; while the thief, leaving it in her grasp, made his escape by the door.

The king, when word was brought him of this fresh success, amazed at the sagacity and boldness of the man, sent messengers to all the towns in his dominions to proclaim a free pardon for the thief, and to promise him a rich reward, if he came and made himself known. The thief took the king at his word, and came boldly into his presence; whereupon Rhampsinitus, greatly admiring him, and looking on him as the most knowing of men, gave him his daughter in marriage.

*Eighty-five*

# The Anger Bargain

*Danish*

There was a man who had three sons. Their names were, of course, Povl and Per and Esben Ashwhipper, who was called this by his brothers because he was always scraping in the ash corner near the place where his mother was sitting. One day when all three of them had grown up their father said to them: "Now listen, boys! You will all have to go out in the world and take care of yourselves. I cannot afford to have you here at home any longer."

Now, Povl immediately wanted to get out and he packed up his knapsack and left. It was not long before he met a little man in grey clothing with a red cap on his head.

"Good day, my son," the old man said, "and where are you going?"

"I am going out to find me a position," answered Povl.

"That suits me fine, I have just gone out to hire me a farmhand. I will give you a bushel full of money when the year is up if you will work for me. You have to do everything I ask of you, and the one of us who first loses his temper shall have a piece cut out of his belly and a piece from his backside. Will you agree to this, my boy?" Povl said yes, he would do that. When the year was up he would get a whole bushel of money, you see, and he had never seen that much money before. He therefore walked home with the man in the mountain.

The following morning the man in the mountain said to him: "It is time to get up, Povl. First you have to clean the stable and groom the horses, and after that you can go plowing; I suppose you know how to plow?"

Yes, he knew how.

"That is fine. I need some plowing done. But I do not suppose that you have a watch to tell the time by?"

No, Povl did not have one.

"That does not matter," said the man in the mountain. "I have a dog here that you can take along; he will lie down at the end of the field, and when he comes home you can come too."

Yes, he would do that. And with that instruction he left. The dog lay down at the end of the field and remained there very peacefully. Noontime came and all the people in the other fields went home, but the dog did not move from the spot. "Shame on that blasted dog," thought Povl. He was so hungry that his stomach was growling, for he had not had anything to eat since he left his home. But he went on plowing till evening came and the dog finally trotted along home.

Povl came home too, but his patience was worn out, and as soon as he came into the courtyard he tore the harness off the horses and threw it on the cobblestones so that it jingled. The man in the mountain came out: "What is the matter, little Povl? It seems to me that you are slinging the harness so violently, you could not be losing your temper, I suppose?"

"I hardly know what to say to that," said Povl, "I have been here since yesterday and have not had one bite to eat. I do not call that decent."

"Oh, so you are not satisfied with your job? If that is the case, you know the terms of our agreement," said the man in the mountain. "Now I will cut a piece from your belly and one from your backside."

When he had done that, Povl was free to go wherever he wanted. He finally dragged himself home to his father, and there was great misery when they were told how Povl had been treated.

Now Per had to go to work, for the father could not feed all of them, and he was given a warning that he had to try to do better. But to make a long story short, the same thing happened to him. He met the man in the mountain, was hired and was of course the first one to lose his temper, and he therefore received the same treatment as Povl. Things looked bad for the father when Per too came home. Now both of the big fellows were lying at home unable to do anything.

"I guess I had better leave now," said Esben, "to see if I can have the same luck as my brothers."

"Yes," said the father, "when those two have not been able to manage, I am afraid things will turn out utterly wrong for you. But take great care that you do not end up at the man in the mountain's."

"Ho ho," said Esben, "he is just the one I want to go to. It should be fun to work for a man in the mountain." He packed his clothes, put spoon and knife and fork in his pocket, and left.

It was not long before he met the man in the mountain, and he hired himself to him on the same conditions as Povl and Per, and walked home with him. It was just evening when they came in and the man in the mountain said: "Can you rock the child while our mother ladles out the supper?"

Yes, he could certainly do that.

The mountain woman served really good bread soup for supper, but there was no talk of Esben eating along with them. However, he was not timid. He let the cradle stand, walked calmly over to the table, and sat down with them. He then took his spoon from his pocket and started eating. They frowned a little but that was none of Esben's concern. He ate a solid supper since it tasted quite good, and when he was done he put his spoon in his pocket again. The man in the mountain now showed him his bed, and Esben slept well until morning.

When morning came, the man in the mountain said: "Now, little Esben, it is time to get up and clean the stable and groom the horses."

He finished that in a hurry and then he went inside to see if breakfast was ready. He was right. Just then the mountain woman carried in a nice big omelet and put it on the table. Esben walked calmly over and sat down at the table, took knife and fork from his pocket, and started eating. They frowned somewhat but he did not mind, and when he was through he put the knife and fork back in his pocket again.

"Now, little Esben, can you go plowing?"

Yes, he could do that.

"I am in need of some plowing. But I do not suppose that you own a watch?"

No, he did not.

"That does not matter either," said the man in the mountain. "I have a dog here that you can take along with you. When he comes home, it is time for you to come too."

Yes, he would do that.

The dog lay down at the end of the field and remained there. Noon came and all of the neighbors went home, but the dog did not move from the spot.

"Shame on the dog," thought Esben. He grabbed one of the plowhandles and gave the dog a great whack on the side. It howled and whined and ran homeward as fast as it could. Now Esben got busy. He grabbed his pocket-knife, cut all four ropes, jumped on one of the horses, and hurried home after the dog.

He had hardly entered the courtyard before the man in the mountain came out. "How is it you came rushing home, little Esben. What is the matter?"

"I will tell you, my old man," said Esben. "I do not know what came over the confounded dog; suddenly it started howling and whining and running home as if something were wrong, and I had to cut the ropes for I was afraid that you would get angry if the dog came home and I did not follow."

"I feel almost cheated," said the man in the mountain.

"You are not angry, master, are you?" said Esben.

Oh, no. What gave him that idea?

Some time passed and Esben was taking care of his daily duties. Then one day the man in the mountain said: "Listen Esben, could you take care of my pigs in the forest?"

Yes, Esben thought he could do that.

"I will tell you something. I usually run my pigs out in the forest in the fall when the beechnuts and the acorns are ripe, so that they may fatten up." He accompanied Esben on the first day. "You can let them run around in the forest, but notice the big mudhole over there. Watch out that they do not run out there, for we will not be able to get them out again."

Yes, Esben would watch out, and the man in the mountain went home. Esben stayed out there for a long time and took care of the pigs, and the man in the mountain was very satisfied with him since they were almost fat now. But then one day he took out his pocket-knife and cut the tails off all of the pigs. He put the tails with the thick end down into the mud, and drove the pigs home to his father, who was very happy to see all that good pork. Esben then ran home to the man in the mountain shouting: "Something is very wrong, master, all of the pigs have run into the mudhole and you can only see their tails."

As soon as the man of the mountain heard this he ran off to the forest with Esben following. The man in the mountain hurried over to the hole and started pulling on one of the tails to bring out the pig, but the tail broke and the man in the mountain fell over backwards into the mud. Esben now arrived and wanted to help pull out the pigs but it was the same story with all of them.

"I thought as much," said the man in the mountain. "They were too fat; the tails are not strong enough for pulling them out. I almost feel cheated," he said.

"I do not suppose that you are angry, master?" said Esben.

But oh no, he was not angry at all.

Some days went by, and then the man in the mountain said to Esben: "We are going to a party today, my wife and I. I suppose that you can take care of things at home. First you can sweep the courtyard and after that is done you can fix up the manure pile. When that is done you can make something good and solid down by the brook, that I can use for crossing it tonight. I think it will be dark when I come home and I will most likely be a little drunk too, so I will not be as sure on my feet as usual. When you have done all that, you can come up to the place where the party is. You can dance and enjoy yourself as long as we are there. Once in a while you should cast an eye in my direction, for that makes me feel good. You must also get some light we can use when we go home. Let me now see, little Esben, that you do exactly as I have told you."

"I will do that, master," said Esben.

The man in the mountain and his wife left for the party, and you can imagine that Esben was busy. First he swept the courtyard, and then he dragged all of their furniture and belongings —chests and cupboards, tables and chairs, as well as pots and pans—out to the manure pile and stacked them up. "Now, that is all fine," thought Esben to himself, "but what shall I find to put over the brook?" He got the idea to take four of their best cows. He pulled them down by the brook, killed them, and put them in the brook in such a way that their horns were sticking up, four to each side, to make a rail. This was all well, and now he had to find some eyes to cast to the man in the mountain. He knew that they had four good sheep which would surely have good eyes that he could use. He got hold of the sheep, killed them and took out their eyes.

"Now then," said Esben, "I am ready to go to the party and it is almost evening. Oh, I almost forgot, I am supposed to find some light; I suppose I could take along the lantern but I do not think I will need it, I think we will be able to see enough to get home if I put fire to the barn." He then put on his best clothes and set fire to the barn before he left.

Everything was as it should be, and he walked up to the place where the party was. He was received quite well, had both food and drink, and was invited to dance in the best room. The man in the mountain was there too and Esben threw one of the sheep's eyes in his direction every time he saw his chance. The man in the mountain did not like that. He could not figure out what the wet lumps were that Esben threw at him every time he looked in his direction.

It was not too long before the man in the mountain came over to his wife and said that they had better go homewards. She thought that they could stay a little longer since Esben had come so recently and he ought to have a chance to enjoy himself too. But nothing persuaded the man in the mountain to stay. He wanted to get home and so they left right away.

"By the way, little Esben," said the man in the mountain when they were outside, "did you bring the lantern?"

"No, you only said that I should get some light, and I put fire to the barn before I left so that we could see to walk home by that. Look there, how nice and bright it burns."

"I feel almost cheated," said the man in the mountain.

"You are not angry, I suppose?" said Esben.

But oh no. There was not a hint of that.

They came to the brook a little while later. The man in the mountain was walking ahead and then he said: "What on earth have you put in the brook, little Esben? It seems to be so lumpy under me."

"I will tell you, master. You told me to put something really good in the brook to cross on, and I did not know anything better than our four best cows. I killed them and put them down here. You can see for yourself master. Here are four horns on each side that you can lean against."

"I feel almost cheated," said the man in the mountain.

"You are not angry, I suppose?" said Esben.

Oh no. Oh no, he was not angry at all.

They finally reached home and the man in the mountain walked quite calmly over to the barn and blew out the fire as if it were a candle. "But what is all the stuff on the manure pile, little Esben?" said the man in the mountain when he noticed all the things that were stacked there.

"I will tell you that, master. You told me to sweep the court-yard and fix up the manure pile, and I knew of nothing more decorative than our furniture and things. It was not easy at all. You must believe me, I have been busy all day."

"I feel almost cheated," said the man in the mountain.

"You are not angry, I suppose?"

But no, there was not a chance of that.

Esben now had to help the man in the mountain carry some of the things in again, and when they had finished, they went to bed.

Esben's bed was in the kitchen and there was only a thin wall between his bed and the man in the mountain's, so that he could hear what the man said to his wife. The man in the mountain was not in a very good mood when he went to bed that night. "It is a mistake if we keep Esben around, little mother. He will spoil everything for us. How on earth am I going to get rid of him?"

The wife did not know how, so he had to figure it out for himself.

"I am afraid that there is no other solution. I will have to kill him, and I might as well do it tonight, since he will be sleeping heavily after the party."

Now Esben heard all of this and didn't know what to do. He got out of bed and carried a big haunch from the kitchen and put it on the pillow. Then he took a large saucepan standing half full of water and put it under the eiderdown. He himself crawled under the bed.

It was not long before the man in the mountain tiptoed in with a large ax. He listened of course to see if everything was quiet and then he swung the ax with all his might and hit the haunch with a loud noise. That was all well but he thought that he had better give him a blow in the stomach too, and it made a squashing sound.

"Now," thought the man in the mountain, "that should take care of him," and he went calmly to bed.

A little later Esben could hear the man snoring loudly. He crawled from under the bed, picked up the haunch and the broken pot, and went to bed, where he slept quietly until day.

You can imagine how the man in the mountain stared when Esben came in for breakfast. "Listen, my good woman," said Esben to the old hag, "could you give me a couple of clean sheets and a shirt? Last night I was bitten by a flea and when I killed it I messed up both the bed and myself." And with that he walked off to his work as if nothing had happened.

"Did you hear that?" said the man to his wife. "He does not consider that blow for anything but a bite of a flea. I do not know what is going to happen. I will have to offer him money to leave, since I cannot see any other way out."

Yes, he would have to take care of that himself, she answered.

Esben came in a little later and the man in the mountain said: "Listen, Esben, do you know what I have been thinking lately?"

No, he had no way of knowing that.

"You see, I have been thinking that I do not need a farm-hand any longer. I can do the work alone and I would like you to leave now on the condition that I pay you your full wages for the year."

"Yes, I would not mind that," said Esben, "but I do not dare to do it because of my father. I am afraid that he will kill me if I come home and tell him that I have left my job prematurely."

"He cannot be angry if I pay your your salary for the full year, can he?"

"That makes no difference. I am still afraid," said Esben.

The man in the mountain was at his wits' end trying to get rid of Esben. He did not dare to offer him all the money he could carry, for he was afraid that Esben could carry more than he owned. He finally got the idea to offer him all of the money he himself could carry in a horse and carriage. "Listen, little Esben, what do you say if I offer you all of the money I can carry in a horse and carriage?"

"Yes," said Esben, "but you have to take it home to my father yourself and tell him that I have been serving you faithfully and that I am not leaving because you are tired of me. I will agree to that if you will, master."

Yes, the man in the mountain accepted that agreement happily and while Esben packed his things the man shoveled the money into the carriage and they both went home to his father. The man in the mountain said that the father should not be angry with Esben for coming home prematurely, for he had been quite satisfied with Esben. And with that he left.

You can imagine how Esben and his father gloated when the man in the mountain had left. They had now received remuneration for the suffering of his brothers, and they lived in wealth and happiness for many years on the money they had got from the man in the mountain.

*Eighty-six*

# Polyphemus, the Cyclops

*Ancient Greek (Homer)*

When I had spoken thus, I went on board my ship, and called my crew to come on board and loose the cables. Quickly they came, took places at the pins, and sitting in order smote the foaming water with their oars. But as we reached the neighboring shore, there at the outer point, close to the sea, we saw a cave, high, overhung with laurel. Here many flocks of sheep and goats were nightly housed. Around was built a yard with a high wall of deep-embedded stone, tall pines, and crested oaks. Here a man-monster slept, who shepherded his flock alone and far apart; with others he did not mingle, but quite aloof followed his lawless ways. Thus had he grown to be a marvelous monster; not like a man who lives by bread, but rather like a woody peak of the high hills, seen single, clear of others.

Now to my other trusty men I gave command to stay there by the ship and guard the ship; but I myself chose the twelve best among my men and sallied forth. I had a goat-skin bottle of the dark sweet wine given me by Maron, son of Evanthes, priest of Apollo, who watches over Ismarus. He gave me this because we guarded him and his son and wife, through holy fear; for he dwelt within the shady grove of Phoebus Apollo. He brought me splendid gifts: of fine-wrought gold he gave me seven talents, gave me a mixing-bowl of solid silver, and afterwards filled me twelve jars with wine, sweet and unmixed, a drink for gods. None knew that wine among the slaves and hand-maids of his house, none but himself, his own dear wife, and one sole house-dame. Whenever they drank the honeyed ruddy wine, he filled a cup and poured it into twenty parts of water, and still from the bowl came a sweet odor of a surprising strength; then to refrain had been no easy matter. I filled a large skin full of this and took it with me, and also took provision in a sack; for my stout heart suspected I soon should meet a man arrayed in mighty power, a savage, ignorant of rights and laws.

Quickly we reached the cave, but did not find him there; for he was tending his fat flock afield. Entering the cave, we looked around. Here crates were standing, loaded down with cheese, and here pens thronged with lambs and kids. In separate pens each sort was folded: by themselves the older, by themselves the later born, and by themselves the younglings. Swimming with whey were all the vessels, the well-wrought pails and bowls in which he milked. Here at the very first my men entreated me to take some cheeses and depart; then quickly to drive the kids and lambs to our swift ship out of the pens, and sail away over the briny water. But I refused—far better had I yielded—hoping that I might see him and he might offer gifts. But he was to prove, when seen, no pleasure to my men.

Kindling a fire here, we made burnt offering and we ourselves took of the cheese and ate; and so we sat and waited in the cave until he came from pasture. He brought a ponderous burden of dry wood to use at supper time, and tossing it down inside the cave raised a great din. We hurried off in terror to a corner of the cave. But into the wide-mouthed cave he drove his sturdy flock, all that he milked; the males, both rams and goats, he left outside in the high yard. And now he set in place the huge door-stone, lifting it high in air, a ponderous thing; no two and twenty carts, stanch and four-wheeled, could start it from the ground; such was the rugged rock he set against the door. Then sitting down, he milked the ewes and bleating goats, all in due order, and underneath put each one's young. Straightway he curdled half of the white milk, and gathering it in wicker baskets, set it by; half he left standing in the pails, ready for him to take and drink, and for his supper also. So after he had busily performed his tasks, he kindled a fire, noticed us, and asked:

"Ha, strangers, who are you? Where do you come from, sailing the watery ways? Are you upon some business? Or do you rove at random, as the pirates roam the seas, risking their lives and bringing ill to strangers?"

As he thus spoke, our very souls were crushed within us, dismayed by the heavy voice and by the monster's self; nevertheless I answered thus and said:

"We are from Troy, Achaeans, driven by shifting winds out of our course across the great gulf of the sea; homeward we fared, but through strange ways and wanderings are come hither; so Zeus was pleased to purpose. Subjects of Agamemnon, son of Atreus, we boast ourselves to be, whose fame is now the widest under heaven; so great a town he sacked, so many men he slew. But chancing here, we come before your knees to ask that you will offer hospitality, and in other ways as well will give the gift which is the stranger's due. O mighty one, respect the gods. We are your suppliants, and Zeus is the avenger of the suppliant and the stranger; he is the stranger's friend and waits on worthy strangers.'

So I spoke, and from a ruthless heart he straightway answered: "You are simple, stranger, or come from far away, to bid me dread the gods or shrink before them. The Cyclops pay no heed to ægis-bearing Zeus, nor to the blessed gods; because we are much stronger than themselves. To shun the wrath of Zeus, I would not spare you or your comrades, did my heart not bid. But tell me where you left your stanch ship at your coming. At the far shore, or near? Let me but know."

He thought to tempt me, but he could not cheat a knowing man like me; and I again replied with words of guile: "The Earth-shaker, Poseidon, wrecked my ship and cast her on the rocks at the land's end, drifting her on a headland; the wind blew from the sea; and I with these men here escaped impending ruin."

So I spoke, and from a ruthless heart he answered nothing, but starting up laid hands on my companions. He seized on two and dashed them to the ground as if they had been dogs. Their brains ran out upon the floor, and wet the earth. Tearing them limb from limb, he made his supper, and ate as does a mountain lion, leaving nothing, entrails, or flesh, or marrow bones. We in our tears held up our hands to Zeus, at sight of his reckless deeds; helplessness held our hearts. But when the Cyclops had filled his monstrous maw by eating human flesh and pouring down pure milk, he laid himself in the cave full length among his flock. And I then formed the plan within my daring heart of closing on him, drawing my sharp sword from my thigh, and stabbing him in the breast where the midriff holds the liver, feeling the place out with my hand. Yet second thoughts restrained me, for there we too had met with utter ruin; for we could never with our hands have pushed from the lofty door the enormous stone which he had set against it. Thus then with sighs we awaited sacred dawn.

But when the early rosy-fingered dawn appeared, he kindled a fire, milked his goodly flock, all in due order, and underneath put each one's young. Then after he had busily performed his tasks, seizing once more two men, he made his morning meal. And when the meal was ended, he drove from the cave his sturdy flock, and easily moved the huge door-stone; but afterwards he put it back as one might put the lid upon a quiver. Then to the hills, with many a call, he turned his sturdy flock, while I was left behind brooding on evil and thinking how I might obtain revenge, would but Athene grant my prayer. And to my mind this seemed the wisest way. There lay beside the pen a great club of the Cyclops, an olive stick still green, which he had cut to be his staff when dried. Inspecting it, we guessed its size, and thought it like the mast of a black ship of twenty oars—some broad-built merchantman which sails the great gulf of the sea; so huge it looked in length and thickness. I went and cut away a fathom's length of this, laid it before my men, and bade them shape it down; they made it smooth; I then stood by to point the tip and, laying hold, I charred it briskly in the blazing fire. The piece I now put carefully away, hiding it in the dung which lay about the cave in great abundance; and then I bade my comrades fix by lot who the bold men should be to help me raise the stake and grind it in his eye, when pleasant sleep should come. Those drew the lot whom I myself would fain have chosen; four were they, for a fifth I counted in myself. He came toward evening, shepherding the fleecy flock, and forthwith drove his sturdy flock into the wide-mouthed cave, all with much care; he did not leave a sheep in the high yard outside, either through some suspicion, or God bade him so to do. Again he set in place the huge door-stone, lifting it high in air, and, sitting down, he milked the ewes and bleating goats, all in due order, and underneath put each one's young. Then after he had busily performed his tasks, he seized once more two men and made his supper. And now it was that drawing near the Cyclops I thus spoke, holding within my hands an ivy bowl filled with dark wine:

"Here, Cyclops, drink some wine after your meal of human flesh, and see what sort of liquor our ship held. I brought it as an offering, thinking that you might pity me and send me home. But you are mad past bearing. Reckless! How should a stranger come to you again from any people, when you have done this wicked deed?"

So I spoke; he took the cup and drank it off, and mightily pleased he was with the taste of the sweet liquor, and thus he asked me for it yet again:

"Give me some more, kind sir, and straightway tell your name, that I may give a stranger's gift with which you shall be pleased. Ah yes, the Cyclops' fruitful fields bear wine in their heavy clusters, for rain from Zeus makes the grape grow; but this is a bit of ambrosia and nectar."

So he spoke, and I again offered the sparkling wine. Three times I brought and gave; three times he drank it in his folly. Then as the wine began to dull the Cyclops' senses, in winning words I said to him:

"Cyclops, you asked my noble name, and I will tell it; but do you give the stranger's gift, just as you promised. My name is Noman. Noman I am called by mother, father, and by all my comrades."

So I spoke, and from a ruthless heart he straightway answered: "Noman I eat up last, after his comrades; all the rest first; and that shall be the stranger's gift for you."

He spoke, and sinking back fell flat; and there he lay, lolling his thick neck over, till sleep, that conquers all, took hold upon him. Out of his throat poured wine and scraps of human flesh; heavy with wine, he spewed it forth. And now it was I drove the stake under a heap of ashes, to bring it to a heat, and with my words emboldened all my men, that none might flinch through fear. Then when the olive stake, green though it was, was ready to take fire, and through and through was all aglow, I snatched it from the fire, while my men stood around and Heaven inspired us with great courage. Seizing the olive stake, sharp at the tip, they plunged it in his eye, and I, perched up above, whirled it around. As when a man bores ship-beams with a drill, and those below keep it in motion with a strap held by the ends, and steadily it runs; even so we seized the fire-pointed stake and whirled it in his eye. Blood bubbled round the heated thing. The vapor singed off all the lids around the eye, and even the brows, as the ball burned and its roots crackled in the flame. As when a smith dips a great axe or adze into cold water, hissing loud, to temper it,—for that is strength to steel—so hissed his eye about the olive stake. A hideous roar he raised; the rock resounded; we hurried off in terror. He wrenched the stake from out his eye, all dabbled with the blood, and flung it from his hands in frenzy. Then he called loudly on the Cyclops who dwelt about him in the caves, along the windy heights. They heard his cry, and ran from every side, and standing by the cave they asked what ailed him:

"What has come on you, Polyphemus, that you scream so in

the immortal night, and keep us thus from sleeping? Is a man driving off your flocks in spite of you? Is a man murdering you by craft or force?"

Then in his turn from out the cave big Polyphemus answered: "Friends, Noman is murdering me by craft. Force there is none."

But answering him in winged words they said: "If no man harms you then when you are left alone, illness which comes from mighty Zeus you cannot fly. But make your prayer to your father, lord Poseidon."

This said, they went their way, and in my heart I laughed—my name, that clever notion, so deceived them. But now the Cyclops, groaning and in agonies of anguish, by groping with his hands took the stone off the door, yet sat himself inside the door with hands outstretched, to catch whoever ventured forth among the sheep; for he probably hoped in his heart that I should be so silly. But I was planning how it all might best be ordered that I might win escape from death both for my men and me. So many a plot and scheme I framed, as for my life; great danger was at hand. Then to my mind this seemed the wisest way: some rams there were of a good breed, thick in the fleece, handsome and large, which bore a dark blue wool. These I quietly bound together with the twisted willow withes on which the giant Cyclops slept—the brute—taking three sheep together. One, in the middle, carried the man; the other two walked by the sides, keeping my comrades safe. Thus three sheep bore each man. Then for myself—there was a ram, by far the best of all the flock, whose back I grasped, and curled beneath his shaggy belly there I lay, and with my hands twisted in that enormous fleece I steadily held on, with patient heart. Thus then with sighs we awaited sacred dawn.

Soon as the early rosey-fingered dawn appeared, the rams hastened to pasture, but the ewes bleated unmilked about the pens, for their udders were well-nigh bursting. Their master, racked with grievous pains, felt over the backs of all the sheep as they stood up, but foolishly did not notice how under the breasts of the woolly sheep men had been fastened. Last of the flock, the ram walked to the door, cramped by his fleece and me the crafty plotter; and feeling him over, big Polyphemus said:

"What, my pet ram! Why do you move across the cave hindmost of all the flock? Till now you never lagged behind, but with your long strides you were always first to crop the tender blooms of grass; you were the first to reach the running streams, and first

to wish to turn to the stall at night: yet here you are the last. Ah, but you miss your master's eye, which a villain has put out—he and his vile companions—blunting my wits with wine. Noman it was,—not, I assure him, safe from destruction yet. If only you could sympathize and get the power of speech to say where he is skulking from my rage, then should that brain of his be knocked about the cave and dashed upon the ground. So might my heart recover from the ills which miserable Noman brought upon me."

So saying, from his hand he let the ram go forth; and after we were come a little distance from the cave and from the yard, first from beneath the ram I freed myself and then set free my comrades. So at quick pace we drove away those long-legged sheep, heavy with fat, many times turning round, until we reached the ship. A welcome sight we seemed to our dear friends, as men escaped from death. Yet for the others they began to weep and wail; but this I did not suffer; by my frowns I checked their tears. Instead, I bade them straightway toss the many fleecy sheep into the ship, and sail away over the briny water. Quickly they came, took places at the pins, and sitting in order smote the foaming water with their oars.

*Eighty-seven*

# Gudbrand on the Hillside

*Norwegian*

Once on a time there was a man whose name was Gudbrand; he had a farm which lay far, far away upon a hillside, and so they called him Gudbrand on the Hillside.

Now, you must know this man and his good wife lived so happily together, and understood one another so well, that all the husband did the wife thought so well done there was nothing like it in the world, and she was always glad whatever he turned his hand to. The farm was their own land, and they had a hundred dollars lying at the bottom of their chest, and two cows tethered up in a stall in their farmyard.

So one day his wife said to Gudbrand:

"Do you know, dear, I think we ought to take one of our cows into town and sell it; that's what I think; for then we shall have some money in hand, and such well-to-do people as we ought to have ready money like the rest of the world. As for the hundred dollars at the bottom of the chest yonder, we can't make a hole in them, and I'm sure I don't know what we want with more than one cow. Besides, we shall gain a little in another way, for then I shall get off with only looking after one cow, instead of having, as now, to feed and litter and water two."

Well, Gudbrand thought his wife talked right good sense, so he set off at once with the cow on his way to town to sell her; but when he got to the town, there was no one who would buy his cow.

"Well, well, never mind," said Gudbrand; "at the worst, I can only go back home again with my cow. I've both stable and tether for her, I should think, and the road is no farther out than in"; and with that he began to toddle home with his cow.

But when he had gone a bit of the way, a man met him who had a horse to sell; so Gudbrand thought 'twas better to have a horse than a cow, so he swapped with the man. A little farther on he met a man walking along and driving a fat pig before him; and he thought it better to have a fat pig than a horse, so he swapped with the man. After that he went a little farther, and a man met him with a goat; so he thought it better to have a goat than a pig, and he swapped with the man that owned the goat. Then he went on a good bit till he met a man who had a sheep, and he swapped with him too; for he thought it always better to have a sheep than a goat. After a while he met a man with a goose, and he swapped away the sheep for the goose; and when he had walked a long, long time, he met a man with a cock, and he swapped with him; for he thought in this wise, " 'Tis surely better to have a cock than a goose." Then he went on till the day was far spent, and he began to get very hungry, so he sold the cock for a shilling, and bought food with the money; for, thought Gudbrand on the Hillside, " 'Tis always better to save one's life than to have a cock."

After that he went on home till he reached his nearest neighbor's house where he turned in.

"Well," said the owner of the house, "how did things go with you in town?"

"Rather so-so," said Gudbrand; "I can't praise my luck, nor do I blame it either," and with that he told the whole story from first to last.

"Ah," said his friend, "you'll get nicely called over the coals, that one can see, when you get home to your wife. Heaven help you, I wouldn't stand in your shoes for something!"

"Well," said Gudbrand on the Hillside, "I think things might have gone much worse with me; but now, whether I have done wrong or not, I have so kind a goodwife, she never has a word to say against anything that I do."

"Oh," answered his neighbor, "I hear what you say, but I don't believe it for all that."

"Shall we lay a bet upon it?" asked Gudbrand on the Hillside. "I have a hundred dollars at the bottom of my chest at home; will you lay as many against them?"

Yes, the friend was ready to bet; so Gudbrand stayed there till evening, when it began to get dark, and then they went together to his house, and the neighbor was to stand outside the door and listen, while the man went in to see his wife.

"Good evening!" said Gudbrand on the Hillside.

"Good evening!" said the goodwife. "Oh, is that you? Now God be praised."

Yes, it was he. So the wife asked how things had gone with him in town?

"Oh, only so-so," answered Gudbrand; "not much to brag of. When I got to the town there was no one who would buy the cow, so you must know I swapped it away for a horse."

"For a horse," said his wife; "well, that is good of you; thanks, with all my heart. We are so well-to-do that we may drive to church, just as well as other people; and if we choose to keep a horse we have a right to get one, I should think. So run out, child, and put up the horse."

"Ah," said Gudbrand, "but you see I've not got the horse after all; for when I got a bit farther on the road I swapped it away for a pig."

"Think of that, now," said the wife; "you did just as I should have done myself; a thousand thanks! Now I can have a bit of bacon in the house to set before people when they come to see me, that I can. What do we want with a horse? People would only say we had got so proud that we couldn't walk to church. Go out, child, and put up the pig in the sty."

"But I've not got the pig either," said Gudbrand, "for when I got a little farther on I swapped it away for a milch goat."

"Bless us!" cried his wife, "how well you manage everything! Now I think it over, what should I do with a pig? People would only point at us and say, 'Yonder they eat up all they have got.' No, now I have got a goat, and I shall have milk and cheese, and keep the goat too. Run out, child, and put up the goat."

"Nay, but I haven't got the goat either," said Gudbrand, "for a little farther on I swapped it away, and got a fine sheep instead."

"You don't say so!" cried his wife; "why, you do everything to please me, just as if I had been with you; what do we want with a goat? If I had it I should lose half my time in climbing up the hills to get it down. No, if I have a sheep, I shall have both wool and clothing, and fresh meat in the house. Run out, child, and put up the sheep."

"But I haven't got the sheep any more than the rest," said Gudbrand; "for when I had gone a bit farther I swapped it away for a goose."

"Thank you, thank you, with all my heart," cried his wife; "what should I do with a sheep? I have no spinning-wheel, nor carding-comb, nor should I care to worry myself with cutting, and shaping, and sewing clothes. We can buy clothes now, as we have always done; and now I shall have roast goose, which I have longed for so often; and, besides, down to stuff my little pillow with. Run out, child, and put up the goose."

"Ah," said Gudbrand, "but I haven't the goose either; for when I had gone a bit farther I swapped it away for a cock."

"Dear me!" cried his wife, "how you think of everything! Just as I should have done myself. A cock! think of that! Why, it's as good as an eight-day clock, for every morning the cock crows at four o'clock, and we shall be able to stir our stumps in good time. What should we do with a goose? I don't know how to cook it; and as for my pillow, I can stuff it with cotton-grass. Run out, child, and put up the cock."

"But, after all, I haven't got the cock," said Gudbrand; "for when I had gone a bit farther, I got as hungry as a hunter, so I was forced to sell the cock for a shilling, for fear I should starve."

"Now, God be praised that you did so!" cried his wife; "whatever you do, you do it always just after my own heart. What should we do with the cock? We are our own masters, I should think, and can lie abed in the morning as long as we like. Heaven be thanked that I have got you safe back again; you who do everything so well that I want neither cock nor goose, neither pigs nor kine."

Then Gudbrand opened the door and said:

"Well, what do you say now? Have I won the hundred dollars?" and his neighbor was forced to allow that he had.

*Eighty-eight*

# Clever Elsie and Her Companions

*Italian*

Once upon a time there were a husband and wife who had a son. This son grew up, and said one day to his mother: "Do you know, mother, I would like to marry!" "Very well, marry! Whom do you want to take?" He answered: "I want the gardener's daughter." "She is a good girl; take her; I am willing." So he went, and asked for the girl, and her parents gave her to him. They were married, and when they were in the midst of the dinner, the wine gave out. The husband said: "There is no more wine!" The bride, to show that she was a good housekeeper, said: "I will go and get some." She took the bottles and went to the cellar, turned the cock, and began to think: "Suppose I should have a son, and we should call him Bastianelo, and he should die. Oh! how grieved I should be! oh! how grieved I should be!" And thereupon she began to weep and weep; and meanwhile the wine was running all over the cellar.

When they saw that the bride did not return, the mother said: "I will go and see what the matter is." So she went into the cellar, and saw the bride, with the bottle in her hand, and weeping, while the wine was running over the cellar. "What is the matter with you, that you are weeping?" "Ah! my mother, I was thinking that if I had a son, and should name him Bastianelo, and he should die, oh! how I should grieve! oh! how I should grieve!" The mother, too, began to weep, and weep, and weep; and meanwhile the wine was running over the cellar.

When the people at the table saw that no one brought the wine, the groom's father said: "I will go and see what is the matter. Certainly something wrong has happened to the bride." He went and saw the whole cellar full of wine, and the mother and bride weeping. "What is the matter?" he said; "has anything wrong happened to you?" "No," said the bride, "but I was thinking that if I had a son and should call him Bastianelo, and he should die, oh! how I should grieve! oh! how I should grieve!" Then he, too, began to weep, and all three wept; and meanwhile the wine was running over the cellar.

When the groom saw that neither the bride, nor the mother, nor the father came back, he said: "Now I will go and see what the matter is that no one returns." He went into the cellar and saw all the wine running over the cellar. He hastened and stopped the cask, and then asked: "What is the matter, that you are all weeping, and have let the wine run all over the cellar?" Then the bride said: "I was thinking that if I had a son and called him Bastianelo and he should die, oh! how I should grieve! oh! how I should grieve!" Then the groom said: "You stupid fools! are you weeping at this, and letting all the wine run into the cellar? Have you nothing else to think of? It shall never be said that I remained with you! I will roam about the world, and until I find three fools greater than you I will not return home."

He had a bread-cake made, took a bottle of wine, a sausage, and some linen, and made a bundle, which he put on a stick and carried over his shoulder. He journeyed and journeyed, but found no fool. At last he said, worn out: "I must turn back, for I see I cannot find a greater fool than my wife." He did not know what to do, whether to go on or to turn back. "Oh!" he said, "it is better to try and go a little farther." So he went on and shortly he saw a man in his shirt-sleeves at a well, all wet with perspiration and water. "What are you doing, sir, that you are so covered with water and in such a sweat?" "Oh! let me alone," the man answered, "for I have been here a long time drawing water to fill this pail and I cannot fill it." "What are you drawing the water in?" he asked him. "In this sieve," he said. "What are you thinking about, to draw water in that sieve? Just wait!" He went to a house near by, and borrowed a bucket, with which he returned to the well and filled the pail. "Thank you, good man, God knows how long I should have had to remain here!" "Here is one who is a greater fool than my wife."

He continued his journey and after a time he saw at a distance a man in his shirt who was jumping down from a tree. He drew near, and saw a woman under the same tree holding a pair of breeches. He asked them what they were doing, and they said that they had been there a long time, and that the man was trying on those breeches and did not know how to get into them. "I have jumped, and jumped," said the man, "until I am tired out and I cannot imagine how to get into those breeches." "Oh!" said the traveler, "you might stay here as long as you wished, for you would never get into them in this way. Come down and lean against the tree." Then he took his legs and put them in the breeches, and after he had put them on, he said: "Is that right?" "Very good, bless you; for if it had not been for you, God knows how long I should have had to jump." Then the traveler said to himself: "I have seen two greater fools than my wife."

Then he went his way and as he approached a city he heard a great noise. When he drew near he asked what it was, and was told it was a marriage, and that it was the custom in that city for the brides to enter the city gate on horseback, and that there was a great discussion on this occasion between the groom and the owner of the horse, for the bride was tall and the horse high, and they could not get through the gate; so that they must either cut off the bride's head or the horse's legs. The groom did not wish his bride's head cut off, and the owner of the horse did not wish his horse's legs cut off, and hence this disturbance. Then the traveler said: "Just wait," and came up to the bride and gave her a slap that made her lower her head, and then he gave the horse a kick, and so they passed through the gate and entered the city. The groom and the owner of the horse asked the traveler what he wanted, for he had saved the groom his bride, and the owner of the horse his horse. He answered that he did not wish anything and said to himself: "Two and one make three! that is enough; now I will go home." He did so and said to his wife: "Here I am, my wife; I have seen three greater fools than you; now let us remain in peace and think about nothing else." They renewed the wedding and always remained in peace. After a time the wife had a son whom they named Bastianelo, and Bastianelo did not die, but still lives with his father and mother.

*Eighty-nine*

# The Master Thief

*Scottish*

There was formerly a farmer, who had rented a farm from a gentleman, and he and the gentleman lived near each other.

The farmer had a son called Billy, who used to be stealing things from people. He would not leave anything that he could steal if he only got an opportunity of doing so, and besides, he used to steal from the gentleman. The gentleman came to the farmer, and told him that he ought to give his son a thorough training in a trade, and that he could not teach him a better trade than thieving.

"Would I not as soon wish him dead," said the farmer, "as to go and teach him thieving—I would prefer it that he were dead."

"Not so, not at all," said the gentleman, "we will leave it to his own inclination, and see what he himself would prefer to learn."

Word was sent for Billy, and when he came in, the gentleman asked him whether he would be willing to go and learn thieving. Billy said he would be willing indeed, that there was no trade he liked better than thieving.

Since he himself was so keen, his father determined that it would be as well to let him have his own way, seeing that as he had a great desire for it, there would be no keeping him from it in any case, and that it were just as well for him to be a clever thief as to be an awkward, clumsy one, since he intended to be a thief.

So his father got him ready to go away to learn thieving. So Billy started forth. On the road he met a man, who asked him where he was going. He told him that he was going to learn thieving, and that he wanted a master to teach him.

"It is a bad trade you are going to learn," said the man, "and there is no fear but that you will find a master."

He let that man pass.

He had not gone much farther when three men met him, who asked him where he was going.

From *More West Highland Tales* by J. G. Mackay. Reprinted by permission of Oliver & Boyd Ltd., Edinburgh.

He replied that he was going to learn thieving, and that his intention was, if any one met him who wanted an apprentice for such a trade, to take service with him.

"What?" said one of them, "I am looking for a lad for that trade myself, and I am willing to engage you."

"I am quite willing," said Billy. So Billy set off with him.

There was a change-house near, and this man wanted to steal all the most valuable things. He got ready for it, and took Billy with him to the change-house.

They had a rope with them with which to slip down the chimney. "Now," said his master to Billy, "you must go down the chimney on the rope, and send up to me all the most valuable things, and after sending them up, I will haul you up yourself."

In the night, when the people of the house had gone to rest, they got up on the roof of the house, and Billy's master let him down the chimney, and when he had got down, he sent up all the most váluable things that there were in the room, and when everything had been sent up, the man above bolted with all he had got, and left Billy down below in the room.

Billy was now in a tight fix, and could not think what to do. He looked round about him, and what should he see but a cow's hide with the horns attached. He seized it, and put it over himself, and began to scream and shriek up and down the room.

The maid-servant arose, and lit a light, and opened the door of the room, and when she saw him, she went back again in a fright, and shouted to her master.

"What ails you?" said her master.

"A great deal," said she: "I have seen the devil—he is in the room."

"How could he be there?" said her master, "surely it must be through the chimney that he came in."

The change-house man went into the room, and saw what seemed to be the devil.

"What brought you here?" said the change-house man.

"It is here that I ought to be, and where I often am," said the seeming devil, "and when I come for the last time, I will not even leave you as much as a needle is worth."

"What will you take for not coming any more? will you accept fifty pounds sterling?"

"I will not: a hundred is little enough: if I get a hundred, I will go away and come no more."

The change-house man gave him one hundred pounds sterling, and he went away.

He went home to his father, and his father was astonished at his returning so soon. The gentleman also heard that Billy had returned, and sent for him.

"Are you trained and proficient already, Billy?" said the gentleman.

"I am," he replied.

"I do not believe that you are. If you are indeed proficient, I shall set you a certain test, which, if you are a clever thief, you will accomplish. Now, I am sending off some carts and carters, and if you are a good thief, you will steal one of the horses from them out of one of the carts."

Said Billy, "Many a thing have I attempted, quite as difficult as that."

The carters departed, and so did Billy; he went to the back of a hillock, by the side of the road by which the carters would return. There was a rabbit hole there. When the carters were returning and getting near, Billy caught a rabbit, broke its leg, and then let it go at the back of the hill; and when the carters saw the rabbit limping, away they went after it.

He let slip one or two rabbits in that way, and the carters went on chasing them.

When the carters were at the back of the hill, after the rabbits, and no one near the carts, Billy came and unharnessed one of the horses from the carts. On to its back he got, and came to the gentleman's house with it. When the carters got back, the horse had gone, and they did not know what to do. So they came home, and said that the horse had been stolen from them. "I see that it has been stolen," said their master.

"I see that you are indeed a good thief," said the gentleman to Billy, "but I will set you another test. I will put a horse in a stable, with five people to guard, four on the floor, and one outside."

"That," said Billy, "is as difficult a thing as any I have yet tried."

The five men went to guard the horse. Billy betook himself to the change-house, and brought away four bottles of whiskey. There was a herd of pigs near the stable, and Billy went down to where the pigs were, with the bottles in his pocket, and laid himself down there as if he were dead. The people who were guarding the horse noticed something going on where the pigs were. So one of them said, "Go down and have a look, lest one of the pigs be stolen from the herd, without our master's knowledge."

So they went down: and they found a dead man among the pigs. They brought back the dead man, and then they noticed some bottles in his pocket. They took two bottles out of that pocket, and began drinking. They did not leave a drop in them. Then they turned the dead man over, and found two other bottles in the pocket on the other side.

They began on these, and never left a drop in them, and now they were completely drunk. No longer would they stay to watch, but they left the horse and the dead man there, and arrived at the change-house. When they had gone, Billy was on his feet at once, and taking the horse with him, came to his father's house.

The gentleman heard that Billy had stolen the horse, and sent word for him.

"So you stole the horse," said the gentleman.

"Yes, I did," said Billy.

"I shall try you with another test yet. I shall have a sword on the table, and a pistol, full of shot, and unless you can carry off the bed-sheet from under my wife, you shall live no longer."

"Truly, you might just as well kill me where we now stand."

"Unless you do what I said, you shall not have long to live after this."

"It is the hardest thing that was ever set before me."

That night Billy set forth, and went to the church-yard, and dug up a body that had been newly buried, and dressed it up. Then he carried it off. He came to the gentleman's house, and ascended to the roof. Then he let the corpse down the chimney.

The gentleman arose, and lit a light, and saw feet coming down the chimney. "The son of the fiend! Here comes this fellow! I'll see to it that he shall not live any longer. I shall not take the trouble of firing at his feet, but when he shows his body, it is then, then, that I will fire."

When the corpse had come right down, he fired. "There! let him stay there. I shall let him remain there, till day comes."

"For the love of God, do not do so," said his wife; "carry him away, and bury him, lest he be the cause of your own death."

So he hoisted him on to his back, and carried him out of the house. When Billy observed that the gentleman had gone off with the corpse, in he went.

"He is so heavy," said he to the gentleman's wife, "I cannot carry him away just now."

She supposed that Billy was her own husband. And Billy went to bed with the gentleman's wife. Little by little, he worked away until he had got the bed-sheet to himself. When he had got it quite away, he arose, and went out.

The gentleman returned, having buried the corpse. "I am tired, and quite worn out."

"What, my love, could have made you tired? it is not two minutes since you left me in the bed."

The gentleman looked, and noticed that the bed-sheet was wanting. "You may have him also. I shall be off."

The gentleman departed accordingly, and Billy had the house, and the wife.


*Ninety*

# Shemiaka the Judge

*Russian*

In a certain village there lived two brothers, one rich and the other poor. The poor brother came to the rich one to borrow a horse to bring wood from the forest. The rich brother gave him a horse. The poor brother also asked for a yoke; the rich one angrily refused. So the poor one tied his sledge to the horse's tail, went to the forest, cut a huge load of wood, so heavy that the horse could hardly drag it, came to his own yard, and opened the gate, but forgot to remove the board across the gate. The horse tried to push through the board and tore off its tail. The poor brother brought the now tailless horse back to the rich brother, who refused to take it back and set out to bring complaint against the poor one before Shemiaka, the judge. The poor man knew that he was in sore trouble, for he had nothing to give to the judge. Sadly he followed his brother.

The two brothers came to a rich peasant's house and asked to be allowed to spend the night. The peasant drank and made merry

From *Russian Fairy Tales*, edited and translated by Norbert Guterman. Copyright 1945 by Pantheon Books, Inc. Reprinted by permission of Pantheon Books, a Division of Random House, Inc.

with the rich brother, but refused to invite the poor one to his table. The poor brother lay on the stove, looking at them; suddenly he fell from the stove and crushed to death a child lying in a cradle below. So the peasant also set out to see Shemiaka the judge, to lodge a complaint against the poor brother.

As they walked to the town (the rich brother, the peasant, and the poor brother, who walked behind them), they happened to cross a high bridge. The poor brother, thinking that he would not escape with his life from Shemiaka the judge, jumped from the bridge, hoping to kill himself. Under the bridge a man was carrying his sick father to the bathhouse; the poor brother fell onto the sledge and crushed the sick man to death. The son went to complain to Shemiaka the judge on the ground that the poor man had killed his father.

The rich brother came to Shemiaka the judge and lodged a complaint against the poor one for having torn off the tail of his horse. In the meantime the poor brother had picked up a stone and wrapped it in a kerchief. Standing behind his brother he thought: "If the judge judges against me I will kill him with this stone." But the judge, thinking that the poor man had prepared a bribe of a hundred rubles, ordered the rich brother to give the horse to the poor one to keep until it grew another tail.

Then the rich peasant came before the judge and lodged his complaint about the death of his child. The poor man took out the same stone and showed it to the judge from where he stood behind the peasant. The judge, thinking that he was being offered another hundred rubles, for the second case, ordered the peasant to give his wife to the poor man to keep until she gave birth to another child, adding: "And then take back your wife and the child."

The third plaintiff accused the poor man of having crushed his father to death. The poor man showed the same stone to the judge. The judge, thinking that he was being offered still another hundred rubles, ordered the dead man's son to go to the bridge and said: "And you, poor man, stand under the bridge, and you, son, jump from the bridge and crush the poor man to death."

Shemiaka the judge then sent a servant to the poor man to ask for three hundred rubles. The poor man showed his stone and said: "If the judge had judged against me, I would have killed him with this stone." The servant came to the judge and said: "If you had judged against him, he would have killed you with a stone." The judge crossed himself and said: "Thank God that I judged in his favor."

The poor brother went to the rich brother to get the horse, in accordance with the verdict, until it should grow another tail. The rich brother did not want to give away his horse; instead, he gave the poor brother five hundred rubles, three measures of grain, and a milk goat, and made peace with him.

The poor man went to the peasant and, citing the verdict, asked for the peasant's wife until she should give birth to a child. Instead, the peasant gave him five hundred rubles, a cow with her calf, a mare with her colt, and four measures of grain, and made peace with him.

The poor man went to the plaintiff whose father he had killed and told him that in accordance with the judge's verdict he, the son, must stand on the bridge, and he himself, the poor man, under the bridge, and that the son must jump on him and crush him to death. The son thought: "If I jump from the bridge I shall not crush him but shall smash myself to death." He gave the poor man two hundred rubles, a horse, and five measures of grain, and made peace with him.

*Ninety-one*

# Little Claus and Big Claus

*Danish (literary: Hans Christian Andersen)*

There lived two men in one village, and they had the same name —both were called Claus; but one had four horses, and the other only a single horse. To distinguish them from each other, folk called him who had four horses Big Claus and the one who had only a single horse Little Claus. Now we shall hear what happened to each of them, for this is a true story.

The whole week through Little Claus was obliged to plow for Big Claus, and to lend him his one horse; then Big Claus helped him out with all his four, but only once a week, and that was on Sunday. Hurrah! how Little Claus cracked his whip over all five horses, for they were as good as his own on that one day. The sun shone gaily, and all the bells in the church tower were ringing to church. The people were all dressed in their best, and were going, with their hymn-books under their arms, to hear the parson preach, and they saw Little Claus plowing with five horses. And he was so pleased that he cracked his whip again and again, and cried, "Gee up, all my horses!"

"You must not say that," said Big Claus, "for only the one horse is yours."

But when some more people went by to church Little Claus forgot that he was not to say this, and he cried, "Gee up, all my horses!"

"Now, I tell you, you must stop it," said Big Claus, "for if you say it again I shall hit your horse on the head, so that he will fall down dead, and then that will be the end of him!"

"I will certainly not say it any more," said Little Claus.

But when some people came by soon after and nodded "Good day" to him he was so pleased, and thought it looked so fine, after all, to have five horses to plow his field, that he cracked his whip again, and cried out, "Gee up, all my horses!"

"I'll 'gee up' your horses for you!" said Big Claus. And he took a mallet and hit the only horse of Little Claus on the head, so that he fell down, and was dead instantly.

"Oh, now I haven't any horse at all!" said Little Claus; and he began to cry.

But after a while he flayed the horse, and let the hide dry in the wind, and put it in a sack and hung it over his shoulder, and went to the town to sell his horse's skin.

He had a very long way to go, and was obliged to pass through a great dark wood, and the weather became dreadfully bad. He went quite astray, and before he got into the right way again it was evening, and it was too far to get to the town or back home again before nightfall.

Close by the road stood a large farmhouse. The shutters were closed outside the windows, but the light could still be seen shining out over the top of them.

"I may be able to get leave to stop here for the night," thought Little Claus; and he went and knocked.

The farmer's wife unlocked the door; but when she heard what he wanted she told him to go away, as her husband was not at home, and would not let her admit strangers.

"Then I shall have to lie out here," said Little Claus. And the farmer's wife shut the door in his face.

Close by stood a great haystack, and between this and the

farmhouse was a little shed with a flat thatched roof.

"I can lie there," said Little Claus, when he looked up at the roof; "that is a capital bed. I suppose the stork won't fly down and bite me in the legs." For a living stork was standing on the roof, where it had its nest.

Now Little Claus climbed up to the roof of the shed, where he lay down, and turned about to settle himself comfortably. The wooden shutters did not cover the windows to the top, and he could look straight into the room. There was a big table, with the cloth laid, and wine and roast meat and a lovely fish upon it. The farmer's wife and the sexton were seated at table, and nobody besides. She was filling his glass, and he was sticking his fork into the fish, for that was his favorite dish.

"If one could only get some too!" said Little Claus, and he stretched out his head towards the window. Heavens! what a splendid cake he saw there! Yes, certainly, that *was* a feast.

Now he heard someone riding along the highroad. It was the woman's husband, who was coming home. He was a good man enough, but he had the strange peculiarity that he could never bear to see a sexton. If a sexton appeared before his eyes he got very angry. And that was the reason why the sexton had called on the wife to wish her "Good day" when he knew that her husband was not at home; and the good woman had put the best fare she had before him. But when they heard the man coming they were frightened, and the woman begged the sexton to creep into a big empty chest which stood there. And he did so, for he knew the husband could not bear the sight of a sexton. The woman quickly hid all the excellent meat and wine in her baking-oven; for if her husband had seen that he would have been sure to ask what it meant.

"Ah, yes!" sighed Little Claus up on the shed when he saw all the good fare put away.

"Is there anyone up there?" asked the farmer; and he looked up and saw Little Claus. "What are you lying up there for? Better come down indoors with me."

And Little Claus told him how he had lost his way, and asked leave to stay there for the night.

"Yes, certainly," said the farmer; "but first we must have something to live upon."

The woman received them both very kindly, spread the cloth on a long table, and gave them a great dish of groats. The farmer was hungry, and ate with a good appetite, but Little Claus could not help thinking of the lovely roast meat, fish, and cake which he knew were in the oven. Under the table, at his feet, he had laid the sack with the horse's hide in it; for, as we know, he had left home to sell it in the town. He could not relish the groats at all, so he trod upon the sack with his foot, and the dry skin inside creaked quite loud.

"Hush!" said Little Claus to his sack, at the same time treading on it again till it squeaked louder than before.

"Why, what have you in your sack?" asked the farmer.

"Oh, that's a magician," said Little Claus. "He says we are not to eat groats, for he has conjured the oven full of roast meat, fish, and cake."

"Wonderful!" said the farmer; and he opened the oven door in a hurry, and found all the dainty food which his wife had hidden there, but which, as he thought, had been conjured there by the wizard under the table. The woman dared not say anything, but put the things at once on the table; and so they both ate of the meat, the fish, and the cake. Then Little Claus again trod on his sack and made the hide creak.

"What does he say now?" asked the farmer.

"He says," said Claus, "that he has conjured three bottles of wine for us too, and that they are standing there in the corner behind the oven."

So the woman was obliged to bring out the wine which she had hidden, and the farmer drank it, and became very merry. He would have been very glad to have such a conjurer as Little Claus had there in the sack.

"Can he conjure up the devil?" asked the farmer. "I should like to see him, for now I am merry."

"Oh, yes," said Little Claus, "my conjurer can do anything that I ask of him—can you not?" he asked, and trod on the hide till it squeaked. "Do you hear? He answers yes. But the devil is very ugly to look at; we had better not see him."

"Oh, I'm not at all afraid. Pray, what will he look like?"

"Well, he'll look the very image of a sexton!"

"Ha!" said the farmer, "that *is* ugly! You must know, I can't bear the sight of a sexton. But it doesn't matter now, for I know that he's the devil, so I shall easily stand it. Now I have got up my courage, but do not let him come too near me."

"Now I will ask my conjurer," said Little Claus; and he trod on the sack and held his ear down.

"What does he say?"

"He says you may go and open the chest that stands in the corner, and you will see the devil crouching inside it; but you must hold the lid so that he doesn't slip out."

"Will you help me to hold it?" said the farmer. And he went to the chest where the wife had hidden the real sexton, who now lay inside, very much frightened. The farmer opened the lid a little way and peeped in under it.

"Hu!" he cried, and sprang backward. "Yes, indeed, now I've seen him, and he looked exactly like our sexton. Oh, it was dreadful!"

After this he had to drink again. So they sat and drank until late into the night.

"That conjurer you must sell to me," said the farmer. "Ask for him what you will! I'll give you a whole bushel of money for him, at once!"

"No, that I can't do," said Little Claus! "Only think how much use I can make of this conjurer."

"Oh, I should so much like to have him!" said the farmer; and he went on begging.

"Well," said Little Claus at last, "as you have been so kind as to give me shelter for the night I will let it be so. You shall have the conjurer for a bushel of money, but I must have the bushel heaped up."

"That shall you have," said the farmer. "But you must take the chest away with you as well. I will not keep it in my house another hour. One cannot tell—perhaps he may be there still."

Little Claus gave the farmer his sack with the dry hide in it, and got in exchange a whole bushel of money, and that heaped up. The farmer also gave him a big wheelbarrow on which to carry off his money and the chest.

"Farewell!" said Little Claus; and he went off with his money and the big chest, in which the sexton was still sitting.

On the other side of the wood was a wide, deep river. The water rushed along so rapidly that one could scarcely swim against the stream. A fine new bridge had been built over it. Little Claus stopped on the middle of the bridge, and said quite loud, so that the sexton could hear it:

"Oh, what shall I do with this stupid chest? It's as heavy as if stones were in it. I shall only get tired out if I drag it any farther, so I'll throw it into the river. If it swims home to me, well and good; and if it does not it will be no great matter."

And he took the chest with one hand and lifted it up a little, as if he meant to throw it into the river.

"No! let be!" cried the sexton from within the chest. "Let me out first!"

"Hu!" said Little Claus, pretending to be frightened, "he's in there still! I must make haste and throw him into the river, so that he may be drowned."

"Oh, no! oh, no!" screamed the sexton. "I'll give you a whole bushel of money if you'll let me go."

"Why, that's another thing!" said Little Claus; and he opened the chest.

The sexton crept quickly out, pushed the empty chest into the water, and went to his house, where Little Claus received a whole bushel of money. He had already received one from the farmer, and so now he had his whole wheelbarrow full of money.

"See, I've been well paid for the horse," he said to himself when he had got home to his own room and was emptying all the money into a heap in the middle of the floor. "That will vex Big Claus when he hears how rich I have grown through my one horse, but I won't tell him about it outright."

So he sent a boy to Big Claus for the loan of a bushel measure.

"What can he want with it?" thought Big Claus. And he smeared some tar underneath the measure, so that some part of whatever was measured should stick to it. And so it happened, for when he got the measure back there were three new silver shillings sticking to it.

"What's this?" cried Big Claus; and he ran off at once to Little Claus. "Where did you get all that money from?"

"Oh, that's for my horse's skin. I sold it yesterday evening."

"That's really being well paid," said Big Claus. He ran home in a hurry, took an axe, and killed all his four horses; then he flayed them, and drove off to the town with their hides.

"Hides! hides! Who'll buy any hides?" he cried through the streets.

All the shoemakers and tanners came running, and asked how much he wanted for them.

"A bushel of money for each!" said Big Claus.

"Are you mad?" said they all. "Do you think we have money by the bushel?"

"Hides! hides!" he cried again; and to all who asked him what the hides cost he replied, "A bushel of money."

"He wants to make fools of us," they all said together. And the shoemakers took their straps, and the tanners their aprons, and began to beat Big Claus.

"Hides! hides!" they shouted mockingly after him. "Yes, we'll tan your hide for you till the blood runs. Out of the town with you!" And Big Claus made off at top speed, for he had never before had such a thrashing in his life.

"Well," said he, when he got home, "Little Claus shall pay for this. I'll kill him for it."

Now at Little Claus's house the old grandmother had died. She had been very cross and unkind to him, but still he was very sorry, and took the dead woman and put her in his warm bed to see if she would not come to life again. There he meant her to lie all night, and he himself would sit in the corner and sleep on a chair, as he had often done before. As he sat there in the night the door opened, and Big Claus came in with his axe. He knew where Little Claus's bed stood, and, going straight to it, he hit the old grandmother on the head, thinking she was Little Claus.

"There now!" said he. "You shall not make a fool of me any more." And so he went home again.

"That's a bad fellow, that man," said Little Claus. "He wanted to kill me. It was a good thing for my old granny that she was dead already, or else he would have taken her life."

So he dressed his old grandmother in her Sunday clothes, borrowed a horse of his neighbor, harnessed it to the cart, and sat the old grandmother up against the back seat, so that she could not fall out when the cart started off. And off they drove through the wood. As the sun rose they came to an inn. There Little Claus pulled up, and went in to get something to eat.

The innkeeper was very, very rich; he was a very good man too, but as hot-tempered as if he was full of pepper and snuff.

"Good morning," said he to Little Claus. "You've put on your Sunday clothes early today."

"Yes," said Little Claus. "I am going to town with my old grandmother; she's sitting out there in the wagon. I can't bring her into the room—will you take her a glass of mead? But you must speak pretty loud, for she can't hear well."

"Yes, that I will," said the innkeeper. And he poured out a big glass of mead, and went out with it to the dead grandmother, who had been propped up in the wagon.

"Here's a glass of mead from your son," said the innkeeper. But the dead woman said not a word, but sat quite still. "Don't you hear?" cried the innkeeper, as loud as he could. "Here is a glass of mead from your son!"

Once more he bawled out the same thing, and yet again, but as she did not move he flew into a passion, and threw the glass in her face, so that the mead ran down over her nose, and she tumbled backwards into the wagon, for she had only been propped up, and not bound fast.

"Hallo!" cried Little Claus, as he rushed out of the door and seized the innkeeper by the throat. "You've killed my grandmother now! See, there's a big hole in her forehead."

"Oh, what a misfortune!" cried the innkeeper, wringing his hands. "That all comes of my hot temper. Dear Little Claus, I'll give you a whole bushel of money, and have your grandmother buried as if she were my own; only keep quiet, or they will cut my head off, and that is so unpleasant!"

So Little Claus again received a whole bushel of money, and the innkeeper buried the old grandmother as if she had been his own. And when Little Claus came home with all his money he at once sent his boy to Big Claus to ask to borrow a bushel measure.

"How is this?" said Big Claus. "Have I not killed him? I must go myself and see to this." And so he went over himself with the bushel to Little Claus.

"Now, where did you get all that money from?" he asked; and he opened his eyes wide when he saw it all together.

"You killed my grandmother, and not me," replied Little Claus; "and I've been and sold her, and got a whole bushel of money for her."

"That's really being well paid," said Big Claus; and he hastened home, took an axe, and killed his own grandmother forthwith, put her on a wagon, drove off to the town with her, to where the apothecary lived, and asked him if he would buy a dead person.

"Who is it, and where did you get him from?" asked the apothecary.

"It's my grandmother," said Big Claus. "I've killed her to get a bushel of money for her."

"Heaven save us!" cried the apothecary. "You're raving! Don't say such things, or you may lose your head." And he told him earnestly what a bad deed he had done, and what a bad man he was, and that he ought to be punished. And Big Claus was so frightened that he sprang out of the apothecary's shop straight into his wagon, whipped up the horses, and drove off home. But the apothecary and all the people thought him mad, and so they let him drive wherever he liked.

"You shall pay for this!" said Big Claus when he got out upon the highroad. "Yes, you shall pay me for this, Little Claus!" And directly he got home he took the biggest sack he could find, and went over to Little Claus's, and said, "Now, you've tricked me again! First I killed my horses and then my old grandmother! And it's all your fault, but you shall never trick me any more." And he seized Little Claus round the body and pushed him into the sack, and took him upon his back, and shouted out to him, "Now I am going to drown you."

It was a long way he had to go before he came to the river, and Little Claus was no light weight to carry. The road passed close by a church: the organ was playing, and the people were singing so beautifully! So Big Claus put down his sack, with Little Claus in it, close to the church door, and thought it would be a very good thing to go in and hear a psalm before he went farther. Little Claus could not get out, and all the people were in church, and so he went in.

"Oh, dear! oh, dear!" sighed Little Claus in the sack. And he turned and twisted, but he found he could not loosen the cord. Soon there came by an old drover with snow-white hair, and a great staff in his hand. He was driving a whole herd of cows and oxen before him, and they stumbled against the sack in which lay Little Claus and knocked it over.

"Oh, dear!" sighed Little Claus. "I'm so young still, and so soon going to heaven!"

"And I, poor fellow," said the drover, "am so old already, and yet I can't get there!"

"Open the sack," cried Little Claus; "creep into it instead of me, and you will soon get to heaven."

"With all my heart," said the drover; and he untied the sack, out of which Little Claus jumped quickly.

"But will you look after the cattle?" said the old man, and he crept into the sack, whereupon Little Claus tied it up, and went his way with all the cows and oxen.

Soon after Big Claus came out of the church. He took the sack on his shoulders again, but it seemed to him as if the sack had become lighter, for the old drover was not more than half as heavy as Little Claus.

"How light he is to carry now! Yes, that is because I have heard a psalm."

So he went on to the river, which was deep and broad, threw the sack with the old drover in it into the water, and called after him, thinking that it was Little Claus, "You lie there! Now you shan't trick me any more!"

Then he went homeward; but when he came to a place where two roads crossed there he met Little Claus driving all his cattle.

"What's this?" cried Big Claus. "Have I not drowned you?"

"Yes," said Little Claus, "you threw me into the river less than half an hour ago."

"But wherever did you get all those fine beasts from?" asked Big Claus.

"They are sea-cattle," said Little Claus. "I'll tell you the whole story—and thank you for drowning me, for now I'm at the top of the tree. I am really rich! I was so frightened when I lay in the sack, and the wind whistled about my ears when you threw me from the bridge into the cold water! I sank to the bottom immediately; but I did not hurt myself, for the most beautiful soft grass grows down there. Upon that I fell; and immediately the sack was opened, and the loveliest maiden, with snow-white clothes and a green wreath upon her wet hair, took me by the hand, and said, 'Are you come, Little Claus? Here you have some cattle to begin with. A mile farther along the road there is a whole herd more, which I will give to you.' And then I saw that the river formed a great highway for the people of the sea. Along its bed they were walking and driving straight from the sea, right up into the land, to where the river ends. It was all covered with flowers and the freshest grass; the fishes which swam in the water darted past my ears, like the birds in the air. What nice people there were there, and what fine cattle grazing in the hills and valleys!"

"But why did you come up again to us so quickly?" asked Big

Claus. "I should not have done so, if it is so beautiful down there."

"Why," said Little Claus, "that was just good policy on my part. You heard me tell you that the sea-maiden said, 'A mile farther along the road'—and by the road she meant the river, for she can't go anywhere else—'there is a whole herd of cattle for you.' But I know what bends the stream makes—sometimes this way, sometimes that; it's a long way to go round. No, it can be done in a shorter way by coming up to the land and driving across the fields to the river again. In this manner I save myself almost half a mile, and get all the quicker to my sea-cattle!"

"Oh, you are a lucky man!" said Big Claus. "Do you think I should get some sea-cattle too if I went down to the bottom of the river?"

"Yes, I think so," said Little Claus. "But I cannot carry you in the sack as far as the river; you are too heavy for me! But if you will go there, and creep into the sack yourself, I will throw you in with a great deal of pleasure."

"Thanks!" said Big Claus; "but if I don't get any sea-cattle when I am down there I shall beat you, you may be sure!"

"Oh, no; don't be so fierce!"

And so they went together to the river. When the cattle, which were thirsty, saw the stream they ran as fast as they could to get at the water.

"See how they hurry!" cried Little Claus. "They are longing to get back to the bottom."

"Yes, but help me first," said Big Claus, "or else you'll get a thrashing!"

And so he crept into the great sack, which had been laid across the back of one of the oxen.

"Put a stone in, I'm afraid I shan't sink else," said Big Claus.

"There's no fear of that," said Little Claus. Still, he put a big stone into the sack, tied the rope tightly, and gave it a push. Plump! Into the river went Big Claus, and sank at once to the bottom.

"I'm afraid he won't find any cattle!" said Little Claus; and then he drove home those he had.

Ninety-two

# The Man from Paradise

*French*

Once upon a time there was a beggar who went to ask alms at the door of a widow who had remarried. "Where are you from, good man?" she said. "From Paris," answered the beggar. "From Paradise?" cried out the good woman, who had misunderstood; "have you heard from there news of my late husband?" "Yes," answered the beggar, "he keeps an inn at the entrance, and he is not too warm." "Ah!" she answered, "that does not surprise me; he was scarcely dressed when they buried him; but wait, I am going to give you clothes to take to him." The woman made a package of the best clothes in the house, and gave them to the beggar, requesting him to be careful in taking them to her late husband.

After the beggar had left the woman's husband returned. She said to him, "A man came who brought me news of my late husband; he keeps an inn at the entrance of Paradise, and he is not too warm; so I sent him a package of clothes to put on." "Poor simpleton!" the husband cried out; "you have let yourself be trapped. Which way did the beggar go?" The woman told him which road the beggar had taken, and he jumped on his horse and hastened along the road.

However, the beggar met a man who was breaking up rocks on the highway.

"You seem tired, my friend," the beggar said to him; "if you wish, I will break the stones in your place in order to warm myself while you take a little walk to stretch your legs." The workman accepted, and the beggar got down on his knees, the sledge-hammer in his hand, after having hidden his package in a hollow of the ditch. The husband soon arrived. "Workman," he said, "have you not seen a man pass by carrying a package?" "Yes; he went into that field." "Hold my horse, good man, I am going to run after him in order to catch him." After the husband had crossed over the stile, the false workman hastened to retrieve his package, jumped upon the horse, and soon disappeared. The good soul looked in vain everywhere, but he could not see the thief; when he returned to the road, he did not find his horse. Shamefacedly he returned home, and when his wife learned the end of the adventure she said to him: "You told me that I was a poor simpleton; if I wished, I could call you John the Idiot, for you have been trapped worse than I."

*Ninety-three*

# The Just Reward

*Russian*

The king of a certain country lost his ring while on a drive through his capital. He at once placed a notice in the newspapers, promising that whoever might find and return the ring would receive a large reward in money. A simple private was lucky enough to find it. "What shall I do?" thought the soldier. "If I report my find at regimental headquarters, the whole affair will be referred to my superiors, each in his turn, from the sergeant to the company commander, from the company commander to the battalion commander, from the battalion commander to the colonel, and from the colonel to the brigadier general—there will never be an end to it. I would rather go straight to the king."

IIe came to the palace. The officer on guard asked him: "What do you want here?" "I have found the king's ring," said the soldier. "Very well, brother! I will announce you, but only on condition that I get half the reward that the king gives you." The soldier thought to himself: "For once in my life I have had a piece of luck, and now I have to share it!" However, he answered the officer on guard: "Very well, I agree. Only give me a note stating that half the reward is for you and half for me."

The officer gave him the note and announced him to the king. The king praised the soldier for having found the ring. "Thank you, brave soldier!" he said. "I shall give you two thousand rubles as a reward." "No, your royal Majesty! That is not a soldier's reward. A soldier's reward is two hundred lashes." "What a fool

From *Russian Fairy Tales*, edited and translated by Norbert Guterman. Copyright 1945 by Pantheon Books, Inc. Reprinted by permission of Pantheon Books, a Division of Random House, Inc.

you are!" said the king, and ordered that the sticks be brought in.

The soldier began to undress, unbuttoned his tunic, and the note dropped on the floor. "What paper is that?" asked the king. "Your Majesty, that is a note stating that only half the reward is for me, and that the other half must go to the officer on guard." The king laughed, called the officer on guard, and ordered that he be given a hundred lashes. The order was carried out, and when it was time to count the last ten lashes, the soldier drew near to the king and said: "Your Majesty, since he is so greedy, I will give the other half of the reward to him too." "How kind you are!" said the king, and ordered that the officer on guard be given the second hundred lashes. After this reward the officer could hardly crawl home. As for the soldier, the king gave him an honorable discharge from the service and presented him with three thousand rubles.

*Ninety-four*

# The Brave Little Tailor

*German*

One summer morning a tailor was sitting on his bench by the window, was in good spirits, and was sewing away for dear life. Then a farmer's wife came down the street, crying, "Jam for sale! jam for sale!" That sounded good to the tailor's ears, and putting his little head out the window, he called, "Come up, madam, you can dispose of your wares here." With her heavy basket the woman climbed the three flights to the tailor's and had to unpack all her jars in front of him. He examined them all, lifted them up, sniffed at them, and finally said, "It seems like good jam to me, just weigh me out two ounces, madam—no matter if it's a quarter of a pound." The woman, who'd hoped to make a good sale, gave him what he asked for but went away grumbling and out of sorts. "Well, God bless my jam," cried the tailor, "and may it give me

From *German Folk Tales*, collected and edited by Grimm Brothers. Translated by Francis P. Magoun, Jr. and Alexander H. Krappe. Copyright © 1960, by Southern Illinois University Press. Reprinted by permission of the Southern Illinois University Press.

strength and vigor!" He fetched a loaf of bread from the cupboard, cut off a full slice, and spread it with jam. "That won't taste bad," he said, "but I want first to finish the jacket before I start eating." He put the bread down beside him, went on sewing, and out of sheer joy made bigger and bigger stitches. Meanwhile, the smell of the sweet jam reached the wall, where lots of flies were sitting; they were attracted to it and settled on it in swarms. "Well, who invited you?" said the tailor and drove the unbidden guests away. But the flies, who understood no German, didn't let themselves be dismissed and came back in even greater numbers. Finally the tailor lost his temper and fetching a piece of cloth from behind the stove, said, "Just wait, you'll catch it!" and struck at them unmercifully. When he drew back and counted, no less than seven were lying dead before him with their legs in the air. "Are you as brave as all that!" he said to himself and couldn't help marveling at his own valor; "the whole town must know about this!" He hastily cut out a belt, sewed it together, and in big letters embroidered on it "Seven at one blow." "Just the town!" he said, "why, the whole world shall know about it!" and his heart jumped for joy like a lamb's tail.

The tailor put the belt around his waist and wanted to go out into the world, thinking his workshop was too small for his bravery. Before leaving, he searched about in the house to see if there wasn't something to take along, but he found only an old cheese, which he put in his pocket. Outside the town gate he noticed a bird caught in the bushes; it had to join the cheese in his pocket. Now he bravely put the miles behind him and, being light of weight and nimble, felt no fatigue. His way led him up on a mountain, and when he reached the highest peak, there sat a powerful giant, taking his ease and looking around. The tailor approached him fearlessly and accosted him, saying, "Good morning, comrade! You're sitting there and viewing the wide world, aren't you? I'm just on my way there and want to test myself. Do you want to come along?" The giant looked at the tailor scornfully and said, "You tramp, you miserable fellow!" "Is that so?" replied the tailor, unbuttoned his coat and showed the giant his belt. "You can read for yourself what sort of man I am." The giant read, "Seven at one blow," thought it was men slain by the tailor, and began somewhat to respect the little fellow.

But he wanted to test him first, took a stone in his hand, and squeezed it so that water trickled out. "Now you do the same," said the giant, "if you've got the strength." "Is that all?" said the tailor, "for a man like me that's mere child's play," put his hand in his pocket, took out the soft choose, and squeezed it so that the liquid came out. "Well," he said, "wasn't that even a little better?" The giant didn't know what to say and couldn't really believe the little chap had done it. Then he picked up a stone and threw it so high that one could hardly see it with the naked eye. "There, you miserable little creature, now do the same." "That was a good throw," said the tailor, "but after all the stone was bound to fall back to earth; I'm going to throw one that won't come back at all," put his hand in his pocket, took out the bird, and threw it up in the air. The bird, glad to be free, rose, flew away, and didn't come back. "How do you like that, my friend?" asked the tailor. "You can throw all right," said the giant, "but now let's see whether you can carry a decent load."

He led the tailor to a huge oak which had been felled and was lying on the ground, and said, "If you're strong enough, help me carry this tree out of the forest." "Gladly," answered the little man, "you just take the trunk on your shoulder, and I'll lift the branches and twigs and carry them. That's the heaviest part, of course." The giant took the trunk on his shoulder, but the tailor sat down on a branch while the giant, who couldn't look around, had to carry away the whole tree and the tailor in the bargain. Back there on the branch the tailor was quite merry and in high spirits and whistled the ditty, "Three tailors were riding out of the gate," as if carrying trees was mere child's play. After dragging the heavy load for quite a way, the giant couldn't go on and called out, "Listen, I've got to drop the tree." The tailor jumped lightly down, seized the tree with both arms as if he'd been carrying it and said to the giant, "You're such a big fellow and can't even carry the tree."

They went on their way together, and as they were passing a cherry tree, the giant seized the top of the tree, where the ripest fruit was hanging, bent it down, put it in the tailor's hand, and told him to eat some. But the tailor was much too weak to hold the tree, and when the giant let go, the tree went up, jerking the tailor into the air. When he came down again unharmed, the giant said, "What does this mean? Aren't you strong enough to hold on to that little shoot?" "It isn't that I'm not strong enough," answered the tailor, "do you think that that would be anything for a man who laid out seven at one blow? I jumped over the tree, because huntsmen were shooting down there in the bushes. Jump over it yourself, if you can." The giant tried to but couldn't get over the tree and remained stuck in the branches. So here, too, the tailor had the best of it.

The giant said, "If you're such a brave fellow, come along to our cave and spend the night with us." The tailor was willing and followed him. When they reached the cave, other giants were sitting there by the fire, and each had a roasted sheep in his hand and was eating. The tailor looked around and thought, "It's a good deal roomier here than in my workshop." The giant showed him a bed and told him to lie down and to sleep as late as he wanted. But the bed was too big for the tailor, so he didn't lie down in it but crept into a corner of the cave. At midnight the giant thought the tailor was sound asleep, got up, took a big iron bar, and smashed the bed in two with one blow, thinking he'd finished the grasshopper off. Early in the morning the giants went into the forest and had quite forgotten the tailor, when all at once he came walking along quite merrily and fearlessly. The giants were terrified and, fearing he might kill them all, took to their heels.

The tailor went on his way, always following his pointed nose. After traveling a long while he came to the courtyard of a royal palace and feeling tired, lay down in the grass and fell asleep. While he was lying there, people came up, looked at him from all sides, and read on his belt, "Seven at one blow." "My!" they said, "what does this great warrior want here in peacetime? He must be a mighty lord." They went and reported it to the king, thinking that if war were to break out, he'd be an important and useful man whom they shouldn't let go at any price. The king liked the idea and dispatched one of his courtiers to the tailor; he was to propose military service once he waked up. The messenger stayed near the sleeping man, waited till the latter had stretched himself and opened his eyes, and then carried out his mission. "That's just what I've come here for," he replied, "and I'm ready to enter the king's service." Accordingly, he was honorably received and was assigned a special dwelling.

The soldiers, however, were jealous of the tailor and wished he were a thousand miles away. "What would happen," they said to one another, "if we got into a quarrel with him and he struck us? Seven would fall with each blow. The likes of us can't stand up to that!" They drew up a resolution and, going to the king in a body, asked for their discharge. "We aren't cut out," they said, "to hold our own against a man who kills seven at one blow." The king was sorry to lose all his faithful servants on account of one man, wished he'd never laid eyes on the tailor, and would have been glad to be rid of him. Still, he didn't dare dismiss him, fearing he might kill him and all his people and usurp the royal throne. For a long time he deliberated this way and that and finally hit on a solution. He sent word to the tailor, saying since he was so great a warrior that he wanted to make him a proposal. In a forest in his country were two giants who were doing great damage by robbing, murdering, and putting the country to fire and sword. No one might venture near them without risking his life. Should he overcome and kill these two giants, he'd give him his only daughter in marriage and half his kingdom as a dowry. Furthermore, a hundred horsemen were to accompany him and help him. "That would be just the thing for a man like you," thought the tailor, "a beautiful princess and half a kingdom aren't offered every day." "Oh yes," he answered, "I'll tame the giants easily enough, nor do I need the hundred horsemen to help me. A man who lays out seven at one blow doesn't need to be afraid of two."

The tailor set out, and the hundred horsemen went with him. When he got to the edge of the forest, he said to his escorts, "You just stop here. I'll settle things easily enough with the giants by myself." Then he skipped into the forest, looking to right and to left. After a while he saw both giants: they were lying asleep under a tree and snoring so as to make the branches wave up and down. The tailor quickly gathered both pockets full of stones and then climbed the tree. When he was halfway up, he hitched out on a branch until he was exactly over the sleeping giants and then dropped one stone after another on one of the giants' chests. For a long time the giant didn't notice anything, but finally he woke up, and giving his companion a poke, said, "What are you hitting me for?" "You're dreaming," said the other, "I'm not hitting you." So they lay down to sleep again. Then the tailor dropped a stone on the other giant. "What's that mean?" cried the latter. "Why are you throwing things at me?" "I'm not throwing anything at you," growled the first giant. For a while they quarreled over the matter, but because they were both tired, they let it go at that, and their eyes closed again. Then the tailor resumed his old game, picked out the biggest stone and dropped it with full force on the first giant's chest. "That's too much!" he exclaimed, jumped up like a madman and bashed his companion against the tree so that it shook. The other paid him back in the same coin, and they fell into such a furious rage that they tore up trees and struck at one another, until finally both fell dead on the ground at the same time.

Now the tailor jumped down. "It was sheer luck," he said, "that they didn't tear up the tree I was sitting in; otherwise I'd have had to jump like a squirrel onto another. Still, a man like me is nimble." He drew his sword and dealt each a couple of good blows on the chest, then went out to the horsemen and said, "The job's done. I've finished off both of them. But it was hard going: in their desperation they tore up trees and defended themselves with them, but nothing does any good when a man like me comes along who lays out seven at one blow." "Aren't you wounded?" asked the horsemen. "No, it turned out all right," answered the tailor, "they didn't ruffle a hair of my head." The horsemen simply wouldn't believe him and rode into the forest; there they found the giants swimming in their own blood and round about lay the torn-up trees.

The tailor now demanded of the king the promised reward, but the latter regretted his promise and reflected anew as to how he might disburden himself of the hero. "Before you get my daughter and half the kingdom," he said to him, "you've got to perform still another heroic feat. In the forest a unicorn is at large and is doing a lot of damage: you must first catch it." "I'm even less afraid of one unicorn than of two giants. Seven at one blow, that's me!" He took along a rope and an ax, went out into the forest, and again bade his companions wait outside. He didn't have to search long. The unicorn soon appeared and rushed straight at the tailor as if it meant to run him through without further ado. "Easy! easy!" he said, "it doesn't go so fast as all that," stopped and waited until the animal was quite near, and then nimbly jumped behind a tree. The unicorn rushed against the tree with all its might and ran its horn so hard into the tree that it wasn't strong enough to pull it out again, and thus it was caught. "Now I've got the bird," said the tailor, came out from behind the tree, first put a rope around the unicorn's neck, and then with his ax chopped the horn free of the tree. When everything was fixed up, he led the animal off and took it to the king.

The king still wouldn't grant him the promised reward and made a third demand. Before his wedding the tailor would have to catch a wild boar that was doing great damage in the forest, and the huntsmen were to help him. "I'll be glad to do it," said the tailor; "it's child's play." He didn't take the huntsmen along into the forest, and they didn't object, for the wild boar had often given them such a warm reception that they had no desire to waylay it. When the boar saw the tailor, it rushed at him, foaming at the mouth and gnashing its tusks, and was going to throw him to the ground. The nimble hero, however, jumped into a near-by chapel and immediately out again up through one of the windows. The boar followed him, but he skipped around outside and shut the door on it, and the enraged animal was caught, since it was far too heavy and too clumsy to jump out the window. Then the little tailor called the huntsmen to see the prisoner with their own eyes. The hero, however, betook himself to the king, who now willy-nilly had to keep his promise and surrender to him his daughter and half the kingdom. Had he known that it was no heroic warrior who was standing before him but only a little tailor, it would have pained him even more. The wedding was celebrated with much pomp and little joy, and a king was made out of a tailor.

After some time the young queen one night heard her husband say in a dream, "Boy, fix the jacket and patch the trousers, or I'll give you a rap over the ears with the yardstick." Then she realized in what circles the young lord had been born, on the following morning complained to her father, and begged him to help her get rid of a husband, who was a mere tailor. The king tried to console her, saying, "Leave your bedroom door open tonight. My servants will be standing outside and once he's asleep, they'll go in, tie him up, and carry him aboard a ship that will send him out into the wide wide world." That satisfied the woman, but the king's squire, who had overheard the whole thing and had a liking for the young lord, reported the plot to him. "I'll put a stop to that," said the tailor. That evening he went to bed with his wife at the usual time. When she thought he'd fallen asleep, she got up, opened the door, and lay down again. The little tailor, however, who'd only been pretending to be asleep, began to cry out in a loud voice, "Boy, fix the jacket and patch the trousers, or I'll give you a rap over the ears with the yardstick. I laid out seven at one blow, killed two giants, led off a unicorn, and captured a wild boar, and am supposed to be afraid of the fellows standing outside the bedroom!" When the men heard the tailor talking like that,

they became terribly frightened, ran off as if the Wild Host was after them, and not one was willing to venture near him any more. Thus the tailor was a king and remained a king as long as he lived.

# Crab

*Italian*

There was once a king who had lost a valuable ring. He looked for it everywhere, but could not find it. So he issued a proclamation that if any astrologer could tell him where it was he would be richly rewarded. A poor peasant by the name of Crab heard of the proclamation. He could neither read nor write, but took it into his head that he wanted to be the astrologer to find the king's ring. So he went and presented himself to the king, to whom he said: "Your Majesty must know that I am an astrologer, although you see me so poorly dressed. I know that you have lost a ring and I will try by study to find out where it is." "Very well," said the king, "and when you have found it, what reward must I give you?" "That is at your discretion, your Majesty." "Go, then, study, and we shall see what kind of an astrologer you turn out to be."

He was conducted to a room, in which he was to be shut up to study. It contained only a bed and a table on which were a large book and writing materials. Crab seated himself at the table and did nothing but turn over the leaves of the book and scribble the paper so that the servants who brought him his food thought him a great man. They were the ones who had stolen the ring, and from the severe glances that the peasant cast at them whenever they entered, they began to fear that they would be found out. They made him endless bows and never opened their mouths without calling him "Mr. Astrologer."

Crab, who, although illiterate, was, as a peasant, cunning, all at once imagined that the servants must know about the ring, and this is the way his suspicions were confirmed. He had been shut up in his room turning over his big book and scribbling his paper for a month, when his wife came to visit him. He said to her: "Hide yourself under the bed, and when a servant enters, say: 'That is one'; when another comes, say: 'That is two'; and so on." The woman hid herself. The servants came with the dinner, and hardly had the first one entered when a voice from under the bed said: "That is one." The second one entered; the voice said: "That is two"; and so on. The servants were frightened at hearing that voice, for they did not know where it came from, and held a consultation. One of them said: "We are discovered; if the astrologer denounces us to the king as thieves, we are lost." "Do you know what we must do?" said another. "Let us hear." "We must go to the astrologer and tell him frankly that we stole the ring, and ask him not to betray us, and present him with a purse of money. Are you willing?" "Perfectly."

So they went in harmony to the astrologer, and making him a lower bow than usual, one of them began: "Mr. Astrologer, you have discovered that we stole the ring. We are poor people and if you reveal it to the king, we are undone. So we beg you not to betray us, and accept this purse of money." Crab took the purse and then added: "I will not betray you, but you must do what I tell you, if you wish to save your lives. Take the ring and make that turkey in the court-yard swallow it, and leave the rest to me." The servants were satisfied to do so and departed with a low bow. The next day Crab went to the king and said to him: "Your Majesty must know that after having toiled over a month I have succeeded in discovering where the ring has gone to." "Where is it, then?" asked the king. "A turkey has swallowed it." "A turkey? very well, let us see."

They went for the turkey, opened it, and found the ring inside. The king, amazed, presented the astrologer with a large purse of money and invited him to a banquet. Among the other dishes, there was brought on the table a plate of crabs. Crabs must then have been very rare, because only the king and a few others knew their name. Turning to the peasant the king said: "You, who are an astrologer, must be able to tell me the name of these things which are in this dish." The poor astrologer was very much puzzled, and, as if speaking to himself, but in such a way that the others heard him, he muttered: "Ah! Crab, Crab, what a plight you are in!" All who did not know that his name was Crab rose and proclaimed him the greatest astrologer in the world.

*Ninety-six*

# Salt

*Russian*

In a certain city there lived a merchant who had three sons: the first was Fyodor, the second Vasily, and the third Ivan the Fool. This merchant lived richly; he sailed in his ships to foreign lands and traded in all kinds of goods. Once he loaded two ships with precious merchandise and sent them beyond the sea with his two elder sons. Ivan, his youngest son, always went to inns and alehouses, and for that reason his father did not trust him with any business; but when Ivan learned that his brothers had been sent beyond the sea, he straightway went to his father and begged him to be allowed to show himself in foreign lands, see people, and earn money by his wits. For a long time the merchant refused, saying: "You'll spend everything on drink and come home without your head!" However, when he saw that his son persisted in his prayers, he gave him a ship with the very cheapest cargo— beams, boards, and planks.

Ivan made ready for the voyage, lifted anchor, and soon overtook his brothers. They sailed together on the blue sea for one day, two days, three days; but on the fourth strong winds arose and blew Ivan's ship to a remote and unknown island. "Very well, boys," cried Ivan to his crew, "make for shore!" And they reached the shore. Ivan stepped out on the island, told his crew to wait for him, and started walking along a path. He walked and walked until he reached a very high mountain. And he saw that in this mountain there was neither sand nor stone but pure Russian salt. He returned to the shore and ordered his sailors to throw all the beams and planks into the water and to load the ship with salt. As soon as this was done, Ivan lifted anchor and sailed away.

After some time, a long time or a short time, and after they had sailed some distance, a great distance or a short one, the ship approached a large and wealthy city, sailed into its harbor, and cast anchor. Ivan, the merchant's son, went into the city to make obeisance to the king of the country and to obtain permission to trade freely, and he took a bundle of his merchandise, Russian salt, to show to the king. His arrival was immediately reported to the sovereign, who summoned him and said: "Speak! What is your business, what do you want?" "Just this, your Majesty! Permit me to trade freely in your city!" "And what goods do you sell?" "Russian salt, your Majesty." The king had never heard of salt; in his kingdom the people ate without salt. He wondered what this new and unknown merchandise might be. "Come," he said, "show it to me." Ivan, the merchant's son, opened his kerchief; the king glanced at the contents and thought to himself: "This is only white sand!" And he said to Ivan with a smile: "Brother, this can be had here without money!"

Ivan left the palace feeling very downcast. Then it occurred to him to go to the king's kitchen and see how the cooks prepared meals there and what kind of salt they used. He went into the kitchen, asked to be allowed to rest for a while, sat on a chair, and watched. The cooks ran back and forth: one was busy boiling, another roasting, another pouring, and still another crushing lice on a ladle. Ivan, the merchant's son, saw that they were not the least bit concerned with salting the food. He waited till a moment came when everyone else was out of the kitchen; then he seized the chance to pour the proper amount of salt into all the stews and sauces. The time came to serve the dinner, and the first dish was brought in. The king ate of it, and found it savory as never before. The second dish was served, and he liked it even better.

Then the king summoned his cooks and said to them: "I have been king for many years, but never before have you cooked me such savory dishes. How did you do it?" The cooks answered: "Your Majesty, we cooked as of old and did not add anything new. But the merchant who came to ask permission to trade freely is sitting in the kitchen. Perhaps he has added something." "Summon him to my presence!" Ivan, the merchant's son, was brought before the king to be questioned. He fell on his knees and asked forgiveness. "Your Majesty, I confess my guilt. I have seasoned all the dishes and sauces with Russian salt. Such is the custom in my country." "And for how much do you sell this salt?" Ivan realized that his business was in a fair way and answered: "It is not very dear—for two measures of salt, one measure of silver and one of gold." The king agreed to this price and bought the whole cargo.

Ivan filled his ship with silver and gold and sat down to wait for a favorable wind. Now the king of that land had a daughter, a beautiful princess. She wanted to see the Russian ship and asked her father's permission to go down to the port. The king gave her permission. So she took her nurses, governesses, and maidservants with her and drove forth to see the Russian ship. Ivan, the merchant's son, showed her every part and told her its name—the sails, the rigging, the bow, and the stern—and then he led her into the cabin. He ordered his crew to cut away the anchor, hoist the sails, and put out to sea; and since they had a good tail wind, they were soon a good distance from the city. The princess came up on deck, saw only the sea around her, and began to weep. Ivan, the merchant's son, spoke to her, comforted her, and urged her to dry her tears; and since he was handsome, she soon smiled and ceased grieving.

For some time, a long time or a short time, Ivan sailed on the sea with the princess. Then his elder brothers overtook him, learned of his audacity and good fortune, and greatly envied him. They came on board his ship, seized him by his arms, and threw him into the sea; then they cast lots between them and divided the booty: the eldest brother took the princess, and the second brother took the ship full of silver and gold.

Now it happened that when they flung Ivan from the ship he saw one of the boards that he himself had thrown into the sea. He clutched this board and for a long time drifted on it above the depths of the sea. Finally he was carried to an unknown island. He went ashore and walked along the beach. He met a giant with an enormous mustache, on which hung his mittens, which he was drying thus after the rain. "What do you want here?" asked the giant. Ivan told him everything that had happened. "If you so desire, I will carry you home. Tomorrow your eldest brother is to marry the princess. Sit on my back." He took Ivan up in his hands, seated him on his back, and ran across the sea. Ivan's cap dropped off. "Ah me," he said, "I've lost my cap!" "Never mind, brother," said the giant, "your cap is far away now, five hundred versts behind us." He brought Ivan to his native land, put him on the ground, and said: "Now promise that you will not boast to anyone about having ridden on my back; if you do boast, I shall crush you." Ivan, the merchant's son, promised not to boast, thanked the giant, and set out on the homeward journey.

When he arrived, everyone was already at the wedding table, preparing to go to church. As soon as the beautiful princess saw him, she jumped from her seat and threw herself on his neck. "This is my bridegroom," she said, "and not he who sits here by my side." "What is this?" asked the father. Ivan told him everything—how he had traded in salt, how he had carried off the princess, and how his elder brothers had pushed him into the sea. The father was very angry at his elder sons, drove them out of the house, and married Ivan to the princess.

Now a gay feast began. The guests got drunk and began to boast, some about their strength, some about their wealth, and some about the beauty of their young wives. And Ivan sat and sat and then drunkenly boasted: "What are your boasts worth? I have something real to boast about. I rode horseback on a giant across the entire sea!" The moment he said these words, the giant appeared at the gate. "Ah, Ivan, son of the merchant," he said, "I told you not to boast about me. Now what have you done?" "Forgive me," Ivan implored him, "it was not I who boasted, but my drunkenness!" "Come, show me. What do you mean by drunkenness?"

Ivan gave orders that a hundred gallon barrel of wine and a hundred gallon barrel of beer be brought. The giant drank the wine and the beer, got drunk, and began to break up and ruin everything in his path; he knocked down trees and bushes and tore big houses asunder. Then he fell down and slept three days and nights without awakening. When he awoke, he was shown all the damage he had done. The giant was terribly surprised and said: "Well, Ivan, son of the merchant, now I know what drunkenness is. Henceforth you may boast about me all you like."

*Ninety-seven*

# Peter Ox

*Danish*

There were once upon a time a peasant and his wife who lived in Jutland, but they had no children. They often lamented that fact and were also sad to think that they had no relatives to whom to leave their farm and other possessions. So the years went by and they became richer and richer, but there was no one to inherit their wealth.

One year the farmer bought a fine calf which he called Peter, and it was really the finest animal that he had ever seen, and so clever that it seemed to understand nearly everything that one said to it. It was also very amusing and affectionate, so that the man and his wife soon became as fond of it as if it were their own child.

One day the farmer said to his wife, "Perhaps the sexton of our church could teach Peter to talk; then we could not do better than to adopt him as our child, and he could then inherit all our property."

"Who can tell?" said the wife, "Our sexton is a learned man and perhaps he might be able to teach Peter to talk, for Peter is really very clever. Suppose you ask the sexton."

So the farmer went over to the sexton and asked him whether he did not believe that he could teach his calf to talk, because he wanted to make the animal his heir. The crafty sexton looked around to see that no one was near, and then said that he thought he could do so. "Only you must not tell anybody," he said, "for it must be a great secret, and the minister in particular must not know anything about it, or I might get into serious trouble as such things are strictly forbidden. Moreover it will cost a pretty penny as we shall need rare and expensive books." The farmer said that he did not mind, and handing the sexton a hundred dollars to buy books with, promised not to say a word about the arrangement to anyone.

That evening the man brought his calf to the sexton, who promised to do his best. In about a week the farmer returned to see how his calf was getting on, but the sexton said that he did not dare let him see the animal, else Peter might become homesick and forget all that he had already learned. Otherwise he was making good progress, but the farmer must pay another hundred dollars, as Peter needed more books. The peasant happened to have the money with him, so he gave it to the sexton and went home filled with hope and pleasant anticipations.

At the end of another week the man again went to make inquiry about Peter, and was told by the sexton that he was doing fairly well. "Can he say anything?" asked the farmer.

"Yes, he can say 'Ma,' " answered the sexton.

"The poor animal is surely ill," said the peasant, "and he probably wants mead. I will go straight home and bring him a jug of it." So he fetched a jug of good, old mead and gave it to the sexton for Peter. The sexton, however, kept the mead and gave the calf some milk instead.

A week later the farmer came again to find out what Peter could say now. "He still refuses to say anything but 'Ma,' " said the sexton.

"Oh! he is a cunning rogue"; said the peasant, "so he wants more mead, does he? Well, I'll get him some more, as he likes it so much. But what progress has he made?"

"He is doing so well," answered the sexton, "that he needs another hundred dollars' worth of books, for he cannot learn anything more from those that he has now."

"Well then, if he needs them he shall have them." So that same day the farmer brought another hundred dollars and a jug of good, old mead for Peter.

Now the peasant allowed a few weeks to elapse without calling on Peter, for he began to be afraid that each visit would cost him a hundred dollars. In the meantime the calf had become as fat as he would ever be, so the sexton killed him and sold the meat carefully at a distance from the village. Having done that he put on his black clothes and went to call on the farmer and his wife. As soon as he had bid them good day he asked them whether Peter had reached home safe and sound.

"Why no," said the farmer, "he has not run away, has he?"

"I hope," said the sexton, "that after all the trouble I have taken to teach him, that he has not been so tricky as to run away and to abuse my confidence so shamefully. For I have spent at least a hundred dollars of my own money to pay for books for him. Now Peter could say whatever he wanted, and he was telling me only yesterday that he was longing to see his dear parents. As I wanted to give him that pleasure, but feared that he would not be able to find his way home alone, I dressed myself and started out with him. We were hardly in the street when I suddenly remembered that I had left my stick at home, so I ran back to get it. When I came out of the house again, I found that Peter had run on alone. I thought, of course, that he had gone back to your house. If he is not there I certainly do not know where he can be."

Then the people began to weep and lament that Peter was lost, now especially when they might have had such pleasure with him, and after paying out so much money for his education. And the worst of it was that they were again without an heir. The sexton tried to comfort them and was also very sorry that Peter had deceived them so. But perhaps he had only lost his way, and the sexton promised that he would ask publicly in church next Sunday whether somebody had not seen the calf. Then he bade the farmer and his wife goodbye and went home and had some good roast veal for dinner.

One day the sexton read in the paper that a new merchant, named Peter Ox, had settled in the neighboring town. He put the paper into his pocket and went straight to the farmer and read this item of news to him. "One might almost believe," he said, "that this is your calf."

"Why yes," said the farmer, "who else should it be?" Then his wife added, "Yes father, go at once to see him, for I feel sure that it can be no other than our dear Peter. But take along plenty of money for he probably needs it now that he has become a merchant."

On the following morning the farmer put a bag of money on his shoulder, took with him some provisions, and started to walk to the town where the merchant lived. Early next morning he arrived there and went straight to the merchant's house. The servants told the man that the merchant had not gotten up yet. "That does not make any difference for I am his father; just take me up to his room."

So they took the peasant up to the bedroom where the merchant lay sound asleep. And as soon as the farmer saw him, he recognized Peter. There were the same thick neck and broad forehead and the same red hair, but otherwise he looked just like a human being. Then the man went to him and bade him good morning and said, "Well, Peter, you caused your mother and me great sorrow when you ran away as soon as you had learned something. But get up now and let me have a look at you and talk with you."

The merchant, of course, believed that he had a crazy man to deal with, so he thought it best to be careful. "Yes I will get up," he said, and jumped out of bed into his clothes as quickly as possible.

"Ah!" said the peasant, "now I see what a wise man our sexton was; he has brought it to pass that you are like any other man. If I were not absolutely certain of it, I should never dream that you were the calf of our red cow. Will you come home with me?" The merchant said that he could not as he had to attend to his business. "But you could take over my farm and I would retire.

Nevertheless if you prefer to stay in business, I am willing. Do you need any money?"

"Well," said the merchant, "a man can always find use for money in his business."

"I thought so," said the farmer, "and besides you had nothing to start with, so I have brought you some money." And with that he poured out on the table the bright dollars that covered it entirely.

When the merchant saw what kind of man his new-found acquaintance was, he chatted with him in a very friendly manner and begged him to remain with him for a few days.

"Yes indeed," said the farmer, "but you must be sure to call me father from now on."

"But I have neither father nor mother living," answered Peter Ox.

"That I know perfectly well," the peasant replied, "for I sold your real father in Copenhagen last Michaelmas, and your mother died while calving. But my wife and I have adopted you as our child and you will be our heir, so you must call me father."

The merchant gladly agreed to that and kept the bag of money; and before leaving town the farmer made his will and bequeathed all his possessions to Peter after his death. Then the man went home and told his wife the whole story, and she was delighted to learn that the merchant Peter Ox was really their own calf.

"Now you must go straight over to the sexton and tell him what has happened," she said, "and be sure to refund to him the hundred dollars that he paid out of his own pocket for Peter, for he has earned all that we have paid him, because of the joy that he has caused us in giving us such a son and heir."

Her husband was of the same opinion and went to call on the sexton, whom he thanked many times for his kindness and to whom he also gave two hundred dollars.

Then the farmer sold his farm, and he and his wife moved into the town where the merchant was, and lived with him happily until their death.

*Ninety-eight*

# "What Should I Have Said?"

*Russian*

In a certain family there was an arrant fool. Not a day passed on
which they did not receive complaints about him; every day he
would either insult someone or injure someone. The fool's mother
pitied him and looked after him as if he were a little child;
whenever the fool made ready to go somewhere, she would explain to him for half an hour what he should do and how he
should do it. One day the fool went by the threshing barn and saw
the peasants threshing peas, and cried to them: "May you thresh
for three days and get three peas threshed!" Because he said this
the peasants belabored him with their flails. The fool came back
to his mother and cried: "Mother, mother, they have beaten up a
fellow!" "Was it you, my child?" "Yes." "Why?" "Because I
went by Dormidoshkin's barn and his family were threshing peas
there." "And then, my child?" "And I said to them: 'May you
thresh for three days and get three peas threshed.' That's why
they beat me up." "Oh, my child, you should have said: 'May you
have to do this forever and ever.' "

The fool was overjoyed. The next day he went to walk in the
village and met some people carrying a coffin with a dead man in
it. Remembering his mother's words, he roared in a loud voice:
"May you have to carry this forever and ever!" Again he was
soundly thrashed. The fool returned to his mother and told her
why he had been beaten up. "Ah, my child," she said, "you should
have said: 'May he rest in peace eternal.' " These words sank
deep into the fool's mind.

Next day he happened again to walk in the village and met a
gay wedding procession. The fool cleared his throat and as soon
as he came up to the procession, he cried: "May you rest in peace
eternal!" The drunken peasants jumped down from the cart and
beat him up cruelly. The fool went home and cried: "O my dear

mother, they've beaten me up terribly." "What for, my child?" The fool told her. His mother said: "My child, you should have danced and played for them." "Thank you, mother," he said. He went to the village once more and took his reed pipe with him.

At the end of the village a corn loft was on fire. The fool ran there as fast as he could; he stopped in front of the corn loft and began to dance and to play on his reed pipe. Again he was thrashed. Again he came in tears to his mother and told her why he had been beaten up. His mother said: "You should have taken some water and helped them to quench the fire." Three days later, when the fool's sides were healed, he went again to walk in the village. He saw a peasant singeing a pig. The fool snatched a pail of water from a woman who was going by with her cowlstaff, ran to the peasant, and poured water over the fire. Again he was soundly thrashed. Again he returned to his mother and told her why he had been beaten up. Then his mother swore never again to let him go to the village, and until this day he has never gone farther than his own back yard.

*Ninety-nine*

# Is He Fat?

*English*

It happened once that two young men met in a churchyard, about eight o'clock in the evening.

One of them said to the other, "Where are you going?"

The other answered, "I'm going to get a bag of nuts that lies underneath my mother's head in this churchyard. But tell me, where are you going?"

He said, "I'm going to steal a fat sheep out of this field. Wait here till I come back."

Then the other man got the nuts that were under his dead mother's head, and stood in the church porch cracking them. In those days it was the custom to ring a bell at a certain time in the evening, and just as the man was cracking the nuts the sexton came into the churchyard to ring it. But when he heard the cracking of the nuts in the porch he was afraid, and ran to tell the parson, who only laughed at him, and said, "Go and ring, fool."

However, the sexton was so afraid, that he said he would not go back unless the parson would go with him. After much persuasion the parson agreed to go, but he had the gout very badly, and the sexton had to carry him on his back. When the man in the porch who was cracking the nuts saw the sexton coming into the churchyard with the parson on his back he thought it was the man who had just gone out to steal the sheep, and had returned with a sheep on his back. So he bawled out, "Is it a fat one?" When the sexton heard this he was so frightened that he threw the parson down and said, "Aye, and thou canst take it if thou lik'st." So the sexton ran away as fast as he could, and left the parson to shift for himself. But the parson ran home as fast as the sexton.

*One Hundred*

# The Pancake

*Norwegian*

Once upon a time there was a good housewife, who had seven hungry children. One day she was busy frying pancakes for them, and this time she had used new milk in the making of them. One was lying in the pan, frizzling away—ah! so beautiful and thick —it was a pleasure to look at it. The children were standing round the fire, and the goodman sat in the corner and looked on.

"Oh, give me a bit of pancake, mother, I am so hungry!" said one child.

"Ah, do! dear mother," said the second.

"Ah, do! dear, good mother," said the third.

"Ah, do! dear, good, kind mother," said the fourth.

"Ah, do! dear, good, kind, nice mother," said the fifth.

"Ah, do! dear, good, kind, nice, sweet mother," said the sixth.

"Ah, do! dear, good, kind, nice, sweet, darling mother," said the seventh. And thus they were all begging for pancakes, the one more prettily than the other, because they were so hungry, and such good little children.

"Yes, children dear, wait a bit till it turns itself," she answered

—she ought to have said "till I turn it"—"and then you shall all have pancakes, beautiful pancakes, made of new milk—only look how thick and happy it lies there."

When the pancake heard this, it got frightened, and all of a sudden, it turned itself and wanted to get out of the pan, but it fell down in it again on the other side, and when it had been fried a little on that side too, it felt a little stronger in the back, jumped out on the floor, and rolled away, like a wheel, right through the door and down the road.

"Halloo!" cried the goodwife, and away she ran after it, with the frying-pan in one hand and the ladle in the other, as fast as she could, and the children behind her, while the goodman came limping after, last of all.

"Halloo, won't you stop?—Catch it, stop it. Halloo there!" they all screamed, the one louder than the other, trying to catch it on the run, but the pancake rolled and rolled, and before long, it was so far ahead, that they could not see it, for the pancake was much smarter on its legs than any of them.

When it had rolled a time, it met a man.

"Good day, pancake!" said the man.

"Well met, Manny Panny," said the pancake.

"Dear pancake," said the man, "don't roll so fast, but wait a bit and let me eat you."

"When I have run away from Goody Poody and the goodman and seven squalling children, I must run away from you too, Manny Panny," said the pancake, and rolled on and on, till it met a hen.

"Good day, pancake," said the hen.

"Good day, Henny Penny," said the pancake.

"My dear pancake, don't roll so fast, but wait a bit and let me eat you," said the hen.

"When I have run away from Goody Poody and the goodman and seven squalling children, and from Manny Panny, I must run away from you too, Henny Penny," said the pancake, and rolled on like a wheel down the road. Then it met a cock.

"Good day, pancake," said the cock.

"Good day, Cocky Locky," said the pancake.

"My dear pancake, don't roll so fast, but wait a bit and let me eat you," said the cock.

"When I have run away from Goody Poody and the goodman and seven squalling children, from Manny Panny, and Henny

Penny, I must run away from you too, Cocky Locky," said the pancake, and rolled and rolled on as fast as it could. When it had rolled a long time, it met a duck.

"Good day, pancake," said the duck.

"Good day, Ducky Lucky," said the pancake.

"My dear pancake, don't roll so fast, but wait a bit and let me eat you," said the duck.

"When I have run away from Goody Poody and the goodman and seven squalling children, from Manny Panny, and Henny Penny, and Cocky Locky, I must run away from you too, Ducky Lucky," said the pancake, and with that it fell to rolling and rolling as fast as ever it could. When it had rolled a long, long time, it met a goose.

"Good day, pancake," said the goose.

"Good day, Goosey Poosey," said the pancake.

"My dear pancake, don't roll so fast, but wait a bit and let me eat you," said the goose.

"When I have run away from Goody Poody and the goodman and seven squalling children, and Manny Panny, and Henny Penny, and Cocky Locky, and Ducky Lucky, I must run away from you too, Goosey Poosey," said the pancake, and away it rolled. So when it had rolled a long, very long time, it met a gander.

"Good day, pancake," said the gander.

"Good day, Gander Pander," said the pancake.

"My dear pancake, don't roll so fast, but wait a bit and let me eat you," said the gander.

"When I have run away from Goody Poody and the goodman and seven squalling children, and from Manny Panny, and Henny Penny, and Cocky Locky, and Ducky Lucky, and Goosey Poosey, I must run away from you too, Gander Pander," said the pancake, and rolled and rolled as fast as it could. When it had rolled on a long, long time, it met a pig.

"Good day, pancake," said the pig.

"Good day, Piggy Wiggy," said the pancake, and began to roll on faster than ever.

"Nay, wait a bit," said the pig, "you needn't be in such a hurry-scurry; we two can walk quietly together and keep each other company through the wood, because they say it isn't very safe there."

The pancake thought there might be something in that, and so they walked together through the wood; but when they had gone some distance, they came to a brook.

The pig was so fat it wasn't much trouble for him to swim across, but the pancake couldn't get over.

"Sit on my snout," said the pig, "and I will ferry you over."

The pancake did so.

"Ouf, Ouf," grunted the pig, and swallowed the pancake in one gulp, and as the pancake couldn't get any farther—well, you see we can't go on with this story any farther, either.

435

# NOTES AND SOURCES

Those wishing more information about folktales and especially about particular tales than that given in the slight suggestions below are referred to Stith Thompson, *The Folktale* (New York, 1946) and to Antti Aarne and Stith Thompson, *The Types of the Folktale* (FF Communications No. 184, Helsinki, 1961). For those without language difficulties very valuable works are: Waldemar Liungman, *Vårefrån Kommer vore Sagor* (Djursholm, Sweden, 1952) and Johannes Bolte and Georg Polívka, *Anmerkungen zu den Kinder- und Hausmärchen der Brüder Grimm* (5 vols., Berlin, 1913–31).

Sources of tales are given in the following notes. Permissions for the use of copyrighted tales are indicated in the list of principal sources given below or in the notes.

## Principal Sources

| | |
|---|---|
| Brækstad | H. L. Brækstad, *Round the Yule Log.* Philadelphia, n.d. |
| Cosquin | Emmanuel Cosquin, *Contes populaires de Lorraine.* Paris, 1886. |
| Crane | T. F. Crane, *Italian Popular Tales.* Boston, 1885. |
| Dasent | G. W. Dasent, *Popular Tales from the Norse.* London, 1889 (first edition 1858). |
| Dawkins | R. M. Dawkins, *Modern Greek Folktales.* Oxford, 1953. |
| Delarue | Paul Delarue, *The Borzoi Book of French Folk Tales.* Translated by Austin Fife. New York, 1956. |
| Grimm | F. P. Magoun and A. H. Krappe (trans.), *The Grimms' German Folk Tales.* Carbondale, Ill., 1960. |
| Guterman | A. N. Afanasief, *Russian Folk Tales.* Translated by Norbert Guterman. New York, 1945. |
| Liungman | W. Liungman, *Sveriges Samtliga Folksagor.* 3 vols. Djursholm (Sweden), 1949–52. Translated by Barbro Sklute. |
| Sébillot | P. Sébillot, *Contes populaires de la Haute Bretagne.* 3 vols. Paris, 1880 ff. Translated by Louise Thompson. |
| Types | Aarne-Thompson, *The Types of the Folktale.* |

## Notes on the Individual Tales

The tale types indicated are based on *The Types of the Folktale* by Aarne and Thompson, Helsinki, 1961.

1 Type 122. Norwegian: Dasent, *Norwegian Fairy Tales* (London, 1910), pp. 248 ff. A Scandinavian folktale for children, now well-known everywhere.
2 Type 155. Italian: Crane, No. 38. An Aesop fable with almost worldwide distribution as an oral tale.
3 Type 301. French: Cosquin, No. 1. Very popular throughout Europe and Near East, sporadic elsewhere.
4 Type 302. Norwegian: Dasent, pp. 59 ff. Popular throughout Europe and Western Asia to India and sporadically elsewhere.
5 Type 303 (including 300). Spanish: A. M. Espinosa, *Cuentos Populares Espanolas*, No. 139 (Stanford University, 1923). A tale with a long and complicated history. More than one thousand versions available. Europe, Asia, and sporadically elsewhere.
6 Type 306. Russian: Guterman, pp. 224 ff. Well-known in Europe but rare outside.
7 Type 310. French: *Revue des traditions populaires* VI, pp. 590 ff. A French literary tale of the eighteenth century. Occasionally heard by story-tellers with some changes. Grimm's "Rapunzel."

8 Type 311. Italian: Crane, No. 16. Popular only in Central and Northern Europe but known as far as India. Sporadic in Africa and America.

9 Type 313C. French: Cosquin, No. 32. Though showing some variety in the opening and in the development of its episodes, this is one of the most popular of all folktales and is known in all parts of the world.

10 Type 314. French: Sébillot, pp. 74 ff. Abridged somewhat. One of the best known of all folktales.

11 Type 318. Literary (Ancient Egyptian, 13th century B.C.): *Land of Enchanters.* Translated by Battiscombe Gunn. Edited by Bernard Lewis (London, 1948), pp. 55–65. Used by permission of Harvill Press. Still current as a widely distributed folktale.

12 Type 325. French: Delarue, No. 15. Probably originating in India but also popular in Europe since antiquity.

13 Type 326. German: Grimm, No. 4. Popular in various forms through Northern and Central Europe. Well-known in America.

14 Type 327A. German: Grimm, No. 15. Some Oriental elements. Has entered literature and opera. Now worldwide in popularity.

15 Type 328. Norwegian: Dasent, p. 215. Often mixed with other similar types. Note especially the English "Jack the Giant Killer." Popular from Ireland to India; sporadic elsewhere.

16 Type 330. Norwegian: Dasent, pp. 105 ff. Elements from antiquity and Middle Ages. Told over most of Europe, rarely elsewhere.

17 Type 331. French: *Revue des traditions populaires* VIII, pp. 216 ff. A popular medieval devil story. Versions differ in their details.

18 Type 332. Swedish: Liungman, pp. 98 ff. From medieval literary sources. As oral tale general in Europe, rare elsewhere. Modern literary and dramatic handlings.

19 Type 333. Literary (French): Charles Perrault, *Contes de ma mère Loye* (Paris, 1697). Translated by Charles Walsh (Boston, 1902). The literary telling of an old folktale.

20 Type 400. Danish: Grundtvig, *Fairy Tales from Afar.* Translated by Mully (London, n.d.), pp. 75–89. One of the most popular tales. The Swan Maiden episode is especially widespread both in literature and in oral tradition.

21 Type 400. Norwegian: Dasent, pp. 181 ff. The same as the previous story with a different beginning.

22 Type 402. Russian: Guterman, pp. 119 ff. Popular in all parts of Europe. The nature of the bride varies (cat, rat, frog, etc.). Told at least since Middle Ages.

23 Type 403. Swedish: G. O. Hylten-Cavallius och G. Stephens, *Svenska Folksagor och Afventyr* (Stockholm, 1844), No. 7 A. One of the most popular of folktales.

24 Type 408. Literary (Italian, 17th century): Giambattista Basile, *Pentamerone*, 5th day, 9th tale. Translated by N. M. Penzer (London, John Lane, 1932). Used by permission of The Bodley Head. Tale essentially South European, sporadically worldwide.

25 Type 410. Swedish: Liungman II, pp. 81 ff. This tale is given as a representative of a French literary concoction of the eighteenth century; it is occasionally heard as an oral tale.

26 Type 425. Norwegian: Dasent, pp. 22 ff. One of the most popular folktales. Known in a variety of forms, both oral and written, since antiquity. The most famous of literary forms is Apuleius's "Cupid and Psyche" (second century after Christ).

27 Type 432. Italian: Crane, No. 3. Literary versions from Middle Ages but somewhat popular with oral story-tellers in Europe and occasionally elsewhere.

28 Type 433B. Swedish: Liungman I, pp. 144 ff. A tale particularly well-known in northern Europe, but not elsewhere in this exact form.

29 Type 440. German: Grimm, No. 1. Belongs to the Cupid and Psyche

group of tales (Type 425) but is known independently in Central and Western Europe.

30 Type 450. Russian: Guterman, pp. 406 ff. Told in Europe and Near East. Some elements found in Ancient Greece.

31 Type 451. Swedish: Liungman I, pp. 146 ff. Mainly Central European.

32 Type 461. Swedish: Liungman I, pp. 148 ff. Very popular in Europe; occasionally elsewhere. Some elements in ancient Greek literature.

33 Type 465A. Greek: Dawkins, No. 18 b. Popular throughout Europe and Asia; sporadic elsewhere.

34 Type 470. Norwegian: Desent, *Tales from the Fjeld* (new ed., New York and London, 1896), pp. 171 ff. Popular throughout Europe. Known in China and America.

35 Type 480. Norwegian: Dasent, pp. 113 ff. Worldwide distribution. More than one thousand versions known.

36 Type 500. English: Jacobs, *English Fairy Tales* (New York and London, 1898), pp. 1 ff. Well-known throughout Europe.

37 Type 501. Norwegian: Dasent, p. 193. Told mostly in northwestern Europe. Frequently printed in chapbooks.

38 Type 503. Irish: Jacobs, *More Celtic Fairy Tales* (New York and London, 1895), pp. 156 ff. Told in all of Europe, especially in north and west.

39 Type 506A. Swedish: Liungman I, pp. 173 ff. A form of the Grateful Dead Man story particularly well known in northern Europe.

40 Type 510A. Portuguese: Consigliori Pedroso, *Portuguese Folk Tales* (London, 1882), pp. 75–79. Probably the best known of all folktales.

41 Type 510B. Norwegian: Dasent, p. 367. Very popular and worldwide. Not always distinguished from Cinderella.

42 Type 511. German: Grimm, No. 130. Popular and worldwide. Often mixed with Types 510A and 510B.

43 Type 513. French: Delarue, No. 18. Principally European.

44 Type 516. German: Grimm, No. 6. Well known from Ireland to India; also in all parts of America.

45 Type 530. Norwegian: Dasent, pp. 92 ff. Popular from Ireland to India; sometimes told in America.

46 Type 531. Greek: Dawkins, No. 34. One of the most popular tales. Nearly worldwide.

47 Type 533. German: Grimm, No. 89. Best known in central Europe.

48 Type 545B. Norwegian: Dasent, pp. 295 ff. Much influenced by literary treatments, though it is a favorite oral tale for children. Sometimes we have a helpful fox.

49 Type 550. German: Grimm, No. 57. Many literary treatments since the Middle Ages, though it has also been popular with story-tellers, especially in Europe.

50 Type 551. Irish: Kennedy, *Fireside Stories of Ireland* (Dublin, 1870), p. 87. Frequently influenced by No. 49.

51 Type 555. Russian: Guterman, pp. 528 ff. Primarily told in German and Slavic countries. Sometimes the husband climbs a beanstalk to heaven and is granted the wishes.

52 Type 560. Greek: Dawkins, No. 9. Nearly worldwide, with literary treatments since the Middle Ages.

53 Type 563. Italian: Crane, No. 32. Like No. 52. Known all over the world. Literary treatments since the Middle Ages.

54 Type 564. Russian: Guterman, pp. 321 ff. Probably a special development of No. 53. This form is popular around the Baltic.

55 Type 566. Russian: Guterman, p. 292. Often known as the Fortunatus legend. Mainly European, though there are Asiatic literary treatments.

56 Type 567. Greek: Dawkins, No. 22. Popular as oral tale, especially in eastern Europe, but is also known elsewhere. Sometimes serves to introduce No. 5.

57 Type 570. Norwegian: Brækstad, pp. 168 ff. Popular especially in Europe

and wherever Europeans have settled. Sometimes known as "The Sack of Lies."

58 Type 571. Hungarian: Jones and Kropf, *Folktales of the Magyars* (London, 1889), pp. 13 ff. The magic animal is frequently a goose. Known from Ireland to India and sometimes elsewhere.

59 Type 590. Norwegian: Dasent, pp. 155 ff. Mainly a central European oral tale. Carried to American Indians, probably by French.

60 Type 613. Norwegian: Dasent, pp. 1 ff. One of the oldest and best known of folktales. In oriental and medieval literature.

61 Type 621. Danish: *Skattegraveren* XI (1889), pp. 235 ff, No. 583. Especially popular in the East Baltic countries.

62 Type 650A. German: Grimm, No. 50. Frequently serves as introduction to No. 3. Versions vary in many details.

63 Type 653. French: Sébillot I, pp. 52 ff. A long literary history in Asia and Renaissance Europe. Orally known especially in Asia.

64 Type 665. Russian: Guterman, pp. 124 ff. Mostly told in Baltic countries and Russia.

65 Type 670. Bulgarian: Wratislaw, *Sixty Folk-Tales from Exclusively Slavonic Sources* (London, 1889), pp. 199 ff. Apparently originated in literary form in India and has traveled to Europe and Africa, but hardly to America.

66 Type 671. Italian: Crane, No. 43. Mainly a central European tale with literary treatments.

67 Type 675. Danish: Grundtvig, *Gamle danske Minder* (1857) II, pp. 308 ff. A tale moderately popular in all parts of Europe and well known elsewhere. I have heard it told by an Ojibway Indian.

68 Type 700. German: Grimm, No. 37. A favorite with story-tellers everywhere.

69 Type 706. Russian: Guterman, pp. 294 ff. Very well known in Europe and Asia, and especially in America.

70 Type 707. Italian: Crane, No. 4. A favorite tale in Europe and Asia. Nearly fifty versions from India. Popular in New World.

71 Type 709. German: Grimm, No. 53. Popular everywhere, especially since its use in the cinema.

72 Type 720. German: Grimm, No. 47. Moderately well known from Ireland to India. The song appears in Goethe's "Faust."

73 Type 750A. German: K. Ranke, *Folktales of Germany* (Chicago, 1966), No. 56, pp. 149 f. Used by permission. Many variations in the details of the numerous versions.

74 Type 756C. Greek: Dawkins, No. 82 b. Essentially an oral tale of Eastern and Southeastern Europe.

75 Type 780. Italian: Crane, No. 8. Very well known, frequently as a ballad.

76 Type 851. Russian: Guterman, p. 115. Mainly European and New World. Sporadic elsewhere.

77 Type 870. Swedish: Liungman I, pp. 341 ff. Principally found in Scandinavia.

78 Type 875. Italian: Crane, No. 108. One of the most popular tales. Possibly it originated in India.

79 Type 877. Italian: Crane, No. 25. A Mediterranean story.

80 Type 900. Italian: Crane, No. 29. A tale probably originating in Italy or central Europe in the Middle Ages. Known from Ireland to borders of Russia.

81 Type 910B. Greek: Dawkins, No. 75a. Certainly an Oriental tale but known in Europe in the Middle Ages. Primarily literary.

82 Type 922. Danish: *Skattegraveren* VI, pp. 153 f. An old jest appearing both in folktales and ballads. Perhaps the most thoroughly studied of all folktales.

83 Type 945. Czech: Wratislaw, *Sixty Folk-Tales from Exclusively Slavonic Sources* (London, 1889), pp. 33 ff. Oriental and primarily literary, though occasionally heard from story-tellers.

84 Type 950. Literary (Ancient Greek, 5th century B.C.): Herodotus, *History*, Book II. Though many oral versions depend on memories of Herodotus, the tale was doubtless known earlier.
85 Types 1000, 1003, 1004, 1010, 1006, and 1008. Danish: *Skattegraveren* VII, pp. 5 ff. A jest well known in all of Europe since the Middle Ages.
86 Type 1137. Greek: *The Odyssey of Homer*. Translated by G. H. Palmer (Boston and New York, 1891), pp. 134 ff. Heard from story-tellers probably having no knowledge of Homer. Possibly it was popular before Homer.
87 Type 1415. Norwegian: Dasent, *Norse Folk Tales* (London, 1910), pp. 151–56. Known over Europe eastward to India and sporadically elsewhere.
88 Types 1180, 1286, 1384, and 1450. Italian: Crane, No. 93. Popular throughout Europe and elsewhere as a Noodle story.
89 Type 1525. Scottish: J. G. MacKay, *More West Highland Tales* (Edinburgh, 1939), No. 11. Used by permission. Appears with many variations in detail and is nearly worldwide.
90 Type 1534. Russian: Guterman, pp. 625 ff. A favorite Oriental tale. Known in Italian novelle.
91 Type 1535. Literary (Danish, 19th century): Hans Christian Andersen. This favorite folktale retold by a master story-teller.
92 Type 1540. French: *Revue des traditions populaires* XI, 447 f. A medieval jest.
93 Type 1610. Russian: Guterman, pp. 39 f. A Renaissance literary tale frequently heard from story-tellers.
94 Type 1640. German: Grimm, No. 20. A jest very well known in Europe and Asia.
95 Type 1641. Italian: Crane, No. 109. This popular jest appears with many variations, depending on the name of the doctor.
96 Type 1651A. Russian: Guterman, pp. 40 ff. This story often concerns the fortune made by taking a cat to a mouse-infested land.
97 Type 1675. Danish: Cramer, *Danish Fairy Tales* (Boston, 1912), pp. 15 ff. A well-known jest, probably originating in the Orient.
98 Type 1696. Russian: Afanasief, pp. 334 ff. One of the best-known jests.
99 Type 1791. English: Addy, *Household Tales*, No. 2. A medieval literary tale, very popular with story-tellers, especially in America.
100 Type 2025. Norwegian: Brækstad, pp. 62 ff. This final story is a good representative of the cumulative tale. Both this and story No. 1 are especially beloved by children.

84 Type 950. Literary (Ancient Greek, 5th century B.C.): Herodotus, *History*, Book II. Though many oral versions depend on memories of Herodotus, the tale was doubtless known earlier.

85 Types 1000, 1003, 1004, 1010, 1006, and 1008. Danish: *Skattegraveren* VII, pp. 5 ff. A jest well known in all of Europe since the Middle Ages.

86 Type 1137. Greek: *The Odyssey of Homer*. Translated by G. H. Palmer (Boston and New York, 1891), pp. 134 ff. Heard from story-tellers probably having no knowledge of Homer. Possibly it was popular before Homer.

87 Type 1415. Norwegian: Dasent, *Norse Folk Tales* (London, 1910), pp. 151–56. Known over Europe eastward to India and sporadically elsewhere.

88 Types 1180, 1286, 1384, and 1450. Italian: Crane, No. 93. Popular throughout Europe and elsewhere as a Noodle story.

89 Type 1525. Scottish: J. G. MacKay, *More West Highland Tales* (Edinburgh, 1939), No. 11. Used by permission. Appears with many variations in detail and is nearly worldwide.

90 Type 1534. Russian: Guterman, pp. 625 ff. A favorite Oriental tale. Known in Italian novelle.

91 Type 1535. Literary (Danish, 19th century): Hans Christian Andersen. This favorite folktale retold by a master story-teller.

92 Type 1540. French: *Revue des traditions populaires* XI, 447 f. A medieval jest.

93 Type 1610. Russian: Guterman, pp. 39 f. A Renaissance literary tale frequently heard from story-tellers.

94 Type 1640. German: Grimm, No. 20. A jest very well known in Europe and Asia.

95 Type 1641. Italian: Crane, No. 109. This popular jest appears with many variations, depending on the name of the doctor.

96 Type 1651A. Russian: Guterman, pp. 40 ff. This story often concerns the fortune made by taking a cat to a mouse-infested land.

97 Type 1675. Danish: Cramer, *Danish Fairy Tales* (Boston, 1912), pp. 15 ff. A well-known jest, probably originating in the Orient.

98 Type 1696. Russian: Afanasief, pp. 334 ff. One of the best-known jests.

99 Type 1791. English: Addy, *Household Tales*, No. 2. A medieval literary tale, very popular with story-tellers, especially in America.

100 Type 2025. Norwegian: Brækstad, pp. 62 ff. This final story is a good representative of the cumulative tale. Both this and story No. 1 are especially beloved by children.